DANIEL, ESTHER, AND JEREMIAH:
THE ADDITIONS

THE ANCHOR BIBLE is a fresh approach to the world's greatest classic. Its object is to make the Bible accessible to the modern reader; its method is to arrive at the meaning of biblical literature through exact translation and extended exposition, and to reconstruct the ancient setting of the biblical story, as well as the circumstances of its transcription and the characteristics of its transcribers.

THE ANCHOR BIBLE is a project of international and interfaith scope: Protestant, Catholic, and Jewish scholars from many countries contribute individual volumes. The project is not sponsored by any ecclesiastical organization and is not intended to reflect any particular theological doctrine. Prepared under our joint supervision, THE ANCHOR BIBLE is an effort to make available all the significant historical and linguistic knowledge which bears on the interpretation of the biblical record.

THE ANCHOR BIBLE is aimed at the general reader with no special formal training in biblical studies; yet, it is written with the most exacting standards of scholarship, reflecting the highest technical accomplishment.

This project marks the beginning of a new era of co-operation among scholars in biblical research, thus forming a common body of knowledge to be shared by all.

William Foxwell Albright
David Noel Freedman
GENERAL EDITORS

Following the death of senior editor W. F. Albright, The Anchor Bible Editorial Board was established to advise and assist David Noel Freedman in his continuing capacity as general editor. The three members of the Editorial Board are among the contributors to The Anchor Bible. They have been associated with the series for a number of years and are familiar with its methods and objectives. Each is a distinguished authority in his area of specialization, and in concert with the others, will provide counsel and judgment as the series continues.

EDITORIAL BOARD

Frank M. Cross   Old Testament
Raymond E. Brown   New Testament
Jonas C. Greenfield   Apocrypha

THE ANCHOR BIBLE

DANIEL, ESTHER AND JEREMIAH:
THE ADDITIONS

A New Translation
with
Introduction and Commentary

by

Carey A. Moore

DOUBLEDAY & COMPANY, INC.
GARDEN CITY, NEW YORK
1977

Library of Congress Cataloging in Publication Data

Bible. O. T. Apocrypha. English. Selections. 1977.
Daniel, Esther, and Jeremiah.

(The Anchor Bible; 44)
Includes bibliographies and indexes.
1. Bible. O. T. Apocrypha—Commentaries.
I. Moore, Carey A., 1930–   II. Title.   III. Series.
BS192.2.A1 1964.G3 vol. 44 [BS1695] 220.6′6s [229]
ISBN 0-385-04702-9
Library of Congress Catalog Card Number 76–42376

In grateful memory of
a gifted and dedicated teacher
William Frederick Shaffer,
Franklin Professor of Greek
Gettysburg College, 1931-1962

THE APOCRYPHA

The term Apocrypha (or "Deuterocanonical Books" in Roman Catholic usage) is popularly understood to describe the fifteen books or parts of books from the pre-Christian period that Catholics accept as canonical Scripture but Protestants and Jews do not. This designation and definition are inaccurate on many counts. An apocryphon is literally a hidden writing, kept secret for the initiate and too exalted for the general public; virtually none of these books makes such a claim. Not only Roman Catholics but also Orthodox and Eastern Christians accept these books, wholly or partially, as canonical Scripture. Roman Catholics do not accept all of them as canonical Scripture, for I and II Esdras and the Prayer of Manasseh are not included in the official Catholic canon drawn up at the Council of Trent (1545-1563). Many Protestant churches have no official decision declaring these books to be non-canonical; and, in fact, up to the last century they were included in most English Protestant Bibles. What is certain is that these books did not find their way into final Jewish Palestinian canon of Scripture. Thus, despite their Jewish origins (parts of II Esdras are Christian and Latin in origin), they were preserved for the most part in Greek by Christians as a heritage from the Alexandrian Jewish community and their basic text is found in the codices of the Septuagint. However, recent discoveries, especially that of the Dead Sea scrolls, have brought to light the original Hebrew or Aramaic texts of some of these books. Leaving aside the question of canonicity, Christians and Jews now unite in recognizing the importance of these books for tracing the history of Judaism and Jewish thought in the centuries between the last of the Hebrew Scriptures and the advent of Christianity.

PREFACE

Originally, *The Additions to Esther* were to have been part of my Esther volume in the Anchor Bible series; however, it soon became apparent to the General Editors that the deuterocanonical portions of Esther were deserving of a more extended treatment than first envisioned. Thus, at the suggestion of Professors W. F. Albright and D. N. Freedman, I removed the Additions from my Esther volume, published the latter in 1971 as volume 7B of the Anchor series, and agreed to do *The Additions to Esther and Jeremiah* as part of Vol. VI of the Anchor Apocrypha, with Father Louis F. Hartman of Catholic University doing *The Additions to Daniel* for the same volume. However, as the result of the untimely death of Father Hartman in 1970, the General Editors asked me to take over the responsibility for *The Additions to Daniel* as well.

The task of doing the present volume proved more time-consuming and far more fascinating than I had expected. My research was made much easier by the efforts of many persons, known and unknown. Ms. Anna Jane Moyer and her predecessor, Mrs. Sarah B. Westine, librarians in charge of the Interlibrary Loan Service at Gettysburg College, as well as nameless persons working in other libraries near and far, have made quickly available to me books and articles which, at first glance at least, would have seemed very difficult for a professor working in a private liberal arts college to secure. Professor David Noel Freedman, who was so very helpful to me in my Esther volume, has offered many valuable criticisms and suggestions for the present work, as have Mr. Robert W. Hewetson, Ms. Eve H. Roshevsky, and the Anchor Bible staff at Doubleday. Once again, Mrs. Mary Miller did an excellent job of typing the manuscript.

I am most mindful of my indebtedness to those scholars, living and dead, who have struggled with, written on—and sometimes even come to love—the Additions to Daniel, Esther, or Jeremiah. I recognize my great indebtedness to them and hope I have sufficiently acknowledged it throughout this commentary.

In the present commentary I have tried to do two things which, at times, may strike some readers as resulting in needless, if not boring, repetition, i.e. I have tried to make each of the three Additions an independent entity, intelligible in itself without the readers having to peruse the other two Additions as well; at the same time, I have also tried to look at the Additions to Daniel, Esther, and Jeremiah as a unit, consisting of similar or related works rather than as totally dissimilar and unrelated compositions, united only by the fact that they share a common title, "The Additions to . . ." This much I do know: to see the trees is easy; to see the forest is even easier; but to see both clearly at the same time—*that* is very difficult, indeed. Whether I have been reasonably successful in keeping these two perspectives in focus, the reader must decide.

C. A. MOORE

Gettysburg College
December 1975

CONTENTS

"THE PRAYER OF AZARIAH AND
THE HYMN OF THE THREE YOUNG MEN"

"SUSANNA"

"BEL AND THE SNAKE"

THE ADDITIONS TO ESTHER

THE ADDITIONS TO JEREMIAH

I BARUCH

EPISTLE OF JEREMIAH

LIST OF ILLUSTRATIONS

1. A view of the city of Babylon and its justly famous ziggurat in the days of the Neo-Babylonian empire. Eckhard Unger, *Babylon, Die heilige Stadt nach der Babylonier,* 2nd ed., Berlin: W. de Gruyter, 1970.
2. Ancient relief depicting a Mesopotamian deity pursuing a winged monster. Courtesy of the British Museum.
3. A ferocious lioness mauling an Ethiopian; eighth century B.C., from Nimrud. Courtesy of the British Museum.
4. Natural and mythical animals, on colored tiles, decorate the southeastern pillars of Babylon's Ishtar Gate; sixth century B.C. Courtesy of the Oriental Institute, University of Chicago.
5. Gold foundation plaque of Darius I (552-486 B.C.), telling the details of the *apadana*'s construction. Photo G. Bourdelon.
6. An ancient document (a marriage contract in Aramaic) written in 449 B.C. on papyrus, rolled, tied, and sealed. Courtesy of The Brooklyn Museum, Charles Edwin Wilbour Fund.
7. A synagogal mural at Dura-Europos, depicting Esther and Xerxes receiving a message (cf. Esth 9:11); third century A.D. Courtesy of Yale University Art Gallery.
8. View of a procession entering Babylon's famous Ishtar Gate. (For close-up of a portion of the gate, see Plate 4.) Eckhard Unger, *Babylon, Die heilige Stadt nach der Babylonier,* 2nd ed., Berlin: W. de Gruyter, 1970.
9. Line drawing of an ancient relief depicting soldiers of Tiglath-pileser III (745-727 B.C.) carrying on their shoulders captured idols. Courtesy of The Archaeological Museum of Cairo.
10. Seated Canaanite god in bronze, covered with gold leaf, dating to ca. 1350-1100 B.C. Courtesy of the Oriental Institute, University of Chicago.
11. A Syrian god in bronze with silver overleaf, dating to 1600-1400 B.C. Courtesy of the British Museum.
12. Nude, winged Babylonian goddess on the Burney Plaque; early second millennium B.C. Courtesy of Sotheby and Co., London.
13. Dead Sea scroll fragment of vs. 44 of the Epistle of Jeremiah, from Cave VII, dating to the first century B.C. From *Les 'Petites Grottes' de Qumrân* by M. Baillet et al., Plate xxx, fig. 2. Courtesy of Oxford University Press, Oxford.

PRINCIPAL ABBREVIATIONS

1. PUBLICATIONS

AB   The Anchor Bible, 1961-

AfR   *Archiv für Religionswissenschaft*

AJSL   *American Journal of Semitic Languages and Literatures*

ANET²   *Ancient Near Eastern Texts Relating to the Old Testament,* ed. J. B. Pritchard, 2d ed., Princeton University Press, 1955

APOT   *The Apocrypha and Pseudepigrapha of the Old Testament,* ed. R. H. Charles, 2 vols., Oxford at the Clarendon Press, 1913

BA   *The Biblical Archaeologist*

BASOR *Bulletin of the American Schools of Oriental Research*

BDB   F. Brown, S. R. Driver, and C. A. Briggs, eds., *A Hebrew and English Lexicon of the Old Testament,* Boston: Houghton Mifflin, 1906; Oxford University Press, 1907. Repr. 1953, 1955

BH³   *Biblica Hebraica,* ed. Rudolf Kittel, 3d ed., Stuttgart: Privilegierte Württembergische Bibelanstalt, 1937, and after

BR   *Biblical Research*

BSt   Biblische Studien

BZ   *Biblische Zeitschrift*

BZAW   Beihefte zur *Zeitschrift für die Alttestamentliche Wissenschaft*

CBQ   *Catholic Biblical Quarterly*

CJT   *Canadian Journal of Theology*

EJ   *Encyclopaedia Judaica,* 16 vols., Jerusalem, 1971

GKC   *Gesenius' Hebrew Grammar,* ed. by E. F. Kautzsch, the 2d Eng. ed. rev. by A. E. Cowley. From the 28th Ger. rev. ed., Leipzig, 1909. Oxford University Press, 1910, repr. 1946 and after

HDB   *Hastings' Dictionary of the Bible,* 5 vols., New York: Scribner, 1901

HPE   *The History of the Persian Empire,* by A. T. Olmstead, University of Chicago Press, 1948

HTR   *Harvard Theological Review*

HTS   Harvard Theological Studies

HUCA   *Hebrew Union College Annual*

IDB   *The Interpreter's Dictionary of the Bible,* eds. G. A. Buttrick et al., 4 vols., New York: Abingdon, 1962

IOTG   *An Introduction to the Old Testament in Greek,* ed. by H. B. Swete and rev. by R. R. Ottley, Oxford at the University Press, 1914

JBL   *Journal of Biblical Literature*

JJGL	*Jahrbuch für jüdische Geschichte und Literatur*
JQR	*Jewish Quarterly Review*
JTS	*Journal of Theological Studies*
LSJ	Henry G. Liddell and Robert Scott, eds., *A Greek-English Lexicon*, rev. by Henry S. Jones, 9th ed., Oxford at the University Press, 1940, repr. 1948 and after
OTTV	*The Old Testament Text and Versions: The Hebrew Text in Transmission and the History of the Ancient Versions,* by B. J. Roberts, University of Wales Press, 1951
PAAJR	*Proceedings of the American Academy for Jewish Research*
PSBA	*Proceedings of the Society of Biblical Archaeology*
RB	*Revue Biblique*
REJ	*Revue des Études Juives*
RHR	*Revue de l'Histoire des Religions*
RSR	*Recherches de science religieuse*
SEÅ	*Svensk Exegetisk Årsbok*
ThR	*Theologische Revue*
TQ	*Theologische Quartalschrift*
VT	*Vetus Testamentum*
ZAW	*Zeitschrift für die alttestamentliche Wissenschaft*
ZDMG	*Zeitschrift der deutschen morgenländischen Gesellschaft*
ZRGG	*Zeitschrift für Religions- und Geistesgeschichte*

2. VERSIONS

AT	Greek "A-text," the so-called "Lucianic recension" of Esther
LXX	The Septuagint, or B-text
LXX^A	Codex Alexandrinus, fifth century A.D.
LXX^B	Codex Vaticanus, fourth century
LXX$^\aleph$	Codex Sinaiticus, fourth century
LXX^L	Lucianic Recension
LXX^Q	Codex Marchalianus, sixth century
LXX^V	Codex Venetus, eighth-ninth centuries
⊕	The "Theodotion" version
OL	The *Vetus Latina,* or Old Latin
SyrH.	The Syro-Hexaplar
Vulg.	The Vulgate
JB	The Jerusalem Bible, 1966
KJ	The King James or Authorized Version of 1611
NEB	The New English Bible, 1961, 1970
RSV	The Revised Standard Version, 1946, 1952. (Unless otherwise identified, quotations from other books of the Bible or Apocrypha are from the RSV.)

3. OTHER ABBREVIATIONS

Akk.	Akkadian
Ar.	Arabic
Aram.	Aramaic
Arm.	Armenian
Bab.	Babylonian
Gr.	Greek
Heb.	Hebrew
Pers.	Persian
Ant.	The *Jewish Antiquities* of Josephus
MS/S	Manuscript/s
NT	New Testament
OT	Old Testament

GLOSSARY OF TERMS

Aramaism, a characteristic feature of Aramaic occurring in another language or dialect.

dittography, the accidental repetition by a scribe, as he copies a manuscript, of a letter, word, or section of material.

gloss, a brief note in the margin or between the lines which some later scribe incorporated into the text he was copying.

haplography, the accidental omission by a scribe, as he copies a manuscript, of a letter, word, or section of material.

Hebraism, a characteristic feature of Hebrew occurring in another language or dialect, e.g. Gr. *kai egeneto* is a Hebraism for Heb. *wyhy.*

hendiadys, a rhetorical figure using two words to express one idea.

passim, Latin for "at different places."

recension, a version brought about by the revision of a text based on a critical evaluation of other texts; here especially, the stages reached in a series of attempts to bring the Greek translation of the Old Testament into line with a Hebrew text prevailing at each stage and in a given location.

Semiticism, here a characteristic feature of either Hebrew or Aramaic occurring in a non-Semitic language.

terminus a quo, Latin for "end from which," i.e. the highest date.

terminus ad quem, Latin for "end to which," i.e. the lowest date.

uncial, either as adjective or noun, pertaining to early medieval Greek manuscripts copied in large, capital letters; uncials are conventionally designed with upper case sigla, e.g. Codex Vaticanus is LXX[B].

Vorlage, German for "prototype," i.e. the original or model after which anything is copied or patterned.

TRANSCRIPTION EQUIVALENTS

Hebrew and Aramaic

'-aleph	k-kaph
'-ayin	q-qoph
h-he	s-samekh
ḥ-heth	ṣ-tsade
ṭ-teth	ś-sin
y-yodh	š-shin

Apart from the above, the remaining Hebrew letters have natural English equivalents. Often, in this commentary especially where the vocalization of the Hebrew word is not in question, only the consonants have been written, this being, of course, the way in which Hebrew was written in the pre-masoretic stage.

In our English translation of the personal names in the Additions are the familiar anglicized spellings of the masoretic text rather than transliterations of the Greek, e.g. the Gr. *Ananias* is rendered as Hananiah.

Greek

e-epsilon	*u-upsilon*
z-zeta	*ph-phi*
ē-eta	*ch-chi*
th-theta	*ps-psi*
x-xi	*ō-omega*
o-omicron	

Apart from the above, the remaining Greek letters have natural English equivalents.

GENERAL INTRODUCTION

The Additions to Daniel, Esther, and Jeremiah consist of those eleven extended passages in the Septuagint which have no counterpart in the Hebrew Bible.[1] Because Christians living outside of Palestine regularly used the Greek translation of the Old Testament rather than the Semitic text, these "Additions" were, quite naturally, accepted as canonical by most Christians. To be sure, here and there a Church Father would question or even reject a particular Addition[2]; but the Additions withstood the attacks from critics inside the Christian Church and so continued to be part of the Christian canon until the sixteenth century, at which time the Protestants rejected them, calling them "apocryphal," while the Roman Catholic Church at the Council of Trent reaffirmed their canonicity in 1546, calling them "deuterocanonical," i.e. of the second canon.[3]

A BRIEF DESCRIPTION OF THE ADDITIONS

Before going any further, we should identify and very briefly describe the particular Additions in question. The Additions to Daniel consists of three extended passages: "The Prayer of Azariah and the Hymn of the Three Young Men" (sixty-eight verses), these being offered by the three martyrs who had been thrown into the fiery furnace for refusing to commit idolatry; "Susanna" (sixty-four verses), the story of a devout Jewess who was

---

[1] The Additions to Daniel consist of 174 verses, to Esther of 107, and to Jeremiah of 212.

[2] The canonical status of the Additions in each book will be discussed at the appropriate point in the present commentary. Complete lists of the canonical books of Church Fathers, Councils, and Synods may be found conveniently in H. B. Swete, *IOTG*, 200-214; and in Albert Sundberg, *The Old Testament of the Early Church*, HTS, XX (1958), 58-59. For brief introductions to the many Church Fathers mentioned in this commentary, the interested reader should see Berthold Altaner, *Patrology*, tr. H. C. Graef, Edinburgh-London: Nelson, 1960. The original texts of the Fathers may be found in J. P. Migne, *Patrologiae cursus completus*, Series *Graeca* and *Latina*. For the dates of relevant Church Fathers, and of classical writers, see Appendix I, p. 359.

[3] According to the Council, the Deutero-Canon consisted of the Additions to Daniel, Esther, and Jeremiah, I and II Maccabees, Judith, Tobit, Ecclesiasticus, and the Wisdom of Solomon. Later on, three other works were added by the Roman Catholic Church as appendixes to the New Testament, namely, III and IV Esdras and the Prayer of Manasseh.

falsely accused of committing adultery; and "Bel and the Snake" (forty-two verses), which tells how Daniel, at the risk of his life, sought out and destroyed two "gods" of the Babylonians.

The Additions to Esther consists of six extended additions: Mordecai's dream (Addition A) and its interpretation (Addition F), verbatim transcripts of Haman's letter announcing a pogrom against the Jews (Addition B) and of Mordecai's letter counteracting it (Addition E), the prayers of Mordecai and Esther (Addition C), and a description of Esther's going before the king unsummoned (Addition D).

Actually, the Additions to Jeremiah consist of two separate books. I Baruch is a collection of miscellaneous literary genre: a confession for the Palestinian remnant (I Bar 1:15-2:5), prayers for the exiled community (2:6-3:8), a poem in praise of Wisdom (3:9-4:4), and a psalm of encouragement (4:5-5:9). The Epistle of Jeremiah, which in the Vulgate is ch. 6 of I Baruch, is a seventy-three-verse harangue against idols and idolatry.

These Septuagint passages, then, are quite diverse in their content, function, and literary genre. Consequently, it is very difficult to make generalizations that are equally applicable to all of them, whether one is speaking of such things as their origin, original language, place of composition, or the like. Nonetheless, as we shall see, the Additions to Daniel, Esther, and Jeremiah do, indeed, share much more with one another than just the common title, "The Additions to. . . ."

THEIR INTRUSIVE CHARACTER

On one point virtually all modern scholars agree, namely, all the Additions with one possible exception,[4] are secondary and intrusive, that is, each of them was added after the particular book in question had attained its final form.[5] In other words, with the possible exception of one passage in Daniel, none of these Additions is a "survivor" or witness to a passage that was in the Semitic text of Daniel, Esther, or Jeremiah when that particular book *was first written*.

How do we know this? Sometimes, as with the Additions to Esther, inconsistencies and contradictions between the canonical and the deuterocanonical portions prove that the Additions had not been an integral

---

[4] I.e. the Prose Narrative concerning the three martyrs in the fiery furnace in "The Prayer of Azariah and the Hymn of the Three Young Men," vss. 23-28[48-51], see pp. 63-65.

[5] By "final" is meant that Semitic text closest to the completed text which the rabbis ultimately approved in the second century A.D. and from which the present MT presumably descends.

part of the book but were added later. Sometimes, as with "Susanna," "Bel and the Snake," and, especially "The Prayer of Azariah and the Hymn of the Three Young Men," the Septuagint (the LXX), in contrast with the later "Theodotion" version (℗), shows that the particular Addition in question was originally separate and circulated quite independently of the biblical book in which it is now found. Other times, as with I Baruch, the presence of certain religious teachings and historical errors argue against the authenticity of the material in question (see NOTES and COMMENTS *passim*).

Probably none of these arguments would be very important in itself, let alone conclusive, were it not for the fact that the external evidence supports and reinforces the impression drawn from the internal evidence, i.e. there are no ancient Hebrew or Aramaic texts containing any of these Additions,[6] no indisputable instances of their being quoted in the Talmud, and no extant Greek translation of them by Aquila, the Jewish convert of the second century A.D. who translated the then-current masoretic text (MT) into slavishly literal Greek.[7]

ORIGINAL LANGUAGE

When were these Additions added to the canonical books? Where did they come from? In what language/s were they originally composed? To these questions Septuagint scholars of the nineteenth century, especially O. F. Fritzsche, E. Schürer, and E. C. Bissell, answered that these Additions never had been part of the Hebrew text, let alone part of the Jewish canon in Palestine; all these Additions had originally been composed in Greek and had been added to the Septuagint around the beginning of the Christian era, give or take a hundred or so years. According to these scholars, the Council of Jamnia, that Jewish council ca. A.D. 90 which ultimately fixed the Hebrew canon, had not rejected these Additions for the simple reason that these Additions never had existed in the Hebrew or Aramaic texts of the Old Testament. As support for these conclusions, modern critics pointed to the statements of ancient scholars such as Origen (185-?254) and, especially, Jerome (340-420), who at various places in their writings expressly stated that they knew of no Hebrew version of this or that Addition. Moreover, modern scholars knew of no external evi-

---

[6] To be sure, Hebrew and Aramaic texts of some of these Additions do occur in the works of the medieval Jewish historians Josippon and Jerahmeel; but in all likelihood, these Semitic texts are not survivors but rather Hebrew and Aramaic translations of the Septuagint and Vulgate; see p. 154, n. 3.

[7] For details of Aquila and his translation, see Swete, *IOTG*, pp. 31-42; and B. J. Roberts, *OTTV*, pp. 120-123.

dence for the one-time existence of any of these Additions in Hebrew or Aramaic, i.e there were no ancient Semitic texts concerning these particular additions, no indisputable quotations of them in the Talmud, and no Greek translation of them by Aquila.

In this matter of the original language/s of the Additions, few twentieth-century scholars agree with the logic of nineteenth-century giants like Fritzsche, Schürer, or Bissell. Moreover, among the advantages that present-day scholars have had over scholars as recent as those in the first half of the present century are the Dead Sea scrolls. These copies of several apocryphal and pseudepigraphal works, formerly known only from the Greek or one of the other ancient versions,[8] have been found in Semitic texts, namely, Tobit (in both Hebrew and Aramaic), Jubilees, Enoch, and the Testament of the Twelve Patriarchs, not to mention a number of other heretofore unknown apocryphal or pseudepigraphical works, including Pseudo-Daniel *a, b,* and *c* (see p. 120). Thus, there is today an almost irresistible disposition on the part of scholars to consider the possibility of a Semitic *Vorlage* (or prototype) for most, if not all, books of the apocrypha and pseudepigrapha.

As for the three books treated in this commentary, each of them probably has at least one Addition which originated in Greek. In Esther, for instance, it is indisputable that the letters of Haman and Mordecai (Additions B and E) were originally Greek compositions; in Jeremiah Stanza vii of the Poem (I Bar 5:5-9) was almost certainly composed in Greek; and in Daniel the story of Bel may have been, too (see NOTES and COMMENTS *passim*).

On the other hand, it is also virtually certain that several Additions in our three books were originally composed in a Semitic language. "The Prayer of Azariah and the Hymn of the Three Young Men" in Daniel, the Epistle of Jeremiah, and the first half of I Baruch (1:1 - 3:8) were almost certainly composed in Hebrew, whereas, in Daniel the Prose Narrative concerning the three martyrs in the fiery furnace (vss. 23-28[45-51]) and the story of Susanna were, in all likelihood, originally in Aramaic. Still other Additions, which seem to have had a Semitic *Vorlage,* may have been written originally in either Hebrew or Aramaic, the evidence being too vague for scholars to be sure. (The justification for all of these assertions will be worked out in detail at the appropriate place in the treatment of each of these Additions.)

---

[8] Until the discovery of the Dead Sea scrolls, the Wisdom of Sira was the only apocryphon for which scholars had the Semitic *Vorlage,* the ancient Hebrew text having been recovered in 1896-1900 from several medieval manuscripts in the Old Cairo Genizah.

ORIGINS OF THE ADDITIONS

The origins of the Additions are almost as varied as their literary genre. Several of them seem to be original compositions deliberately written for their present context, for example, the letters of Haman and Mordecai (Additions B and E in Esther), the prayers of Mordecai and Esther (Addition C), the account of Esther's going before the king unsummoned (Addition D), and the interpretation of Mordecai's dream (Addition F). On the other hand, several of the Additions were independently circulating works, originally having no relationship whatever to their present context, e.g. "The Prayer of Azariah,"[9] "The Hymn of the Three Young Men," the prayers and psalm in I Baruch (I Bar 1:15 - 3:8, 4:5 - 5:4), and, possibly, Mordecai's dream (Addition A). Several of the aforementioned Additions were probably independent works taken from some liturgy of the synagogue or temple. By contrast, "Susanna" was a purely secular tale which only later on was thoroughly judaized and related to the prophet Daniel. "Bel and the Snake" and the Epistle of Jeremiah are probably haggadic or priestly expositions of passages of Scripture, notably, of Jer 51:34-35,44 and Jer 10:11, respectively. As for the origins of the poem in praise of Wisdom (I Bar 3:9 - 4:4) and the Prose Narrative in the fiery furnace Addition (Dan 3:48-51 of the LXX), these may have been composed for their present context; but, more likely, they had prior independent existence. (It cannot be stressed too often that the various generalizations so easily offered here in the General Introduction are pursued in detail at the appropriate places in the commentary.)

In sum, the Additions have very diverse sources, both pagan and Jewish, as well as secular and religious. As the NOTES and COMMENTS will illustrate, many of the prayers and psalms in the Additions are redolent of earlier biblical phrases and images, especially those of Isaiah, Jeremiah, Psalms, and Deuteronomy.

---

[9] "The Prayer of Azariah and the Hymn of the Three Young Men" is the general title given to that material in the LXX which actually consists of at least three distinct compositions, each of which probably had a separate and independent existence apart from its present context in Daniel, namely, "The Prayer of Azariah," the prose narrative concerning the fiery furnace incident, and "The Hymn of the Three Young Men" (see pp. 40-44).

EFFECT OF THE ADDITIONS

It would be very helpful for one's understanding of the Additions if one could know their purpose, that is, why an ancient editor supplied this or that Addition, and what he had hoped the Addition would accomplish. It is, however, much easier and safer to describe the Addition's effect; for the particular effect, which may or may not have been the one intended by the ancient editor, is nonetheless objectively observable, whereas the ancient editor's purpose can only be inferred.

The effect of the Additions on our three books depends upon the particular book in question. Obviously Jeremiah's message and reputation as a religious figure and writer are in no way affected by the addition of these five chapters expressly stated as having been written by someone else, even if that "someone else" were Jeremiah's own personal secretary, Baruch. And assuming for the moment that the Epistle of Jeremiah actually was written by the prophet himself (which it certainly was not), one must admit that the Epistle does nothing to enhance Jeremiah's reputation as a thinker or writer; but the Addition is also too brief to diminish it, either.

On the other hand, the Book of Esther is totally transformed by the presence of its Additions. Because of them, *God,* not Esther or Mordecai, is the hero in the Greek version.[10] Then too, whereas in the MT the establishment of the historical basis for the Jewish festival of Purim is the matter of central concern, in the Greek version, primarily because of the Additions, the establishment of Purim is played down and religious matters are strongly emphasized, namely, God's providential care of his people, his miraculous intervention to save Esther (*the* highpoint, or climax, in the Greek version), the efficacy of prayer, and the importance of *kašrût* (see p. 157, n. 7). In short, the Additions correct what some Jewish and Christian critics have regarded as "deficiencies" in the Hebrew version of Esther.

In this matter of the effect of the Additions upon the canonical book, the Additions to Daniel occupies a middle ground, in that it alters the character of the canonical book only slightly. "The Prayer of Azariah and the Hymn of the Three Young Men" shifts the spotlight from the MT's center of interest (i.e. the pagan king and his lavish court) to the faith of the three martyrs and the greatness of their God. The story of Susanna, not only provides the sole female model for righteousness in the entire

---

[10] For instance, God, who is not mentioned even once in the Hebrew text of Esther, is referred to over fifty times in the Greek version!

Book of Daniel, but it also showed the ancient readers that the young Daniel had been very courageous and spiritually precocious long before he attained full adulthood. "Bel and the Snake" confirmed the ancient reader's hope that, unlike King David, Daniel did not change for the worse as he grew older and more powerful, that is, "Bel and the Snake" showed that even after serving long years as a courtier of the king, Daniel was still God's man first and was still willing to risk his life for his religion. Nonetheless, these Additions, unlike the Additions to Esther, can be removed without drastically affecting the character and message of the Greek version.

RELIGIOUS IDEAS

With the possible exception of "Bel and the Snake,"[11] all the Additions are deeply imbued with the spirit of Judaism such as we find it, in all its variety of beliefs and practices, in the first two centuries before the Christian era. God is depicted in the Additions as being the omnipotent and transcendent deity (cf., especially, "The Hymn of the Three Young Men" and the Epistle of Jeremiah), who is also the personal, anthropomorphic God of the Fathers (see especially "The Prayer of Azariah," Addition C of Esther and I Baruch),[12] guiding the fortunes of his chosen people in general (cf. I Baruch, Additions A and F of Esther) and miraculously saving those individuals who trust in him and are suffering for the sake of their religion (so the Additions to Daniel and Addition D of Esther). He hears their prayers ("The Prayer of Azariah," "Susanna," Addition C of Esther, and I Baruch) and forbids worship of any god other than himself ("The Prayer of Azariah," Addition C of Esther, and the Epistle of Jeremiah). Other important items, such as covenant, the Law of Moses, kašrût, temple, strong ethnic and religious consciousness, and the like, are stressed in varying degrees in this or that Addition. Strangely enough, neither sacrifice nor apocalypticism is a matter of any great concern, although Additions A and F of Esther do include ingredients of the latter.

In any event, whatever the particular reason may have been for the various Additions being excluded from the Jewish canon, the reason cannot

---

[11] In "Bel" the spotlight is centered almost exclusively on Daniel and his cleverness, with God scarcely getting into the act; and were it not for the Habakkuk episode (which was added only later), the same would be true of "The Snake." Not surprisingly, among the Church Fathers "Bel and the Snake" was the least quoted of the three Additions to Daniel.

[12] I.e. I Bar 1:1 - 3:8 and 4:5 - 5:9.

have been that the Additions contained heretical teachings or ideas unacceptable to normative Judaism as defined, for instance, by the Council of Jamnia.[13]

LITERARY MERIT

There is a certain risk involved in determining the literary merit of a work known only in translation, for there is always the possibility that either the particular translator has done an injustice to the original or, at the opposite extreme, that he has considerably improved upon the original. With respect to the Additions, however, our problem is somewhat simplified by the fact that, so far as we can tell, the same Greek translator was responsible for both the canonical and the deuterocanonical portions of each book (see below). There is, however, no reason to think that the same translator did Daniel, Esther, and Jeremiah.

With respect to the Additions to Daniel, a distinction must be made here between the literary merit of the LXX (or better, its presumed Semitic *Vorlage*) and the ϴ (and its presumed Semitic *Vorlage*). For instance, "Susanna" and "Bel" are told far better in ϴ than in the LXX; and, on the whole, ϴ is far better edited than the LXX, especially in "The Prayer of Azariah," "Susanna," and "Bel" (see NOTES and COMMENTS *passim*). Moreover, as literary creations in their own right, "Susanna" and "Bel" are very effectively told tales, although, interestingly enough, the Church Fathers alluded to Susanna herself and ignored "Bel," probably out of religious considerations. If usage be an important criterion of literary merit, i.e. the extent, frequency, and length of time a literary work is quoted or alluded to by Church Fathers or is used in the liturgy of the Christian Church, then the "Hymn of the Three Young Men" is much superior to the "Prayer of Azariah" or "The Snake," the latter two being virtually ignored by the Fathers.

In the canonical portions of the Greek version of Esther, the LXX (or B-text) disagrees appreciably with the A-text, or so-called "Lucianic recension" (see pp. 163-164). In the Additions themselves, however, there is substantial agreement between the two, probably because the A-text borrowed its Additions from the B-text. In any event, the two royal edicts, the one composed by Haman (Addition B) and the one by Mordecai (Addition E), are both very effectively constructed political and psychological documents, written, as befitting their undeniable Greek origins, in a highly rhetorical and florid style. The other Additions are far

---

[13] One possible exception to this generalization, at least according to one interpretation, is "Susanna" (see p. 80).

more simple in their style and content. The description of Esther's going before the king unsummoned is very effectively told in Addition D and is the one passage in the Additions to Esther which Church Fathers, like Augustine, quoted. The prayers of Mordecai and Esther (Addition C), though appropriate for their context, are little more than a mosaic of older biblical phrases and ideas. Addition A, consisting of both poetry and prose, is clear enough but hardly memorable for its style, while Addition F (the interpretation of the dream) is confusing and even contradictory. In sum, the Additions to Esther do not represent excellent writing; and, not surprisingly, they were ignored by the Church Fathers, although, in all fairness to the Additions, it should be noted that the Church Fathers also rarely alluded to canonical Esther (see p. 156).

As for the Additions to Jeremiah, the Greek version itself offers no great problems, perhaps because there is no extant text of Theodotion to point them up. In any event, I Baruch, which is actually a composite of the works of several authors, consists of a prose introduction (1:1-14) and four prayers and psalms of uneven quality (see NOTES and COMMENTS *passim*), bound together only by their having the same assumed historical background, namely, the Exile. In terms of content and style, the prayers and psalms offer nothing new but are faint or distorted echoes of well-known images and phrases from such books as Psalms, Isaiah, and Jeremiah. The book suffers from the additional burden of being very poorly edited: the prose introduction is imprecise and confusing, and the major sections of the book are arranged in a most illogical fashion (see COMMENT, p. 275). Had it not been for 3:36-38, which the Church Fathers regarded, erroneously it would seem, as predictive of the Incarnation, I Baruch would have been completely ignored by the ancient writers.

Essentially the same criticisms must be leveled against the Epistle of Jeremiah. The Epistle has little in the way of imagery or phraseology which is new or memorable, the poem—for that is what it really is, despite its title—being little more than a mosaic created out of words and images from Jeremiah, Isaiah, Psalms, and Deuteronomy. The "epistle" is also lacking in any clear organization and development of thought, this in spite of the fact that it does have essentially the same refrain after eight of its ten strophes. However, the Epistle evidently was more appreciated by the Church Fathers, or at least, it seems to have been referred to more often than was I Baruch.

Authors of the Additions

There is no reason to think that the authors of these Additions were other than Jewish. Their distinctive Jewish piety[14] and theology,[15] their occasional strong anti-Gentile spirit,[16] and, most important of all, their probable date of composition (see below) definitely preclude their being Christian compositions. Not only do the Additions in our three books have different authors; but, as implied earlier, the Additions within any one of the three books also have at least a couple of authors. In Daniel, for instance, "The Prayer of Azariah," "The Hymn of the Three Young Men," "Susanna," and "Bel and the Snake" each had its own particular author, and he is not to be confused or identified with the Jewish editor/s who inserted these Additions into their present contexts. Moreover, "Bel and the Snake" consists of at least three originally separate tales: the Bel narrative, the Snake story, and the Habakkuk episode. As for the Additions to Esther, even if Additions A, C, D, and F were composed by the same author (which they probably were not), Additions B and E, being composed originally in Greek, were obviously not the product of that same writer. As for the Additions to Jeremiah, each of the four major sections of I Baruch probably has its own separate author; the Epistle of Jeremiah is obviously a pseudepigraphon.

Date

In fixing the dates for the Additions one must carefully distinguish three different types of dates: (1) the *terminus ad quem,* which is usually established by the earliest external evidence, i.e. the earliest quoting or alluding to the Addition by another datable ancient source; (2) the date of the Addition's insertion, or inclusion, in the canonical text (which may or may not be the date of its composition)[17]; and (3) the date of original composition.

The *terminus ad quem,* or latest possible date, is set definitively by the

[14] Cf. Addition C of Esther, "Susanna," and I Baruch.
[15] Cf. "The Prayer of Azariah" and I Baruch.
[16] See especially Additions A, C, and F of Esther.
[17] For example, the date of Addition E's insertion in the Septuagint version of Esther is identical with its date of composition, whereas "The Hymn of the Three Young Men" had existed sometime before it found itself in its present place.

external evidence. Additions B, C, D, and E of Esther are the earliest attested Additions, being paraphrased by Josephus in his *Jewish Antiquities* (ca. A.D. 93-94); but Additions A and F, as well as the Additions to Daniel and to Jeremiah, were not even alluded to, let alone quoted, until the middle of the second century A.D. (see NOTES *passim*).

However, the date of insertion for the Additions, at least for those that had existed in the Semitic text, must be pushed back to no later than the end of the second century B.C., that being the time by which the Semitic texts of Daniel, Esther, and Jeremiah had been translated into Greek; and, in most cases, the translator of the Additions in a given book is the same as the translator of the canonical text as well (see below). In most instances, scholars have never been able to detect syntactical, stylistic, or vocabulary differences between the Greek of the Additions and the Greek of the canonical portions of Daniel.

As for their dates of composition, here there is greater latitude—and uncertainty. "Susanna" and the Epistle of Jeremiah may have been composed as early as the late Persian period, while "Bel and the Snake" may not have been written until shortly before the Greek translation of Daniel, that is, ca. 100 B.C. With the exceptions of the letters of Haman and Mordecai (Additions B and E), the Additions to Esther were almost certainly products of the second century B.C. On the other hand, it is virtually impossible to give a date for those Additions which may have been taken from existing synagogal or temple liturgy, for example, "The Prayer of Azariah," "The Hymn of the Three Young Men," and the prayers in I Baruch.

Nonetheless, when all things are taken into consideration, it is reasonable to conclude that most of the Additions to Daniel, Esther, and Jeremiah were composed sometime during the second century B.C. This century, it will be remembered, was an especially trying one for the Jews living in Palestine. It began with their enthusiastic switch of allegiance from the Egyptian Ptolemies to the Seleucids of Syria (ca. 198 B.C.), included the terrible Maccabean revolt against Antiochus IV (Epiphanes) ca. 167-163 B.C., and ended with the Hasmonean period during which the Jews ruled themselves, relatively free of threats from without but very much divided by cultural and religious tensions and conflicts within.[18]

---

[18] During the reign of the Hasmonean king John Hyrcanus (135-105 B.C.) such diverse religious parties as the Pharisees, Sadducees, and Essenes, including the group at Qumran, were clearly in existence and were contending with one another.

PLACE OF COMPOSITION

An Addition's provenance, or place of composition, must be inferred from
two kinds of internal evidence: (1) the Addition's presumed original language, i.e. a priori, a Greek original argues for an Egyptian provenance; a
Semitic original, for a Palestinian or Babylonian one; and (2) any in-
cidental clues in the Addition's setting, particular emphases, or theology.
As will be illustrated *passim* by NOTES and COMMENTS, the Additions to
Daniel and to Jeremiah[19] very probably had a Palestinian origin.[20] The letters of Haman and Mordecai (Additions B and E of Esther), being original Greek compositions, may very well have had an Egyptian provenance,
but there is every reason to believe that the other Additions to Esther originated in Palestine.

REJECTION FROM THE HEBREW CANON

If, as has been argued here, most of the Additions were originally second
century B.C., Palestinian works composed in Hebrew or Aramaic, then
why were they not included in the Hebrew canon as fixed by the Jewish
Fathers at the Council of Jamnia? The simple truth is that no one knows.
The decisions of the Pharisaic schools at Jamnia were "unofficial" (there
is not even an accurate record of what was determined there) and only
gradually did their decisions become the accepted positions through Judaism.

It is reasonable to assume, however, that there is no simple answer which
applies equally to all the Additions. Rather, there were specific reasons for
rejecting each of the Additions. (Perhaps the word "rejected" is too strong
here. For, in point of fact, many of the Additions probably never were accepted by all Palestinian Jews *in the first place,* that is, these Additions entered some, but not all, of the then-current Semitic scrolls of the second
century B.C.; but when the Greek translation of the particular book in

[19] Except Stanza VII of I Baruch (i.e. 5:5-9), which may have had a Greek origin
(see pp. 315-316).

[20] It is quite possible, of course, that the very earliest form of the story of Susanna
(or of the Snake) originated in Babylon; but the thoroughly judaized version we now
have is almost certainly a Palestinian creation. In any event, an Egyptian provenance
for the Additions, as was so often suggested in the last century by Septuagint specialists, is out of the question.

question was made, the particular Semitic text chosen happened to be one which contained the Additions.)

In any event, it is unlikely that the Additions were rejected because of their religious or theological content. Certainly none of the Additions (with the possible exception of "Susanna")[21] seems to contain heretical ideas or teachings unacceptable to normative Judaism as defined and interpreted by the Pharisaic schools at Jamnia. Quite to the contrary, most of the Additions are saturated with Jewish piety and orthodox Jewish theology.[22] Nonetheless, with the exception of Josephus (see p. 13 above), no ancient Jewish writer alluded to, let alone quoted, any of them.

As to why the Additions to Jeremiah were rejected by the Jews, the answer seems simple enough: both I Baruch and the Epistle of Jeremiah were adjudged by Jamnia as being of inferior religious and literary quality, a conclusion that the early Christian Church evidently shared with the Jewish Fathers, if we may judge from the extent to which Church Fathers ignored these two Additions. As for the Additions to Daniel, the likelihood is that they were rejected because the Jewish Fathers, who themselves were not very far removed from the actual "publication date" of the original Book of Daniel, knew that the Additions were interpolations; and, to make matters worse, the literary and religious inadequacies of these passages added to the handicap.

But exactly why the Semitic Additions to Esther (i.e. Additions A, C, D, and F) were rejected by the Council of Jamnia is very puzzling indeed, especially since the Additions to Esther seem to correct the so-called "deficiencies" of the canonical text (see p. 157). The truth is that the *Hebrew* version of Esther almost did not make it at the Council of Jamnia, and that as late as the third and fourth centuries A.D. there were still Jews who contested the book's canonicity.[23] Yet the Book of Esther must have been quite popular among the Jews, if one may judge from the extent of the allusions to it in the Talmud and the great number of extant medieval *megillot*.[24]

The Council of Jamnia probably preferred a Hebrew version of Esther without the Additions for one of two reasons: either the rabbis knew that the Additions were secondary and that fact, in and of itself, was sufficient justification for the Additions' being rejected; or the rabbis realized that these obviously religious Additions ran an excellent chance of being unin-

---

[21] "Susanna" does contradict a Pharisaic *Halakhah* in the Mishnah (see p. 80).

[22] Especially is this true of "The Prayer of Azariah and the Hymn of the Three Young Men," "Susanna," Additions A, C, D, and F of Esther, and I Baruch.

[23] For a full discussion of the canonicity of the Book of Esther, see AB 7B, XXI-XXXV.

[24] *Megillot* (Hebrew for "scrolls") refers to the Hebrew text of Esther written on vellum; for details, see AB 7B, Appendix III.

tentionally profaned and desecrated because of the boisterous and exuberant manner in which some Jews evidently celebrated Purim. For instance, according to one ruling in the Mishnah, Jews celebrating Purim were to drink until they were unable to distinguish between "Blessed is Mordecai" and "Cursed is Haman" (*Megillah 7b*). If Purim, in fact, was celebrated in such an uninhibited fashion, then certainly these obviously religious passages were better left out. Of the two explanations, the former strikes the present writer as the more probable (see AB 7B, XXXIII-XXXIV).

THE GREEK VERSIONS

Not surprisingly, in the matter of the Greek versions of the Additions, each book has its own particular set of problems, although in the Additions to Jeremiah the problems are, by comparison, very minimal.

As is well known among scholars, the Book of Daniel has two Greek versions, the Septuagint (LXX) and the "Theodotion" (Θ); and for reasons that are not known to us, by A.D. 250 the LXX had been displaced by Θ in the Christian Church.[25] The very puzzling relationship that exists between the LXX and Θ throughout the canonical portions of Daniel also obtains in the Additions. For instance, in "The Prayer of Azariah and the Hymn of the Three Young Men" the LXX and Θ are virtually identical, whereas, in "Susanna" these two versions differ considerably from one another in both wording *and* content (see NOTES *passim*). In this particular matter, "Bel and the Snake" holds a middle position between the two extremes. Moreover, Θ, which in the deuterocanonical portions, at least, also has a tendency to present its material in a more clear and effective manner, also has the greater number of Semiticisms (in both the canonical and deuterocanonical portions). It is certainly hard to explain the appearance of these Semiticisms in the later version (i.e. in Θ) if they are not simply the result of someone trying to bring the Greek text into a closer conformity with a Semitic one.

However, the problem of the Greek versions of Daniel, both the canonical and deuterocanonical portions, is greatly complicated by the fact that the so-called "Theodotion" version (Θ) is obviously not one of those many texts translated by the well-known second-century A.D. Jewish proselyte, Theodotion; for "Pre-Theodotion" readings, whose presence has been long recognized in the New Testament, have now also been found among the Dead Sea scrolls. Scholars are now debating the question of whether the "Θ" of Daniel is an earlier translation by a century or more (so A.

---

[25] The Septuagint version, whose Greek text until 1772 was known to scholars only indirectly through the Syro-Hexaplar, is even now represented by just two manuscripts: Kölner Papyrus 967 and Codex Chisianus 88.

Schmitt and P. Grelot) or just a recension (so J. Schüpphaus). In any event, the LXX is still regarded as being the older of the two.

Unfortunately, the date of the translation of the LXX of Daniel is far from certain; but a date somewhere around 100 B.C. is generally accepted by scholars. And, since scholars have never been able to distinguish significant differences in the diction and literary style of the Additions as over against the canonical portions of Daniel, the Additions must have been part of the Septuagint at the time of the latter's creation. (All of these rather complex matters concerning the Greek versions are dealt with in greater detail on pp. 30-33.)

Because the so-called "Theodotion" version has been the one used by the Christian Church for almost two thousand years, that version will be the basic starting point for all discussions of Daniel in the present commentary; but at all important points along the way the LXX will be examined carefully as well.

With regard to the Book of Esther in general, its Greek texts offer a different set of problems. The Greek Esther has two quite distinct versions, the Septuagint (or B-text) and the so-called "Lucianic recension" (or A-text), neither of which corresponds closely to Esther's masoretic text. Evidently, the translator of the B-text was more concerned with preserving the meaning or content of his Semitic text than he was with making a literal, word-for-word rendering of it; at points, for instance, his translation is quite paraphrastic. On the other hand, the A-text, which has in it the greater number of literalisms and Hebraisms, is shorter than the LXX, primarily because of certain "omissions" and "abbreviations." (Actually, the A-text is not a recension by Lucian, as is commonly thought, but an independent translation of a Hebrew text that was, in many ways, quite different from both the MT and the Semitic *Vorlage* of the LXX [see pp. 163-164].)

Fortunately for our purposes here, however, in the Additions the B-text and the A-text are in substantial agreement with one another, probably because the A-text borrowed the Additions from the B-text (see pp. 327-328). In any event, though the B-text will be this commentary's starting point for translation and discussion of the Additions to Esther, the A-text will also be given full treatment.

Judging from the clues given in the colophon of the Greek Esther (i.e. F 11; see pp. 250-251), we may safely conclude that the Septuagint version was made ca. 114 B.C., and that, with the exception of the letters of Haman and Mordecai (Additions B and E), the Additions to Esther were already a part of the Hebrew text at the time of the Septuagint translation. Additions B and E must have been added to the LXX some time later.[26]

The Greek texts of the Additions to Jeremiah offer relatively few

---

[26] They were part of the Septuagint before the end of the first century A.D., for Josephus paraphrased them in his *Jewish Antiquities* (ca. A.D. 93-94).

problems—possibly only because some of the potentially troublemaking evidence, such as Theodotion's version, has been lost. That that particular version of I Baruch once existed is known only because the Syro-Hexaplar has five very brief readings with the ⊕ *siglum* accompanying them. In spite of the fact that I Baruch had two separate Greek translators for its Septuagint text,[27] both sections of the translation were sufficiently literal so that R. R. Harwell could easily yet accurately "retranslate" the Greek back into good Biblical Hebrew, even to the point of recovering the probable metrical patterns of the two poems in 3:9 - 5:9 (see p. 262). In neither I Baruch nor the Epistle of Jeremiah are there many significant variants among the Septuagint manuscripts (see NOTES *passim*).[28] Vaticanus (LXX^B) seems to be the best text to use as the basis for the English translation of the Additions to Jeremiah, even as it is the best text for the Additions to Daniel (⊕^B) and to Esther (the B-text).

OTHER ANCIENT VERSIONS

The ancient and modern[29] versions of the Additions to Daniel, Esther, and Jeremiah are all based upon a Greek version, usually the Septuagint. The qualifying phrase, "usually the Septuagint," is required because of the Additions to Daniel, where only the Syro-Hexaplar and the oldest texts of the *Vetus Latina* (OL) are based upon the LXX. The Vulgate, Coptic, Ethiopic, Arabic, Armenian and Aramaic[30] are all based upon ⊕. Usually these translations are quite literal renderings of the Greek, the one exception being the Syriac, which follows "Bel and the Snake" quite literally but in "Susanna" is sometimes more free. (The justification for these generalizations, as well as a more precise qualification of them, will be found, as usual, in the NOTES *passim*.)

As for the Additions to Esther, versions such as the *Vetus Latina*, the Coptic, and Ethiopic are clearly based upon the LXX (or B-text), although the OL does have a number of readings agreeing with the A-text. In spite of the fact that in the canonical portions of Esther the Vulgate and Syriac rendered a Hebrew text, they were still quite free at points; and it appears that the same is true of their rendering of the Septuagint Additions to Esther. Likewise, in the Additions to Jeremiah the ancient ver-

---

[27] I Baruch 3:9 - 5:9 was done by someone other than the translator of I Bar 1:1 - 3:8, the latter translator being the same one who was also responsible for doing chs. 29-52 of Jeremiah (see p. 262).

[28] Unfortunately, for the Additions to Jeremiah there is no Sinaiticus (LXX^ℵ).

[29] For example, the KJ, RSV, JB, and NEB.

[30] I.e. the Aramaic text in the medieval *Chronicles of Jerahmeel*, see p. 49.

sions rendered the Septuagint version with varying degrees of literalness (see NOTES *passim* for details).

The principal difficulty in using the ancient versions for explicating or emending the Greek texts is that the ancient versions are either so fragmentary,[31] late,[32] mixed,[33] or unscientific[34] that their variant readings must be viewed with considerable caution. Nonetheless, this commentary will note interesting or important variants in the various ancient versions and, when in order, will discuss them in some detail.

[31] For example, the OL often consists of only very brief quotations from the Church Fathers.

[32] The Arabic version, for instance, may date to as late as the ninth century.

[33] E.g. the Peshitta, or Syriac.

[34] With the exception of the Septuagint and the Vulgate, none of the ancient versions is represented by what might be properly called a critical, scientific edition.

THE ADDITIONS TO DANIEL

Introduction

Description of Additions

The Additions to Daniel consists of three extended passages in the Septuagint which have no counterpart in the canonical text of Daniel, namely, "The Prayer of Azariah and the Hymn of the Three Young Men" (sixty-eight verses in the Greek text), "Susanna" (sixty-four verses), and "Bel and the Snake" (forty-two verses). Exactly where in the Septuagint each of these Additions occurs depends sometimes upon the specific Greek manuscript under consideration; but generally speaking, one may say that "The Prayer of Azariah and the Hymn of the Three Young Men" is always found between what would correspond to vss. 23 and 24 of the third chapter of canonical Daniel, and that "Susanna" and "Bel and the Snake" come, in that order, after the canonical chapters of Daniel.

As for their contents, "The Prayer of Azariah and the Hymn of the Three Young Men" contains the prayer and hymn uttered by Azariah and his two companions, Hananiah and Mishael, after they had been tossed into the fiery furnace for refusing to worship a gold image set up by King Nebuchadnezzar. They could pray and sing in the still blazing furnace, which had burned to death people just standing near it, because God had sent an angel down inside it to protect them. "Susanna" is the story of a beautiful and devout Jewess who was falsely accused of adultery by two rejected lovers. She was saved from public execution by the last-minute intervention of the young Daniel who, inspired by an angel, reopened the case and convicted her false accusers by their own testimony. "Bel and the Snake" is actually two stories. "Bel" tells of how, at the risk of his own life, the courtier Daniel proved, by means of a cunning trap, that the large quantities of food regularly "eaten" at night by the statue of Bel-Marduk were actually being stolen by the priests of Bel. "The Snake" is the story of how Daniel killed a "divine" snake in Babylon by feeding it a special concoction. In retaliation, Daniel's enemies compelled the king to throw Daniel into the Lions' Pit. Miraculously, the ravenous lions did not eat him; and when on the sixth day Daniel himself was hungry, God had an angel bring the Palestinian-based Habakkuk to feed Daniel. Upon Daniel's release the next day, his enemies were tossed into the pit and were devoured instantly. In short, all three Additions have their setting in Babylon and describe how some Jew who trusted in the Lord was delivered from certain death through the intervention of an angel.

Other generalizations can be made; but as will be evident from this commentary later, it is very difficult to make generalizations which are equally applicable to all three Additions. (The term "Addition" will be reserved here for the three major passages in Daniel; whenever a component part of any one of these Additions is spoken of, it will be referred to as an "addition," i.e. with a small "a.")

Their Intrusive Character

Perhaps the one incontestable generalization that can be made concerning these Greek Additions is that, with the possible exception of one passage within the first Addition (i.e. the Prose Narrative [see pp. 63-65]), all the Additions to Daniel are clearly intrusive and secondary, that is, they were added at various times after what we call canonical Daniel had taken its "final" form.[1] Both the external and the internal evidence clearly support this conclusion.

As for the external evidence, not only are these Additions lacking in the present MT, but there is no manuscript evidence for their existence among the Jews of antiquity. No Jewish writer in the Talmud either quotes or alludes to these specific Additions; nor does Josephus, even though in his *Jewish Antiquities* (ca. A.D. 93-94) he provides his readers with other apocryphal stories about the prophet Daniel (*Ant.* x 11.6-7). Nor has any evidence of them been found among the Dead Sea scrolls, this in spite of the fact that at least seven copies of Daniel, some of them admittedly quite fragmentary, have been found at Qumran, as well as three heretofore unknown stories about Daniel in Aramaic fragments (see p. 120). Nor do scholars know of any Greek translation of these Additions by Aquila, the second-century Jewish convert who translated the then-current rabbinic text into ridiculously literal Greek (on Aquila, see Roberts, *OTTV*, 120-123). All the ancient Semitic versions of Daniel, including the Syriac, the Syro-Hexaplar, the Arabic, and the Aramaic, as well as other versions such as the Old Latin, the Vulgate, the Ethiopic, Bohiaric, and Sahidic, are clearly based upon the Greek versions, i.e. upon either the Septuagint (LXX) or "Theodotion" (ϴ). Finally, Jerome himself (340-420) expressly stated that he knew of no current Semitic text of the Additions.

The internal evidence certainly corroborates the case made by the external evidence. "Susanna" is unquestionably intrusive (see pp. 90-91). The same must be said for "The Prayer of Azariah and the Hymn of the Three Young Men" (see p. 60) and "Bel and the Snake" (pp. 132-133), with the additional observation that each of these Additions had substantial material added to it. Although these generalizations and assertions will be discussed in detail later on at the appropriate places (as will all the

---

[1] By "final" is meant that Semitic text closest to the completed text which the rabbis ultimately approved in the second century A.D. and from which the present MT presumably descends.

generalizations made in this introduction), we may take just one example to illustrate the point. Not only does "Bel and the Snake" represent the union of two originally separate stories which circulated independently of one another, but the Snake story itself consists of at least two independent stories which circulated separately (see pp. 121-122).

Original Languages

To say that the three Additions are secondary is not to say that they were originally composed in Greek, as has been so often argued in the past. On the contrary, there is strong internal evidence that most, if not all, of the Additions and their component parts existed in an ancient Semitic text of Daniel. So far as we now know, Julius Africanus (d. after A.D. 240) was the first to suggest that at least one of the Additions ("Susanna") was composed in Greek (see p. 81); but apart from an occasional dissenting voice, not until the nineteenth century did scholars argue strongly for the Additions being Greek in origin, notably Fritzsche, Schürer, and Bissell.

The lack of external evidence notwithstanding (see above), the internal evidence argues for a Semitic original or prototype (*Vorlage*) for all these Additions, although admittedly not always with the same degree of probability.[2] Nonetheless, Hebraisms can be found in "The Prayer of Azariah and the Hymn of the Three Young Men" (see p. 45), "Susanna" (pp. 82-83), and "Bel and the Snake" (pp. 119-120). In fact, sometimes the only way to account for a variant reading in the LXX and ⊙ is by positing a particular Semitic word or phrase (see p. 116); other times, a puzzling Greek word or phrase is best explained by positing a specific Hebrew or Aramaic word as the *Vorlage* (see p. 96*f*). Nonetheless, it is exceedingly difficult to say whether Hebrew or Aramaic was the particular language of an Addition, especially since the LXX and ⊙ may not have even had the same Semitic *Vorlage*. (The problem, of course, is not confined to the Additions; for the question of *the original language/s* of the canonical Book of Daniel is by no means an easy question, either.) Most likely, "The Prayer of Azariah and the Hymn of the Three Young Men" was originally in Hebrew, whereas the story of Susanna was probably in Aramaic, as were the stories of Bel and the Snake. However, using a method of syntactical analysis for determining whether a given passage in Greek is "translation-Greek" or "original-Greek,"[3] Raymond A. Martin, in an unpublished study of the syntactical features of "Susanna" and "Bel and the Snake,"

---

[2] Of the three Additions, "The Prayer of Azariah and the Hymn of the Three Young Men" was almost certainly in Hebrew, while "Susanna" was probably in Aramaic; and "Bel and the Snake" has the least likelihood of being in either Hebrew or Aramaic.

[3] For details on the method, see Martin, pp. 5-38.

has tentatively concluded that "probably a Semitic original lies behind most of Susanna" (vss. 50–59 of the LXX, he thinks, were originally in Greek) and that the ℗ of " 'Bel' is mostly original Greek, whereas 'The Snake' is probably mostly translation of a Semitic *Vorlage*" (from personal correspondence with the present writer).

Origin of Additions

Several of the Additions, as well as some of their component parts, were originally separate works, circulating independently of their present context in the Book of Daniel. "The Prayer of Azariah and the Hymn of the Three Young Men" contains at least two, and probably three, pieces that may originally have been in the Temple or synagogal liturgy. The story of Susanna was evidently a secular folk tale, originally having nothing at all to do with the prophet Daniel (see p. 109); and the same must be said for "Bel and the Snake" (pp. 132-133). In all likelihood, "Bel and the Snake" is fiction, i.e. one of the Haggadic tales inspired by Jer 51:34-35, 44 (see pp. 122-123).

Effect of Additions

Regardless of what languages the Additions were composed in originally, they appreciably affect the character of the Septuagint text of Daniel. Intended or not, the effect of "The Prayer of Azariah and the Hymn of the Three Young Men" is to shift the spotlight from the pagan king and the story's lavish setting to the faith of three martyrs and the greatness of their God (see p. 44). "Susanna" introduces the readers to the young Daniel and illustrates, especially in ℗, the lad's spiritual precociousness (pp. 115-116); moreover, the story demonstrates that God is also with pious women who trust in him (see p. 91). Finally, "Bel and the Snake" well illustrates the fulfillment of Jeremiah's predictions in Jer 51:34-35,44 (see pp. 122-123).

In theory at least, these Additions should considerably increase the interest and dramatic effect of the Book of Daniel. After all, in "Susanna" and "Bel and the Snake" interesting new plots are introduced, the Bel story often being referred to by scholars as one of literature's earliest detective stories. Then too, the cast of characters in the Book of Daniel is enlarged by the entrance of the fascinating Susanna and the precocious Daniel, as well as by the appearance of the villainous elders. Moreover, the three martyrs in the furnace, who in the MT were little more than faceless names in the chorus, emerge as men whose faith the readers can understand and applaud.

Yet something is obviously amiss here, because the Jews ultimately chose to omit the Additions while the Christians tended to ignore them. To be sure, Church Fathers would sometimes cite Susanna, along with Esther or Judith, as being a fine example of a good, God-fearing woman; and "The Hymn of the Three Young Men" has figured prominently in the liturgies of the Christian churches down through the ages, even to the present (see p. 50). On the other hand, "Bel and the Snake" was rarely cited (see p. 126). All in all, these Additions to Daniel were not very popular among Christians. And this brings us to the question of their literary merit.

Literary Merit of Additions

With regard to this question, two qualifications must be made at the outset. First, it is risky, if not impossible, to judge the literary merits of the presumed Semitic *Vorlage* of these Additions, that is, we have no assurance that the Greek translation was either better or worse than the original. (Who is to say, for instance, that the Greek translation was not far superior to the Semitic text, and that it was the literary insufficiencies of the Semitic text that was the principal reason for these Additions not being included in the Jewish Canon?) Second, one must carefully distinguish between the literary merits of the Additions reflected in the LXX as over against the later ⊕.

While it might be conceded that the story of Susanna and "The Prayer of Azariah" are true gems, it is indisputable that their present settings do not show them off to best effect, although in this respect ⊕ does do a better job than the LXX of minimizing or obscuring the intrusive character of these two Additions (see NOTES *passim*). Nor does "Bel and the Snake," which in all manuscripts and versions always comes after the canonical chapters of Daniel, seem to be in an appropriate place, especially in the LXX (see pp. 132-133). For, in terms of typology, "Bel and the Snake" clearly belongs with the stories in Daniel 1-6, not with the visions in Daniel 7-12.

In terms of presenting an effectively told story, the difference between the LXX and ⊕ are minimal in "The Prayer of Azariah and the Hymn of the Three Young Men." "Susanna," however, is unquestionably better told in ⊕ (see pp. 78-79), and, to a lesser extent, so is "Bel" (see p. 139); but the Snake story is better told in the LXX (see pp. 146-147). (It is assumed here that most of these internal differences between the LXX and ⊕ represent different Semitic originals rather than highhanded editing on the part of the Greek translators [see below].)

Ultimately, the best criterion for establishing the literary merit of an artistic creation is the "test of time," i.e. the frequency, extent, and length of time a literary work is quoted or alluded to. In this respect, "The Hymn of the Three Young Men" and "Susanna" have fared the most favorably; but even then, they were not used by the Church Fathers as extensively as other materials in Daniel. For instance, Daniel's one-night experience in the lions' den (Daniel 6) is referred to far more often by the Church Fathers than is his seven-day stay with the lions in the Snake story. But literary merit, important though it is, is but one element in the survival of a religious work; content and teachings are also relevant factors.

Religious Teachings

All three Additions are "deliverance stories." Each tells of how an individual chose death in preference to violating some basic religious principle of the Jewish faith: Azariah, Hananiah, Mishael, and Daniel would not commit idolatry; Susanna would not commit adultery. And because of their faith and piety, God miraculously delivered them from certain death, using an angel as part of his plan; and then, in keeping with the justice of divine retribution, the enemies of our heroes experienced the type of death they had originally planned for their victims.

Taking the three Additions together, we get a clear impression that God is the omnipotent Lord of the Universe (so "The Hymn of the Three Young Men"), the Lord of History who is very much concerned, among other things, with his people Israel (so "The Prayer of Azariah"), who is also genuinely concerned with the fate of individual men and women, especially those who suffer in the name of their religion.

Of the three Additions, only "Bel and the Snake" does not always fit the pattern. For example, unlike Susanna and the three young men, Daniel in "Bel and the Snake" actively courted a confrontation with the king and his enemies; and apart from a few pious remarks on Daniel's part, the ancient author, by keeping the spotlight centered on Daniel, made Daniel rather than God the real hero of the story—which is probably the reason why the Habakkuk story was later added to the Snake narrative (see p. 127).

Date of Additions

In terms of the external evidence, no Addition was definitely mentioned by an ancient writer until the second century A.D., when a portion of "The Prayer of Azariah and the Hymn of the Three Young Men" was quoted by Justin Martyr (d. 165) in his *Apologia* I 46, and verses from "Susanna" and "Bel and the Snake" were quoted by Irenaeus of Lyons (140-?202) in his *contra Haereses* IV 26, and IV 5,2, 26,3, respectively.

The internal evidence, however, gives a quite different picture. But first a distinction must be made between two types of dates: an Addition's date of composition, and the date of its inclusion in the Book of Daniel. For instance, in its earliest form the Susanna story may have been told as early as the Persian period (see p. 91); but it was not inserted into the Book of Daniel until sometime after the latter had been written, i.e. sometime after ca. 167-163 B.C., else why was the Semitic version of "Susanna" not a part of the MT of Daniel, and how can we better explain the fact that in its earliest Greek form (i.e. the LXX) this Addition fits so awkwardly into its larger context (see pp. 90-91)? The same arguments are also applicable to "The Prayer of Azariah and the Hymn of the Three Young Men," some parts of which were probably in existence prior to the writing of the Book of Daniel but were inserted into the latter only later (see pp. 45-46, 47-48). By contrast, the Bel and Snake narratives may not have even come into existence until after the Semitic Book of Daniel had been first published, a late second- or early first-century B.C. date making the most sense for this addition (see p. 128). In other words, some of the Additions or at least some of their component parts probably existed prior to the first publication of the Book of Daniel (ca. 167-163 B.C.), but none of them was added to Daniel until sometime later. Nor were they all added at the same time.

In any case, most, if not all, of them were added prior to the translation of the Semitic Daniel into Greek. The reason for this last assertion is that scholars have never been able to detect syntactical, stylistic, or vocabulary differences between the Greek of the Additions and the Greek of the canonical portions of Daniel. Thus, the *terminus ad quem* for the Additions and most of their component parts is the date of the Greek translation of the Semitic text of Daniel, i.e. ca. 100 B.C.

Rejection from the Jewish Canon

But if the Additions were a part of the Semitic text of Daniel which was translated into Greek, thus becoming a part of the Alexandrian canon of the Jews and from there becoming a part of the Christian canon, then why were these Additions ultimately rejected from the Palestinian canon as fixed by the Council of Jamnia in A.D. 90?[4] The simple truth is that no one knows. The decisions at Jamnia were "unofficial" and only gradually became the accepted positions throughout Judaism.

It is a reasonable inference, however, that the Additions were not rejected from the Hebrew canon because they contained heretical ideas or teachings unacceptable to normative Judaism, i.e., "Judaism" as inter-

---

[4] Many scholars of the past century as well as a few of the present one would argue, of course, that the Additions, being Greek compositions originally, never were part of the Palestinian canon.

preted by the Council of Jamnia. Not only was the Fiery Furnace incident
a very popular story with many variations among the ancient Jews (see p.
65), but "The Prayer of Azariah and the Hymn of the Three Young
Men" contains three of the most important themes of the entire Old Testament (see p. 51) and no teachings even slightly offensive to Judaism, let
alone heretical. And even if, as seems quite likely, the story of Susanna
was originally a secular folk tale, it has been thoroughly judaized and saturated with religious elements of Judaism (see pp. 89-90); the story's
only "weakness" is the clear implication that people in authority, including
elders, cannot always be blindly trusted (see p. 92).[5] By comparison,
"Bel and the Snake" is admittedly somewhat lacking in religious stature
(see pp. 126-127); but even so, "Bel and the Snake" is typologically very
similar to the canonical tales of Daniel 1-6 (see p. 121); and like the
other two Additions, it contains no heretical ideas or teachings unacceptable to normative Judaism around the beginning of the Christian era.

Why, then, were these Additions rejected by the rabbis? The most probable answer is that the ancient Jewish leaders recognized, even as do we
today, the intrusive or secondary character of the Additions. Interesting
though the story of Susanna may be in its own right, as "Susanna" stands
in the Septuagint text of Daniel, it is decidedly out of place—in a variety
of ways (see p. 80); and so is "The Prayer of Azariah" (see p. 65). As
for "Bel and the Snake," the rabbis may have known for an incontestable
fact that this Addition, which was probably added after the first two Additions, was not part of the "original" Book of Daniel (pp. 125-126).
Had the three Additions been masterpieces of religious literature, they
might have overcome the handicap of being known for what they actually
were, i.e. later additions to the original Book of Daniel. In sum, by the
time of the Council of Jamnia, if not earlier, Jews had come to prefer an
older and more authentic text of Daniel, one "uncontaminated" by the
Additions.

Greek Versions

The relationship of the LXX to Θ in the Additions is a very puzzling one.
On the one hand, the LXX and Θ are virtually the same in "The Prayer of
Azariah and the Hymn of the Three Young Men" (see p. 52); on the
other hand, in "Susanna" the LXX and Θ disagree considerably in wording *and content* (see pp. 78-80). "Bel and the Snake" occupies a middle position, that is, the LXX and Θ agree with one another more in "Bel

---

[5] However, it should be noted that it was the "people in authority," be they priests,
rabbis, or Church Fathers, who ultimately decided what books would be included in
the various canons.

and the Snake" than they do in "Susanna" but less than in "The Prayer of Azariah and the Hymn of the Three Young Men."

Perhaps the explanation for this puzzling situation, i.e. the lack of a consistent relationship between the LXX and ℗ in all three Additions, should not be sought in the Additions themselves but rather in the Book of Daniel. For, as is well known, a very strange thing happened to the Septuagint text of Daniel, namely, by A.D. 250 the LXX had been replaced by ℗ in the Christian Church. Why, we do not know. The oft-quoted words of Jerome state the problem rather than explain it: "The churches of the Lord Savior do not read the prophet Daniel according to the Seventy Interpreters [i.e. the LXX], using the edition of Theodotion; and why this happened I do not know. . . . This only am I able to assert: that [the LXX] disagreed greatly from the truth, and was rightly rejected."[6] By the phrase "the truth" Jerome meant, of course, the Hebrew-Aramaic text of Daniel. But what does *that* mean? Should we, with F. Field, S. R. Driver, and J. A. Montgomery, understand by it that the original LXX was poorly done or was too paraphrastic? Or, does it simply mean, as R. H. Charles thought, that the LXX was too different from Jerome's Hebrew-Aramaic text of Daniel, that is, that the LXX was a translation of the old Aramaic text, whereas ℗ was based upon the then-current Hebrew-Aramaic version of Daniel? Or, quite possibly, there was some theological objection to the LXX; for example, Dan 9:24-27 in the LXX, in contrast to ℗, could not be used as a Messianic prediction for Christ (so A. Bludau, *BSt* 2 [1897], 23-24).[7]

The problem is further complicated by the fact that scholars cannot agree on the origin and nature of ℗ in the Book of Daniel. Is it really a translation by Theodotion, a Jewish translator in the first third of the second century A.D., whose work elsewhere in the Greek Bible is designated by the siglum "℗,"[8] or was the so-called ℗ of Daniel actually translated by someone else and erroneously attributed to Theodotion; or, finally, is "℗" just a recension, i.e. an editorial revision of the Greek text without reference to a Semitic text at all?

This is an exceedingly confusing and complex question arising out of the long-recognized fact that "Theodotion" renderings of Daniel occur in texts that clearly antedate Theodotion himself. "Pre-Theodotion" readings occur not only in Church Fathers such as Justin Martyr, Hermas (fl. 140-155), and Clement of Rome (30?-?99), but even in the New Testament,

---

[6] From his Preface to Daniel; see Migne, *Patrologiae Latina* XXVIII, 1291.

[7] On the general problem of the Church's preference for the ℗ of Daniel, the interested reader should consult the very helpful introductory remarks on the subject by Pfeiffer, pp. 438-444; as well as the more detailed remarks by Driver, pp. xcviii-cii; Montgomery, pp. 46-50; and Charles, pp. l-lvii.

[8] For brief introductory remarks on Theodotion and his well-known translation, see Swete, *IOTG*, pp. 42-49, and Roberts, *OTTV*, pp. 123-126.

notably in the Book of Revelation.[9] Now the matter has been further complicated by the presence of "Theodotion" readings among the Dead Sea scroll materials.

In a more recent study of the problem, Armin Schmitt rightly concluded that whoever was responsible for translating the canonical and deuterocanonical portions of Daniel in the version identified as "Θ," he most definitely *was not* the well-known Theodotion of the second century A.D. (Schmitt, pp. 11-16, 112). More debatable, however, is Schmitt's conclusion (pp. 100-112) that the canonical and deuterocanonical portions of Θ were done by different translators, the Additions possibly being done by Symmachus, another Jewish translator of the second century A.D.[10] If the Additions of Θ are the work of Symmachus, that would be additional evidence for the existence of a Semitic *Vorlage* for the Additions, inasmuch as Symmachus always translated Semitic texts rather than revised Greek originals.

Building upon the epoch-making work of Dominique Barthélemy,[11] Pierre Grelot[12] has argued with considerable persuasiveness that Θ of Daniel actually antedates the version of Aquila and that it represents a Palestinian version made some year between 30 and 50 of the Christian era and that the Additions were part of that version.

The debate, of course, rages on and probably will continue to do so until some of the larger Septuagint problems are better understood. In an even more recent article, J. Schüpphaus,[13] while willing to concede to Schmitt and Grelot that Θ may not have been translated by Theodotion, is nevertheless quite certain that the Θ of Daniel is, at least as far as the Additions are concerned, an extensive re-editing of both the style and content of the LXX, and not a new translation. Differences in content between the LXX and Θ, says Schüpphaus (p. 72), are the result of "thematic alignment," that is, whereas the LXX had been more concerned with encouraging the Jewish community to greater religious activity, Θ was more concerned with consoling and offering hope to Jews living in a time of a very aggressive paganism. Schüpphaus ignores the question of whether there was a Semitic *Vorlage* for the Additions, although in n. 4 on p. 50 of his article he seems to think so.

In short, confused though the present state of the problem is, there is a

---

[9] The relevant readings in "pre-Theodotion" texts may be conveniently found in Charles, pp. lii-lvii, cxvi-cxxii; Montgomery, pp. 46-50; and A. Bludau, *BSt* 2 (1897), 14f.

[10] According to Jerome (*Commentary on Amos* iii 11), whereas Aquila was more concerned with literalism, i.e. with exact verbal rendering of his Semitic text, Symmachus was more concerned with conveying its sense. On Symmachus and his translation of the Hebrew Bible, see Swete, *IOTG*, pp. 49-53, and Roberts, *OTTV*, pp. 126-127.

[11] *Les devanciers d'Aquila*, Supplements to Vetus Testamentum, X, Leiden: E. J. Brill, 1963.

[12] *Biblica* 47 (1966), 381-402.

[13] *ZAW* 83 (1971), 49-72.

growing consensus among Septuagint scholars that the ℗ of Daniel was not
done by the second-century translator Theodotion but by an earlier Palestinian translator, and that the Additions seem to have been part of that
translation.

The LXX

Because the so-called Theodotion of Daniel had replaced the LXX in
the Christian Church by A.D. 250, there are at present only three surviving
witnesses to the Septuagint of Daniel: (1) the Kölner Papyrus 967, which
dates from ca. A.D. 150 and preserves Daniel 5-12, together with "Susanna" and "Bel and the Snake" (but not "The Prayer of Azariah and the
Hymn of the Three Young Men")[14]; (2) the Codex Chisianus 88 ["87" in
F. Field, *Origenis Hexapla*], a ninth-century cursive manuscript which
also contains Hippolytus' *Commentary on Daniel* and a ℗ text of Daniel[15];
and (3) the Ambrosian Syro-Hexaplar (SyrH.), a very literal Syrian
translation of Origen's text made by Paul of Tella at Alexandria in
616-17. The scarcity of LXX manuscripts is unfortunate, for there are
several points where the LXX is unclear or even unintelligible (see NOTES
passim).

That the LXX of Daniel probably existed by ca. 100 B.C., if not earlier,
is clear from the fact that it was used by the translator of I Maccabees
(see A. Bludau, *BSt* 2 [1897], 8, n. 6). Virtually all scholars agree that the
place of translation was Egypt, probably Alexandria. Inasmuch as the literary style and diction of the Additions do not differ from the rest of the
LXX of Daniel,[16] we may safely assume that the Additions had the same
date and place of translation as the canonical Daniel.

The ℗

℗ usually presents the material in a more clear and effective fashion
than does the LXX (see NOTES *passim*); but ℗ also contains the greater
number of Hebraisms, the LXX usually being more successful in avoiding
clumsy Semiticisms (see NOTES *passim*). One is certainly hard pressed to
explain the introduction of Semiticisms and Hebraisms into the more recent text (i.e. into ℗) by any other explanation than that ℗ was either a
new Greek translation of a Semitic text or the revision of a Greek text in
light of a Semitic text.

In any event, because the ℗ of Daniel has been the Greek version used
by the Christian Church down through the ages and is still the text followed in most modern translations of the Additions to Daniel, ℗ will be
the text used as the starting point for translation and discussion in the
present commentary; however, the LXX will be discussed regularly.

---

14 The text and notes may be found in Angelo Geissen (see BIBLIO I).
15 For details, see Montgomery, pp. 25-26.
16 See Fritzsche, p. 114; A. Bludau, *BSt* 2 (1897), 161.

Other Ancient Versions

With the exception of the Syro-Hexaplar and the earliest edition of the *Vetus Latina* or Old Latin (OL),[17] all the ancient versions of Daniel as well as modern ones, including the KJ, RSV, JB, and NEB, are based upon ℮. The same must be said about the three Additions to Daniel. With a few exceptions, the SyrH. follows the LXX quite slavishly (see NOTES *passim*), while the rest of the ancient versions, the Vulgate, the Arabic, the Armenian, the Coptic (both in the Sahidic dialect of the South and the Bohairic of the North), and the Ethiopic are quite literal translations of the ℮. Moses Gaster's Aramaic text (see p. 49) also agrees with ℮. Only the Syriac, or Peshitta, which is also based upon ℮, is sometimes quite free (see NOTES *passim*). Despite the fact that Joseph Ziegler has done an excellent job of providing an *apparatus criticus* (for title, see BIBLIO I), using all these ancient versions, they still do not provide as much insight into the Greek text as one would hope.

---

[17] I.e. the one attested in quotations from the very early Latin Fathers; for details, see Montgomery, pp. 29-32, and Charles, p. 1viii.

BIBLIOGRAPHY I

Commentaries

Ball, Charles James. *The Additions to Daniel*, Apocrypha of the Speaker's Commentary, ed. Henry Wace, II. London: John Murray, 1888. *Cited as* Ball.

Bennett, William Henry. *The Prayer of Azariah and the Song of the Three Children*, in *APOT*, I, 625-637. *Cited as* Bennett.

Bissell, Edwin Cone. *Additions to Daniel*, The Apocrypha of the Old Testament. New York: Scribner, 1880. *Cited as* Bissell.

Charles, Robert Henry. *A Critical and Exegetical Commentary on the Book of Daniel*. Oxford at the Clarendon Press, 1929. *Cited as* Charles.

Davies, Witton. *Bel and the Dragon*, in *APOT*, I, 652-664. *Cited as* Davies.

Delcor, Matthias. *Le Livre de Daniel*. Paris: Gebalda, 1971.

Driver, Samuel R. *Daniel*, Cambridge Bible for Schools and Colleges. Cambridge at the University Press, 1901. *Cited as* Driver.

Fritzsche, Otto F. *Zusätze zu dem Buche Daniel*, Kurzgefasstes exegetisches Handbuch zu den Apokryphen des Alten Testaments, eds. O. Fritzsche and C. Grim, I. Leipzig: Hirzel, 1851. *Cited as* Fritzsche.

Kay, David M. *Susanna*, in *APOT*, I, 638-651. *Cited as* Kay.

Kuhl, Curt. *Die drei Männer im Feure*, BZAW 55, 1940. *Cited as* Kuhl.

Montgomery, James A. *A Critical and Exegetical Commentary on the Book of Daniel*, International Critical Commentary. New York: Scribner, 1927. *Cited as* Montgomery.

Plöger, Otto. *Historische und legendarische Erzählungen Zusätze zu Daniel*, Jüdische Schriften aus hellenistisch-römischer Zeit, I/1. Gütersloh: Mohn, 1973. *Cited as* Plöger.

Rothstein, Johann W. *Die Zusätze zu Daniel*, Die Apokryphen und Pseudepigraphen des Alten Testaments, ed. E. E. Kautzsch, I. Tübingen: Mohr, 1900. *Cited as* Rothstein.

Scholz, Anton. *Commentar über das Buch "Esther" mit seinen Zusätzen und über "Susanna."* Würzburg-Wien: Leo Woerl, 1892. *Cited as* Scholz.

——— *Commentar über das Buch "Judith" und über "Bel und Drache,"* 2d ed. Leipzig: Leo Woerl, 1898.

Zöckler, Otto. *Die erzählenden Zusätze zu Daniel: Susanna, Bel und der Drache*, Die Apokryphen des Alten Testamentes, Kurzgefasstes Kommentar zu den Heiligen Schriften des Alten und Neuen Testamentes sowie zu den Apokryphen, eds. O. Zöckler und H. Strack, IX. München: Oskar Beck, 1891. *Cited as* Zöckler.

Other Books

Brown, F., S. R. Driver, and C. A. Briggs, eds. (abbr. BDB). *A Hebrew and English Lexicon of the Old Testament.*

Daubney, William H. *The Three Additions to Daniel.* Cambridge: Deighton, Bell, 1906. *Cited as* Daubney.

Eissfeldt, Otto. *The Old Testament: An Introduction, including the Apocrypha and Pseudepigrapha, and also the works of similar type from Qumran,* tr. from the 3d Ger. ed. by Peter R. Ackroyd. New York: Harper & Row, 1965. *Cited as* Eissfeldt.

Gaster, Moses. *The Chronicles of Jerahmeel.* London: Royal Asiatic Society, 1899.

Ginzberg, Louis. *The Legends of the Jews.* Philadelphia: Jewish Publication Society, 1909.

Kautzsch, E. F., ed. *Gesenius' Hebrew Grammar,* the 2d Eng. ed. rev. by A. E. Cowley (abbr. GKC).

Kittel, Rudolf, ed. *Biblia Hebraica,* 3d ed. (abbr. *BH³*).

Liddell, Henry G., and Robert Scott, eds. *A Greek-English Lexicon,* rev. by Henry S. Jones (abbr. LSJ).

Martin, Raymond A. *Syntactical Evidence of Semitic Sources in Greek Documents,* Society of Biblical Literature, Septuagint and Cognate Studies, III. Missoula, Mont.: Scholars Press, 1974. *Cited as* Martin.

Metzger, Bruce. *An Introduction to the Apocrypha.* Oxford University Press, 1957. *Cited as* Metzger.

Oesterley, W. O. E. *The Books of the Apocrypha.* New York: Revell, 1914.

―――― *An Introduction to the Books of Apocrypha.* New York: Macmillan, 1935. *Cited as* Oesterley.

Pfeiffer, Robert H. *History of New Testament Times, with an Introduction to the Apocrypha.* New York: Harper, 1949. *Cited as* Pfeiffer.

Plessner, J. *Die apocryphischen Bücher ins Hebräische übersetzt,* I. Berlin, 1833.

Pritchard, J. B., ed. *Ancient Near Eastern Texts Relating to the Old Testament,* 2d. ed. (abbr. *ANET²*).

Pusey, Edward Bouvier. *Daniel the Prophet.* New York: Funk & Wagnalls, 1886.

Roberts, B. J. *The Old Testament Text and Versions: The Hebrew Text in Transmission and the History of the Ancient Versions* (abbr. OTTV).

Schmitt, Armin. *Stammt der sogenannte "ᴼ"-Text bei Daniel wirklich von Theodotion?,* Mitteilunger des Septuaginta des Septuaginta-Unternehmens, IX. Göttingen: Vandenhoeck und Ruprecht, 1966. *Cited as* Schmitt.

Schürer, Emil. *Geschichte des jüdischen Volkes im Zeitalter Jesu Christi,* 4th ed., III, Leipzig, Hinrichs, 1909. *Cited as* Schürer.

Swete, Henry Barclay. *An Introduction to the Old Testament in Greek* rev. by R. R. Ottley (abbr. *IOTG*).

Torrey, Charles C. *The Apocryphal Literature.* Yale University Press, 1945. *Cited as* Torrey.

Articles

Baumgartner, Walter I., "Susanna—Die Geschichte einer Legende." *AfR* 24 (1926), 259-280.

—— "Der Weise Knabe und die des Ehebruchs beschuldigte Frau," *AfR* 27 (1929), 187-188.

Both articles are reprinted in *Zum Alten Testament und seiner Umwelt,* (Leiden: Brill, 1959), 42-67.

Bludau, August, "Die alexandrinische Übersetzung des Buches Daniel und ihr Verhältnis zum massoretischen Texten," *BSt* 2 (1897), 1-30, 140-200, 330-368.

Brüll, Nehemiah, "Das apokryphische Susanna Buch," *JJGL* 3 (1877), 1-69.

—— "Das Gebet der drei Männer im Feuerofen," *JJGL* 8 (1887), 22-27.

—— "Die Geschichte von Bel und dem Drachen," *JJGL* 8 (1887), 28-29.

Christie, Elmer B., "The Strophic Arrangement of the Benedicte," *JBL* 47 (1928), 188-193.

Fenz, Augustinius K., "Ein Drache in Babel. Exegetische Skizze über Daniel 14:23-42," *SEÅ* 35 (1970), 5-16.

Gaster, Moses, "The Unknown Aramaic Original of Theodotion's Additions to the Book of Daniel," *PSBA* 16 (1894), 280-290, 312-317; 17 (1895), 75-94.

Gehman, Henry S., "The Sahidic and the Bohairic Versions of the Book of Daniel," *JBL* 46 (1927), 279-330.

Grelot, Pierre, "Les versions grecques de Daniel," *Biblica* 47 (1966), 381-402.

Heller, Bernhard, "Die Suzannerzählung: ein Märchen," *ZAW* 54 (1936), 281-287.

Hoenig, Sidney B., "Bel and the Dragon," *IDB*, I, 376-377.

—— "Song of the Three Young Men," *IDB*, IV, 426.

Howorth, Henry H., "Some Unconventional Views on the Text of the Bible, VII," *PSBA* 29 (1907), 31-38, 61-69.

Huet, Gedeon, "Daniel et Susanne: Note de littérature comparée," *RHR* 65 (1912), 277-284.

—— "Daniel et Suzanne," *RHR* 76 (1917), 129-130.

Jones, B. W., "The Prayer in Daniel ix," *VT* 18 (1968), 488-493.

Julius, Caspar, "Die Griechischen Danielzusätze und ihre kanonische Geltung," *BSt* 6 (1903), 1-183.

Landersdorfer, Simon, "Der Drache von Babylon," *BZ* 11 (1913), 1-4.

Lévi, Israel, "L'Histoire 'de Suzanne et les deux vieillards' dans la littérature juive," *REJ* 95 (1933), 157-171.

MacKenzie, Roderick A. F., "The Meaning of the Susanna Story," *CJT* 3 (1957), 211-218.

Marshall, John T., "Bel and the Dragon," *HDB*, I, 267-268.

—— "Susanna," *HDB*, IV, 630-632.

—— "Three Children, Song of the," *HDB*, IV, 754-756.

Papadopoulos, N., "The Deuterocanonical Sections of Daniel" (in Greek), *Theologia* 40 (1969), 458-489; 41 (1970), 340-364.

Roth, Wolfgang M. W., "For Life, He Appeals to Death (Wis 13:18): A Study of Old Testament Idol Parodies," *CBQ* 37 (1975), 21-47.

Rowley, Harold H., "The Unity of the Book of Daniel," in *The Servant of the Lord and Other Essays on the Old Testament,* ed. H. H. Rowley, London: Lutterworth Press, 1952.

Schüpphaus, Joakim, "Der Verhältnis von LXX-und Theodotion-Text in den apokryphen Zusätzen zum Danielbuch," *ZAW* 83 (1971), 49-72.

Toy, Crawford H., "Bel and the Dragon," *The Jewish Encyclopaedia,* ed. I. Singer (New York: Funk & Wagnalls, 1905), II, 650-651.

——— "Susanna, The History of," *The Jewish Encyclopaedia,* XI, 602-603.

Wevers, J. W., "Septuaginta-Forschungern seit 1954," *ThR* 33/1 (1968), 26-38.

Wiederholt, Theodor von, "Die Geschichte der Susanna," *TQ* 51 (1869), 287-321, 337-399.

Wurmbrand, Max, "A Falasha Variant of the Story of Susanna," *Biblica* 44 (1963), 29-37.

Zimmermann, Frank, "Bel and the Dragon," *VT* 8 (1958), 438-440.

——— "The Story of Susanna and Its Original Language," *JQR* 48 (1957/58), 236-241.

Ancient Versions

Geissen, Angelo. *Der Septuaginta-Text des Buches, Daniel: Kap. 5-12, zusammen mit Susanna, Bel et Draco, sowie Esther Kap. 1,1a-2,15, nach dem Kölner Teil des Papyrus 967,* Papyrologische Texte und Abhandlungen, V. Bonn: Rudolf Habelt, 1968.

Swete, Henry Barclay, ed. *Daniel.* The Old Testament in Greek According to the Septuagint, III. Cambridge University Press, 1894.

Ziegler, Joseph. *Susanna, Daniel, Bel et Draco.* Septuaginta. Vetus Testamentum Graecum auctoritate Societatis Gottingensis editum, ed. J. Ziegler, XVI/2. Göttingen, 1954.

"THE PRAYER OF AZARIAH AND THE HYMN OF THE THREE YOUNG MEN"

Introduction

"The Prayer of Azariah and the Hymn of the Three Young Men" is one of several titles[1] given to that additional Septuagint material between what would correspond presently to vss. 23 and 24 of the third chapter of the canonical Book of Daniel. According to ch. 3 of the MT, three Jewish youths named Shadrach, Meshach, and Abednego[2] were thrown into a fiery furnace by King Nebuchadnezzar because they had refused to bow down and worship a huge gold idol the king had set up in the plain of Dura. Even though their executioners were themselves burned to death as they were tossing the three young martyrs into the blazing furnace (which had been heated seven times hotter than usual), the three young men themselves were not burned because, as the king soon found out, God had sent an angel into the oven to protect them. Letting them out of the furnace, the king exclaimed:

> "Blessed be the God of Shadrach, Meshach, and Abednego, who has sent his angel and delivered his servants, who trusted in him, and set at nought the king's command, and yielded up their bodies rather than serve and worship any god except their own God. Therefore I make a decree: Any people, nation, or language that speaks anything against the God of Shadrach, Meshach, and Abednego shall be torn limb from limb, and their houses laid in ruins; for there is no other god who is able to deliver in this way" (Dan 3:28-29).

[1] No separate title is given to this work in the ancient Greek manuscripts, except in codex Alexandrinus, where the Prayer and the Hymn (with no connecting Prose Narrative) are chs. 8 and 9 in Odes (an appendix to Psalms in the Septuagint) and are entitled "Prayer of Azariah" and "Hymn of Our Fathers," respectively. In the KJ the title for the work is "The Song of the Three Holy Children," the word "children" connoting, not tender age, but religious affiliation as, for example, the phrase "the children of Israel" to denote Jews.

[2] Because the third chapter of the MT is in Aramaic, the Babylonian names of the youths were used, whereas in the first two chapters of the MT, which are in Hebrew, they are called by their Hebrew names: Hananiah, Azariah, and Mishael, respectively. On the probable meaning of their Hebrew and Aramaic names, see NOTE on vs. 66.

With one possible exception (see COMMENT, pp. 63-65), the story is well told in the MT. And judging from the frequency with which the story of the three martyrs is told or alluded to in the Talmud and Mishnah (see Ball, pp. 305-306), one may infer that the story was very popular among the ancient Jews and that it existed in variant forms other than those of the MT and the Septuagint.

Description of Component Parts

Contrary to what its title might suggest, "The Prayer of Azariah and the Hymn of the Three Young Men" contains four (three, according to most scholars) separate and independent works: (1) the Prayer of Azariah (vss. 1-22[24-45][3]); (2) the Prose Narrative (vss. 23-28[46-51]); (3) the Ode (vss. 29-34[52-56]); and (4) the Psalm (vss. 35-68[57-90]). In this commentary, when the Ode and Psalm are taken together and spoken of as a unit, the combined work is referred to as the Hymn.

The Prayer of Azariah

This prayer (vss. 1-22 [24-45]), although often ascribed to Azariah (so vs. 2 of ☉) was actually offered, according to vss. 1-2 of the LXX, by all three of the martyrs. In spite of the fact that Azariah and his two companions were in a terrible predicament, they being yet unaffected by the searing flames or heat but still inside the blazing furnace, the martyrs did not so much pray for their own deliverance (but see vss. 18-21); rather, they confessed the sins of their nation (cf. vss. 4-9, 14-15). Verses 7-8 [30-31] sound the basic note, or theme, of the Prayer: "We have not obeyed your commandments; we have not observed or done as you commanded us for our own good. So in all that you have brought upon us, and all that you have done to us, you have acted justly."

Yet, these verses contradict the situation the three martyrs found themselves in, i.e. their confession of sinfulness and apostasy was clearly not applicable to themselves. In fact, these men were in their present predicament precisely *because they had obeyed* God's commandments: they had refused to bow down and worship the gold idol! The inappropriateness of a number of verses in the Prayer,[4] especially vss. 5-8, together with some

---

[3] For the third chapter of Daniel, the MT has thirty verses; the Greek, ninety-seven. In order to avoid confusion, in this commentary "The Prayer of Azariah and the Hymn of the Three Young Men" is numbered consecutively, starting with vs. 1 and ending with vs. 68; and the corresponding verse number of the Greek text, when used, will be in square brackets.

[4] "The author [or editor of the Prayer] makes Azariah review the history of the Jewish nation as calmly as an aged saint might do under the fig-tree of solitude at the time of evening prayer" (Marshall, *HDB*, IV, 755). C. C. Torrey, however, denied that there was anything inappropriate about the Prayer, arguing that "Azariah's long

other lines of evidence (see COMMENT, p. 65) indicate that the Prayer was a separate and independent entity that originally had nothing to do with the Fiery Furnace incident but was inserted by a later scribe for reasons known only to him. Where that scribe got the Prayer from is unknown; many scholars believe that it may have originally been part of the temple or synagogal liturgy of the day. Certainly the Prayer is not unlike such national laments as those in the Psalter (e.g. Psalms 44, 74, 79 and 80) and in prose confessions elsewhere, notably, Dan 9:4-19; Ezra 9:6-15; Neh 9:6-37; and I Bar 1:15 - 3:8.

The Prose Narrative

This brief narrative (vss. 23-28[46-51]), coming between the Prayer of Azariah and the Hymn (vss. 29-68[52-90]), tells how God's angel kept the interior of the fiery furnace safe and cool for the three martyrs, even though the flames shooting out of the furnace were so hot that some Chaldeans standing around the oven were burned to death.

Brief though the narrative passage is, it has nonetheless raised for scholars a number of questions. For instance, some scholars[5] pointing to what they regard as a "gap" or deficiency in the masoretic narrative of the Fiery Furnace, have argued that the Prose Narrative (or something very similar to it) stood between what are now vss. 23 and 24 of the third chapter of the Semitic text of Daniel *from the very beginning;* other scholars, including Charles and Kuhl, have found different explanations for the "gap" (see COMMENT, p. 64). But those scholars who support the Prose Narrative as being original and therefore erroneously edited out of the Semitic text of ch. 3, possibly at the same time that the Prayer and Hymn were "edited out," must contend with the fact that vss. 23-25 [46–48] of the Prose Narrative obviously contradict vs. 22 of the MT concerning the question of exactly when the Chaldeans near the oven were burned to death (see COMMENT, p. 65). On one point, however, virtually all modern scholars agree, namely, the relative position of the Prayer to the Prose Narrative is totally illogical, i.e. the Prayer of Azariah was offered up inside the fiery furnace *prior* to any mention of the miraculous intervention on the part of God's angel who cools off the oven and continues to protect the three martyrs. The most obvious, and certainly correct, explanation for the last-mentioned phenomenon is that the narrative or Prose Narrative was already a part of the Semitic text of Daniel when a Jewish scribe proceeded to insert the Prayer (see COMMENT, p. 65).

---

prayer is not for deliverance from the fire; it was too late for such a petition. . . . He prays for his people" (Torrey, p. 155)—all of which seems a rather lame explanation.

[5] For example, von Gall, Bludau, and Rothstein.

The Ode

Uttered by all three of the martyrs while they were still inside the fiery furnace, this brief hymn of praise (vss. 29-34[52-56]) consists of six verses[6] or bicola. The first colon always blesses God while the second colon is always a refrain with essentially the same meaning but slightly different phraseology in each verse, as seen in the following representative example:

> 29[52] Blessed are you, O Lord, God of our fathers,
> praiseworthy and highly exalted for ever.
> 30 and blessed is your glorious and holy name,
> to be highly praised and highly exalted for ever.

Most biblical scholars do not distinguish between what the present commentary calls the Ode (vss. 29-34) and the Psalm (vss. 35-69); but various considerations do justify such a distinction (see COMMENT, p. 75).[7]

The Psalm

This beautiful hymn of praise (vss. 35-68[57-90]), consisting of four stanzas, reflects the message and content of canonical psalms, notably Psalm 148[8]; and it resembles the structure of Psalm 136 where one refrain ("for his steadfast love endures for ever") occurs in the second colon of all twenty-six bicola. In the Psalm, the refrain "sing his praise and highly exalt him for ever" occurs thirty-one times under the same conditions (but see NOTE on vs. 35).

In terms of general content, the Psalm is far more logically structured than Psalm 148; instead of skipping around from one subject to another like the composer of Psalm 148, the author of our Psalm proceeded very systematically to call the various groups within the universe to worship the Lord, ever moving from the general to particulars. The first stanza (vss. 35-41) deals exclusively with the psalmist's addressing God's creations in

---

[6] So this commentary and most modern translations. The Greek versions erroneously regarded the same material as being only five verses, failing to see that the first "verse" of the Ode actually consisted of two lines, or verses. Originally, however, the Ode had seven lines (see second NOTE on vs. 32).

[7] The mere fact that quite often in the liturgies of the Western churches the Ode (conventionally called the *Benedictus Es* after the opening words of its Latin translation) and the Psalm, or *Benedicite* as it is commonly called, have separate settings and uses does not prove that the two psalms were originally separate and independent compositions. But the varying usages made of them by Christian churches in their liturgies do reflect genuine differences between the Ode and the Psalm. For a discussion of the liturgical use of the *Benedictus* and the *Benedicite*, see Daubney, pp. 83-97.

[8] Cf. for example, vss. 36-37 with Ps. 148:1-2a: "Praise the Lord! Praise the Lord from the heavens, praise him in the heights! Praise him, all his angels"; or vss. 39-41 with Ps 148:2b-3: "Praise him, all his host! Praise him, sun and moon, praise him all you shining stars!"

the Highest Heaven, i.e. things like the angels (vs. 37), the cosmic ocean
(vs. 38), the stars (vs. 41), and the like; whereas in Stanza II (vss.
42-51) the psalmist addresses only elements coming down from heaven,
things like rain (vs. 42), snow (vs. 50), etc. Stanza III (vss. 52-59) en-
joins the earthly creations, such as mountains and hills (vs. 53), plants
(vs. 54), fish (vs. 57), and others, to praise God. The final stanza (vss.
60-68) addresses mankind in general and various groups within Israel in
particular, including priests (vs. 62), the humble in heart (vs. 65) and,
most inappropriately, the three martyrs themselves (see first NOTE on vs.
66).

Typical of the Psalm's content and structure are such verses as the following:

Stanza I

36[58] Bless the Lord, you heavens,
   sing his praise and highly exalt him for ever.
40[62] Bless the Lord, you sun and moon,
   sing his praise and highly exalt him for ever.

Stanza II

43[65] Bless the Lord, all you winds,
   sing his praise and highly exalt him for ever.
51[73] Bless the Lord, you lightnings and clouds,
   sing his praise and highly exalt him for ever.

Stanza III

54[76] Bless the Lord, all you things that grow in the ground,
   sing his praise and highly exalt him for ever.
58[80] Bless the Lord, all you birds of the air,
   sing his praise and highly exalt him for ever.

Stanza IV

60[82] Bless the Lord, you sons of men,
   sing his praise and highly exalt him for ever.
63[85] Bless the Lord, you servants of the Lord,
   sing his praise and highly exalt him for ever.

In summary, with the possible exception of the Prose Narrative (see
COMMENT, pp. 63-65), the Septuagint's sixty-eight verses between what
would correspond to vss. 23 and 24 of ch. 3 of the MT are unquestionably
additions, that is, they are not surviving witnesses to material in the Semitic text of Daniel when the Book of Daniel was *first* written (ca. 167-
163 B.C.). The Prayer itself is not only inappropriate by virtue of its content but also by its position, i.e. it precedes instead of follows the Prose
Narrative. In the LXX, the Prose Narrative, which serves to introduce the
Hymn, glaringly contradicts the MT (see COMMENT, p. 64). And finally,

the Hymn, while admittedly not inappropriate in terms of both its content and its context, gives every indication of being originally a separate and independent entity (see COMMENT, pp. 47-48), which was probably added later, else how can we explain the fact that it is not contained in the MT?

Effect of Additions

Regardless of the original intent of the Jewish editors who first supplied these additions to the Fiery Furnace incident, the effect of the interpolations is quite clear, namely, the spotlight has shifted from the king and the story's lavish setting to the faith of the martyrs and the greatness of their God. As the drama is presented in the masoretic text, the pagan king has the stage most of the time, whether it is his decree being discussed (3:1-11), or he himself speaking (vss. 13-15), or his orders being carried out (vss. 19-23). Even more surprising, the reader of the MT knows far more about how the king felt before (vss. 13-15, 19-20), during (vss. 24-26), and after the intended incineration (vss. 28-30) than he knows about the feelings and conduct of the heroes themselves (vss. 16-17). Having bravely given their stirring speech in the witness chair, so to speak, did the young men continue in the same heroic way, or did they later falter or have some misgivings? Weren't they grateful to be miraculously saved at the very last minute? The reader assumes so, but the masoretic text does not say; it is only Nebuchadnezzar that afterwards gives the stirring speech in praise of the Lord (vss. 28-29 of the MT).

But the inclusion of the Addition changed all that. For the Prayer underscores the humility and piety of the martyrs while the Prose Narrative and the Hymn call to mind the majesty and power of the Lord God of Israel. In the MT the martyrs were models *by what they did*. By means of its additions the Septuagint showed *what they were*.

Original Language, Date, and Place of Composition

The most crucial question that must be asked about each of the four additions is this: In what language was it originally written? The answer to that question goes a long way toward answering the related questions of provenance and date of composition, i.e. a Greek original would argue for an Alexandrian provenance while evidence of an Aramaic or Hebrew *Vorlage* for a Babylonian or Palestinian origin. One thing is certain: questions concerning original language, date, and place of composition must be asked of each addition separately, there being no justification for treating the four additions en masse and some clear evidence for not doing so (see below).

Despite the fact that ancient scholars such as Jerome[9] knew of no current proto-masoretic text containing any of the Septuagint "additions" to the Fiery Furnace, it was not until Eichhorn (ca. 1824) that the Semitic origin of these passages was first questioned by modern scholars, and not until Fritzsche (ca. 1871) that these additions were strongly argued as being Greek compositions rather than translations. While Fritzsche's view is probably not the position held by a majority of scholars today, such an opinion was quite understandable. Not only are there very few Hebraisms that one can point to in the additions, but there is not one indisputably clear example of a Greek word or phrase which can only be explained by positing a Semitic *Vorlage*. (In the present commentary, Hebraisms are not listed all together in one place but are dealt with in their appropriate contexts, e.g. the Hebraisms in the Prayer, or in the Psalm, etc.; such lists can, however, be found in Daubney, pp. 49-53; Bennett, p. 628; Marshall, *HDB*, IV, 775; and A. Bludau, *BSt* 2 [1897], 160.)

The Prayer

The evidence of a Hebrew original for this prayer takes several forms. First, in the Prayer itself both the LXX and ⊕ used the Hebrew names for the three martyrs, this in spite of the fact that elsewhere in the same chapter the Greek texts follow the MT by using only the Aramaic names (see NOTES on vs. 1 and vs. 2). Were the Prayer a Greek composition, one would surely expect its author to have followed the name types of the Greek text into which he was inserting his prayer; and yet in ch. 3 of the Septuagint, apart from the Prayer itself, the names of the three martyrs occur thirteen times—but only in Aramaic! Evidently then, the Septuagint translator was following a Semitic text, preferring to render the names in the Prayer as his Semitic text had them rather than, for the sake of consistency, changing them to agree with the Aramaic names elsewhere in the chapter. Second, the Prayer has several Hebraisms, some of which are admittedly quite commonplace (see first NOTES on vs. 4 and on vs. 10); but others are unusual, if not corrupt (see NOTE on vs. 11 and second NOTE on vs. 17). Third, the mere fact that this addition is a prayer argues for its having originally been in Hebrew, the latter being ipso facto the Jews' sacred language of prayer and praise.[10]

The most compelling reason for believing that the Prayer had a Hebrew original is the relative ease with which it can be translated into Biblical

---

[9] Before vs. 1[24] Jerome wrote in the Vulgate, "What follows I have not found in the Hebrew texts"; and after vs. 68[90] he noted, "These occur nowhere in the Hebrew, and what we have is translated from Theodotion's edition."

[10] Without citing linguistic evidence, Charles (p. 73) asserted that the Prayer and Hymn were in Aramaic, a view which would have the advantage of making these additions consistent with the language of the particular section in which they currently find themselves (Dan 2:4b - 7:28 is in Aramaic). But the situation concerning the original language/s of the canonical Book of Daniel is so complex and uncertain, that to say ch. 3 of the MT was in Aramaic "at first" just cannot be proved.

Hebrew, i.e. literally and yet without too many liberties being taken with the Greek text. In this regard, Kuhl did a fairly good job of reconstructing the Hebrew Prayer (Kuhl, pp. 132-154), and an excellent job with the Ode (pp. 154-159) and Psalm (pp. 111-129), showing that in Hebrew the Prayer probably had a metrical pattern of 3+3 (or 2+2+2)/3+3 (or 2+2+2), the Ode a 4/4, and the Psalm a 2+2/3, usually.[11] In Hebrew prosody, where, for instance, a verse is divided into two cola (or bicola), a 3+3/2+2+2 means that the first colon is divided in half, each half having three beats or stresses, while the second colon is divided into thirds, each third having two beats. For instance, Kuhl rendered the Greek of vss. 5-6[28-29]

kai drimata alētheias epoiēsas kata a epēgages ēmin kai epi tēn polin tēn agian tēn tōn paterōn ēmōn Ierousalēm, oti en alētheia kai krisei epēgages panta tauta dia tas amartias ēmōn. Oti ēmartomen kai ēnomēsamen apostēnai apo sou, kai exēmartomen en pasin.[12]

into Hebrew as

wmšpṭy-ṣdq ʿšyt	*blk-ʾšr hbʾt ʿlynw*		3+3
wʾl yrwšlym	*ʿyr hqdš*	*ʾšr lʾbtynw*	2+2+2
ky bʾmt wbmšpṭ	*hbʾt kl-zʾt*	*byd-ʿwnnw*	2+2+2
ky hršʿnw whʿwynw	*lrḥq mʿlyk*	*whṭʾnw bkl*	2+2+2

Such verses as the above are typical of the way in which Kuhl reconstructed most of the verses in the Prayer, Ode, and Psalm, i.e. literally and yet within the presumed metrical pattern (but see NOTES on vss. 8 and 64). Taking all the evidence together, we may conclude that the case for a Hebrew original for the Prayer, while not proved, is probable.

The only clues to the date and place of the Prayer's composition are the melancholy tone of the Prayer in general,[13] and vss. 9, 15, and 17 in particular (see NOTES), where the presumed background seems to correspond best with Israel's darkest days under Antiochus Epiphanes IV, a Seleucian king who tried to wipe out Judaism ca. 167-163 B.C. Though written quite possibly in the same general period as the Book of Daniel itself, the Prayer was inserted evidently only later but, in any case, prior to the Septuagint's translations of the Semitic text of Daniel (see Introduction to the Additions to Daniel, pp. 28-29). Palestine would have been the place of its composition.

---

[11] According to Kuhl, the "theme" verse of each of the three stanzas is a 3/3, namely, vss. 36[58], 52[74], and 61[83].

[12] "You have passed just sentence in everything that you have brought upon us, and upon Jerusalem, the holy city of our fathers; for in true justice you have brought about all these things on account of our sins. For we have sinned and acted lawlessly by deserting you; we have sinned in everything."

[13] As exemplified, for instance, in vss. 5-7,10,19, and 21 (see NOTES).

The Ode

Being quite brief, the Ode offers little opportunity for finding in it evidences of a Hebrew original. But the simple fact that it was an antiphonal psalm appropriate for public worship suggests that it would have been composed in Hebrew; and the likelihood of that is strengthened considerably by the ease and accuracy with which Kuhl has retranslated the Ode back into Biblical Hebrew with a 4/4 meter. Verse 29[52] is typical of what Kuhl has done with all seven verses:

> *eulogētos ei Kurie o theos tōn paterōn ēmōn*
> *kai ainetos kai uperupsoumenos eis tous oiōnas.*

> brwk yhwh 'lhy 'btynw   4
> wmhll wmrwmm m'd l'wlm   4

As for the date of its composition, there are only two clues given, both ambiguous. The phrase "temple of your sacred glory" (vs. 31[53]) has been taken by some scholars to refer to Yahweh's being in the temple at Jerusalem, in which case that would seem to contradict vs. 15 of the Prayer where the Temple was still in ruins (or at least, was inaccessible). According to that logic, the Ode would have been written at a time other than that of the Prayer. More likely, however, the reference in vs. 31 is to the Heavenly Temple, not the one in Jerusalem (see NOTE on vs. 31), in which case there is no reason why the Ode could not have been composed at the same time as the Prayer, although it need not have been.

The other "clue" to the date is that Tobit 8:5,[14] containing as it does the opening lines of the Ode as well as the general theme of both the Ode and the Psalm (see NOTE on vss. 29-30), *may* have inspired the writing of the Ode (or at least, its inclusion with the Psalm), in which case we have a *terminus a quo* for the Ode since the Book of Tobit was composed in the second century B.C. The Ode's probable place of composition would be Palestine. In any event, the Ode was added to the Semitic text of Daniel prior to the latter's being translated into Greek.

The Psalm

Despite the fact that the Psalm (vss. 35-68) is the longest of the four additions, it offers perhaps the fewest clues as to its original language, date, and provenience. It has, for instance, only one indisputable Hebraism (see NOTE on vs. 68); and it is far from certain that that particular Hebraism should be taken with the Psalm, i.e. originally it could have

---

[14] I.e. "Tobias began to pray, 'Blessed are you, O God of our Fathers, and blessed is your holy and glorious name for ever. Let the heavens and all your creatures bless you!'"

been the concluding part of the Prose Narrative and then later separated from the latter by the insertion of the Hymn (see below). Moreover, the fact that in vs. 66 the *Hebrew* names for the heroes are used does not preclude the possibility that the Psalm itself was originally in Aramaic and that the scribe who inserted it into the Book of Daniel just happened to have used Hebrew names as he was tailoring this once-separate psalm to the Semitic text of Daniel (see NOTE on vss. 66-67).

More likely, however, the Psalm would have been originally in Hebrew, the reasons for our saying this being the same as those for the Ode. First, this antiphonal psalm, with its oft-repeated refrain "sing his praise and highly exalt him for ever" (thirty-one times), is clearly designed for public worship, which would presumably have been in Hebrew. Second, virtually every verse of the Psalm can be literally yet poetically reconstructed into a Hebrew line with a metrical pattern of 2+2/3. Verse 40[62] is very typical of Kuhl's excellent rendering of the Psalm:

> *eulogeite, ēlios kai selēnē, ton kurion*
> *umneite kai uperupsoute auton eis tous aiōnas.*
> *brkw yhwh šmš wyrḥ*   2+2
>
> *hllhw wrwmmhw l'wlmym*   3

Taken together, the evidence permits a presumption of a Hebrew original for the Psalm but no certainty.

Apart from the ambiguous clue mentioned in vs. 31 concerning the Book of Tobit providing the *terminus a quo* for the Hymn, there is virtually no internal evidence as to the original date of the Psalm. In any case, it was inserted after the Book of Daniel had been written but before the Prayer was added.[15] Evidently, it was part of the Semitic text of Daniel when the latter was translated into Greek. *If* the Psalm was composed in Hebrew, Palestine would have been its probable place of composition. Certainly the frequency with which water in its various forms of dew, rain, and snow is mentioned in the Psalm (cf. vss. 38,42,46,50,55-56) probably precludes an Egyptian provenance for the Psalm.

The Prose Narrative

If, as some scholars have contended, vss. 23-28[46-51] are actually a portion of the original Fiery Furnace story that was erroneously deleted when the Prayer and Hymn were rightfully deleted later on from the Se-

---

[15] One must distinguish carefully between the date of composition and the date of insertion into the Book of Daniel. It is not invalid, for instance, to argue as have some scholars that the strikingly different moods of the Prayer and the Hymn (the former is rather despondent, the latter quite jubilant) necessarily prove that they were composed in different historical periods, i.e. the Prayer during the Maccabean struggle, the Hymn either before or after that time. But that the Prayer was *inserted* later than the Hymn seems fairly certain from its awkward position in relationship to the Prose Narrative which introduces the Hymn.

mitic Book of Daniel, then the Prose Narrative would have been in the same Semitic language as the rest of the Fiery Furnace narrative, which was, to judge from the present MT, Aramaic. But if the Prose Narrative was designed as an introduction for the Hymn, as seems more likely (see COMMENT, p. 65), then vss. 23-28 would have been in the same language as the Hymn, i.e. in Hebrew. Certainly a Hebrew *Vorlage* is made even the more probable by the use of the Hebrew name Azariah in vs. 26[49], as well as by the fact that vs. 91a of the LXX has a clear Hebraism (Gr. *kai egeneto*), regardless of whether the latter is a detached part of the Prose Narrative or a part of the Hymn's transition to vs. 24 [91b] of the MT. Assuming that the Prose Narrative was composed as an introduction for the Hymn, one may conclude that vss. 23-28[46-51] were composed at the time that the Hymn was inserted into the Semitic text, i.e. after the Book of Daniel was written but before it was translated into Greek.

Before leaving the subject of the original language/s of the four additions, we should say a word about a thesis or body of evidence that was quite popular in studies on the apocrypha of Daniel at the turn of the last century, namely, the work of Moses Gaster, who claimed that in a medieval work entitled *The Chronicles of Jerahmeel* he had found the Aramaic original from which Theodotion had made his Greek translation of the Additions to Daniel.[16]

There can be no doubt that the Prayer, the Prose Narrative, and the Hymn as found in Gaster's Aramaic text are strikingly similar to the Greek ⊙, especially in those few places where the LXX and ⊙ disagree with one another. The problem, however, is that when the Aramaic and the Greek texts are compared to one another, there is no reading which decisively shows that the one version was necessarily based upon the other. In other words, Gaster's text could just as easily be an Aramaic translation of ⊙. Such a possibility cannot be lightly dismissed since it has been shown, in some instances at least, Hebrew and Aramaic materials in medieval writers like Josippon and Jerahmeel were actually Semitic translations based on the Septuagint or Vulgate! (For details on Josippon, see p. 154), n. 3.) Nonetheless, readings from Gaster's Aramaic version will sometimes be noted and discussed in the present commentary.

Literary Merit

Regardless of whether the four additions to Daniel were composed in Hebrew or not, any judgment on their literary merit must confine itself to

---

[16] M. Gaster, "The Unknown Aramaic Original of Theodotion's Additions to the Book of Daniel," *PSBA* 16 (1894), 280-290, 17 (1895), 75-94; *The Chronicles of Jerahmeel*.

the additions as they exist in the Greek and other ancient versions. "Literary merit" is a rather subjective thing to establish, in part, because in poetry especially, it is a matter of one's "ear" and a sensitivity to nuance. Equally able scholars can listen to the same thing and "hear" it differently. For instance, of the refrain in the Psalm ("Sing his praise and highly exalt him for ever") it has been said: "The monotony of form is itself effective. It is like the monotony of the wind on the waves" (Ball, p. 307); "a certain solemnity is achieved by the regularly recurring refrain" (Metzger, p. 101); "a refrain apt to linger in the ear either in Greek or English" (Daubney, p. 56). While all three scholars were speaking favorably of the same refrain, apparently they were not saying or "hearing" the same thing.

If, however, the criterion of literary merit is usage or popularity, i.e., the frequency, extent, and length of time a particular passage is quoted or alluded to, then the answer is quite clear. For from the early Church Fathers on, the Ode and the Psalm (but not the Prayer) figured prominently in the liturgies of both the Eastern and Western churches (see p. 42, n. 7), the Ode, or *Benedictus,* still being used today in the Roman Catholic Church by the priest in his obligatory early morning private devotions.

Ancient Use of Addition as Scripture

Although in its broadest outlines the Fiery Furnace incident was quite popular among ancient Jews, citations from its "Greek" additions are slight and rather late. Josephus (*Ant.* x 10.5) tells the story of the three martyrs in the fiery furnace but gives no indication that he was aware of the Additions. (That he had no special aversion to using deuterocanonical materials is clear from the fact that he paraphrased some of the Additions to Esther.) Nor is there any clear evidence of the apocryphon being specifically quoted in the numerous rabbinic accounts of the Fiery Furnace prior to the Middle Ages, when these additions finally appeared in Josippon and Jerahmeel.[17] Nor did the writers of the New Testament use any of this material.[18]

The early Church Fathers, then, provide the first indisputable evidence that the additions to the Fiery Furnace were regarded as Holy Scripture, passages from it being quoted or alluded to by Justin Martyr (d. 165) in

---

[17] Pfeiffer (p. 442) argued that since I Macc 2:59; IV Macc 16:21 and 18:12 had the same name sequence as vs. 66 of the Hymn (i.e. Hananiah, Azariah, and Mishael), the Alexandrian Jews knew our additions and regarded them as canonical.

[18] To be sure, there are several instances where the New Testament has phrases reminiscent of our additions, namely, *tapeinos tē kardia* in Matt 11:29 (cf. *tapeinoi tē kardia* in vs. 65[87]; *eurein eleos* in II Tim 1:18 (cf. vs. 15[38]); and *pneumata dikaiōn* in Heb 12:23 (cf. *pneumata . . . dikaiōn* in vs. 64[86]). These NT passages, however, are too brief to justify the view that their NT writers were actually quoting from the additions.

his *Apologia* I 46; Clement of Alexandria (d. before 215) in *Eclogae propheticae* I; Hippolytus of Rome (170-235); Tertullian (160?-220) in his *de Oratione* 15; and Cyprian of Carthage (d. 258) in his *de Lapsis* 31.

Julius Africanus (d. after 240) in his letter to Origen (185?-?254) was, so far as we now know, the first Church Father to question the canonicity of these additions. He was followed in this by Jerome (340?-420), who although he had his doubts about the canonicity of these additions (see p. 45, n. 9), nonetheless left them in ch. 3 of the Vulgate instead of, as he had done with "Susanna" and "Bel and the Snake," putting them at the end of the canonical Daniel. Polychronius, brother of Theodore of Mopsuestia (350?-428), was adamant in regarding these additions as not being part of the original Book of Daniel.

Nonetheless, judging from the citations of these additions as Scripture by the Church Fathers, we may say that the overwhelming majority of the Fathers continued to regard these additions as an integral part of the canonical text of Daniel.[19]

Religious Teachings

Whatever the real reason for this Addition to Daniel not being included by the Jewish Fathers in the Hebrew canon, it cannot have been that it was judged by them to contain heretical ideas or teachings unacceptable to normative Judaism as interpreted, for instance, by the Council of Jamnia. Moreover, when the Prayer, Prose Narrative, and Hymn are taken together, our Addition affirms three of the most important and basic themes of the Old Testament: God works in human history, especially for his chosen people (so the Prayer); God is also with his people as individuals, delivering those who serve and trust in him (so the Prose Narrative); and God is the Lord of all, the Creator who is exalted above his creation rather than identified with it (the Hymn). Such teachings are quite compatible with post-exilic Judaism in general, and with the canonical Book of Daniel in particular. (There is no reason to think that any of these component parts of the Addition is Christian in origin.) Ideas, phrases, and entire lines in the Addition are redolent of older biblical passages, notably, in Isaiah, I and II Chronicles, Nehemiah, and Psalms for the Prayer; and Psalms, especially Psalm 148, for our Hymn (see NOTES *passim*).

---

[19] Daubney (pp. 76-80) lists citations from the Fathers down through the sixth century. For the most exhaustive list of citations, see Caspar Julius, *BSt* 6 (1903), 1-183.

Ancient Versions

LXX and ⊕ Compared

Unlike the situation in "Susanna" and "Bel and the Snake," the LXX and ⊕ are in almost total agreement with one another in the four additions now under discussion. Apart from a few disagreements on the correct verse sequence,[20] which in this case does not really affect the content, the only striking variants are around "the edges," i.e. only vss. 1-2[24-25], which introduce the Prayer, and vs. 23[46], which is the opening line of the Prose Narrative, greatly differ in the LXX and ⊕.

To be sure, here and there ⊕ evidently added or omitted a word or phrase (see textual notes *passim*), but most verses in the LXX and ⊕ are the same, word for word. Almost totally absent in ⊕ are variant synonyms; in other words, rarely did ⊕ replace a noun, verb, or adjective of the LXX with a synonym. Moreover, in those few instances where ⊕ *may* have a substitute synonym, there is no clear indication that a Semitic text governed that substitution. Therefore, either the author of ⊕ did not correct the LXX by a Semitic text or, more likely, he had essentially the same Semitic text as the translator of the LXX. The latter explanation is more likely if the ⊕ of Daniel was not done in the second century A.D. by Theodotion, but by someone earlier (see Introduction to "The Additions to Daniel," pp. 30-33).

The LXX, which is represented by one Greek manuscript directly (the Chigi MS, Codex 88) and by the Syro-Hexaplar indirectly, sometimes has the support of the Vulgate (see NOTES *passim*). The ⊕ is represented by a number of manuscripts, the most important being Vaticanus ($⊕^B$) and Alexandrinus ($⊕^A$). In contrast to most manuscripts of ⊕, $⊕^B$ omits two verses—and rightly so (see NOTES on vss. 45-46).

Other Ancient Versions

With a few exceptions, the Syro-Hexaplar (SyrH.) faithfully follows the LXX rather than the ⊕. Both the Old Latin (*Vetus Latina*), which is quite fragmentary, being primarily quotations from the Latin Fathers, and the Vulgate are literal translations of the Greek; and the Arabic text is even more literal. The Ethiopic and Bohairic are also very literal, while the Syriac is quite free. Gaster's Aramaic text, as noted on p. 49, agrees

---

[20] Inasmuch as the LXX's sequence of verses seems somewhat more logical than ⊕'s (see NOTE on vss. 44-51), there would seem to be little justification for the editor of ⊕ to change the sequence of his verses unless he was reflecting the verse sequence of his Semitic text.

with ☉ rather than LXX. In terms of their usefulness in establishing the original readings of the Greek texts, the relative merits of these versions are reflected in the order in which they have been mentioned above, the most important coming first and the least, last.

I. THE PRAYER OF AZARIAH

(Vss. 1-22[3:24-45 in LXX, ℗, and Vulgate])

1[24] And they walked about in the heart of the flames, singing hymns to God and blessing the Lord. 2[25] Then Azariah stood still and uttered this prayer—in the midst of the fire he opened his mouth and said:

3[26] "Blessed *and praiseworthy*^a are you, Lord, the God of our
      fathers; and your name is glorified for ever!

4[27] For you are just in all that you have done^b.
      All your deeds are true, and your ways right;
      and all your judgments are true.

5[28] You have passed just sentence in everything
      that you have brought upon us,
      and upon Jerusalem, the holy city of our fathers;
   For in true justice you have brought about all these
      things^c on account of our sins.

6[29] For we have sinned and acted lawlessly by deserting you;
      we have sinned in everything.

7[30] We have not obeyed your commandments;
      we have not observed or done as you commanded us
      for our own good.

8[31] *So in*^d *all that you have brought upon us*^e,
      and all that you have done to us,
      you have acted justly.

---

a-a So ℗^B and SyrH.; see NOTE.
b Most Greek MSS and versions add, with LXX, "to us."
c Many MSS and versions add "upon us."
d-d ℗ "and all"; LXX "and now"; Vulg. *omnia ergo.*
e-e ℗^A Q omit; see NOTE.

9[32] You have delivered us into the power of our *enemies,
       lawless and most hateful rebels*,
       and to an unjust king, the vilest in the whole world.

10[33] Yet we dare not open our mouths,
        shame and disgrace are the lot of your servants
        and those who worship you.

11[34] For your name's sake do not abandon us for ever;
        do not annul*g* your covenant.

12[35] And do not withdraw your mercy from us,
        for the sake of Abraham your friend,
        for the sake of Isaac your servant
        and of Israel your holy one.

13[36] You promised them descendants
        as numerous as the stars of the sky
        and as the grains of sand on the seashore.

14[37] Yet, Lord, we have dwindled among the nations,
        and we are abject throughout the world today
        because of our sins.

15[38] Right now we have no prince, no prophet, no leader;
        no burnt offering, no sacrifice, no oblation, no
        incense;
        no place to make an offering before you and find
        mercy.

16[39] Yet with contrite soul and *h*the humbled spirit*h* may we
        be as acceptable

17[40] As with burnt offerings of rams and bulls
        and with thousands of fattened lambs.
        So may our "sacrifice" be in your sight this day
        *i*and so may we wholeheartedly follow you*i*;
        for those who trust in you will*j* not be disappointed*k*.

18[41] Now that we earnestly*l* follow you
        and fear you and seek your face,

---

f-f So ⊕ᴮ, with LXX; most MSS of ⊕ have "lawless enemies, most hateful rebels."
g Gr. "scatter"; see NOTE.
h-h So LXX; ⊕ and SyrH. have "the spirit of humility," an obvious Hebraism.
i-i ⊕ "and be complete after you"; LXX "and make atonement before you"; Vulg. *ut
placeat tibi;* Aramaic omits; see NOTE.
j LXX has present tense.
k LXX (but not SyrH.) adds "and so may we wholeheartedly follow you," an obvious
gloss from ⊕.
l Gr. "with whole heart."

19[42] Do not let us be put to shame,
            but treat us in keeping with your leniency
            and in keeping with your great mercy.
20[43] Rescue us in your miraculous manner
            and glorify your name, Lord.
21[44] Let all those who abuse your servants be disgraced;
            let them be stripped of all their power,
            and their strength broken.
22[45] Let them know that you *alone are Lord God*,
            and glorious over the whole world.

ᵐ-ᵐ So ⊙ᴮ; most MSS of ⊙ have "the Lord, the only God," as in II Kings 19:19 of LXX.

NOTES

1. *they*. I.e. Hananiah, Azariah, and Mishael, whose Aramaic names were Shadrach, Abednego, and Meshach, respectively (Dan 1:7). The use of only their Hebrew names in the Addition (so vs. 1 of the LXX and vs. 66 of LXX and ⊙) is a clear indication of the latter's secondary, or intrusive, character; for in the MT's Aramaic account of the experience in the fiery furnace (ch. 3) these men are always called by their *Aramaic* names (thirteen times, to be exact), and in the first two chapters of the MT they were, with but one exception (1:7), referred to by their Hebrew names (cf. 1:6,11,19; 2:17).

The corresponding verse in the LXX is quite different, namely: "So then Hananiah, Azariah, and Mishael prayed and sang hymns to the Lord when the king commanded them to be thrown into the furnace." Neither the LXX nor ⊙, however, is particularly smooth in its treatment here: the LXX reads like an intrusive superscription, and ⊙ prepares the reader to hear a hymn of praise when, in actual fact, a *communal* confession of sin will follow (see COMMENT, p. 60).

2. *Azariah*. That Azariah offered the prayer rather than Hananiah is curious and is further evidence of the secondary character of the Addition. Azariah, it seems, was not the most important of the three young men; for in the MT regardless of whether they are listed by their Hebrew or Aramaic names, Azariah was *always* mentioned last. The fact that even in the Addition itself he is never mentioned first when the others are also named (vs. 66, and vs. 1 of the LXX) has prompted some scholars to think that the Prayer of Azariah (vss. 3-22) may originally have referred to an Azariah other than Meshach, and that the identity of names explains why this rather inappropriate prayer (see COMMENT) was inserted here. Certainly the name was quite common, there being at least twenty-five Azariah's mentioned in the Bible (see F. T. Schumacher, *IDB*, I, 324-325).

In the LXX, however, all three men uttered the prayer together: "Azariah stood and uttered this prayer; he, together with his companions, opened his mouth and praised the Lord—in the heart of the furnace, vigorously stoked [lit. "greatly heated from below with fire"] by the Chaldeans, they said." Repeating awkwardly and needlessly the content of vs. 1, the verse in the LXX adds little of real significance; ⊙, however, represents a smooth and natural progression of the narrative introduction. Possibly, the verse in ⊙ was influenced by Jonah 2:2 of the LXX which, in introducing Jonah's prayer, is remarkably similar in structure and wording.

3. *Blessed . . . God of our fathers.* Cf. I Chron 29:10,20.

praiseworthy [ainetos]. In the LXX ("Blessed are you, Lord, the God of our fathers; and praiseworthy [aineton] and glorified is your name for ever"), "praiseworthy" modifies name, not God (so ⊙). The LXX's reading is preferred by M. Gaster on the basis of his Aramaic version (*PSBA* 17 [1895], 75) and by Kuhl (pp. 132-134) on the basis of the presumed Hebrew meter.

4. *you are just in [epi] all.* This "ungreek" use of *epi*, "upon," is a clear Hebraism; cf. Dan 9:14 and Neh 9:33.

your judgments are true. Literally "your judgments are truth"; this use of the predicate noun as an adjective is also a Hebraism.

5. *just sentence.* Literally "judgments of truth."

in true justice. Cf. Ps 111:7 and Jer 4:2. Literally "in truth and judgment," which is really hendiadys, just as the Aramaic rightly renders it (Gaster, *PSBA* 17 [1895], 76).

6. *sinned [ēmartomen] and acted lawlessly . . . have sinned [exēmartomen].* Cf. Dan 9:5,15. Fritzsche would have deleted *exēmartomen* as a later gloss; but Kuhl (p. 136) rightly observes that considerations of meter require the retention of the verb, i.e. its retention preserves for the reconstructed Hebrew the necessary meter of 2+2+2. Evidently the Greek renders the well-known Hebrew triad for sin, namely, the Hebrew verbs *ršʿ*, "to be wicked," *ʿwh*, "to act perversely," and *ḥṭʾ*, "to fail" (cf. Dan 9:5; Ps 106:6; I Kings 8:47; II Chron 6:37).

7. *obeyed . . . observed or done.* The Greek apparently renders another well-known trinity of Hebrew verbs: *šmʿ*, "to hear," *šmr*, "to keep," and *ʿśh*, "to do" (cf. Deut 4:1f, 5:1, 6:3, 7:12; I Kings 11:38).

8. *all that you have brought upon us.* The difficulties—not to mention the pitfalls and arbitrary decisions—involved in reconstructing the presumed Hebrew original from a verse surviving only in the Greek and the versions is well illustrated by this clause. On the one hand, because this clause is omitted by ⊙^(A Q) and because its meaning is essentially the same as the next clause, Rothstein (p. 180), Bennett (p. 633), and others would delete it as a gloss; on the other hand, Kuhl (p. 137), in the interest of preserving for the verse the usual metrical pattern of 3+3/3+3, would not only retain the clause but add "in truth and righteousness you have brought it," a reading for which there is no manuscript support whatever in the Greek or the versions.

9. *rebels [apostatōn].* A Hebraism. Meaning "runaways," *apostatai* is used in Num 14:9 and Josh 22:19 to render the Hebrew verb *mrd*, "to rebel"; although ostensibly referring to the Babylonians, the word is rather inappropriate for them and is universally understood by scholars as a veiled allusion to

Hellenistic Jews, i.e. to apostate Jews such as described in I Macc 1:11-15,41-43. Noting that the Aramaic version omits "most hateful rebels," Gaster (*PSBA* 17 [1895], 77) regarded the phrase as a later interpolation, it being added by a copyist who regarded the situation as being applicable to the Hellenists.

unjust king, the vilest. At face value the phrase refers to Nebuchadnezzar (but see Jer 25:9); actually, however, it is a veiled allusion to a new "Nebuchadnezzar," the detested Antiochus Epiphanes (cf. I Macc 1:20-28, 41-64).

10. *we dare not.* Literally "there is not to us"; a Hebraism which seems to render the Heb. *'ên lānû* (cf. II Sam 21:4; II Chron 35:3).

those who worship [tois sebomenois] you. Cf. vs. 68. This represents a poetic parallel with the previous phrase, not a gloss (so Rothstein) or "proselytes" (so *sebomenoi* in Acts 17:17).

11. *annul [diaskedasēs] your covenant.* In the MT the Hebrew idioms for breaking a covenant are *škḥ bryt,* "to forget a covenant" (cf. Deut 4:31) and *prr bryt,* "to annul a covenant" (cf. Lev 26:15; Judg 2:1).

12. *Abraham your friend.* Cf. Isa 41:8: "But you, Israel, my servant, Jacob, whom I have chosen, the offspring of Abraham, my friend." While the epithet of "God's friend" as applied to Abraham was continued in the Apocrypha Jub 19:9) as well as in Christian (cf. James 2:23 and *I Clement* xvII 2) and Muslim writings (cf. Koran 4:125), nowhere in the Bible except here are these particular epithets applied to Isaac and Israel, respectively. (To be sure, the *people* Israel are often characterized as "holy" [cf. Exod 19:6; Deut 7:6], but never the wily, devious patriarch of that name; for justification of such an unflattering characterization of him, see L. Hicks, "Jacob (Israel)," *IDB,* II, 782-787.)

13. *You promised them.* Literally "to them you promised." Though this promise was made specifically to Abraham (Gen 22:17), it was, in the judgment of various biblical writers, reaffirmed to others (cf. Exod 32:13 and Jer 33:22).

14. *we have dwindled [esmikrunthēmen].* Cf. Jer 29[36]:6; I Bar 2:34.

15. *Right now we have . . . no prophet.* Literally "And there is not at this time . . . a prophet." Although the ancient author may have found inspiration for this verse in some such biblical passage as Hosea 3:4 or II Chron 15:3, he nonetheless slipped up by attributing the appalling conditions of a later period, i.e. Israel's darkest days under Antiochus Epiphanes in 167 B.C., to the days of Nebuchadnezzar, a period when two of Israel's greatest prophets *were* laboring, namely, Jeremiah and Ezekiel.

no burnt offering . . . no incense. In accordance with Deut 12:11-18, the Deuteronomic Reformation of Josiah had centralized all public worship in Jerusalem (on the Reformation, see J. Bright, *A History of Israel,* rev. 2d ed. [Philadelphia: Westminster Press, 1972], 317-321); but with the Jerusalem temple destroyed, Jews, or at least those Jews outside of Palestine (cf. Jer 41:5), could no longer offer whole burnt offerings (Gr. *olokautōsis*=Heb. *'ōlāh*); animal sacrifices (Gr. *thusia*=Heb. *zebaḥ*); oblation (Gr. *prosphora*=Heb. *minḥāh* in Ps 40[39]:7); or incense (Gr. *thumiama*=Heb.

q^etōret). For an excellent introduction to this involved subject, see T. H. Gaster, "Sacrifices and Offerings, OT," *IDB*, IV, 147-159.

to make an offering [karpōsai]. Literally "to offer the fruits" (cf. III Esd 4:52), but in Lev 2:10 this verb is used for "burning a cereal offering."

16. *contrite soul [psuchē suntetrimmenē].* The word "soul" is somewhat surprising; for, ordinarily, "contrite heart" is the Hebrew idiom in parallel with "humbled spirit" (cf. Pss 34:18[33:19], 51[50]:17, 147[146]:3; but see also III Macc 2:20). On the meaning of "soul," see NOTE on vs. 64.

17. *So may our "sacrifice" be in your sight.* While the theological position here is reminiscent of great passages such as Pss 51:16-17 and 141:2, the verse in no way denies the importance or efficacy of sacrifice; as T. H. Gaster has so accurately observed: "Contrary to a widespread impression that there was a fundamental antithesis on this subject between the religion of the law and that of the prophets, the truth is that the latter were not against sacrifice per se, but simply against the abuse of it. . . . Nowhere, however, in all the prophetic literature of the OT, is there any denial of the premise that *within its prescribed limits* [italics added], sacrifice was indeed an effective religious vehicle; the advance beyond this assumption is entirely postbiblical" (*IDB*, IV, 157). For the exilic Jew living in Babylon (the presumed setting for our story) and the Palestinian Jew living in the dark days of Antiochus Epiphanes (the actual setting for the prayer) sacrificing at the Temple was not an option open to him.

and so may we wholeheartedly follow you. Scholarly discussions of this obviously corrupt clause have produced much heat but little light, the discussion of the problem not having been advanced much since the days of Bennett (cf. Bennett, pp. 628, 634). Consider, for a moment, the way this clause is translated in various recent English versions:

RSV: "and may we wholly follow thee."
Chicago Bible: "So let our sacrifice rise . . . and fully
follow after you,"
JB: "and may it be your will that we follow you
wholeheartedly,"
NEB: "Accept our pledge of loyalty to thee,"

The Greek in ⊕ [*ektelesai opisthen sou*] literally means "be complete after you," which, in turn, sounds very much like a very literal Greek rendering of the Hebrew idiom *mallē' 'ah^areykā,* "to wholly follow you" (cf., for example, Num 14:24; Deut 1:36; Josh 14:8); unfortunately, however, our Greek verb *ekteleō* is never used in the LXX to render this Hebrew phrase. The corresponding clause in the LXX is somewhat more appropriate: *kai exilasai opisthen sou,* "and make atonement before you" (cf. Mal 1:9 and Zech 7:2, 8:22 of the LXX). Thus far, efforts to produce a Hebrew text from which both the LXX and ⊕ could have originated have been unsuccessful.

19. *your leniency [epieikeian].* Cf. Wisd Sol 2:19 and 12:18.

20. *your miraculous manner [ta thaumasia sou].* Literally "your wonderful things" (cf. Ps 9:1); the plagues against Pharaoh in Moses' day were called *thaumasia* (cf. Exod 3:20 of LXX). As it turned out, the survival of the three young men in the fiery furnace could only be termed "miraculous." This verse,

incidentally, is one of the few in the prayer which seems especially appropriate
to its context.

21. *be stripped of* [*kataischuntheiēsan apo*]. Cf. Jer 2:36. Literally "be disgraced from."

22. *the whole world* [*olēn tēn oikoumenēn*]. In the Greek Bible *oikoumenē* is
used to render the Heb. *tēbēl*, "world" (Prov 8:31), as well as *'ereṣ*, "earth"
(Isa 10:23).

COMMENT

Three arguments, none of them decisive in itself, prove that the Prayer of
Azariah was a separate and independent entity that originally had nothing to do
with the Fiery Furnace story: (1) the clumsy and repetitious character of
the prayer's own introduction to itself as preserved in vss. 1-2[24-25 of the
LXX]; (2) the use in vs. 1 of the Hebrew names for our three heroes, whereas
in masoretic account of the Fiery Furnace the MT always used their
Aramaic names; and (3) the obvious inappropriateness of much of the prayer
for its situation or context.

Concerning the third point, scholars have been almost unanimous in regarding the prayer as *a national lament,* or communal prayer of repentance and
supplication, something that would have been used in the liturgy of the synagogue or the public temple worship, like Psalms 44, 74, 79, or 80. While such a
prayer may never be out of date, emphasizing as it does the community's sinfulness and God's justice, neither is it always appropriate for every particular
moment or crisis. Given the fact that the three young men were in their present
terrible predicament precisely because they had been true to their God by refusing to bow down to the gold image which Nebuchadnezzar had set up in the
plain of Dura (Dan 3:1,16-18), scholars usually regard vss. 5-8 as glaringly inappropriate:

> You have passed just sentence in everything
> > that you have brought upon us,
> > and upon Jerusalem, the holy city of our fathers;
> For in true justice you have brought about all these
> > things on account of our sins.
> For we have sinned and acted lawlessly by deserting you;
> > we have sinned in everything.
> We have not obeyed your commandments;
> > we have not observed or done as you commanded us
> > for our own good.
> So in all that you have brought upon us,
> > and all that you have done to us,
> > you have acted justly.

Why was a prayer inserted at this point in the Fiery Furnace narrative?
Only the ancient Jewish scribe responsible for inserting it could answer that

question; but, quite possibly, he felt that inasmuch as in 3:28 of the MT Nebuchadnezzar, a pagan king, would himself bless and praise Israel's God, the three Jewish martyrs should not be outdone but should also praise God.

To be sure, there are also those verses, especially toward the end of the prayer, which are very appropriate for the youths in the furnace, namely vss. 18-21:

> Now that we earnestly follow you
>   and fear you and seek your face,
> Do not let us be put to shame,
>   but treat us in keeping with your leniency
>   and in keeping with your great mercy.
> Rescue us in your miraculous manner
>   and glorify your name, Lord.
> Let all those who abuse your servants be disgraced;
>   let them be stripped of all their power,
>   and their strength broken.

Where, when, or by whom the prayer was originally written is unknown; for almost no clues are given. Being a prayer, it was probably composed in Hebrew, the Jewish language of worship; and there are a few indications of a Hebrew *Vorlage* (see first NOTE on vs. 4). As for the date of composition, several passages suggest vivid memories of, if not a present experiencing of, the terrible events of the persecution of Antiochus Epiphanes in 167-165 B.C. (see esp. vss. 6,9,15,17). Whoever the ancient poet was, he found his inspiration, if one may judge from biblical parallels, primarily in Psalms, Isaiah, Jeremiah, and Chronicles (see NOTES *passim*).

The likelihood that the prayer was originally in Hebrew has been strengthened considerably by the efforts of Kuhl (pp. 132-154), who did an excellent job of reconstructing a Hebrew text with a metrical pattern of 3+3 (or 2+2+2)/ 3+3 (or 2+2+2), although sometimes Kuhl was too willing to use his metrical pattern as a Procrustean Bed in which, without any manuscript support from the Greek or versions, he deleted or added Hebrew phrases and clauses to his reconstructed Hebrew text. Kuhl's task was made easier and his results somewhat more certain by the fact that the texts of the LXX and ⑨ are virtually identical—at least in comparison to their striking lack of agreement with one another in the other Additions to Daniel, i.e. in "Susanna" and in "Bel and the Snake."

II. GOD PRESERVES THE MARTYRS
IN THE FIERY FURNACE
(Vss. 23-28[46-51])

23[46] Now the king's servants who had thrown them in did not stop stoking the furnace with naphtha, pitch, tow, and brush— 24[47] so that the flame rose seventy-some feet above the furnace.

25[48] Then it shot out and burned to death those Chaldeans it found about the furnace. 26[49] But the angel of the Lord came down and joined Azariah and his companions in the furnace, and drove the scorching blaze out of the furnace, 27[50] and made the middle of the furnace as though a dew-laden breeze were blowing through it, so that the fire did not touch them at all—it did not hurt or even annoy them.

28[51] Then in unison the three praised and glorified and blessed[a] God in the furnace, saying:

[a] LXX and SyrH. add "and exalted."

NOTES

23. *had thrown them in.* Cf. Jer 29:22. Regardless of whether the Fiery Furnace incident is essentially true or not, it is a fact that Nebuchadnezzar did indeed use fire as a means of execution (see Kuhl, pp. 34-39).

naphtha [*naphtha*]. This is not the distilled oil we know but some naturally occurring inflammable liquid, probably petroleum, such as is mentioned in II Macc 1:20-22,30-36. For Talmudic references to naphtha, see Ball, p. 315.

The corresponding verse in the LXX is hopelessly corrupt: "Now when they had thrown the three into the furnace at the same time, and the furnace was seven times hotter than usual—and when those who had thrown them in (they who had thrown them in were above them) while those underneath them were feeding the fire with naphtha, pitch, tow, and brush—." The SyrH. compounds the verse's infelicities, if not difficulties for the reader, by prefixing to this verse: "Now the king's servants who had thrown them in did not stop stoking the furnace." Marginal readings, dittographies, or both have evidently crept into the Septuagint text. But corrupt though this verse in the LXX obviously is, it (in both the LXX and ℮) clearly contradicts Dan 3:22 of the MT, where those who tossed the three heroes into the furnace were themselves *immediately* consumed. Verse 23 [46] of ℮ does not, however, contradict vss. 22-23 of ℮.

24. *seventy-some feet.* Literally "forty-nine cubits," i.e. seven cubits times seven, "seven" being a favorite sacred number in Daniel (4:25, 9:2,25, 10:2, 13) and elsewhere in the literature of the Hebrews and other ancient Near Eastern peoples (see M. H. Pope, "Seven, Seventh, Seventy," *IDB*, IV, 294-295).

25. *those . . . about the furnace.* According to Daubney, vs. 25[48] "is not a repetition of vs. 22 of the MT, but refers to the *scorching of the onlookers* [italics added], while vs. 22 speaks of those who executed the king's order" (p. 42). While this interpretation is possible, another one is more likely (see COMMENT).

26. *drove the scorching blaze out of.* "Drove out" represents a not too satisfactory attempt at rendering *exetinaxe*, "he shook off." Gaster's Aramaic text has "it [i.e. the fire] cooled down," which makes eminently good sense; but that fact alone is no guarantee that it represents the original idea in the Semitic *Vorlage* of the Greek Daniel.

27. *a dew-laden breeze [pneuma drosou] . . . blowing through [diasurizon].* Literally "a wind of dew, whistling through"; a Hebraism. Cf. Wisd of Sol 17:17[18] for *pneuma surizon.* Dew, representing an agent of physical relief here and in Sir 18:16 and 43:22, has a variety of symbolic meanings in the Old Testament (see R. B. Y. Scott, "Dew," *IDB*, I, 839).

COMMENT

Brief though the Prose Narrative is, vss. 23-28[46-51] are riddled with problems, this in spite of the almost complete identity of the LXX and ℮ (vs. 23 [46] being an exception to this generalization). Ironically, the very fact that the LXX and ℮ are identical in vss. 24-28 is itself a problem, or at least it raises the question of why there is no disagreement between the two Greek versions, when there is such striking disagreement between them in the prose introduction to the Prayer of Azariah, i.e. in vss. 1-2[24-25].

It may be that the canonical text of the MT is itself at the root of the problem, for in Dan 3:21c-25 of the MT we read:

> [21] . . . and they were cast into the burning fiery furnace. [22] Because the king's order was strict and the furnace very hot, the flame of the fire slew those men who took up Shadrach, Meshach, and Abednego. [23] And these three men, Shadrach, Meshach, and Abednego, fell bound into the burning fiery furnace.
>
> [24] Then King Nebuchadnezzar was astonished and rose up in haste. He said to his counselors, "Did we not cast three men bound into the fire?" They answered the king, "True, O king." [25] He answered, "But I see four

men loose, walking in the midst of the fire, and they are not hurt; and the appearance of the fourth is like a son of the gods." (RSV)

Numerous scholars have observed that vs. 24 of the MT seems surprisingly abrupt and unexpected: the reader of the MT has no idea whatever that the three martyrs are still alive and that an angel is with them there in the fiery furnace. But the king knows! It is almost as if something had "fallen out" of the Aramaic text. Not surprisingly, as early as the last century, some scholars, including von Gall, Bludau, Rothstein, and Jahn, suggested that what had "fallen out" was either the Prose Narrative (vss. 23-28[46-51] or something very much like it (so Oesterley and Bennett).

To concede the existence of a "gap" between vss. 23 and 24 of the MT's third chapter does not, however, automatically prove that the Prose Narrative was an original part of the Semitic Daniel and that, somehow or other, it was erroneously dropped when the Prayer of Azariah and the Hymn of the Three Young Men were edited out of the finally approved Semitic text of Daniel. Kuhl (pp. 84-86), for instance, maintains that the "gap" between vss. 23 and 24 of the Aramaic text was quite deliberate and original, it being a well-known literary device for increasing the tension and interest of the story, i.e. with vs. 24 the reader wonders what the king saw that was so astonishing. Thus, according to Kuhl, vss. 23-28[46-51 of the LXX] represents a later construction, designed to give the setting for the Hymn when the latter was added to the Semitic text of Daniel. (The "dispensability" of the Prose Narrative is, perhaps, indirectly confirmed by the fact that the Prayer and Hymn [without the Prose Narrative] occur in LXX[A] as an appendage to the canonical Book of Psalms, the Prayer and Hymn being chs. 8 and 9, respectively, of Odes.) R. H. Charles, on the other hand, eliminated the "gap" by, ironically enough, deleting vs. 23 of the MT as a gloss. Therefore, the king's astonishment in vs. 24 was his immediate response to seeing his trusted executioners burned to death just as they tossed the three martyrs into the fire (vs. 22 of the MT). According to Charles, both linguistic and manuscript evidence indicate that vs. 23 of the MT is a gloss, probably composed by the same Jewish scribe who added the already independently existing Aramaic(!) Prayer and Hymn to his particular copy of the Semitic Book of Daniel. Thus, argued Charles, when the officially approved text of the Semitic Daniel was finally established by the rabbis, the Prayer, the Prose Narrative, and Hymn had been removed; but vs. 23 of the MT was retained erroneously (Charles, pp. 72-75).

But even if one rejects the explanations of the "gap" offered by Kuhl and Charles, he is still hard-pressed to view the Prose Narrative *in its present form* as being originally an integral part of the Semitic Daniel, i.e. as having been between vss. 23 and 24 of the Semitic text *prior to* the Hymn's (and the Prayer's [see below]) being added to it. For vss. 23-25[46-48] of the Prose Narrative obviously repeats and contradicts vs. 22 of the MT (but see NOTE on vs. 25), the latter clearly stating that those who threw the three martyrs into the fire were themselves immediately burned to death, whereas the Prose Narrative has these same men continue to stoke the fire *after* they had pushed the martyrs in and only somewhat later do they perish in an erupting flame (vss. 23-25 [46-48].

Pointing out, quite correctly, that the Θ's translation of vss. 22-23 of the canonical Daniel makes no mention of the king's executioners being burned to death just as they tossed the three martyrs into the furnace (ergo, in Θ there is no contradiction), Oesterley (*The Books of the Apocrypha,* p. 388) argued for "something like" the Prose Narrative being originally between vss. 23 and 24 of the MT. The objection to that argument, however, is that the LXX's translation of vss. 22-23 of the canonical Daniel *does have* the would-be executioners being burned to death at the time. Clearly then, the LXX's Semitic *Vorlage* did contain and perpetuate the contradiction; and it remained for Θ, or more likely, for Θ's Semitic *Vorlage,* to perceive the problem and to "correct" it by deleting what is still recorded in 3:22 of the MT.

One point is indisputably true: either the Prose Narrative or, more likely, the Prayer of Azariah is misplaced. Both logically and chronologically, the Prayer of Azariah should follow rather than precede the Prose Narrative since only the angel's first cooling off the inside of the fiery furnace, as described in vss. 23-28, would have prevented Azariah from being incinerated and would thus have provided him with the opportunity to offer the prayer in vss. 3-22. Yet, not only does the Prayer precede the Prose Narrative, but in the prose introduction to the prayer we learned that the fire was burning furiously *before* the prayer was offered ("Azariah stood and uttered this prayer . . . in the heart of the furnace, vigorously stoked by the Chaldeans" [vs. 2 of the LXX]; "And they walked about in the heart of the flames. . . . Then Azariah stood still and uttered this prayer—in the midst of the fire he opened his mouth and said" [vss. 1-2 of Θ]). The most probable explanation for all this, one offered by numerous scholars, including Kuhl (pp. 161-164), is that the Prose Interlude was originally a prelude to the Hymn which a scribe inserted, and that still later on another Jewish scribe prefixed what we now call "The Prayer of Azariah" to the prose narrative, thereby making what was once a logical prose prelude an illogical and contradictory interlude.

Such a theory also explains why the LXX and Θ are identical in the Prose Narrative (except for vs. 23) and yet are so very different from one another in the prose introduction to the Prayer (vss. 1-2[24-25]). When first the Hymn, along with its prelude, and then later the Prayer were added, in the Semitic *Vorlage* of the LXX the section immediately before the Prayer remained unchanged, while the Semitic *Vorlage* of Θ better accommodated itself to its larger context, first by dropping that material in 3:22 of the MT which conflicted with the Prose Narrative, and then later by making the prose introduction to the Prayer less repetitious and more smooth.

Finally, from exactly where the scribe who added the Prose Narrative got the account itself is unknown. He may have composed it himself, imaginatively elaborating on the "details of fact" now found in 3:24-28 of the MT. Or, he may have used a variant form of the story of the three martyrs circulating independently of the narrative as found in the MT. (For numerous Talmudic and Midrashic references to the various versions of the story of the three young men, including some brief summaries as well as actual quotation of some stories, see Ball, pp. 305-306.)

III. THE HYMN OF THE THREE YOUNG MEN

(Vss. 29-68[52-90])

29[52] "Blessed are you, O Lord, God of our fathers,
      praiseworthy and highly exalted for ever.
30 And blessed is your glorious and holy name,
      to be highly praised and highly exalted for ever*a*.
31[53] Blessed are you in the temple of your sacred glory,
      to be highly praised and greatly glorified for ever.
32[54] *b*Blessed are you who sit upon the cherubim
      and look upon the depths,
      praiseworthy*c* and *d*highly exalted*d* for ever.
33[55] Blessed are you on your*e* royal throne,
      to be highly praised and highly exalted for ever.
34[56] Blessed are you in the dome of heaven,
      to be hymned and glorified for ever.

35[57] Bless the Lord, all you works of the Lord,
      sing his praise and highly exalt him for ever.
36[58] *f*Bless the Lord, you heavens,
      sing his praise and highly exalt him for ever.
37[59] Bless the Lord, you *g*angels of the Lord*g*,
      sing his praise and highly exalt him for ever.
38[60] Bless the Lord, *h*all you waters*h* above the heavens,
      sing his praise and highly exalt him for ever.

---

a So many Greek MSS; but ⦵ᴮ and Vulgate have, with LXX and SyrH., "for all times"; see NOTE.
b In several Greek MSS, Vulgate, and Aramaic, vss. 32 and 33 are, with LXX and SyrH., given in reverse order; see NOTE.
c Gr. *ainetos;* ⦵ᴬ has *uperainetos,* "be highly praised," as in vs. 30.
d-d The LXX (but not SyrH.) has "glorified."
e Many MSS add, with LXX, "glorious."
f In LXX and Vulgate, vss. 36 and 37 are in reverse order; cf. Ps 148:1,2, and 4.
g-g SyrH. omits "of the Lord," while Bohairic and Syriac have "all angels of the Lord" (cf. Ps 148:2 of LXX).
h-h ⦵ᴮ and SyrH.: "waters and all things," an obvious error.

39[61] *Bless the Lord, all you powers*,
>   sing his praise and highly exalt him for ever.

40[62] Bless the Lord, you sun and moon,
>   sing his praise and highly exalt him for ever.

41[63] Bless the Lord, you stars of heaven,
>   sing his praise and highly exalt him for ever.

42[64] *Bless the Lord, all you rain and dew,*
>   sing his praise and highly exalt him for ever.

43[65] Bless the Lord, all you winds,
>   sing his praise and highly exalt him for ever.

44[66] Bless the Lord, you fire and heat,
>   sing his praise and highly exalt him for ever.

45[67] *Bless the Lord, you *cold and heat*,
>   sing his praise and highly exalt him for ever.

46[68] *Bless the Lord, you dews and falling snows,
>   sing his praise and highly exalt him for ever.

49[69] Bless the Lord, you *cold and heat*,
>   sing his praise and highly exalt him for ever.

50[70] Bless the Lord, you frosts° and snows,
>   sing his praise and highly exalt him for ever.

47[71] Bless the Lord, you nights and days,
>   sing his praise and highly exalt him for ever.

48[72] Bless the Lord, you light and darkness,
>   sing his praise and highly exalt him for ever.

51[73] Bless the Lord, you lightnings and clouds,
>   sing his praise and highly exalt him for ever.

52[74] Let the earth bless the Lord,
>   let it sing his praise and highly exalt him for ever.

53[75] Bless the Lord, you mountains and hills,
>   sing his praise and highly exalt him for ever.

54[76] Bless the Lord, all you things that grow *in the ground*,
>   sing his praise and highly exalt him for ever.

---

i-i Only ⊖^{B} has "Let every power bless the Lord."

j-j ⊖$^{B\ L\ V}$ have "Let all rain and dew bless the Lord."

k ⊖^{B} omits the verse, and probably rightly so; see NOTE.

l-l So ⊖^{A} and SyrH.; LXX "frost and cold."

m ⊖^{B} and Syriac omit entire verse.

n-n So ⊖$^{B\ Q}$; but ⊖^{A}, Vulgate, Bohairic, and Eth. have "ice and cold"; LXX has "ices and cold"; see NOTE on vs. 45.

o So most Greek MSS and versions; but ⊖^{B}, SyrH., and Arabic have the singular.

p-p So ⊖ and SyrH. (*en tē gē*); LXX "on the earth" (*epi tēs gēs*); see NOTE.

55[78] *q*Bless the Lord, you seas and rivers,
  sing his praise and highly exalt him for ever.
56[77] Bless the Lord, you *r*rains and springs*r*,
  sing his praise and highly exalt him for ever.
57[79] Bless the Lord, you sea monsters and all things that
      swim in the waters,
  sing his praise and highly exalt him for ever.
58[80] Bless the Lord, all you birds of the air,
  sing his praise and highly exalt him for ever.
59[81] Bless the Lord, all you *s*wild beasts and cattle*s*,
  sing his praise and highly exalt him for ever.

60[82] Bless the Lord, you sons of men,
  sing his praise and highly exalt him for ever.
61[83] *t*Bless the Lord, O Israel*t*,
  *u*sing his praise and highly exalt*u* him for ever.
62[84] Bless the Lord, you priests *v*of the Lord*v*,
  sing his praise and highly exalt him for ever.
63[85] Bless the Lord, you servants *w*of the Lord*w*,
  sing his praise and highly exalt him for ever.
64[86] Bless the Lord, you spirits and souls of the just,
  sing his praise and highly exalt him for ever.
65[87] Bless the Lord, you who are holy and humble in heart,
  sing his praise and highly exalt him for ever.
66[88] Bless the Lord, Hananiah, Azariah, and Mishael,
  sing his praise and highly exalt him for ever.
    For he has snatched us *x*from the nether world*x*
      and saved us from the hand of death.
    He has rescued us from the burning fiery furnace,
      and has rescued*y* us from the heart of the fire.
67[89] Give thanks to the Lord; for he is good,
      for his mercy endures for ever.

---

q In the LXX, vss. 55 and 56 are in reverse order.
r-r So LXX and SyrH.; Θ has "the springs"; see NOTE.
s-s So Θ (*thēria kai ta ktēnē*), as in the LXX of Gen 1:24; LXX has "the cattle and wild beasts" (*tetrapoda kai thēria tēs gēs*), as also in LXX of Gen 1:24.
t-t Θ^A Q V "Let Israel bless the Lord."
u-u Θ^Q V "Let him sing his praise and let him highly exalt."
v-v So most Greek MSS, Vulgate, and many versions; Θ^B and Armenian omit; LXX "servants of the Lord"; see NOTE.
w-w So all Greek MSS and versions except Θ^B and Armenian, which omit; see NOTE.
x-x Gr. *ex adou;* Syriac "from death"; Aramaic "from Sheol"; see NOTE.
y So Θ (*errusato*); LXX has "delivered" (*elutrōsato*).

68[90] Bless the God of gods, all you who worship the Lord,
        sing his praise and give thanks,
        for his mercy endures for ever."[z]

[z] Vulgate adds, "These occur nowhere in the Hebrew, and what we have is translated from Theodotion's edition."

NOTES

29-30. These two verses strikingly agree with the Greek of LXX[A B] in Tobit 8:5: "Tobias began to pray, 'Blessed art you, O God of our fathers, and blessed is your holy and glorious name for ever. Let the heavens and all your creatures bless you.' " Even more noteworthy is the fact that the second half of Tobit 8:5, i.e. "Let the heavens and all your creatures bless you," is in capsule form what the Psalm elaborates in detail. Thus, Tobit 8:5, containing as it does both elements of the Ode and a summary of the Psalm, may have been the inspiration for the Hymn (see COMMENT). Perhaps of some relevance for establishing the *terminus a quo* for the Hymn is the fact that the Book of Tobit is usually dated to some time during the second century B.C.

29. *highly exalted* [*uperupsoumenos*]. Either the Greek translator of Daniel or a later editor (so Fritzsche) had a preference for compound words using the prefix *uper-;* for although this particular compound word does occur elsewhere in the Septuagint (cf. Pss 36:35, 96:9), the translator used in the ode three other compound words found nowhere else in the Septuagint, namely, *uperainetos*, "be highly praised" (vs. 30); *uperumnētos*, "be highly exalted" (vs. 31); and *uperendoxos*, "be greatly glorified" (vs. 31).

30. *for ever* [*eis tous aiōnas*]. Even though many Greek manuscripts, including both LXX and ⊛[B], also have *pantas*, "all," i.e. "for *all* times," *pantas* is probably a gloss since it does not occur elsewhere in the refrains of this seven-verse ode, which in the liturgy of the Western Church is known by the opening words of its Latin translation, *Benedictus es*, "Blessed are You."

With respect to this phrase, the Aramaic version makes an interesting distinction which the Greek does not: whereas in vss. 29-68[52-90] both the LXX and ⊛ have *eis tous aiōnas* ("for ever"), the Aramaic version sometimes has *l'lm'* "for ever," and sometimes *b'lm'*, "in the world," because, wrote M. Gaster, "God's Name is to be praised for ever; His *creatures* cannot very well praise Him for ever . . . but they can praise Him in this world" (*PSBA* 17 [1895], 80). But although such a distinction may be appealing to the Western mind, there is no reason to think that in this matter Gaster's Aramaic text accurately reflects the original Hebrew *Vorlage* of the psalm, because the canonical Book of Psalms does not observe such a fine distinction with regard to mortal creatures not being able to praise for ever.

31. *temple of your sacred glory*. This is probably an allusion to God's Heavenly Temple (as in Ps 11:4; Hab 2:20); but the Greek could be translated as

"in thy holy and glorious temple" (so NEB), in which case we have a clear Hebraism (i.e. a substantive used as an adjective) *and* an apparent allusion to the earthly temple at Jerusalem. But even if the latter interpretation should be the case, that fact does not necessarily indicate, as some scholars have insisted, that Hymn and Prayer were composed in different historical periods; for vs. 15 [38] may only mean that, in keeping with the ostensible Babylonian setting of the story, the Jerusalem temple was "destroyed" for Jews in Babylon, not that it was actually unavailable to Jews in the later days of the Ode's actual author.

32. *sit upon the cherubim*. See also the LXX of I Sam 4:4; II Sam 6:2; II Kings 19:15; and Ps 80:1. A winged celestial creature on which Yahweh rode (II Sam 22:11; Ps 18:10), the mythical cherub (pl. cherubim) was often depicted in the form of a bull with a human head. Adopted by the Israelites from their pagan Canaanite and Mesopotamian neighbors and then adapted to Israelite literature and art, the cherubim figured prominently in both Israelite myths (cf. Gen 3:24) and cult (cf. Exod 25:18-20; I Kings 6:23-28). For details on cherubim and related celestial creatures, see T. H. Gaster, "Angel," *IDB*, I, 128-134, especially pp. 131-132.

and look upon the depths. Kuhl (p. 157) and E. B. Christie (*JBL* 47 [1928], 188-193) undoubtedly were correct in viewing the phrase as a surviving witness to a once-separate verse. Christie has persuasively argued that this ode, like each of the four stanzas in the psalm (vss. 35-68), originally had seven verses, or bicola, with the first colon of each verse having one separate and distinct thought, the one seeming exception to this generalization being the first colon of vs. 32 which has *two* thoughts. Moreover, a further expression of the early corruption of the passage is the disagreement in ⊕ and LXX over the proper order of vss. 32 and 33.

34. *the dome [stereōmati] of heaven*. Usually translated as "firmament," *stereōma* renders the Heb. *rqy'*, as in Gen 1:6-8; Ps 18:2[19:1H]; and Dan 12:30. "The Hebrew term means properly a 'strip of beaten metal' (cf. Exod. 39:3; Num. 17:3; Jer. 10:9 . . .) and harks back to the conception of the sky as a mirrorlike surface—a conception which recurs in Job 37:18, and which finds a classical counterpart in the common Homeric expression 'brazen heaven' (*Iliad* V.504; XVII.425; *Odyssey* III.2; Pindar *Pythian Odes* X.22, *Nemean Odes* VI.3)" (T. H. Gaster, "Firmament," *IDB*, II, 270).

35. *sing his praise [umneite] and highly exalt [uperupsoute] him for ever*. This refrain, like the one in Psalm 136, will be repeated in every verse of the psalm (vss. 35-68) without variation, except in vs. 52 where a change in the refrain coincides with a change in the addressee, and in vss. 66-68 where a later scribe has been at work (see NOTE on vss. 66-67). Kuhl's reconstruction of this Hebrew refrain, or half verse, is *hllhw wrwmmhw l'wlmym*, which has three stresses or beats (see Kuhl, pp. 111-113).

36. *you heavens [ouranoi]*. I.e. the sky or canopy of the earth. In the Old Testament, "the heavens" (Heb. *šmym*) were sometimes thought of as being like a curtain or garment, as well as being the upper part of the cosmic ocean (for details, see T. H. Gaster, "Heaven," *IDB*, II, 551-552).

38. *you waters above the heavens*. Cf. Ps 148:4 of LXX. These are the celestial waters, or upper cosmic ocean, above the dome of the earth (cf. Gen 1:7, 7:11).

39. *all you powers* [*dunameis*]. The first half of the verse is quite similar to the LXX of Ps 102[103H]:21, where *dunameis* renders the Heb. *ṣb'wt* ("hosts"), a word which in the Old Testament has a variety of meanings, including army (Gen 21:22), angels (Ps 148:2), and celestial bodies (Ps 33:6). In this verse, "powers" is probably a collective term for the celestial bodies to be mentioned by name in vss. 40-41. (For further details, see B. W. Anderson, "Hosts, Host of Heaven," *IDB*, II, 654-656.)

40-41. *sun and moon . . . stars.* Cf. the LXX of Ps 148:3. Verse 41 marks the end of the psalm's first stanza, in which the heavenly bodies, erroneously worshiped as gods by Israel's pagan neighbors, were quite rightly called upon to worship the Lord (cf. Deut 4:19).

42. *you rain* [*ombros*] *and dew* [*drosos*]. Cf. the LXX of Deut 32:2. Because dew was so important to the Near East's rainless summer months, that fact alone may explain why dew is mentioned twice in the same stanza (here and in vs. 46 [but see NOTE there]).

43. *winds* [*pneumata*]. Were this verse an original Greek composition, one would expect to find here *anemoi* rather than *pneumata,* the latter being the less exact yet standard Septuagint rendering of the Heb. *rwḥwt,* "winds" (cf. Ps 148:8).

44-51. As can be seen from the following chart, vss. 44-51[66-73] have a very different order among the various Greek MSS and ancient versions:

LXX, ⊕ᵛ ᴸ *Vulgate*	⊕ᴬ, *Arabic, Bohairic*	⊕ᴮ ᵠ	*Sahidic*	*Ethiopic*	*Syriac*
44	44	44	44	44	44
45	45	47	45	47	64 (*sic*)
46	46	48	46	46	47
49	47	49	47	49	48
50	48	50	48	48	45
47	49	51	50	45	50
48	50	(omits vss. 45-46)	51	50	51
51	51		(omits vs. 49)	51	(omits vss. 46, 49)

Because the order of verses in the LXX appears somewhat more logical and is, presumably, older and more original (see COMMENT), the LXX's verse order is followed in our translation; but ⊕'s verse numbering is retained, this numbering being the one followed in most English translations, including the RSV Apocrypha.

45. *cold* [*psuchos*] *and heat* [*kausōn*]. This verse and the next are omitted by ⊕ᴮ, and rightly so, because they are probably a gloss. For in this verse the LXX's *rigos kai psuchos,* "frost and cold," parallels, in part, the LXX's *pagoi kai psuchos,* "ices and cold," in vs. 47, while in vs. 49, ⊕ᴬ has *pagos kai psuchos,* "ice and cold," and ⊕ᴮ has *psuchos kai kauma,* "cold and heat."

46. *dews* [*drosoi*] *and falling snows* [*niphetoi*]. Cf. LXX of Deut 32:2. This is a curious combination, the two parts of the pair being neither obviously similar (as the pair in vs. 44) nor antithetic (as those in vs. 45). Thus, there is some merit to Ball's suggestion (p. 319) that *drosoi* should be translated here as "snows," inasmuch as in Prov 26:1 the LXX rendered the Heb. *šeleg,*

"snow," by *drosos,* "dew." More likely though, we are dealing here with a gloss; for not only does ⊕ᴮ omit the verse, but the dew (*drosos*) had already been addressed by the psalmist in the first verse of the present stanza (vs. 42).

47. *nights and days.* The order of these nouns reflects the ancient Jewish view that "a day" was from sunset to sunset, a view which finds expression in the Genesis cosmogony of the "P-Source" (cf. Gen 1:5,8,13, etc.). In earlier days, however, the ancient Israelites may have reckoned "a day" as being from sunrise to sunrise (cf. Num 11:32; Judg 19:5-9; and Exod 24:18).

48. *light and darkness.* In the Old Testament these two nouns are frequent companions, but usually in a context where "darkness" has less than positive connotations about it (cf. Isa 5:20, 45:7, 59:9; Ps 112:4; Job 12:25). For further details, see O. A. Piper, "Light, Light and Darkness," *IDB,* III, 130-132.

51. With this verse, Stanza II (vss. 42-51) of the psalm comes to an end. Whereas Stanza I (vss. 35-41) concerned itself with the psalmist's addressing God's works in the Highest Heavens, Stanza II centered on the psalmist's calling to worship those elements that *come down from heaven.* Although Stanza II currently has ten verses, it is highly probable that, like the Ode (vss. 29-34) and Stanzas I, III, and IV of the psalm, it originally had seven verses. Assuming that the ancient author would not have repeated the same ideas so quickly and clumsily in the same stanza, E. B. Christie (*JBL* 47 [1928], 188-193) argued, quite plausibly, that we, with ⊕ᴮ, delete vss. 44 and 45 of the LXX, they being repetitious of vs. 50 (which is the same in both the LXX and ⊕), and that we also delete vs. 49, which is repetitious of elements in vss. 44 and 50. Thus, we would end up with only seven verses in the stanza and no repetitious material.

Persuasive though Christie's solution is, it must be adopted with some caution because those "repetitious" elements that one sees in the Greek texts may not really be that at all but rather careless or inaccurate Greek renderings of quite different Hebrew words. Elsewhere in the Septuagint, for example, a word like *pagos* (and *pachnē*) is used to render the Heb. *kᵉpôr,* "hoar frost," *as well as* the Heb. *keraḥ,* "cold"; and, as already noted earlier, the Gr. *drosos,* "dew," is used elsewhere in the Septuagint to translate not only the Heb. *ṭal,* "dew," but also *šeleg,* "snow."

52. *Let the earth bless . . . let it sing.* The shift to a new category of addressee in Stanza III, namely, to animate and inanimate things on the earth (vss. 52-59), is marked here by the use of the jussive in both cola of the verse.

53. *you mountains and hills.* Cf. Ps 148:9. This pair, an expression of permanence and solidity, frequently occurs in the Bible, especially in Isaiah and Jeremiah.

54. *that grow in the ground.* Most English translations erroneously translate this as "that grow on the earth"; but cf. Gen 2:9, 19:25, and Job 5:6 where the LXX uses *gē* to render the Heb. *'dmh,* "soil."

56. *rains [ombroi] and springs [pēgai].* The LXX's reading has been adopted in preference to that of ⊕ (*ai pēgai,* "the springs") because the latter cannot be fitted into the required 2+2 metrical pattern which, as Kuhl has so convincingly shown (Kuhl, pp. 110-133), the Hebrew psalm had for the first colon, or line, of each verse. Kuhl's own suggestion that the Hebrew was originally *m'yny-hmym,* "springs of water" (as in I Kings 18:5; II Kings 3:19) is metrically possible but without manuscript support. Somewhat more plausible is

Louis Hartman's conjecture that the Greek was originally *cheimarroi*, "winter streams" (as in Ps 73:15, *pēgas kai cheimarrous*), which was corrupted into *cheimerinoi*, "winter storms," which was, in turn, replaced by a simpler, if not synonymous word, *ombroi*, "rains."

Christie (*JBL* 47 [1928], 190) would solve the problem by simply deleting the verse as a later gloss, arguing that this verse is corrupt, it being the only verse in Stanza III (vss. 52-59) where the LXX and ⊕ disagree with one another in both their content and verse order. Moreover, if this verse is deleted as a gloss, then the third stanza would have the "requisite" seven verses. Cf. NOTE on vs. 51.

57-60. *sea monsters . . . birds . . . wild beasts and cattle . . . men.* Cf. Ps 148:7,10,11-12. Even though the aforementioned psalm was obviously the model, if not also the actual inspiration, for our psalmist, he nonetheless chose to follow the order of creation as presented in Gen 1:21-26, i.e. sea monsters, birds, wild beasts and cattle, and, finally, man.

57. *sea monsters* [*kētē*]. Cf. Ps 148:7, where the LXX has *drakōn*. In the Septuagint, *kētos* is used for a variety of Hebrew words, including *tnynm* (the larger sea monsters such as mentioned in Gen 1:21) and *dg* (the whale in Jonah 2:1), as well as mythical creatures like Rahab (Job 26:12) and Leviathan (Job 3:8).

59. *wild beasts and cattle.* Cf. Ps 148:10. This verse marks the conclusion of the psalm's Stanza III, in which God's earthly creations, both the inanimate (vss. 52-56) and the animate (vss. 57-59), are enjoined to worship the Lord. As indicated in the NOTE on vs. 56, Christie would reduce the present stanza's eight verses to seven by deleting vs. 56.

60-65. *men . . . Israel . . . priests . . . servants . . . spirits and souls of the just . . . the holy and humble.* As in the previous stanza, Stanza IV lists the addressees in an ascending order of importance.

62. *priests of the Lord.* The presumed meter for a regular verse in this psalm, namely 2+2/3, requires that the reading of ⊕ᴮ be rejected (see textual footnote *v-v*). The mention here, first of Israel (vs. 61) and then of her priests (vs. 62), is a frequent progression of thought in Psalms (cf. 115:9-10, 118:2-3, 135:19-20).

63. *servants* [*douloi*] *of the Lord.* The reading of ⊕ᴮ (see textual footnote *w-w*) must be rejected for the same metrical considerations as in vs. 62. The addressees here are evidently temple personnel, probably Levites (cf. Pss 134:1, 135:1-2,20; and I Chron 9:33). On the very complex question of the respective roles of the priests and Levites, see R. Abba, "Priests and Levites," *IDB*, III, 876-889.

64. *spirits* [*pneumata*] *and souls* [*psuchai*] *of the just.* I.e. men who are righteous and alive, not disembodied spirits or immortal souls. In the Septuagint, *psuchē*, "soul," is often used in the sense of "living creature," be it animal (cf. LXX of Gen 1:20,24, 9:10,12,15,16) or man (cf. Gen 2:7). For further details, see N. W. Porteous, "Soul," *IDB*, IV, 428-429.

Unable to convert the Greek into literal Hebrew within the "prescribed" metrical limits of the verse, Kuhl (pp. 123-124) has substituted the phrase *bḥwrym wzqnym*, "youth and old men" (cf. Ps 148:12). While this emendation has the merit of "fitting the meter" and being logical and providing a quite specific addressee for vs. 87, Kuhl's proposal is without a shred of manuscript support, and, thus, it raises again the question of whether "considerations of meter" cannot sometimes be a Procrustean bed. Besides, there is such a thing as artistic variation, i.e. the poet may have varied from a standard meter at times.

66-67. Because these verses "are somewhat out of tune with the form and thought" of the preceding verses (so Christie, *JBL* 47 [1928], 190), he, and others, rightly regarded them as being a later interpolation into the original seven-verse stanza. The interpolation would have been made by that scribe who inserted the Hymn into the Semitic text of Daniel and then tried to tailor it to its specific context by adding vss. 66-67.

66. *Hananiah, Azariah, and Mishael.* So I Macc 2:59. These Hebrew names mean, respectively, "Yahu has been gracious," "Yahu has helped," and, possibly, "Who is what God is?" For the possible forms and meanings of their Babylonian, or Aramaic, names, see B. T. Dahlberg, "Shadrach, Meshach, and Abednego," *IDB*, IV, 302-303.

For the three martyrs to have used the *second person* plural form in exhorting themselves to worship the Lord (so vs. 66a) is certainly unnatural, and suggests that the entire verse, including b and c where they revert to the more natural first person plural, is not part of the psalm as it circulated independently of the Book of Daniel but rather represents a less than skillful adaptation of the psalm to the third chapter of Daniel.

from the nether world [*ex adou*]. Cf. Pss 48:16, 88:49, and Hosea 13:14 of the LXX. Literally "from Hades," which may suggest to some readers a place of torment (as in Matt 11:23 and Luke 16:23); but as T. H. Gaster has correctly observed, "Nowhere in the OT is the abode of the dead regarded as a place of punishment or torment. The concept of an infernal 'hell' developed in Israel only during the Hellenistic period," "Dead, Abode of the," § 6, *IDB*, I, 788. Our psalm is undoubtedly a creation of the Hellenistic age, but the clause "and saved us from the hand of death," which stands parallel with "he has snatched us *ex adou*," clearly shows that the grave, or Sheol, must have been intended here.

67. The Greek of the verse is identical with that of Pss 105:1, 106:1, and 135:1 of the LXX.

68. With this verse the Hymn ends. However, the scribe who first inserted the Hymn into the Book of Daniel evidently supplied a few additional words so as to "integrate" it into what would follow, that is, after inserting the Hymn, he added in Hebrew, "When [*kai egeneto*] the king heard them singing, and when, on standing up, he saw them alive." (In ⊕, the transition from the Hymn to the narrative in 3:24 of the MT is more brief: "Now Nebuchadnezzar heard them singing.") The important point to note in all this is that the LXX's *kai egeneto* is a Hebraism (=Heb. *wyhy*) and constitutes the final linguistic evidence that the Hymn was in Hebrew because the narrative itself, at least as it presently stands in Dan 3:1-23,24-30 of the MT, was in Aramaic.

COMMENT

There are three good reasons for regarding vss. 29-34 (what we have been calling "the Ode") and vss. 35-69 ("the Psalm") as having been originally separate and independent works: (1) they have different addressees, God himself being addressed in the Ode, his creations, in the Psalm; (2) in the Greek, and presumably in the Hebrew, the Ode and Psalm have different refrains, the Psalm always has the same (see NOTE on vs. 35), whereas the refrain of the Ode is always changing, be it ever so slightly; and (3) in their presumed Hebrew forms, the Ode and the Psalm had different metrical patterns.

Concerning the last point, one cannot be dogmatic; but it does seem clear that Kuhl has successfully, i.e. literally and yet without taking too many liberties with the Greek text, reconstructed the Ode so that it appears to have been originally a Hebrew poem of seven verses, each verse (or bicola)in 4/4 meter (Kuhl, pp. 154-159), while the Psalm must usually have had a 2+2/3 (Kuhl, pp. 111-129); for specific examples, see Introduction. That Kuhl has been so successful in rendering the Ode and Psalm back into *poetic* Hebrew form, without usually doing any injustice to the sense of the Greek, is perhaps the strongest argument for the Hymn having originally been in Hebrew. (For Kuhl to have "successfully" translated Greek prose back into Hebrew prose would not have been nearly as conclusive a proof of a Semitic *Vorlage*, let alone a Hebrew one.) On the other hand, it must be conceded that there is little internal evidence for a Semitic original for the Hymn, although neither the Ode nor the Psalm is without some faint traces or Hebraisms (see NOTES on vss. 31,43, and 68).

The biblical sources for the ancient author seem clear enough. Psalm 148 not only contains many of the ideas that were later incorporated into the Psalm, but sometimes even its sequence of ideas is preserved in the Psalm:

Psalm 148		Psalm
vss. 1-2a	=	36-37
2b-3	=	39-41
9, 10, 11-12	=	53, 59, 60

In terms of content, our Psalm is more systematically structured than Psalm 148, there being an obvious consistency of subject within each stanza (i.e. going from general to particulars) as well as a more logical progression of thought from stanza to stanza:

Stanza I	(vss. 35-41)	Creations in the Highest Heavens should praise God.
Stanza II	(vss. 42-51)	Elements coming from heaven should praise God.
Stanza III	(vss. 52-59)	Earthly creations should praise God.
Stanza IV	(vss. 60-68)	All mankind should praise God.

But our psalmist also drew phrases and ideas from elsewhere in the Book of Psalms as well as, to a far lesser extent, from the Pentateuch (see NOTES *passim*), but, surprisingly enough, not from Isaiah or Jeremiah. The Psalm is quite reminiscent of Psalm 136 (see NOTE on vs. 35), although whether the latter was the model our psalmist consciously followed cannot be determined. Pfeiffer (p. 448) would see the Psalm (and Psalm 148) as possibly being inspired by Sirach 43; but this view is questionable.

Perhaps the most fascinating, if ultimately unanswerable, question is the relationship of Tobit 8:5 (see NOTE on vss. 29-30) to the Hymn. It may, of course, be pure coincidence that the first two cola of Tobit 8:5 correspond fairly accurately to the general theme and opening lines of the Ode, and that its third colon is a capsule statement of our Psalm. However, it is just possible that Tobit 8:5 inspired a later scribe to add the Ode to the Psalm, i.e. the Psalm had already been incorporated into the Semitic Book of Daniel by an earlier scribe when a later scribe, inspired by Tobit 8:5, added the Ode, the latter being either composed by him or, more likely, taken from a Hebrew prayerbook.

"SUSANNA"

INTRODUCTION

The story of Susanna concerns a brief but terrifying experience in the life of a very good and lovely Jewess, Susanna daughter of Hilkiah. Had it not been for the last-minute intervention of the young Daniel, she would have been put to death for a crime she had not committed.

Résumé of Story

Because Susanna's husband Joakim was very wealthy, their home in Babylon had become a meeting place where Jews regularly gathered to discuss the affairs of the day. Among the frequent visitors to Susanna's house were two elders who had recently been appointed judges. (These two men were totally undeserving of such an honor; for, unbeknown to the Jewish community, throughout their lives they had broken the laws of God and man.) Anyway, each of the judges, as he got a glimpse of Susanna day after day, developed a secret passion for her; and when one day they caught each other spying on her, they agreed to proposition her as soon as they could find her in a compromised situation. They would not have long to wait! (vss. 1-14).

One very hot day, while they were hidden in Joakim's garden, Susanna entered it and had her servants lock the outside gates so she could bathe. No sooner had she dismissed her maids, than the old lechers accosted her, insisting that she either have sexual relations with them, right then and there, or they would frame her, swearing that they had just now caught her in the act of adultery but that the young man involved had escaped. Unwilling to sin against her God by committing adultery, Susanna started screaming, whereupon the elders threw open the garden gates and raised such a commotion that the whole household rushed in from the adjoining house and so learned the shocking "facts" (vss. 15-27).

The next day Susanna's trial for adultery was held at the scene of the "crime." Her two accusers, full of dignity and righteous indignation, told their story. (The presiding elders and the community did not deign to ask Susanna for her version.) The circumstantial evidence, especially since it was undergirded by two witnesses whose age and rank put them above suspicion, was enough to convict her; and the community sentenced her to death (vss. 28-41).

Fortunately, although her own people would not listen to her, her God did! For as Susanna was being led away to be put to death, God inspired the young boy Daniel to challenge the verdict and assert that she had been framed. Resuming the trial at the scene of the crime, Daniel had the villains separated so that they could not hear one another's testimony. Then Daniel asked each of them the same question ("Under what tree did you see them making love?") to which they each gave a different answer, thereby totally discrediting their testimony. So, in accordance with the Law of Moses, the false witnesses were treated by the community in exactly the way these villains had intended Susanna to be treated, i.e. they were stoned to death. Thus, that day was Susanna, an innocent person, saved; and the boy Daniel first came to the attention of his people (vss. 42-64).

Two things should be noted about the above summary. First, the English version given above is that of Theodotion (ϴ) which differs from the older Septuagint (LXX) at a number of important points. But because the Theodotion version of Daniel replaced the older Septuagint version in the early Christian Church, to such an extent that no Septuagint manuscript of Daniel was even published until 1772 (see Introduction, p. 33), this Anchor Bible commentary will take the story of Susanna in ϴ as the basis, or starting point, for translation and discussion. Second, a detailed résumé is not a whole lot shorter than the actual story itself, a fact which underscores the brevity and fast-moving pace of this ancient short story. (The entire story in ϴ occupies only 118 lines of printed Greek in Swete's edition.)

Brief though the story itself is, in both the LXX and ϴ the principal characters are well developed, and the plot is simple and direct, with mounting suspense and sudden resolution. The story is a skillful admixture of three of the most basic and universal fascinations of man: God, sex, and death.

Comparison of the Story in LXX and ϴ

It is very easy to say with certainty how the LXX and ϴ of "Susanna" differ from one another. It is virtually impossible to say why. Unlike the differences between the LXX and ϴ in the other Additions to Daniel, which are minimal, their differences in "Susanna" are considerable. In fact, scholars have usually been far more struck by the differences than by their similarities.

When the two Greek texts are printed side by side for purposes of comparison (as in Scholz), one need not even read a word of the texts to see at a glance that there are striking differences, that each text contains phrases and entire verses which the other does not. For instance, ⊛ contains numerous additions:[1] vs. 11 ("since they were ashamed to admit their passion, that they wanted to have intercourse with her"); vss. 15-18 (the bath scene in the garden); vss. 20-21 (the elders proposition Susanna and explain how they can frame her); vss. 24-27 (Susanna's servants rush in and learn of her alleged crime); vs. 31b (Susanna was shapely); vs. 36b (the villains testify that Susanna had made deliberate preparations for her lover); vs. 39 (her lover was too strong for them to hold and so escaped); vs. 41b ("and they condemned her to death"); vss. 46-47 (Daniel disassociates himself from the verdict and her imminent execution); vss. 49-50 (Daniel counsels resumption of the trial and is invited to sit with the elders); and vs. 63 (Susanna's parents, husband, and relatives praise God for the outcome).

Some of these additions improve the logic of the narrative (see Notes *passim*); more important, many of them increase the story's drama and tension (see Notes *passim*). Verse 51b of the LXX was evidently deleted by ⊛ (see Note). Verses 30 and 62 may have been condensed by ⊛ (or, more likely, "condensed" by the author of the Semitic *Vorlage* which the translator of ⊛ used); and the last verse of the LXX was totally transformed by ⊛ (see Note).

In spite of the above changes, the plot remains essentially the same. Inevitably, there are some differences in "details of fact," such as the time of day the alleged crime occurred ("at dawn" in the LXX; apparently "at midday" in ⊛), the time and place where the trial was held (see Note on vs. 28). By far the most important difference is one of emphasis, namely, in ⊛ Daniel himself is given far greater prominence than in the LXX (see Comment, pp. 115-116).

When the two Greek texts are carefully compared word for word, then the differences between them become even more pronounced. With regard to identical wording, for instance, of the sixty verses "shared" by the LXX and ⊛, only about twenty-three per cent of them have either total (cf. vss. 29, 33-34, 40, 48, 52, 57-58) or even significant partial verbatim agreement (cf. vss. 5b, 10a, 22b, 23a, 36a, 41a). Nor are the parallels in content (but not wording) particularly numerous (cf. vss. 46-47, 49-50, 63). Hebraisms are far more common in ⊛ (see Introduction, p. 83).

And therein lies the problem: assuming, as virtually all Septuagint scholars do, that the LXX is the older text, should one regard ⊛ of Daniel as a *recension,* or re-editing, of the LXX (so Fritzsche in 1851, and Schüpphaus in 1971), or as a *separate translation* of a Semitic text (so Bludau in 1897, and Schmitt in 1966)? And *if* ⊛ does represent a separate

---

[1] Among modern scholars, only Theodor von Wiederholt, *TQ* 51 (1869), 316-321, has argued (unconvincingly) that the "additions" in ⊛ are original and primary, and that the LXX experienced the abridgments and deletions.

translation, was its Semitic *Vorlage* essentially the same as the one used by the LXX, or not? Was one *Vorlage* in Aramaic and the other Hebrew? Should the question of "translation versus recension" be raised and answered in the broad terms of the LXX and ⊕ *of Daniel* or more narrowly, i.e. in terms of the LXX and ⊕ *of only Susanna?* These are exceedingly complex questions, and the existing evidence is so fragmentary and confusing that no one dares be dogmatic about his answer (see Introduction, pp. 30-33). It would seem to the present writer that the differences between the LXX and ⊕ of "Susanna" are sufficiently great in terms of content and diction as to argue for their being separate translations of two Semitic texts which, while similar, were by no means identical, *and* that the translator of ⊕ must have had the LXX before him, otherwise, how can we possibly account for the verbatim agreements in the Greek?

Canonicity of "Susanna"

How did it happen that "Susanna" got into the Christian canon but not into the Jewish Old Testament? The most obvious but least persuasive answer is that, like some other books of the Apocrypha such as II Maccabees, "Susanna" never was a part of the Hebrew canon, that is, that "Susanna" was originally composed in Greek and was erroneously incorporated into the canonical Daniel (so E. B. Pusey and A. H. H. Kamphausen). The objection to this view is that "Susanna" does seem to have had a Semitic *Vorlage* (see Introduction, pp. 81-84).

More persuasive is the view of Solomon Zeitlin (*JQR* 40 [1950], 236) and S. B. Hoenig (*IDB*, IV, s.v. "Susanna") that "Susanna" was finally rejected by the Jewish Fathers because in its present form the story clearly contradicts a Pharisee *Halakhah* in the Mishnah, namely, when witnesses had contradicted one another and were discredited, those witnesses could not be punished unless two other individuals who had not been at the scene of the crime testified that at the time of the alleged crime the accusing witnesses were actually with them, thereby proving that the accusing witnesses had deliberately offered false testimony and had not simply made an honest mistake (*Sanhedrin* v 1).

An even more likely explanation, however, is that the story of Susanna was ultimately, and rightly, regarded by Jews as a very unsuitable introduction to the materials in the canonical Daniel. Not only is the background of the Susanna story basically different from that of Daniel 1-6,[2] but in "Susanna" Daniel himself is poorly presented, primarily because in the earliest form of the story the boy Daniel did not figure at all (see p. 109).

Equally plausible is the ancient view of Hippolytus that the Jewish

---

[2] So R. A. F. MacKenzie, *CJT* 3 (1957), 214; see also Kay, pp. 642-643.

elders ultimately rejected the book because of the unfavorable light it cast upon certain aspects of Jewish life. Or, as David M. Kay in typical English understatement so accurately put it, "The story would not be popular with elders; and it was elders who fixed the canon" (p. 642).

One thing is certain: "Susanna" is not quoted as scripture by any ancient Jewish writer. Unlike the Additions to Esther, none of the Additions to Daniel was utilized by Josephus, possibly because they did not exist at that time (ca. A.D. 93-94); but more likely, they were either circulating as independent stories or were not in the particular Greek manuscripts Josephus had at his disposal. Nor is there a translation of "Susanna" by Aquila, a second-century A.D. Jewish translator of the then-current Hebrew Bible.

The earliest Christian citation of "Susanna" as Scripture is by Irenaeus of Lyons (140-?202) in his *contra Haereses* V 26 (see Migne, *Patrologiae Graeca*, VI, 1054). Unfortunately, the canon lists of Church Fathers and Councils are of no help to us because although Daniel is nearly always mentioned as being canonical, there is usually no indication of whether "Susanna" was included. On the other hand, we know of no Christian reservations concerning "Susanna" until Julius Africanus' letter (Migne, *Patrologiae Graeca*, X, 689) to Origen (185?-?254). The debate was later revived by the anti-Christian critic Porphyry (233-?304) in his *adversus Christianos* XII, as preserved in Eusebius, and, still later, raised anew by Ruffinus (345-410) with Jerome. Nonetheless, that Church Fathers found ample occasion to refer to the book is evident from a perusal of the citations in the Fathers, the most exhaustive list having been compiled by Caspar Julius, *BSt* 6 (1903), 1-183.

Original Language of "Susanna"

There is no external evidence that the Greek "Susanna" is a translation of a Semitic text. None of the seven Semitic copies of Daniel found among the Dead Sea scrolls at Qumran[3] contains any of the Additions to Daniel, although it should be pointed out that some of these copies are far from being intact. Nor in Josephus is there any trace of the Additions to Daniel, this in spite of the fact that Josephus does record some other non-canonical legends concerning Daniel (cf. *Ant.* x 11.6-7). Both Origen and Jerome said that they knew of no Hebrew text of "Susanna." Nor do we have an Aquilan translation of "Susanna," a fact which should not surprise us since Aquila, being a disciple of the very conservative rabbi Akiba, translated into Greek only those books which were in the then-current Hebrew Bible.[4] ("Susanna" did, however, get into the second-century

---

[3] Two copies in Cave I, four in Cave IV, and one in Cave VI.
[4] For details on the translation by Aquila, Swete, *IOTG*, pp. 31-42, and Roberts, *OTTV*, pp. 120-123.

Tetrapla of Origen.) Moreover, all the ancient versions of "Susanna" are clearly based upon either the LXX or ℗ (see p. 92). Finally, claims in the last century by scholars such as Moses Gaster, to the effect that they had found Hebrew or Aramaic survivals of the Additions to Daniel in the tenth- and eleventh-century Jewish works of Josippon and Jerahmeel,[5] have been discredited, some of the texts of Josippon and Jerahmeel having been shown by other scholars to be medieval translations of Greek and Latin versions of Susanna.[6]

There is, however, some internal evidence for a Semitic *Vorlage* for "Susanna," although whether the story was translated from Hebrew or Aramaic is impossible to tell. Scholars readily agree that the LXX and, especially, the ℗ are so simple and straightforward that they can be translated into Hebrew much more easily than is the case with many acknowledged Greek compositions.[7] This task of translating into Hebrew is made much easier, in part, by the fact that the Greek texts of "Susanna" have so many sentences beginning with *kai,* "and," followed immediately by the verb, these two features being very reminiscent of the *waw* consecutive construction of Biblical Hebrew. In the LXX of "Susanna," *kai* introduces over fifty clauses, whereas, in some passages of comparable length in books known to have been composed in Greek we have considerably less use of *kai.* In a passage of comparable length there are twenty instances of *kai* in the Gospel of John, fifteen in the Gospel of Luke, and twelve in Josephus (so Kay, p. 641).

Further evidence of a Semitic *Vorlage* includes the following Heb/Aramaisms: the frequent use of Semitic idioms, including *kai egeneto* (Heb. *wyhy*), "and it happened" (vss. 7,15,19,28 of ℗), *idou* (Heb. *hinnēh*), "Behold!" (vss. 13 and 44 of LXX; and vss. 20 and 43 of ℗), "usual" (see NOTE on vs. 15), and "I'm in a bind" (see NOTE on vs. 22); the very frequent use of the pronominal suffix in both the genitive and accusative cases (e.g. vss. 30, 63, and *passim*); the use of the same Greek root with almost diametrically opposite meanings (see NOTES on "they lusted for her" in vs. 8, and "to have intercourse with" in vs. 11 of ℗); and the use of the definite article for the vocative (vs. 42 of ℗; vs. 48).[8]

Even more suggestive of a Semitic *Vorlage* are those variants between

---

[5] See Moses Gaster, "The Unknown Aramaic Original of Theodotion's Additions to the Book of Daniel," *PSBA* 16 (1894), 280-290; 312-317; and his *The Chronicles of Jerahmeel*, 1-9.

[6] See Israel Lévi, "L'Histoire 'de Suzanne et les deux vieillards' dans la littérature juive," *REJ* 95 (1933), 157-171. For further details on Josippon, see *EJ*, X, 296-298; for Jerahmeel ben Solomon, see IX, 1,345.

[7] For a Hebrew version of "Susanna," see Israel Lévi, *REJ* 95 (1933), 160-166.

[8] These and a number of other Heb/Aramaisms may be conveniently found in Scholz (p. 148), Bludau (*BSt* 2 [1897], 183-185), Daubney (pp. 134-139), and Kay (pp. 641-642). The lists in Scholz and Daubney, however, must be used with some caution, as they represent an exhaustive list of possibilities rather than a judicious selection of probabilities.

the LXX and ℗ which are best explained by viewing them as different renderings of the same Semitic text:

vs. 23 LXX *kallion de me mē praxasan* "But it's better for me not to do it"

℗ *aireton moi esti mē praxasan* "But I would rather not do it"

vs. 53 LXX *kai ton men athōon katekrinas, tous de enochous ēphieis* "you condemned the innocent and dismissed the guilty"

℗ *kai tous men athōous katakrinōn, apoluōn de tous aitious* "condemning the innocent and acquitting the guilty"

For other examples of this same phenomenon, see COMMENT, p. 116.

Most significant of all, perhaps, are those very puzzling Greek phrases which are best explained by presupposing a misreading of a Semitic *Vorlage* (see NOTES on "were lovesick for her," in vs. 10, and "they put them to death" in vs. 62).

Two other lines of argument for a Semitic *Vorlage* should be mentioned here, although neither is a particularly strong argument in itself. First, approximately three-fourths of the Heb/Aramaisms in "Susanna" occur only in ℗. This is in keeping with the well-known fact that elsewhere in the Bible Theodotion sometimes introduced into his recension Heb/Aramaisms which the older LXX did not have, primarily because he was trying to bring his own recension of the LXX into closer conformity with the then-current Hebrew text (so Roberts, *OTTV*, pp. 123-126). Second, inasmuch as there is no perceptible difference in translation style between "Susanna" and the canonical portions of Daniel (see Introduction, p. 29), one is forced to conclude that the Greek translator of Daniel either translated the LXX of "Susanna" from a Semitic text just as he did the canonical portions of Daniel, or that he himself composed "Susanna." Although the second possibility cannot be ruled out, it is much less likely, in part, because the skills of a translator are, ordinarily, sufficiently different from those of an author that one and the same person usually does not possess both types of skill to a high degree.

Admittedly, none of the above lines of argument is decisive in itself; but taken together, they do provide a reasonably strong case for a Semitic *Vorlage* for "Susanna." And finally, the one-time existence of such a Semitic text has been appreciably increased by the discovery at Qumran of three Dead Sea scrolls containing *in Aramaic* hitherto unknown legends about Daniel.[9]

---

[9] These three manuscripts, very fragmentary in nature, have been tentatively named Pseudo-Daniel *a, b,* and *c.*

Before leaving the subject, we should note one piece of internal evidence that commentators, ancient and modern (Julius Africanus, E. B. Pusey, A. H. H. Kamphausen), have insisted proves beyond all doubt that "Susanna," if not the other Additions to Daniel, was originally composed in Greek, namely, the paronomasia, or play on words, in vss. 54-55 ("Under a *schinon* ["mastic"] tree . . . an angel of God . . . *schisei* ["will split"] you in half") and in vss. 58-59 ("Under a *prinon* ["oak"] . . . an angel of God . . . to *prisai* ["to saw"] you in half"). Persuasive at first glance, the argument that these puns preclude any possibility of a Semitic *Vorlage* quickly breaks down. The ancient Greek translator, for instance, may simply have made puns in Greek where none existed in the Semitic text[10]; or more likely, the Greek translator, guided by the fact that puns were in his Semitic text, proceeded, like certain ancient and modern translators of "Susanna," to create—not translate!—comparable puns in his own language (see NOTES on vss. 54-55, 58-59).

Origin of the Susanna Story

Modern scholars began to question the historicity of the Susanna story as far back as 1770 (so J. D. Michaelis). Every year since then new voices have been heard denying the historicity of "Susanna," until today virtually no scholar subscribes to it as pure fact even though most aspects of the story are quite believable. At one time or another over the last two hundred years, however, certain types of interpretation have been especially in vogue.

Early modern commentators, like Johann G. Eichhorn and Gustav Jahn, regarded "Susanna" as "fiction with a moral," although scholars could not agree on exactly what that moral was. In the early twentieth century there were even those scholars who saw "Susanna" as a historicized myth, or at least as having a mythical heroine, Susanna herself being either the virgin goddess Phryne (so Karl Fries), the Swan Maiden (so Wolfgang Schultz), or the sun goddess (so Ernest Siecke). For details, the interested or, more likely, the puzzled reader who cannot see how a case can be made for any of these absurd suggestions should see W. I. Baumgartner, *AfR* 24 (1926), 259-267; and Pfeiffer, pp. 452-453.

With greater justification, other scholars, including Fritzsche (p. 185), viewed the story of Susanna as a legendary or apocryphal story describing the *modus operandi* and subsequent downfall of that infamous pair of arch-adulterers, Ahab ben Kolaiah and Zedekiah ben Maaseiah, the false

---

[10] As illustrative of this phenomenon elsewhere in the LXX, August Bludau (*BSt* 2 [1897], 186) cited Micah 7:11: *ēmeras aloiphēs plinthou exaleipsis sou ē ēmera ekeinē.*

prophets mentioned in Jer 29:21-23. Both Origen (*Epistle to Africanus*) and Jerome (*Commentary on Jeremiah*) were familiar with the following story recorded in the Babylonian Talmud:

> Because they have wrought folly in Israel and have committed adultery with their neighbours' wives, what did they do? They went to the daughter of Nebuchadnezzar.[11] Ahab told her, "Thus says the Lord, 'Indulge Ahab.'" She went and reported to her father. He said to her, "Their God hates unchastity. When they come again to you, send them to me." When they came again to her, she sent them to her father. He asked them, "Who told you (to do so)?" They replied, "The Holy One, blessed be His name." (Said the king), "I have asked Hananiah, Mishael, and Azariah; and they told me that this thing is forbidden." They replied, "We are prophets like them. To them He did not reveal it, but to us He revealed it." Said the king to them, "I want to put you to the test, as I did with Hananiah, Mishael, and Azariah (namely, by the ordeal by fire). They said, "They were three and we are only two." He replied, "Choose anybody you want to be with you." They said, "Let it be Joshua the high priest." They thought, namely, "May Joshua, whose merits are numerous, come and protect us." They brought him and threw (the three of) them (into the furnace). The two were burnt. As to Joshua the high priest, only his vestments were singed. (*Sanhedrin* 93a.)[12]

Scholars who regarded the story of Susanna as an apocryphal tale concerning the downfall of Ahab and Zedekiah pointed to the fact that the villainous elders in the Susanna story are not named and so could very easily be interpreted as being Ahab and Zedekiah, especially since in some ancient Jewish traditions Susanna (or her equivalent) was regarded as being either the wife or daughter of a king (see below). Apart from the obvious fact that such an argument is *ex silentio,* there is an even more formidable, if not irrefutable, argument against the theory: the adulterous elders in "Susanna" are judges, not prophets. Moreover, the theory does not explain the third part of "Susanna," that is, Daniel's role in the story (vss. 42-64).

Difficult though it is to establish the early stages of the Susanna story, i.e. its form prior to the extant LXX version, it is not so difficult for us to spot some of the subsequent stages in its post-biblical development. There is, for instance, the Samaritan version, where the daughter of one Amram, a high priest living on Mount Gerizim, was falsely accused of fornication

---

[11] Other Jewish sources, telling essentially the same story, say she was Nebuchadnezzar's *wife,* Semiramis (cf. *Tanḥuma Buber* III 7; *Tanḥuma Vayikra* 6; *Yalkut Shimeoni*).

[12] This English translation, together with its Hebrew text, is in Max Wurmbrand, *Biblica* 44 (1963), 29-37.

by two rejected suitors. Her father, however, succeeded in establishing the villains' perfidy, and they were summarily executed.[13] As Bernhard Heller pointed out (*ZAW* 54 [1936], 286-287), Daniel was automatically ruled out as the deliverer of the daughter of Amram because Samaritans could not have had as their hero a biblical personage later than the time of Joshua ben Nun, i.e. someone mentioned in biblical books written after the Pentateuch.

The story of Susanna also appears in the tenth-century work of Josippon, with one important exception—*all* the names have been changed: the heroine is called *Anna* wife of *Hannaneh,* her husband being a priest sent to Rome by Herod Agrippa II (A.D. 56-100); and the hero is *Nahman* who, along with the king, played a major role in interrogating the *three* false witnesses.[14] A Hebrew form of "Susanna," corresponding fairly closely to Θ, is to be found in the works of Jerahmeel of the eleventh century[15]; but as noted earlier on p. 82, n. 6, Lévi has shown that the story is based upon the Latin Vulgate.

One of the latest stages in the development of the Susanna story is probably the Falashic version. According to this text from the ancient Jewish black community in Ethiopia,[16] Susanna was the daughter of a king *and* the widow of a king (thereby nicely combining two one-time contradictory Jewish traditions). Out of spite, three of her rejected suitors agreed among themselves falsely to accuse her of fornication; and she would have been stoned had not the angel Michael come to her aid in the appearance of a mortal. Separating the three accusers from one another, Michael asked each of them, in the presence of a jury consisting of Susanna's father and seventy-seven kings, the same two questions, namely: "Where did you see Susanna sinning with her body?" and "At what time of day was it?" The answers to the first question greatly differed from one another ("I saw her under a fig tree," said one; "I saw her in the palace," said another; "I saw her in the women's apartment," said the third); nor could the witnesses agree on the time of day the offense occurred. Delivered from certain death, Susanna was then rewarded by being made queen.[17]

All in all, the principal weakness of the theory that "Susanna" is a leg-

---

[13] For text and translation, see Moses Gaster, "The Story of the Daughter of Amram," *Studies and Texts in Folklore, Magic, Medieval Romance, Hebrew Apocrypha, and Samaritan Archaeology,* 3 vols. (London: Maggs Bros., 1925-28), I, 199-210.

[14] The Hebrew text, along with its translation and discussion, may be found in Israel Lévi, *REJ 95* (1933), 166-171. Lévi characterized the story as "une mélange de folklore et de pseudo-science," which he dated to some time prior to the fifteenth century (p. 171).

[15] Texts, translations, and discussions may be found in Moses Gaster, *Chronicles of Jerahmeel,* and Lévi, pp. 159-166.

[16] For details on this ethnic group, see *EJ*, VI, 1,143-1,154.

[17] The Ethiopic text, translation, and discussion are in M. Wurmbrand, *Biblica 44* (1963), 29-35.

end or apocryphal story is that we know far more about the story's development and history *after* the Greek versions than before them.

Just about a hundred years ago, however, a theory was suggested that was heartily endorsed by many of the best scholars and while probably not *the* prevailing interpretation today, still has its defenders, namely, that the Book of Susanna was originally a Pharisaic polemic of the first century B.C., attacking the court procedures and theory of the Sadducees. This theory was first, and definitively, worked out by Nehemiah Brüll, *JJGL* 3 (1877), 1-69.[18]

Brüll's theory was based upon certain well-known historical facts. Even though the Pharisees and Sadducees were very strongly opposed to one another at various times and on a variety of issues, at few periods were they more hostile toward one another than in the days of the Hasmonean king Alexander Janneus (104-78 B.C.), a Sadducean sympathizer who treated the Pharisees most cruelly (see Josephus *Ant.* XIII 13-14).[19] The leader of the Pharisees at the time was Simeon ben Shetaḥ, brother-in-law of Janneus and a layman of strong convictions whose views and actions created for him some implacable enemies. For instance, contrary to *Halakhah,* Simeon once hanged in Ashkelon on one day eighty Jewish "witches" (cf. *Sanhedrin* VI 4; Jerusalem Talmud, *Sanhedrin* VI 9,23c).

Later, in retaliation for that action, relatives of the executed women falsely accused Simeon's son of a capital offense so that the boy was convicted and sentenced to death. Just before the youth was to be executed, however, his accusers admitted they had accused him falsely, whereupon the young man said to Simeon, "Father, if you want salvation to come through you, let the law take its course" (Jerusalem Talmud, *Sanhedrin* VI 3,23e). In other words, the lad was willing to be put to death so that his false accusers would *have to* be put to death! By doing this, father and son intended to underscore what they regarded as the terrible injustice of the Sadducean interpretation concerning the proper punishment of a false accuser. (On interpreting the Mosaic legislation of Deut 19:18-21 concerning the appropriate punishment of a false witness, the Sadducees and Pharisees were sharply divided. The Sadducees were strict constructionists,

---

[18] Brüll had evidently taken his clue from the work of Moritz Duschak (*Mosaisch-talmudische Strafrecht* [Vienna: W. Braumüller, 1869], pp. 94*ff*) who viewed the story of Susanna as inspired by the conduct of one Johanan ben Zakkai (d. A.D. 80) who, according to the Talmud, regularly cross-examined witnesses and who, on one particular occasion, upon learning that the witness claimed to have observed the murder while standing under a fig tree, proceeded to question that witness as to the exact size of the various parts of the fig tree as well as the color of its figs (cf. Babylonian Talmud, *Sanhedrin* 41a; Mishnah *Sanhedrin* V 2). In the judgment of most scholars today, the principal weakness of Duschak's theory is that it provides too late a historical basis for the Susanna story, i.e. the late first century A.D.

[19] For details on Janneus, see S. B. Hoenig, *IDB,* II, 801. For brief introductory remarks on the history and teachings of the Pharisees and Sadducees, see Matthew Black, *IDB,* III, s.v. "Pharisees"; and A. C. Sundberg, *IDB,* IV, s.v. "Sadducees."

stressing the equivalency principle of vs. 21: "Your eye shall not pity; it shall be life for life, eye for eye, tooth for tooth . . . foot for foot." On the other hand, the Pharisees, including Simeon and his son, emphasized the *intention* of the accuser, as given in vss. 18b-19a: "If the witness is a false witness and has accused his brother falsely, then you shall do to him *as he had meant to do* to his brother" [italics added].)

In his day, Simeon ben Shetaḥ also strongly argued for the cross-examination of witnesses: "Be very searching," he cautioned, "in the examination of witnesses; but be guarded in your words, lest from them they [i.e. the accusers] learn to lie" (*Pirqe Aboth* I 10). For further details on Simeon ben Shetaḥ, see *EJ*, XIV, 1,563-1,565.

Thus, according to Brüll (pp. 43-69), the story of Susanna was really an argument, in narrative form, eloquently supporting two important views of the Pharisee Simeon ben Shetaḥ concerning the problem of false accusers: (1) the necessity of interrogating witnesses with skepticism, care, and cleverness; and (2) the punishment of false accusers in accordance with their intentions for the falsely accused rather than in accordance with the accused's actual fate. That Brüll's theory has some merit is indicated, in part, by the wholehearted support it gained from such first-rate interpreters of "Susanna" as C. J. Ball, J. T. Marshall, D. M. Kay, and W. O. E. Oesterley.

The theory does have, however, several weaknesses. First, in the Susanna story Daniel's own court conduct is not exemplary, being a far cry from sound judicial procedure, that is, Daniel condemned each of the elders *before* he had established through their own testimony their guilt (cf. vss. 49, 52-53, 56-57). That Daniel knew of the elders' guilt through divine revelation (so vs. 45) in no way mitigates this criticism of his courtroom procedures and etiquette; for other interrogators and "jurors" could not have followed his example since, unlike him, they could not count on divine revelation to provide them with the necessary insight. Second, while the story illustrates the importance of a skeptical attitude toward accusers as well as the need for effective interrogation techniques, it is debatable whether the proverbial "man in the street" in ancient Palestine would have seen these fine points of the debate "unless a scholar explained it to him in that sense" (Pfeiffer, p. 452). Finally and most important of all, there is a simpler and more persuasive explanation for the story of Susanna, namely, it was a folk story.

Early in the present century Gedeon Huet[20] suggested that the story of Susanna belongs to the literary genre of the folk tale and that it had as its theme the popular motif of the wise child who intervenes and corrects an unjust decision, a theme found, as Huet correctly pointed out, in *A Thousand and One Nights,* The Tales of Sinbad, and the Mongolian version of

[20] *RHR* 65 (1912), 277-284.

The Throne of Vikramaditya. In a later article, Huet, while reluctantly conceding that the Daniel in "Susanna" may not have been a young child (see NOTE on "a young boy" in vs. 45), offered additional examples of "the wise child" motif (*RHR* 76 [1917], 129-130).

Huet's view was accepted and further refined by Walter Baumgartner who, by briefly summarizing the plots of ten ancient folk tales, showed that while the hero of such stories often was a child, he need not be, there being examples of an old man, a king, or even a woman acting as the wise judge.[21] Not only was the story of Susanna purely secular and profane in origin, said Baumgartner, but it was actually a combination of two folk motifs: (1) the wise judge; and (2) the "Genoveva" theme, i.e. "the widespread tale of the chaste wife falsely accused and repudiated, generally on the word of a rejected suitor." (For specifics on this literary genre, see "Genevieve, Genoveva," *Encyclopaedia Britannica,* 11th ed., XI, 594; better yet, see K. 2,112 in Stith Thompson, *Motif-Index of Folk-Literature* [University of Indiana Press, 1957], IV, 474.)

Although many recent scholars, including Pfeiffer and Eissfeldt, have accepted the views of Baumgartner, they have emphasized (and rightly so) that the Susanna story, while probably originating as a purely secular story and, possibly, originating even outside the Jewish community, had nonetheless been thoroughly judaized, i.e. the story had a strong and distinct Jewish ethnic and religious cast.

Religious Elements in the Story

Even though the story may very well have been originally a secular folk tale with no value apart from entertainment, by the time of its translation into Greek it had become thoroughly religious in character. God is mentioned or alluded to fifteen times in "Susanna's" sixty-four verses. In fact, with the exception of the two villains, *everybody in the story* mentions God: the narrator of the tale (cf. vss. 5, 9, 44, 45; and vs. 62 of the LXX), Daniel (vss. 53, 55, 59), the righteous presiding elders (vs. 50), Susanna's parents and relatives (vs. 63), the congregation (vs. 60), and, of course, Susanna herself who, though she feared God (vss. 2, 23), trusted in him (vs. 35), prayed to him (vs. 42), and so was delivered. It is no coincidence that it was only the wicked elders who did not mention God. *That,* after all, had been their problem all along: they themselves were not at all concerned about him (cf. vs. 9).

With the exception of the villains, the entire Jewish community was apparently religious. There was a strong sense of ethnic identity and in-group pride, or so we may infer from such comments of Daniel's as "You de-

---

[21] "Susanna—Die Geschichte einer Legende," *AfR* 24 (1926), 259-280; and "Der Weise Knabe und die des Ehebruchs beschuldigte Frau," *AfR* 27 (1929), 187-188.

scendant of Canaan, not Judah" (vs. 56); and ". . . daughters of Israel
. . . being afraid of you, they had relations with you two; but this daughter of Judah would not submit" (vs. 57). Susanna herself was a "God-
fearing woman; her parents were also religious and had instructed their
daughter in the Law of Moses" (vss. 2b-3). Twice the Jewish scriptures
were quoted or paraphrased (cf. vss. 5 and 53). The Law of Moses was
held in high esteem and, more importantly, was followed faithfully; the
Jewish community, for instance, regarded false accusation (vs. 62) as well
as adultery (vs. 41) as a capital offense. The community abhorred bloodguilt (cf. 48b and 50a; for details on the general subject, see Moshe
Greenberg, "Bloodguilt," *IDB*, I, 449-450), and rejoiced in the vindication
of the innocent (vs. 60) and the punishment of the wicked (vss. 61-62).

In sum, if the story was originally profane and non-Jewish in origin,
with no theological interests, it has nonetheless been reworked and thoroughly saturated with religious elements of Judaism. We do not have here
a fascinating, titillating tale that was made more acceptable to "prudish"
elements of the Jewish community by having a moral artificially and per-
functorily tacked on at the end. From the beginning and throughout,
religious interests and elements permeate the story.

Purpose of the Story

Originally designed to be enjoyed for its own intrinsic interest and drama,
the story of Susanna was, at the time of the Septuagint translation, a part
of a Semitic version of Daniel (see p. 29). Although some of the other
stories in Daniel 1-6 may very well have had an earlier and separate existence,[22] the story of Susanna is still not at all compatible with them in
their present form and so undoubtedly represents an intrusion or later addition.

As the story currently stands in the Greek versions, it is strangely out of
place. (This is true whether one reads it immediately before ch. 1 of the
canonical version [as in ⊛, OL, Coptic, Ethiopic, Arabic] or after Daniel
12 [as in LXX, SyrH., and Vulg.].) Even though the story of Susanna
originally preceded Daniel 1[23] and served to introduce Daniel who was
only a boy at the time (cf. vs. 45), the story still seems appreciably
different from the other stories in Daniel 1-6. For one thing, Daniel himself is not even mentioned until vs. 45, and he is certainly not the hero of

[22] Cf. Eissfeldt, pp. 522-524; R. H. Pfeiffer, *Introduction to the Old Testament*, rev.
ed. (New York: Harper, 1968), 766-769.
[23] That this was its original place and that it was later put at the end of the
canonical chapters by Jerome, who readily admitted doing that with the Additions to
Esther (see p. 155f), is strongly suggested by the fact that in the oldest extant Greek
text of Daniel, Papyrus 967, a LXX (!) manuscript, the story of Susanna comes *before* Daniel 1.

the Susanna story: Susanna is! (In fact, in the LXX the boy Daniel is little more than a representative of sensitive and idealistic youth [see COMMENT, pp. 115-116].) Moreover, the physical setting in "Susanna" is quite different from the other stories: to be sure, the incident takes place in Babylon, but not in the court as in the other Daniel stories but in the suburbs or countryside. More important, the Jewish community in the Susanna story gives every appearance of being independent and self-governing, having even the right to execute its lawbreakers. Most important of all, and in sharp contrast to the stories in Daniel 1-6, the Jewish community appears to be *unthreatened,* that is, there is no pressure on them to desert their religious heritage or to worship other gods.

While readily conceding the secular and folk origins of "Susanna," Roderick A. F. MacKenzie[24] has maintained that the story well fits the other stories in Daniel 1-6, in that it features the divine intervention whereby a condemned martyr is saved from certain death, the category of women being added to that of men and children. "Thus," wrote MacKenzie, "the three obligations of not worshipping idols, of not committing adultery, and of not eating pork, were for them [i.e. the Jews] practically on the same level. The first is represented in Dan. 3, the second in Susanna, the third in Dan. 1. . . . For any one of these taboos the faithful Jew should be ready to give his life" (p. 217). One may agree with these observations and still conclude that the story does not *really* fit well, a conclusion which the ancient Jewish Fathers long ago arrived at and which, in all likelihood, was the principal reason "Susanna" did not become part of their canon.

The Story's Place and Date of Composition

"It is of course impossible to tell exactly where Susanna originated or when" (Pfeiffer, p. 449). Accurate though that statement is, it is not very helpful. Thus, assuming that the Babylonian setting in vs. 1 of the LXX is not original (see NOTE on "that year" in vs. 5), present-day scholars have often inferred from the internal evidence, i.e. from the social and political situation depicted in the story, that "Susanna" had a Palestinian provenance. MacKenzie asserts rather than proves, however, that the story "comes from a Jewish community far more isolated from Greek influences than one in Egypt. And this again seems to indicate southern Palestine. It is here Susanna is at home, and her story is a lasting monument to the faith and moral standards of the Judean populace" (p. 218).

No particular century can confidently be assigned as the *terminus a quo* for the story, although some time in the Persian period is quite possible, that is, a time when the Jewish community in Palestine enjoyed a

[24] *CJT* 3 (1957), 211-218.

modicum of independence and self-governance, and, most important of all, when its religion was unthreatened from outside. The *terminus ad quem* is, as scholars from Bludau to Plöger all agree, the date of the Greek translation of the LXX of Daniel, which, while uncertain, was probably some time around 100 B.C. (see below). Scholars who follow Brüll's thesis that "Susanna" was a Pharisaic polemic against Sadducean judicial theories and practices also date "Susanna" to the same general period.

The Church's Preference for ℗

Leaving to the specialists the larger question of why the ℗ of Daniel was preferred to the LXX (see pp. 31-33), one can offer two excellent reasons why the ℗ of "Susanna" would have been preferred by the early Christian Church. First, Daniel himself plays, unquestionably, a larger role in the ℗ than in the LXX; in fact, one may even raise the question of whether Daniel himself really figured at all in the earliest form of Susanna (see COMMENT, pp. 115-116). Given the fact that "Susanna" often served as the chapter immediately before Daniel 1 of canonical Daniel, ℗'s greater emphasis on Daniel himself also gave ℗ an edge.

Second, in contrast to ℗, the LXX had in vs. 51 a sentence which, while conceding only that elders were human and fallible, could by easy extension be applied to *all* human authorities and institutions, namely, "Daniel said to the congregation, 'Now don't take into consideration that these are elders, saying (to yourself), "They would not lie."'" Certainly not all bishops and patriarchs appreciated having Daniel call the people's attention to the fact that individuals in positions of power and authority are not automatically above suspicion or exempt from human frailties. Crucial though these two points are for making ℗'s account preferable to that of the LXX, they are probably not *the* reasons for the ultimate triumph of ℗ in the Book of Daniel.

Other Ancient Versions

With the exception of the Syro-Hexaplar and the earliest edition of the Old Latin, all the ancient versions of Daniel are based upon "Theodotion" and not the Septuagint. The same must be said for "Susanna": the Syriac Peshitta, the Coptic (both in the Sahidic dialect of the South and the Bohairic of the North), the Ethiopic, the Vulgate, the Arabic, and the Armenian are all slavishly literal renderings of ℗, not LXX, and contibute little to the explication of the text (see textual footnotes *passim*). Only the Syriac versions provide interesting, though secondary, variants (see NOTES *passim,* or Marshall, *HDB,* IV, 630-631).

IV. TWO ELDERS FALSELY ACCUSE SUSANNA OF ADULTERY

(Vss. 1-27 [ch. 13 in LXX and Vulgate])

1 There once lived in Babylon a man named Joakim. 2 He had married Susanna, daughter of Hilkiah, a very beautiful and God-fearing woman. 3 Her parents too were religious and had instructed their daughter in the Law of Moses. 4 Now Joakim was quite wealthy, and he had a garden adjoining his house; and*a* the Jews used to come to him since he was the most eminent of them all.

5 Now that year two elders of the people were appointed judges (it was of such the Lord had said, "Wickedness came forth from Babylon through elders who as judges only seemed to guide the people"); 6 these were often at Joakim's house, and all who had suits used to come to them*b*. 7 *c*At midday, when the people had left, Susanna would go in *d*and stroll in*d* her husband's garden. 8 These two elders would watch her every day, going in and walking around*e*, and they lusted for her. 9 So they perverted their own minds and averted their eyes, not looking to Heaven or rendering just decisions. 10 Both *f*were lovesick for*f* her; but they did not tell one another of their frustration 11 since they were ashamed to admit their passion, that they wanted to have intercourse with her. 12 So they would eagerly watch, day after day, to get a glimpse of her.

13 *g*One day*g* they said to one another, "Let's go home; it's time for lunch." And leaving, they parted company from one another. 14 But doubling back, they arrived at the same place; and after quizzing one

a Bohairic and Syriac add "all."
b "Him" in OL and Ethiopic.
c Θ adds "And it happened"; see NOTE.
d-d Θ*V* omits.
e Bohairic, Syriac, and Ethiopic add "in the garden."
f-f Greek "were wounded over"; see NOTE.
g-g Lacking in Greek and ancient versions; see NOTE.

another on the reason, they admitted their passion. Then together they
agreed on a time when they might find her alone.
15 So it was that while they were watching closely for the opportune
day, she came in as usual, accompanied only by two maids. And she
wanted to bathe in the garden as it was very hot. 16 Since no one was
there except the two elders who had hidden themselves and were spying on her, 17 she said to her maids, "Bring me oil and cosmetics, and
close the garden gates so I can bathe." 18 So they did as she had ordered: they closed the garden gates and went out by the side doors to
get the things she had asked them for; they did not see the elders because they were hidden. 19 As soon as the maids had left, the two
elders got up and accosted her.
20 "Look!" they said, "the garden gates are shut, and nobody can
see us; and we desire you. So let us have you. 21 If not, we will testify
against you, saying that a young man was with you, and that is why
you had dismissed your maids."
22 Susanna groaned and said, "I'm in a bind! For if I do this thing,
it'll be my death; [h]and if I don't do it, I'll not escape your hands.[h]
23 But[i] I would rather not do it and so fall into your hands than sin in
the Lord's sight."
24 So Susanna screamed, and the two elders shouted against her.
25 And one of them ran to open the garden gates. 26 When the household heard the commotion in the garden, they dashed in through a
side door to see what had happened to her. 27 When the elders had
given their version, the servants were shocked; for nothing of this sort
had ever before been said about Susanna.

[h-h] Θ^{V} omits.
[i] Vulg., Bohairic, and Syriac have the conjunction; Greek omits.

NOTES

1. *Babylon.* For a modern painting of this ancient city, based upon some archaeological evidence, see Plate 1.

Joakim. Unfortunately, the name of Joakim's father is not mentioned. But in any case, the bearer of this good Jewish name (Gr. *iōakim*=Heb. *yhwyqym*, "The Lord will establish") should not be identified with Joakim, the Jewish high priest in Judith's day (cf. Judith 4:6-8,14; 15:8). Nor should he be identified with that Judean king (so Hippolytus, Julius Africanus, and other ancient writers) who was taken captive to Babylon by Nebuchadnezzar and was released from prison later on, i.e. King Jehoiachin (cf. II Kings 24:15, 25:27), although according to II Chron 36:5-7, King Jehoiakim was also taken prisoner to Babylon (but see J. Bright, *A History of Israel*, 2d ed., 324-327). See also NOTE on "most eminent of all them" in vs. 4.

2. *Susanna* [*Sousanna*]. Occurring as a feminine personal name in the New Testament but not in the Old (cf. Luke 8:3; I Chron 2:31-35 has the masculine personal name), this name is derived from the plant world, Heb. *šôšannâ*, "lily" (cf. II Chron 4:5; Song of Songs 2:2; Hosea 14:5).

Hilkiah [*chelkiou*]. A very popular Hebrew name, Hilkiah (Heb. *ḥlqyh*, "The Lord is my portion") was the name of at least nine individuals in addition to Susanna's father (for details, see B. T. Dahlberg, *IDB*, II, s.v. "Hilkiah").

beautiful and God-fearing. These same qualities were also attributed to other Jewish heroines dating from Septuagintal literature of approximately the same general period, namely, to Judith (Judith 8:7-8), Sarah the daughter of Raquel (Tobit 6:12, 3:14-15), and Esther (Esther 2:7 and 20 of the LXX).

3. *religious*. Literally "righteous" (*dikaioi*). There is in Biblical Hebrew no word for the phenomenon we today call "religion."

instructed . . . in the Law. I.e. in accordance with commandments such as those in Deut 4:9-10 and 6:6-7: "And these words which I command you this day shall be upon your heart; and you shall teach them diligently to your children, and shall talk of them when you sit in your house, and when you walk by the way, and when you lie down, and when you rise."

4. *quite wealthy . . . a garden*. Such a high standard of living was evidently quite possible for Jewish exiles in Babylon; consider, for example, Jer 29:5, where Jeremiah advises the Jewish exiles in Babylon, "Build houses and live in them; plant gardens and eat their produce"; also II Esd 3:1b-2, where Ezra says, "I . . . was in Babylon. I was troubled as I lay on my bed, and my thoughts welled up in my heart, because I saw the desolation of Zion and the wealth of those who lived in Babylon."

garden (*paradeisos*). This term is a loanword from the Old Pers. *pairidaēza*, "garden" or "park," the latter entering Biblical Hebrew as *pardes* (cf. Neh 2:8; Eccl 2:5; Song of Songs 4:13). In the LXX, however, *paradeisos* was also used for the Garden of Eden (Genesis 2-3), and as the Abode of the righteous dead in the intertestamental (cf. I Enoch 20:7; Ps Sol 14:2; IV Esd 3:6; II Bar 4:2-7) and NT literature (Luke 23:43; II Cor 12:3; Rev 2:7). For further discussion, see H. K. McArthur, *IDB*, III, s.v. "Paradise."

most eminent of them all. There is, however, no justification for the ancient view that this Joakim was the former king of Judah. Had he been the former king, surely that fact would have been noted by the narrator (see Introduction, pp. 84–85).

5. *that year*. As the text presently stands, the phrase evidently refers to the year that Joakim took a wife (cf. vs. 2). More likely, however, it refers to something in the original but now-lost LXX context; especially is this the case since vs. 30 of the LXX says that Susanna had at this time *four* children.

Until the discovery of Kölner LXX Papyrus 967, scholars, taking their clue from the *sigla* on the margins of the Chigi LXX Codex 88, thought that *all* of vss. 1-5 was supplied from Theodotion. But this LXX papyrus, dating from ca. A.D. 150, has the last two-thirds of vs. 5: "it was of such . . . people"; and

Geissen, the papyrus' editor, believes that probably all of vs. 5 was originally part of the LXX of "Susanna" (Geissen, pp. 33-37).

it was of such the Lord had said. Literally "concerning whom the Master [*o despotēs*] said." The names of the villains are nowhere given in the Greek. Although one Syriac manuscript does identify them as Amid and Abid, there is no reason to regard these names as genuine survivals.

"Wickedness came . . . the people." Occurring nowhere else in the MT or the LXX, this quotation is probably a "confused reminiscence" of Jer 29:20-23 (so Pfeiffer, p. 454, and most scholars), since the Ahab and Zedekiah mentioned there were prophets, not judges.

6. For the verse, the LXX has "And law suits from other cities [Papyrus 967: "from many others"] would come to them."

7. In ⊚, this verse (and vss. 15,19, and 28) begins with *kai egeneto,* the standard Greek rendering of the Heb. *wyhy,* "and it happened." That a later Greek version, namely ⊚, has such Hebraisms as these when the older LXX version does not surely argues for the two versions being based upon a Semitic text—unless, of course, these represent an effort on the part of "Theodotion" to archaize the text.

8. *they lusted for her.* Literally "they were with a desire [Gr. *epithumia*] for her." The use of the noun *epithumia* in a bad sense here and in vss. 14 and 56 of ⊚ and the use of its verb *epithumeō* in a perfectly innocent sense in vs. 15 of ⊚ probably represents a translation from a Semitic original where different roots were involved (so Daubney, p. 134).

Verses 7-8 of the LXX differ considerably from those of ⊚; "7 These two, having seen a woman with a good figure, the wife of their brother from the sons of Israel, by the name of Susanna daughter of Hilkiah, wife of Joakim, strolling in her husband's garden in the afternoon, 8 desired her." These verses, needlessly duplicating much of the material in vss. 1-2 of the LXX, are indisputable confirmation that vss. 1-4 of the LXX are not original but, just as the *sigla* claim, were supplied from ⊚. Nor is there any mention in vss. 7-8 of the LXX, as there was in vs. 6 of ⊚, of the elders regularly holding court at Joakim's house (but see vs. 28 of ⊚) or of their frequently seeing Susanna. Verses 7-8 of the LXX are, however, consistent with vs. 28 of the LXX, where the two elders are said to be living in a different town from Joakim and to hold court at the synagogue, not as in vs. 28 of the ⊚ at Joakim's house.

9. Of vss. 6-27 of ⊚, only this verse is identical with the LXX (see COMMENT).

to Heaven. I.e. to God, a metonym or surrogate for God, as in Dan 4:31,34; Rom 1:18; Luke 5:18; and throughout the Gospel of Matthew, where "kingdom of Heaven" replaces "kingdom of God."

10. *were lovesick for her.* The Greek has *katanenugmenoi peri autēs,* "were wounded over her," which although quite possible, is somewhat awkward. The adopted reading follows Frank Zimmermann (*JQR* 48 [1957/58], 239-240), who suggested that since the Hebrew idiom for being passionately in love is *ḥlh,* "be sick (with love)" (cf. II Sam 13:2; Song of Songs 2:5, 5:8), the Greek translator of "Susanna" confused here in vs. 10 the Hebrew verb *ḥlh,* "be sick," with *ḥll,* "be wounded." That such could easily have happened is clear from

Song of Songs 2:5 and 5:9, where the Greek translator made exactly that mistake.

Verse 10 of the LXX, while identical with ⊖ in the first portion of the verse, is quite different in the latter part: "Both were lovesick for her; but one did not admit to the other the evil which possessed them on account of her (although the woman did not know of this matter)." The LXX has further underscored the villainy of the elders by stressing that Susanna had in no way "encouraged" them.

11. *to have intercourse with.* Literally "to be with." The Greek verb *suggignomai* is used in an opprobrious sense here and in vs. 39 (so also in Gen 19:5 and 39:10 of the LXX) but in a perfectly innocent sense in vss. 30 and 63, which, again, suggests that the same Greek verb was used for two different Semitic roots.

12. In the LXX this verse was quite different: "And when day had dawned, they came furtively, eager who should be the first to appear in her presence and speak with her."

13. *One day.* Although the phrase is in neither the Greek nor the versions, something like it must have originally been in the text. (Possibly some such phrase as this fell out by haplography with *kath ēmeran,* "day after day," of vs. 12.)

For this verse the LXX has: "And, as usual, she was strolling around. The one elder had already arrived when the other got there, so the one questioned the other, saying, 'Why did you come so early in the morning without inviting me along?'"

14. For this verse the LXX had: "They each acknowledged to the other his frustration."

15. Inasmuch as there is no parallel in the LXX for vss. 15-18, the bath scene in ⊖ must have been a later addition. If so, from a literary point of view it is a most welcome one: the bathing scene not only excites the elders, thereby enabling them to attempt their dastardly deed, but it can also fire the imagination of some readers. Of such considerations are good stories made!

as usual. Literally "as yesterday and the third day," an incontestable Hebraism (cf. Gen 31:2,5; Exod 5:7,14; Josh 4:18; II Kings 13:5; I Macc 9:44), which argues for the Greek "Susanna" having been a translation from a Hebrew or Aramaic original. One can scarcely imagine a Greek writer using such a clumsy Semitic idiom as this in an original Greek composition.

17. *cosmetics [smēgmata].* Cf. Esth 2:3,9,12, where *smēgma* is used to translate the Heb. *tmrwq;* and Judith 10:3. Whether one should understand here "soap," "ointments," or "cosmetics" is uncertain. Ball's statement, "Susanna wanted the oil and cosmetics for use *after,* not *before* or *in,* the bath" (p. 335), represents a degree of certainty and precision lying beyond the mind-reading capabilities of most scholars, including the present writer.

19. *accosted [epedramon].* Cf. I Macc 6:45. Literally "run at." In the LXX, which has no bathing scene, the corresponding verb is more graphic and ominous: "And they said to the other, 'Let's go to her!' And together they approached her and tried to force [*exebiazonto*] her."

20. Verses 20-21, which are not a part of the LXX, represent a very dramatic expansion and improvement of the Septuagint story.

gates are shut, and nobody can see us. The elders are emphasizing here, not their safety from discovery, but her helplessness.

So let us have you [dio sugkatathou ēmin kai genou meth ēmōn]. Literally "So assent to us [cf. Exod 23:1], and be with us [cf. Gen 39:10 and Tobit 3:8 of the LXX]." This translation may strike some readers as too colloquial, if not needlessly coarse. It is noteworthy, however, that this indelicate Greek expression for sexual intercourse occurs only here and vs. 21, where the elders are propositioning Susanna. Elsewhere in "Susanna" when the narrator is speaking of the sex act or the elders are testifying, less colorful and more neutral language is used (*suggenesthai,* "to have intercourse with," vss. 11,39; *anepese meth,* "lay down with," vs. 37; *omilountas,* "making love," vs. 54). To the general public these dignified elders may have seemed like distinguished gentlemen. But their blunt ultimatum showed Susanna what they really were. They wanted her body—or her life!

21. *was with you [ēn meta sou].* This Greek idiom, which is the same as the one in the preceding verse, confirms the correctness of the interpretation there, i.e. the elders were not claiming that they would testify that Susanna was *alone with* a young man (even though conduct such as that would probably not have been regarded as proper, it would hardly have been considered as deserving of death); rather the elders were threatening to testify that they saw her actually having sexual intercourse (so vss. 37-39, although there the elders, understandably, use more neutral terms for it).

22. *I'm in a bind [stena moi panthothen].* Literally "narrow for me on all sides" is evidently a Hebraism for "being in a dilemma" (cf. II Sam 24:14 of the LXX).

it'll be my death. I.e. either God himself will punish her or the Jewish community will stone her to death (cf. Deut 22:21-24; Lev 20:10; John 8:4-5).

I'll not escape your hands. Susanna did not try to talk the elders out of their dreadful offer; for as Ball so memorably put it, "The lamb knows itself in the power of the dogs" (p. 336).

In the latter two-thirds of the verse, ⊙ followed rather faithfully the LXX, which had: "The Jewess said to them, 'I know if I do this thing it'll be my death; and if I don't do it, I'll not escape your hands.'"

23. Susanna's logic is reminiscent of Joseph's response to Potiphar's wife: "How can I do this great wickedness, and sin against God?" See also David's response to the prophet Gad in II Sam 24:14.

24. Inasmuch as the LXX has none of the materials in vss. 24-27 of ⊙, this very exciting scene of Susanna screaming and the servants rushing in and hearing the terrible accusations against her of the elders was evidently an expansion by a later writer, writing in either Greek or Hebrew/Aramaic.

screamed. Literally "cried with a loud voice"; cf. Esther A 5, 4:1. Her scream may have been one of fear and frustration; possibly she was crying to the Lord for help (so Scholz). In any case, in keeping with their threat in vs. 21, the elders are now shouting out their accusations against Susanna.

25. *to open the garden gates.* To provide thereby "proof" that Susanna's young lover had really been there but had gotten away (see vs. 39).

COMMENT

Whatever reason/s the early Christian Church may have had for replacing the Septuagint text of Daniel with the "Theodotionic" version, one thing is clear as far as the story of Susanna is concerned: it is told far more skillfully in ⊕. One has only to read a translation of the LXX to see that:

> 5b It was of such the Lord had said, "Wickedness came forth from Babylon through elders who as judges only seemed to guide the people"; 6 and lawsuits from other cities would come to them. 7 These two, having seen a woman with a good figure, the wife of their brother from the sons of Israel, by the name of Susanna daughter of Hilkiah, wife of Joakim, strolling in her husband's garden in the afternoon, 8 desired her. 9 They perverted their minds and averted their eyes, not looking to Heaven or rendering just decisions. 10 Both were lovesick for her; but one did not admit to the other the evil which possessed them on account of her (although the woman did not know of this matter).
>
> 12 And when day had dawned, they came furtively, eager who should be the first to appear in her presence and to speak with her. 13 And, as usual, she was strolling around. The one elder had already arrived when the other got there, so the one questioned the other, saying, "Why did you come so early in the morning without inviting me along?" 14 They each acknowledged to the other his frustration. 19 And the one said to the other, "Let's go to her." And together they approached her and tried to force her. 22 The Jewess said to them, "I know if I do this thing, it'll be my death, and if I don't do it, I'll not escape your hands. 23 But it's better for me not to do it and so fall into your hands than sin in the Lord's sight."

The LXX is appreciably shorter than ⊕, partly because its beginning (vss. 1-5a) has been lost, but primarily because there is no bath scene (vss. 15-18) or account of the servants coming in and learning of Susanna's shocking conduct (vss. 24-27).

The Theodotion version is not only more expansive than the LXX, but it is also more concerned with psychological aspects of the story, with illuminating thought and feeling and not just with describing the outward act. For instance, ⊕ evidently added vs. 11: "since they were ashamed to admit their passion, that they wanted to have intercourse with her," as well as vss. 20-21: " 'Look!' they said, 'the garden gates are shut, and nobody can see us; and we desire you. So let us have you. If not, we will testify against you, saying that a young man was with you, and that is why you had dismissed your maids.' "

When the two Greek texts themselves are printed side by side in parallel columns, as is the case in Scholz, then the differences between the two are, at a glance, graphic—even without making a detailed word-for-word comparison of them. Not only are there gaps, where ⊕ has material lacking in the LXX; but, on closer examination, the ⊕ differs substantially from the LXX even in those verses which are "parallel" to one another. For instance, only vss. 5b,9,10a, 22b, and 23a of ⊕ are identical with the LXX. The remaining eight "parallel" passages are similar in content but quite different in wording. All in all, one is far more struck by the differences between the LXX and ⊕ than by their similarities.

While conclusive proof for a Semitic *Vorlage* of "Susanna" is certainly lacking, evidence of such a *Vorlage* is strongly suggested by the presence of a number of Hebraisms (*kai egeneto* [=Heb. *wyhy*] in vss. 7,15, and 19 of ⊕; "yesterday and the third day" in vs. 15 of ⊕, and "I'm in a bind" in vs. 22 of ⊕), the use of the same Greek root with almost diametrically opposite meanings (see NOTES on "they lusted for her" in vs. 8, and "to have intercourse with" in vs. 11), and, perhaps most decisive of all, the presence of a Greek word which presupposes a misreading of the Hebrew (see NOTE on "were lovesick for her" in vs. 10).

Since, with the exception of the readings in vss. 8 and 10, all of the above Hebraisms are confined to ⊕, it is difficult to explain this phenomenon except by theorizing that Theodotion must have been editing his Greek text with a Semitic text before him. (One could, of course, claim that Theodotion was deliberately archaizing, but see below.)

Whether such additions in ⊕ as vss. 11,15-18,10-21, and 24-27 originated with "Theodotion" himself or were already existent in the particular Semitic text available to him is impossible to say. A priori, one would assume that Theodotion had not taken it upon himself to invent these additions in ⊕. On the other hand, all but two of the eight Hebraisms noted in the paragraph before last occur in passages where LXX and ⊕ "parallel" one another, thereby suggesting that a Semitic text may have been the controlling factor here. This latter point does, however, argue against the Hebraisms in ⊕ being simply efforts on Theodotion's part to archaize the text: had that been his intent, we should certainly have expected stronger evidence of it, i.e. more Hebraisms, in the additions themselves.

V. SUSANNA IS TRIED AND
SENTENCED TO DEATH

(Vss. 28-41)

28 *a*The next day, when the people had gathered at the house of her husband Joakim, the two elders arrived, viciously determined to have her put to death. So in the presence of the people they said, 29 "Summon Susanna daughter of Hilkiah, Joakim's wife." So they summoned her. 30 And she came, accompanied by her parents, her children, and all her relatives. 31 Now Susanna was very refined and shapely. 32 And the scoundrels ordered her to be uncovered *b*(for she was veiled)*b* so that they might feast upon her beauty. 33 But her friends and all who saw her were in tears. 34 The two elders stood up, with the people all around them, and placed their hands upon her head. 35 In her tears she looked upward to heaven, for her heart trusted in the Lord.

36 The elders said, "As we were strolling by ourselves in the garden, this woman came in with two maids. She shut the doors and dismissed the maids. 37 Then a young man, who had been hiding, went over to her and lay down with her. 38 But being in a corner of the garden, we saw this wicked thing and so ran toward them. 39 Though we saw them having relations, we could not hold the man because he was too strong for us; and he opened the gates and took off. 40 But we grabbed this one here and asked who the young man was, 41 but she would not tell us. These things do we testify."

Inasmuch as they were elders of the people and judges, the entire*c* congregation believed them and condemned Susanna*d* to death.

a ⊕ has *kai egeneto;* see NOTE on vs. 7.
b-b A gloss; see NOTE.
c So OL, Bohairic, and Syriac, after LXX; ⊕ omits.
d Greek and versions have "her."

NOTES

28. *viciously determined to have.* Literally "full of wicked intent concerning Susanna." More than fear of detection or desire for self-preservation was probably involved here, i.e. the rejected lover had now rejected the loved one, a phenomenon well illustrated in II Sam 13:15, where it was said of Amnon after he had raped his half-sister Tamar: "Then Amnon hated her with very great hatred; so that the hatred with which he hated her was greater than the love with which he had loved her."

Verse 28 in the LXX is very different from Θ in both wording and content: "But the scoundrels turned, huddled together, and decided that they should have her condemned to death. So they went to the synagogue of the city where they were living; and all the sons of Israel who were there sat in judgment."

One can only speculate on what literary considerations lay behind Theodotion's change of the trial's time and place. It does seem, however, that by staging the trial the following day in the very place where the alleged offense took place, Theodotion (or the author of the Semitic text Theodotion had before him) was not only providing additional time for the vicious rumor mills to work and community resentment to mount against Susanna but he was also heightening the drama by holding the trial at the actual scene of the crime, where all could so easily imagine what had happened. Moreover, Theodotion's placing the trial at the scene of the crime is also more logical because later on, when Daniel cross-examined the false witnesses, the jury could easily see for themselves that neither of the trees mentioned by the wicked elders (vss. 54 and 58) was there in the garden.

Unless in the corresponding verse the LXX has something significantly different from Θ, no translation of LXX will be given in the NOTES. For a translation of the LXX *in toto* (vss. 28-41), see COMMENT.

30. In contrast to Θ, LXX had mentioned specific numbers of people involved: "The woman arrived, accompanied by her father and mother; also there came her servants and maids (being five hundred in number), as well as Susanna's four children." Since the trial was being held in another city (so vs. 28 of LXX), evidently everybody from Susanna's hometown came, whether out of concern or curiosity.

31. *refined [truphera] and shapely [kai kalē tō eidei].* These same two attributes were also possessed by Queen Esther (see Esth D 3 and 2:7, respectively). As will be evident from the NOTE on vs. 32, Susanna's refinement and attractiveness make the conduct of the two elders in vs. 32 all the more villainous. For this verse the LXX has simply: "The woman was very refined."

32. At first glance, the LXX is similar to Θ in both meaning and wording: "So the scoundrels commanded them to uncover her in order that their lust might feast upon her beauty."

(for she was veiled). With this gloss, Theodotion tries to explain why it was

ordered that she be "uncovered." It is more likely, however, that the LXX actually meant "stripped naked" since, according to Ezek 16:37-39, such was part of the penalty for adultery (cf. also Hosea 2:3,10). Frank Zimmermann (*JQR* 48 [1957/58], 236-237) has called attention to the prescribed treatment in the Mishnah (*Sotah* I 5) for a suspected adulteress who refuses to confess: her hair is disheveled by a priest and her clothes ripped and torn until her breasts are exposed, unless, says Rabbi Judah, the woman be beautiful, in which case these things are not to be done. In ordering Susanna's breasts exposed, the elders, argued Zimmermann, not only were adding to her disgrace and discomfort, but they were actually prejudging the verdict against her, thereby further compounding their villainy.

33. *her friends.* Literally "those with her," i.e. those mentioned in vs. 30.

34. *placed their hands upon her head.* For this form of adjuration, see Lev 24:14. The LXX's version ("The two elderly judges stood up and placed their hands upon her head") is, technically speaking, not as procedurally correct as ⊖, because the two elders could not simultaneously act as judges, they being witnesses in the case (so *Kam* 90*b* in the Babylonian Talmud). For a brief but helpful survey on biblical theory and practice with respect to giving witness, see Moshe Greenberg, *IDB*, IV, s.v. "Witness," and its related subject, "Oaths," in M. H. Pope, *IDB*, III, 575-577.

35. At this point the LXX supplied Susanna's prayer itself: "but her heart was trusting in the Lord her God; and lifting up (her head), she sobbed, saying, 'Lord, the eternal God who knows all things before they happen, you know that I did not do what these villains have so falsely testified against me.' And the Lord heard her prayer." Theodotion or, more likely, the author of his Semitic *Vorlage* had evidently removed the prayer from here and had Susanna utter it at the point when she was found guilty and sentenced to death (vss. 42-44 of ⊖). Which context is the more appropriate for such a prayer is debatable, either place being quite suitable, a fact recognized probably by a Syriac version which has the prayer at both points.

36. *As we were strolling.* The Greek of ⊖ here is a genitive absolute, a construction quite characteristic of standard Classical Greek; the corresponding clause in the LXX, however, is a straightforward temporal sentence characteristic of Hebrew narrative (LXX: "The two elders said, 'We were strolling in her husband's garden' "). Had the author of ⊖ been really interested in archaizing a narrative originally composed in Greek (so some scholars), then it is very difficult to understand why he would have introduced in ⊖ a genitive absolute construction.

39. *he was too strong for us.* The LXX had a different and, possibly, less convincing reason for the man not having been recognized: "And on approaching them, we recognized her, but the young man fled in disguise."

41. *Inasmuch as they were elders . . . and judges.* I.e. they were completely above suspicion and so were not cross-examined as provided by Deut 19:15-20.

condemned Susanna to death. In accordance with Lev 20:10: "If a man commits adultery with the wife of his neighbor, both the adulterer and the adulteress shall be put to death" (see also Deut 22:22-23). The penalty for adultery was death by stoning (cf. Ezek 16:38-40; John 8:5).

COMMENT

The LXX version printed below is an interesting and well-told story that certainly could have survived on its own merits without being improved by ⊙:

28 But the scoundrels turned, huddled together, and decided that they should have her condemned to death. So they went to the synagogue of the city where they were living, and all the sons of Israel who were there sat in judgment.

29 The two elderly judges stood up and said, "Summon Susanna daughter of Hilkiah, Joakim's wife." They immediately called for her. 30 The woman arrived, accompanied by her father and mother; also there came her servants and maids (being five hundred in number) as well as Susanna's four children. 31 The woman was very refined. 32 So the scoundrels commanded them to uncover her in order that their lust might feast upon her beauty. 33 And all her friends were in tears as were many who knew her. 34 The two elderly judges stood up and placed their hands upon her head, 35 but her heart was trusting in the Lord her God; and lifting up (her head), she sobbed, saying, "Lord, the eternal God who knows all things before they happen, you know that I did not do what these villains have so falsely testified against me." And the Lord heard her prayer. 36 The two elders said. "We were strolling in her husband's garden, 37 and turning the corner [Gr. *to stadion*] we saw this woman 'sleeping' with a man. Stopping, we saw them having sexual intercourse; 38 but they did not know that we were standing there. Then we agreed on it, saying, 'Let's find out who they are!' 39 And on approaching them, we recognized her; but the young man fled in disguise. 40 But we grabbed this one here and asked her, 'Who's the man?' 41 But she did not tell us who he was. These things do we testify."

Inasmuch as they were elders and judges of the people, the entire congregation believed them.

If one does not include Susanna's prayer in vs. 35 of the LXX, then the narratives in vss. 28-41 of the two Greek versions are approximately of equal length. Although in their wording the two Greek texts parallel one another very closely in vss. 29,33-34,36a, and 40-41a, the similarities end there. One is, again, struck by the differences in the two versions, resulting, in part, because of different details of "fact," such as where and when the trial was held.

Unfortunately, no clear editorial principle emerges as the cause for other differences in the two accounts, although ⊙ does have some details that increase the reader's interest: Susanna was also shapely (vs. 31); her adultery was neither a matter of rape nor pure chance, for she had deliberately made preparations for her lover's visit (cf. vs. 36; for the biblical distinction between being raped and consenting, see Deut 22:25-27); the young man was too strong for the elders to hold (vs. 39); she was sentenced to death (vs. 41). On the other hand, in vs. 30 the author of ℗ seems to have condensed the LXX material for no good reason. It is very difficult to escape the conclusion that at least some of these differences between the two versions reflect differences in their Semitic *Vorlagen* rather than in the editorial principles of the author of ℗.

VI. THE ELDERS ARE DISCREDITED BY DANIEL AND ARE EXECUTED
(Vss. 42-64)

42 Susanna uttered a loud cry and said, "Eternal God, you know all secrets and know everything before it happens, 43 you know that they have framed me. Must I now die, being innocent of what they have so maliciously charged against me?"

44 The Lord heard her cry. 45 Just as she was being led away to be put to death, God roused the holy spirit of a young boy*a* by the name of Daniel; 46 and he shouted out,*b* "I am innocent of this woman's blood!"

47 Then all the people turned to him and asked, "What do you mean by that?" 48 Having taken his stand in their midst, he replied, "Are you such fools, sons of Israel? Would you condemn a daughter of Israel without first cross-examining and discovering its accuracy? 49 Go back to the place of trial; these men have framed her."

50 So all the people hurried back. Then *c*the presiding elders*c* said to him, "Come sit with us and inform us, since God has granted the authority*d* to you."

51 Then Daniel said to them, "Separate them some distance from one another, and I will interrogate them."

52 When they had been separated from one another, he summoned one of them and said to him, "You who have grown old in wickedness, the sins which you committed in the past have now caught up with you: 53 making unjust decisions, condemning the innocent and acquitting the guilty, though the Lord has said, 'You shall not put to death the innocent and righteous person.' 54 Now then, if you really did see this woman, tell us: Under what tree did you see them making love?"

He answered, "Under *e*a clove tree*e*."

a A Syriac version adds "who was twelve years old"; see NOTE.
b Most versions add "and said."
c-c Greek and versions have "the elders."
d Presbeion in ⊕B; Greek and versions usually have presbutereion.
e-e Gr. schinon, "mastic tree"; OL lentiscus; see NOTE.

55 "Very good!" retorted Daniel, "you've perjured yourself!" Already an angel of God has received the sentence from God and will cleave you in half!" 56 Then he set him aside and ordered them to bring in the other one.

"You descendant of Canaan, not Judah," said Daniel*f* to him, "beauty has seduced you, and lust has corrupted your heart! 57 This is how you have been treating the daughters of Israel*g*; and being afraid of you, they had relations with *h*you two*h*. But this daughter of Judah would not submit to your villainy. 58 Now then, tell me: Under what tree did you catch*i* them making love?"

"Under a yew*j*," he answered.

59 "Very good!" retorted Daniel to him, "you, too, have perjured yourself! The angel of God is waiting with drawn sword to hew you in half and destroy *k*the pair of you*k*!"

60 Then all the congregation cheered, and they blessed God who saves those who trust in him. 61 Then they turned on the two elders, for Daniel had convicted them of perjury through their own testimony. So they punished *l*the elders*l* the way *m*the elders*m* had intended to afflict their neighbor. 62 Acting in accordance with the Law of Moses, they put them to death. So an innocent life*n* was saved that day. 63 Hilkiah and his wife praised God*o* for their daughter Susanna*p*, as did her husband Joakim and all her relatives, because she was found innocent of any impropriety. 64 From that day forward Daniel had a great reputation in the eyes of the people.*q*

---

f "He" in Greek and versions.

g ⑯*V* has "Jerusalem," which probably originated from a misread abbreviation for "Israel."

h-h Greek "you" (*umin*), the plural pronoun.

i Gr. *katelabes;* "see" in Syriac and Arabic, cf. vs. 54.

j Greek, OL, and Arabic read "oak"; Vulgate and SyrH. transliterated the Gr. *prinon;* see NOTE.

k-k Greek "you" (*umin*), the plural pronoun.

l-l Greek "them."

m-m Greek "they."

n Greek "blood."

o ⑯*B* *A* omit name; most MSS have.

p ⑯*B* *A* omit name; most MSS have.

q Vulgate adds another verse: "And King Astyages was gathered to his fathers, and Cyrus the Persian took his kingdom"; see NOTE.

NOTES

42. *know all secrets* [*o tōn kruptōn gnōstēs*]. Literally "who knows the se-crets." Cf. Deut 29:29: "The secret things [LXX *ta krupta*] belong to the Lord our God; but the things that are revealed belong to us and to our children for ever. . . ."

everything before it happens. Literally "who knows all things before their creation." For a brief introduction into the OT problem of God's foreknowl-edge and man's freedom, see the relevant discussion in B. W. Anderson, *IDB*, II, s.v. "Foreknow, Foreknowledge"; see also the related articles on "Predes-tination" and "Providence" in *IDB*, III, 869 and 940, by G. E. Mendenhall and C. F. D. Moule, respectively.

This prayer (vss. 42-43), evidently removed from its original place in the LXX (vs. 35), is similar in thought but not in wording to the LXX's prayer, the latter being: "Lord, the eternal God who knows all things before they hap-pen, you know that I did not do what these villains have so falsely testified against me." In its version, ⊖ has added two phrases to the prayer, "you know all secrets" and "Must I now die?", both elements adding to the drama of the situation.

45. *God roused the holy spirit.* The author of ⊖ significantly modified the LXX, which had: "An angel of the Lord appeared just as she was being led away to be put to death. And the angel gave, as he was ordered, a spirit of un-derstanding to a youth named Daniel." Thus, whereas in the LXX an *angel* gave Daniel insight (*suneseōs;* cf. Isa 11:2 and Deut 34:9), a statement per-fectly consistent with Dan 9:21 and 10:5*f*, where an angel assisted the adult Daniel, the author of ⊖ has God rousing the holy spirit *already in* Daniel, a change probably made under the influence of Dan 4:9,18 and 5:11, where Daniel had within himself "the spirit of the Holy God."

a young boy [*paidariou neōterou*]. According to the ⊖, Daniel was a young boy (*paidarion* being the diminutive of *pais*) and not, as in LXX, just "a youth" (*neōtēs*). If Daniel was understood to be a young boy at the time, then that would justify ⊖^A ᴮ, OL, and Arabic versions placing the story of Susanna before ch. 1 of the canonical Daniel instead of at the end as ch. 13, as done by the LXX and the Vulgate.

On the basis of *paidariou neōterou* in ⊖, Gedeon Huet (*RHR* 65 [1912], 277-284) argued that the Susanna story was an example of a "well-known" an-cient literary genre, namely, the correction of an injustice by the intervention of a young child. The Susanna story may indeed be such an example; but as Huet himself was later forced to concede (*RHR* 76 [1917], 129-130), the Septuagint occasionally used the word *paidarion* for males of marriageable age, as in Tobit 5:17.

Daniel. The name, meaning "God has judged," was given to many Jews, in-cluding a son of David (I Chron 3:1), a post-exilic priest (Ezra 8:2; Neh

10:6), and Enoch's father-in-law (Jub 4:20). A most ancient Canaanite name, going back at least to the days of Ugarit (1550-1350 B.C.), when a king *Dnil* figured in the Aqht Legend (see *ANET²*, 149-152), Daniel was a most illustrious name, symbolic of righteousness and wisdom (cf. Ezek 14:14, 28:3). By the intertestamental period, in some quarters at least, just as the once-human Enoch had become an angel (cf. III Enoch 4:2), so had the wisdom-figure of Daniel, albeit a fallen angel (cf. Enoch 6:7, 69:2).

At the Dead Sea community of Qumran, Daniel was a subject of great interest, there being found in Cave IV three Aramaic manuscripts which, while fragmentary, do clearly have a Daniel relating Jewish history to a king. Even though these up till now unknown narratives (tentatively called Pseudo-Daniel *a, b, c*) have not as yet cast any direct light on the story of Susanna, the very presence of such stories in Aramaic certainly strengthens the likelihood of Susanna also having a Semitic *Vorlage*.

Not until vs. 45 is Daniel mentioned! And when he is, in the older account (the LXX) it is *the angel* that gets top billing. This, plus other considerations to be discussed later, suggests that Daniel may not have figured at all in the original Susanna story (see pp. 115-116).

46. Daniel's words are reminiscent of Pontius Pilate's in Matt 27:24. Although divinely inspired (so vs. 45), Daniel was apparently also acting here well within his rights; for according to the Mishnah, "When the person to be stoned is led out, a herald must precede proclaiming these words: 'This person, (name) son of (name), is on the way to being stoned for the crime of (specifics), on the testimony of (name) and (name); whosoever can show his innocence, let him approach and set forth his reasons.' If none appeared, when they came within ten cubits of the place of stoning, the condemned was invited to confess, in deference to Joshua 7:19" (*Sanhedrin* VI 1-2). The condemned was then stripped and either pushed off of a scaffold six cubits high or down a ravine by one of the witnesses; the other witness threw the first stone (*Sanhedrin* VI 3-4). For details on stoning and related types of punishment in the Bible, see J. Greenberg, *IDB*, I, 741-742, and Moshe Greenberg, IV, 447.

47. *"What do you mean by that?"* Literally "What's this thing which you have said?" Neither vs. 46 nor vs. 47 appears in the LXX.

48. *fools [mōroi]*. According to Scholz (p. 174), *mōroi* is used in the Old Testament only in a religious sense, i.e. in referring to those who depart from the Law (cf. Ps 94:8).

With the exception of its opening phrase, the LXX is virtually the same for this verse so it need not be offered here (for a translation of the LXX in toto [vss. 46-64], see COMMENT.

49. *have framed her*. Cf. vs. 43. Literally "falsely have they testified against her"; the Greek adverb is in the emphatic position.

Both this verse and the next represent an expansion by ☉, these verses not being in the LXX.

51. For this verse the LXX has a very significant "addition": " 'Now, separate them for me some distance from one another in order that I may discredit [*etasō*] them.' When they had been separated, Daniel said to the congregation,

'Now don't take into consideration that these are elders, saying (to yourself), "They would not lie." I, however, will interrogate them as things occur to me.'" The LXX is not an expansion (so Plöger, p. 80); but, far more likely, ℮ (or, even more likely, the *Vorlage* of ℮) deleted this LXX material which sensitive authorities later on felt not only undermined the authority of the two villains but authority in general, including their own. Here, then, is one more reason why the early Christian Church preferred ℮ over the LXX (see pp. 30-31).

52. *You who have grown old in wickedness.* Literally "aged in evil days." Daniel was certain of the elders' wickedness and guilt, not through cross-examination, but through prior revelation (so vs. 45). Cross-examination was not necessary for Daniel but for the jury and their verdict.

have now caught up with you [nun ēkasin]. Literally "now have come."

With but a slight change, ℮ virtually reproduced the LXX: "Then he summoned one of them; and they brought the elder to the youth. 'Listen,' said Daniel to him, 'listen, you who have grown old in wickedness, the sins which you committed in the past have now caught up with you.'"

53. *'You shall not . . . righteous person.'* This "quote" is an allusion to Exod 23:7.

54. *a clove tree.* In choosing the names for the two trees mentioned by the wicked elders here and in vs. 58, a translator must decide between two incompatible options: shall he accurately translate the name of the trees, thereby losing the play on words in vss. 55 and 59; or shall he falsely identify the trees so as to make possible the puns? The latter course has been taken here because the paronomasia was, from a literary point of view, probably more important to the ancient Greek editor than the identification of the trees per se. Martin Luther evidently felt the same way; for he identified the tree in vs. 54 as a *Linden*, to rhyme with *finden* (vs. 58); and he chose *zeichen* in vs. 59, to rhyme with *Eiche* (vs. 58). English-speaking writers, in sympathy with this approach, have suggested several possibilities, including "clove" and "cleave" (so Ball, p. 341); "pine tree" and "pine away"; "ash tree" and "turn to ash" (so Pfeiffer, p. 433, n. 10).

The tree actually mentioned in the verse is the *schinon*, or "mastic tree" (*Pistacia Lentiscus* [LSJ, 1,476]). Occurring only here in the Greek Bible, the word *schinon* was, not surprisingly, transliterated by the Vulgate and SyrH.; the OL, however, rightly has *lentiscus*. "Mastic" is really the sweet-smelling gum, or sap, from the tree. (Even today, as every traveler to the Near East knows from being besieged by young peddlers, the word for "chewing gum" is *mastiq*.)

Although in this verse the ℮ and the LXX have the identical answer (LXX: "'Now then, under what tree and in what part of the garden did you see them with one another?' The godless fellow answered, 'Under a clove tree [*schinon*]'"), the verse is probably more skillfully conceived in ℮ where only one question was asked *and answered*, whereas, in the LXX *two* were asked but only one was answered.

55. *"you've perjured yourself!"* Literally "you lied against your own head." *will cleave [schisei].* Literally "will split." The Greek verb is a pun on *schinon*, "mastic tree" (vs. 54), which is rendered as "clove" to play on

"cleave." Essentially the same strategy was long ago carried out by the translator of a Syriac version who used *pāstēqā*, "pistachio tree," and *pēsaq*, "to cut off" (vss. 54-55); and *rummānā*, "a pomegranate tree," and *rumchā*, "a sword" (vss. 58-59).

Since the days of Julius Africanus these two puns in "Susanna" have been the source of great controversy. Africanus maintained that they were prima facie evidence that "Susanna" had originally been composed in Greek because, he argued, no Greek translator could have so cleverly and accurately carried two such puns over into another language. Many more recent scholars have agreed with his argument, especially German scholars of the last century. Kay (p. 650) has pointed out, however, that exactly just such an "impossible" translation did occur in Judg 10:4, where the Heb. *'yrym . . . 'yrym* was accurately rendered into Greek as *pōlous . . . poleis*, "asses . . . cities." *Anesis* and *aphesis* in I Esd 4:62 *may* be another example of such paronomasia (so Daubney, p. 133). In any case, one should never underestimate the skill and ingenuity of biblical translators, be they ancient Greeks or modern scholars. As an example of literal yet brilliant translation of Hebrew into another language, consider the Chicago Bible's English translation of Samson's riddle to the Philistines: "Out of the eater came something to eat. Out of the strong came something sweet" (Judg 14:14).

Starting with Origen (for text, see Kay, p. 650), scholars who believed that "Susanna" had a Semitic *Vorlage* have offered a variety of suggestions as to what the original words might have been, including *pstq'*, "pistachio tree," and *psq*, "to cut off" (so Syriac and Brüll); *prsq*, "peach tree," and *ypsqd*, "shall cut you" (Zimmermann, *JQR* 48 [1957/58], 237). A longer list of other possibilities, mostly far-fetched, may be found in Ball (p. 324). Evidently there was nothing in biblical "etiquette" to preclude punning in even such serious matters as a death sentence (cf. Josh 7:25).

In contrast to Scholz who argued that the Greek translator accurately translated the Greek verbs and then picked trees to match, it could be argued that the exact opposite happened. Otherwise, how can one account for the *total inappropriateness* of the verbs in vss. 55 and 59? The wicked elders were stoned to death, not slaughtered (but cf. vs. 62 of the LXX)! Besides, it was their identification of the trees, albeit erroneous, that established the fact they had perjured themselves.

For this verse the LXX has: " 'Very good!' retorted the youth, 'you've perjured yourself! Today the angel of the Lord will cleave you [cleave your life].' "

56. *descendant of Canaan.* Although obviously intended as a stinging insult, the meaning of the phrase is not clear even after one considers the LXX: "Then he set that one aside and said to bring in to him the other one. And he said to him, 'Why was your progeny corrupted like Sidon and not like Judah? Beauty has beguiled you—petty lust!' " The Canaan mentioned by ℘ was the father of the Sidon alluded to in the LXX (cf. Gen 10:15).

Inasmuch as Canaan had been cursed because of a sexual impropriety of his father Ham (Gen 9:20-25), one might infer that "descendant of Canaan" was a popular expression applied to people guilty of some sexual offense, just as "a Zimri" was applied to assassins and opportunists who murdered for political position (cf. II Kings 9:31). On the other hand, Sidon was the ancestor of many

"Jewish" villains, not the least of which were the wicked Jezebel, wife of King Ahab (cf. I Kings 16:31), and their daughter Athaliah, wife of King Jehoram and later ruling monarch of Judah (II Chron 21:6, 22:10-12), both women being Israelite rulers who, like the two elders, had greatly abused their duly constituted powers by perpetrating gross injustices against their own people. All things considered, we should probably understand the phrase to mean, not that the second elder was literally a descendant of Canaan but that he had *acted like* Canaanites, who, as Zimmermann has reminded us, "were derided for bastardy in midrashic literature" (*JQR* 48 [1957/58], 237).

Given our uncertainty as to the meaning of the allusion to Sidon, we should not conclude, as did Solomon Zeitlin (*JQR* 40 [1949/50], 236), that the choice of that particular name indicates Palestinian authorship of "Susanna," otherwise, argues Zeitlin, a name like Babylon or Nineveh would have been used instead.

not Judah. Nor is the meaning of this phrase clear. Possibly, it is an allusion to Genesis 38, where Judah fulfilled, in actual fact even if not by deliberate intent, a proper and legitimate role in begetting offspring, whereas the second elder certainly had not (so vs. 57).

57. *daughters of Israel . . . this daughter of Judah.* Since Daniel himself had earlier referred to Susanna as "a daughter of Israel" (vs. 48), the invidious comparison here is somewhat puzzling (but see Hosea 4:15). It may, of course, reflect the understandable bias of Babylonian Jews who were primarily Judean exiles; but, more likely, it represents a later prejudice of Palestinian Jews toward their northern neighbors, especially toward the Samaritans who considered themselves the heirs of North Israel (so Pfeiffer, p. 454).

58. *a yew.* Prinos, the tree actually mentioned here, was the holm oak (*Quercus Ilex*, so LSJ, 1,464). Although oak species are frequently mentioned in the Bible, there is, as with so many other flora and fauna of the Bible, considerable vagueness concerning their precise identification; for details, see J. C. Trever, *IDB*, III, s.v. "Oak." In keeping with the logic offered in the NOTE on vs. 54, *a clove tree,* "yew" has been chosen so as to rhyme with "hew" of vs. 59.

As in vs. 54 of the LXX, the LXX here also has two questions but only one answer: " 'Now then, tell me: Under what tree and in which part of the garden did you catch them making love?' 'Under a yew,' he answered."

59. *angel . . . with drawn sword.* Literally "angel . . . holding the sword." For a similar image, see Num 22:31 and I Chron 21:16.

to hew. Literally "to saw"; cf. Amos 1:3 of LXX. *Prisai* here is a play on words with *prinos*, "oak," in vs. 58.

The LXX is somewhat different: "And Daniel said, 'Reprobate [*amartōle*]! The angel of the Lord is now standing with drawn sword until the people have destroyed you that he may hew you down [*kataprisē*].' " Scholz (pp. 179-180) was probably correct in suggesting that the different verbs for the angel's stance go back to a misreading of the Hebrew, i.e. the LXX had *qwm*, "standing," which was read by ☉ as *qwh*, "waiting."

60. *cheered.* Literally "cried out with a loud voice."

they blessed [eulogēsan] God. By being more theocentric in this verse,

Theodotion "improved" the LXX which had: "Then all the congregation raved about [*aneboēsen epi*] the youth."

61. *through their own testimony.* Literally "from their mouth."

punished . . . the way the elders had intended. This was in accordance with the principle of retribution stated in Deut 19:18-21: "If the witness is a false witness and has accused his brother falsely, then you shall do to him as he had meant to do to his brother. . . . it shall be life for life, eye for eye, tooth for tooth. . . ." As noted in the Introduction, the Pharisees and Sadducees were sharply divided over the correct interpretation of the passage. The Sadducees argued that false witnesses could be executed *only if* the falsely accused had already been killed, whereas, the Pharisees maintained that the false witnesses should be killed even when the falsely accused had not been killed (for specifics, see in the Mishnah, *Makkoth* I 6; see also Gamara *Makkoth* v *b;* and the *Sifre* on Deut 19:19).

The LXX was not very different: "How through their own testimony he had established their perjury. In accordance with the Law, they punished them exactly as the elders [they] had intended to afflict their sister."

62. *they put them to death.* For reasons known only to him, the author of ℗ chose to "spare" his readers the bloody details of the LXX: "So they silenced them, led them off, and pitched them into a ravine, whereupon, the angel of the Lord hurled lightning [fire] in their midst. So an innocent life was saved that day." The LXX's "they silenced (*ephimōsan*) them" probably means that the elders' protests of innocence or their cries for mercy were silenced by the crowd (cf. Matt 22:34). However, Zimmermann, noting that the Greek verb literally means "to muzzle" (so I Tim 5:18), has suggested that the Greek translator had read the Heb. *wyzmwm*, "and they gagged them," as if it were from the verb *zmm*, "to muzzle" (*JQR* 48 [1957/58], 240-241). Certainly, gagging a condemned person would seem to run counter to the Talmudic practice of encouraging the condemned to make a last-minute admission of guilt (see NOTE on vs. 46).

63. *any impropriety* [*aschēmon pragma*]. Literally "an unseemly deed." In the Septuagint the word *aschēmos* is used to describe not only a capital offense such as Shechem's rape of Dinah (Gen 34:7) but also the grounds for a divorce (Deut 24:1), which some, such as the Shammai school, would restrict to adultery while others, like the school of Hillel, interpreted in very general terms. Susanna was not just found innocent of the act of adultery: her conduct was found above reproach, i.e. she had in no way encouraged the lecherous men or been responsible for their advances toward her.

64. The last verse in ℗ differs appreciably from that of the LXX, the latter being hopelessly corrupt: "Because of this the young are beloved of Jacob— on account of their simplicity. And let us watch over the young that they be courageous sons. For the young are idealistic, and a spirit of knowledge and understanding will always be in them."

After examining various proposals and emendations from Fritzsche's on, Ball wrote back in 1888 what is still the best comment on the verse: "It is difficult to imagine that Greek was the original language of this closing sentence. As Greek it is intolerable as well as unintelligible; as a bald rendering from a Semitic tongue its peculiarities are intelligible enough" (p. 342). Only two other observations need be added: in this verse the LXX has a pronounced Wisdom-character (so Plöger, p. 81); and youth in general, not Daniel in particular, has the spotlight, all of which suggests that in the LXX's earliest form Susanna was given top billing and Daniel may not have been on the scene at all.

After vs. 64 the Vulgate adds another verse: "And King Astyages was gathered to his fathers, and Cyrus the Persian received his kingdom." This verse obviously provides an error in chronology since we are given to understand here that Daniel was a young boy in 550 B.C.; yet according to Dan 1:5-6 Daniel was a youth in 597 B.C.! The solution of the problem is quite evident: the verse should be taken with Daniel 14, i.e. with "Bel and the Snake," not with "Susanna."

COMMENT

Even more than the two previous sections (vss. 1-27, 28-41), this portion of the LXX differs from ⊚:

45 An angel of the Lord appeared just as she was being led away to be put to death. And the angel gave, as he was ordered, a spirit of understanding to a youth named Daniel. 48 Addressing the crowd, Daniel, having taken his stand in their midst, replied, "Are you such fools, sons of Israel? Would you decide against a daughter of Israel without first cross-examining and discovering its accuracy? 51 Now, separate them for me some distance from one another in order that I may discredit them."

When they had been separated, Daniel said to the congregation, "Now don't take into consideration that these are elders, saying (to yourselves), 'They would not lie.' I, however, will interrogate them as things occur to me."

52 Then he summoned one of them; and they brought the elder to the youth. "Listen," Daniel said to him, "listen, you who have grown old in wickedness, the sins which you committed in the past have now caught up with you: 53 entrusted with hearing and judging cases carrying the death penalty, you condemned the innocent and dismissed the guilty, though the Lord has said, 'You shall not put to death the innocent and righteous person.' 54 Now then, under what tree and in what part of the garden did you see them with one another?" The godless fellow answered, "Under a clove tree [schinon]."

55 "Very good!" retorted the youth, "you've perjured yourself! Today the angel of the Lord will cleave you [cleave your life]." 56 Then he set that one aside and said to bring in to him the other one.

And he said to him, "Why was your progeny corrupted like Sidon and not like Judah? Beauty has beguiled you—petty [small] lust! 57 And this is how you have been treating the daughters of Israel; and being afraid of you, they had relations with you two. But this daughter of Judah would not tolerate [not endure to bear] your villainous sickness. 58 Now then, tell me: Under what tree and in which part of the garden did you catch them making love?'

"Under a yew," he answered.

59 And Daniel said, "Reprobate! The angel of the Lord is now standing with drawn sword until the people have destroyed you that he may hew you down."

60 Then all the congregation raved about the youth, 61 how through their own testimony he had established their perjury. In accordance with the Law, they punished them exactly as the elders ["they"] had intended to afflict their sister. 62 So they silenced them, led them off, and pitched them into a ravine, whereupon, the angel of the Lord hurled lightning in their midst. So an innocent life was saved that day. 64 Because of this the young are beloved of Jacob—on account of their simplicity. And let us watch over the young that they be courageous sons. For the young are idealistic, and a spirit of knowledge and understanding will always be in them.

A careful comparison of the Greek texts of ⊙ and the LXX permits us to make several generalizations. First, the LXX and ⊙ are more different in vss. 45-64 than they are alike. For instance, of those twenty verses, there are only four verses with virtually identical wording (vss. 48,52,57-58), and seven with roughly parallel content (vss. 45,51,53-56,61); furthermore, ⊙ adds five verses to the LXX (vss. 46-47,49-50,63), and has deleted one verse (vs. 51b), greatly abbreviated another (vs. 62), and "replaced" a third (vs. 64).

Second, the primary effect of the changes above is the elevation of young Daniel in ⊙, that is, Daniel was not nearly as dominant a figure in the LXX. Consider the following variants:

vs. 45b LXX   And the angel gave, as he was ordered, a spirit of understanding to the youth named Daniel.

        ⊙   God roused the holy spirit of a young boy by the name of Daniel;

46-47   and he shouted out, "I'm innocent of this woman's blood!"
(*only in the* ⊙) Then all the people turned to him and asked, "What do you mean by that?"

49-50   "Go back to the place of trial; these men have framed
(*only in the* ⊙) her." So all the people hurried back. Then the presiding elders said to him, "Come sit with us and inform us, since God has granted the authority to you."

64   LXX   Because of this the young are beloved of Jacob—on account of their simplicity. And let us watch over the young that they be courageous sons. For the young are idealistic, and a spirit of knowledge and understanding will always be in them!

        ⊙   From that day forward Daniel had a great reputation in the eyes of the people.

One might add, for whatever it is worth, that the LXX mentions Daniel *by name* only four times while the ⊛ does so six times.

Third, in this section (vss. 45-64) of "Susanna," as in vss. 1-41, ⊛ improved upon the LXX by strengthening the story's logic (cf. vss. 54 and 58) and dramatic effect, e.g. the addition of vss. 46-47, 49-50, and 63.

Finally, several consecutive verses seem to represent different Greek translations of the same Semitic *Vorlage:*

> vs. 53   LXX   *kai ton men athōon katekrinas, tous de enochous ēphieis*
> "you condemned the innocent and dismissed the guilty"
>
>   ⊛   *kai tous men athōous katakrinōn, apoluōn de tous aitious*
> "condemning the innocent and acquitting the guilty"
>
> 54   LXX   *nun oun upo ti dendron . . . eōrakas autous ontas sun eautois* "Now then, under what tree . . . did you see them with one another?"
>
>   ⊛   *kai nun . . . upo ti dendron eides autous omilountas allēlois* "Now then . . . under what tree did you see them making love?"
>
> 55   LXX   *orthōs epseusai eis tēn seautou psuchēn o gar aggelos kuriou schisei sou tēn psuchēn sēmeron* "Very good! you've perjured yourself! Today an angel of the Lord will cleave you."
>
>   ⊛   *orthōs epseusai eis tēn seautou kephalēn, ēdē gar aggelos . . . schisei se meson* "Very good! you've perjured yourself! Already an angel of God . . . will cleave you in half."

As noted earlier, a Semitic *Vorlage* for "Susanna" is both believable and likely. As was already noted (see NOTE on vs. 55), the presence of two Greek puns in this section is no insurmountable obstacle (but see p. 25*f* for the *tentative* findings of R. A. Martin); and the recent discovery of three hitherto unknown Daniel stories in Aramaic at Qumran (Pseudo-Daniel *a, b,* and *c*) attests to the great Jewish interest in the Daniel genre and increases the likelihood that the Susanna story is the Greek witness to a Semitic version.

"BEL AND THE SNAKE"

INTRODUCTION

"Bel and the Snake" consists of two "confrontation narratives" in which Daniel, a confidant of King Cyrus of Persia, courted his own destruction by deliberately setting out to disprove the "divinity" of two revered Babylonian gods, the idol called Bel and a very large snake.

Résumé of "Bel and the Snake"

In the first tale (vss. 1-22), the king, noticing that Daniel did not worship the idol Bel, assured Daniel that Bel really was a god and cited as evidence how much food Bel ate every day. When Daniel countered by saying, "Don't be misled, Your Majesty, for it is just clay on the inside, and bronze outside; he has never eaten or drunk anything!" (vs. 7), the offended king demanded that these charges be immediately settled, one way or another. Whereupon the priests of Bel proposed an experiment whereby the king himself, having seen that the offerings for Bel that day were arranged properly, should have the temple door shut in his presence, and sealed by his own signet. Then, if the offerings were still there in the morning, the priests would be put to death; if they were not there, then Daniel would be executed (vss. 1-13).

Now the priests had so fearlessly proposed this contest because they had a secret door leading into the temple, through which they and their families would go that night to carry off, as usual, the offerings to Bel. Daniel had just as fearlessly accepted the proposal because, unbeknown to the priests, he would have the temple floor covered with ashes in the king's presence just before the temple door was shut and sealed for the night (vss. 13-15).

When the king had the temple door opened the next morning, he was elated to learn that Bel had vindicated himself; for he could see that the offering tables were empty. But his joy was turned to fury when Daniel pointed out to him all the human footprints in the ashes on the floor! The convicted Belists were summarily executed by the king; and with the king's permission, Daniel destroyed the idol and its temple (vss. 16-22).

In the second story (vss. 23-42), the king, either because he wanted to strengthen his authority over the victorious Daniel or, more likely, because he himself now had some reservations about the supposed divinity of Babylonian gods, challenged Daniel again, this time by pointing to a large snake the Babylonians worshiped and saying, "You cannot say that this is not a living god, so worship him." "I will worship," replied Daniel, "the Lord my God, for he is a living God"; and then, as if to justify his blunt refusal, Daniel added, "But with your permission, Your Majesty, I will kill the snake without sword or stick" (vss. 23-26).

Then Daniel brewed together a concoction of pitch, fat, and hair, and fed it to the snake who, upon swallowing it, burst open and died. The Persian king may have been content to see another Babylonian fraud exposed, but the Babylonians were not. Applying a great deal of pressure on the king, they finally persuaded him to toss Daniel into a terrible lions' pit, where, ordinarily, its seven lions were fed two human bodies and two sheep every day. But although Daniel was in with the lions for six whole days, during which time the lions were not fed any food, Daniel remained hungry but unharmed (vss. 27-32).

It was on Daniel's sixth day there that an angel of the Lord brought to him the prophet Habakkuk, having carried him through the air from Judea to Babylon by the hair of his head. (Now, in Judea Habakkuk had been in the act of carrying some stew he had just made to the harvesters in the field.) Even as Daniel was eating the food Habakkuk had brought him, Habakkuk himself was being whisked back by the angel to Judea (vss. 33-39).

Thus, Daniel was both unharmed and quite healthy and strong when the king came to the Lions' Pit the next morning. Praising Daniel's God for delivering him, the king hauled Daniel up from the pit and tossed in those who had plotted against him. They, of course, were instantly devoured (vss. 40-42). So it was that Bel was proven to be a false god because he could not eat, and the snake was proven to be a false god because he did eat—and died from it!

The summary offered above, though based on Theodotion's version of "Bel and the Snake," is sufficiently broad and general so as to include most of, but certainly not all, the variant "details of fact" in the LXX (see NOTES passim). In any case, as the résumé should suggest, the two stories are interesting but brief, with their emphasis on plot and action rather than on character or details. Their ancient author told his two stories simply but dramatically; and, unlike later Jewish narrators of these tales, he resisted the temptation to embellish or elaborate on potentially interesting details (see e.g. NOTE on "pitch, fat, and hair" in vs. 27).

Original Language of the Stories

Perhaps the most fascinating problem in "Bel and the Snake" is that the preceding characterization of their literary style is not equally applicable to both stories in either of the Greek versions; or, to put it somewhat differently, the story of Bel is told far more effectively in ☉ (see COMMENT, p. 139), while the story of the Snake is told more effectively in the LXX (see COMMENT I, p. 147).

This rather surprising lack of consistency—a priori, one would normally expect either the LXX or, more likely, the ☉ to be, from a literary point of view, the superior version for both stories—undoubtedly testifies to the originally separate and independent state of the two stories in their Semitic forms. That the literary differences between the LXX and ☉ are not primarily the result of the work of their Greek translators but rather reflect differences in the respective Semitic *Vorlagen* of LXX and ☉ is indicated, in part, by the fact that in both stories ☉ consistently has many more Semiticisms, i.e. the nature and quality of the translation in each version remains consistent for both stories; it is in the substantive matters of "details of fact" where the real differences occur.

To be sure, the evidence of a Semitic original for "Bel and the Snake" is primarily internal in nature,[1] there being only one medieval manuscript which *may* be a descendant of the ancient Semitic text, namely, an Aramaic text of The Snake (but not of Bel), which Jerahmeel incorporated into his chronicles *in addition to* Josippon's Hebrew translation of "Bel and the Snake."[2]

While the case for a Semitic original for "Bel and the Snake" is certainly not as strong as the case for "Susanna" (see pp. 181-183), nonetheless a good case can be built for it.[3] For one thing, in "Bel and the Snake" there

[1] As noted in the Introduction to Daniel (p. 24), the story occurs in none of the Dead Sea scroll copies of Daniel; nor is it paraphrased or alluded to by Josephus. Moreover, both Origen (185?-?254) and Jerome (340?-420) expressly stated that no Hebrew text of it existed in their own day.

[2] This Aramaic text, together with its translation and detailed comparison with the LXX and ☉, is in M. Gaster, *PSBA* 16 (1894), 280-290, 312-317; and 17 (1895), 75-94, respectively. It is highly debatable, however, whether Gaster successfully proved that the Aramaic text was not a translation of ☉. For instance, since Gaster's Aramaic text shares certain readings found elsewhere only in the Vulgate (e.g. "and behold" [vs. 23], "what you worship" [vs. 27], and "from the den of lions" [vs. 42]), Gaster's Aramaic text may, like "Susanna's" Hebrew text (see p. 82, n. 6), be nothing more than a translation of the Vulgate.

[3] Late eighteenth- and nineteenth-century scholars would have denied this, E. C. Bissell representing the last yet strongest statement of their position: "But there are absolutely no traces in the extant text of the LXX of its being a translation" (p. 447).

are those obvious Hebraisms, such as *kai egeneto* (cf. vss. 14,18, and 28 of ⊙; vss. 15 and 33 of the LXX), the predominance of verses beginning with *kai* plus a verb in the past tense (so twenty-eight of the forty-two verses in ⊙), a very "un-Greek" preference for *kai* (used eight times each, for example, in vss. 14[⊙] and 27) and used with all the shades of meaning as the Heb. *wa,* "and" (see NOTE on vs. 26), and awkward "Greek" expressions (cf. NOTES on "at all" in vs. 18, and on "in a gust of wind" in vs. 36). Finally, words like *pissa,* "pitch," and *trix,* "hair," may ultimately represent corruptions in an Aramaic stage of our stories (see NOTE on "pitch, fat, and hair" in vs. 27).[4]

Two other points should be noted. Both Greek versions of "Bel and the Snake" are so utterly simple in their literary style that it is highly likely that they are translations of Semitic *Vorlage* rather than original Greek compositions, the latter tending to have a more involved and rhetorical character. Finally, since by scholarly consensus there is no discernible difference in the Greek of the deuterocanonical as over against the canonical portions of Daniel, then, unless the Greek translator of Daniel composed the Additions himself (which is highly unlikely), he must have rendered them from his Aramaic or Hebrew text. But just as it is highly problematical what the original language of the Book of Daniel was— whether it was totally in Hebrew, Aramaic or, as now, in some combination of the two—so it is problematical whether "Bel and the Snake" was originally all in Hebrew (so Brüll, Davies, Oesterley, and Torrey), Aramaic (Gaster, Ball, Marshall, Toy, Daubney, and Zimmermann), or the LXX was based upon one Semitic language, and ⊙ upon the other. (Interestingly enough, many scholars discuss the problem in some detail without ever indicating what they themselves have concluded.)

Given the greater number of Hebraisms in ⊙, the most logical hypothesis is that the stories in their earliest and independent form were in Aramaic, the language of both Palestine and Babylon in the Persian period (see below), and that ⊙ was based upon a Hebrew translation of the Aramaic. Such a possibility has been considerably strengthened by the fact that at the Dead Sea community at Qumran there was discovered in Cave IV three heretofore unknown narratives, *in Aramaic,* featuring a Daniel who is relating Jewish history to a king.[5]

---

[4] For still other Hebraisms, see NOTES *passim;* longer lists of Hebraisms may conveniently be found in Davies (pp. 655-656) and Daubney (pp. 204-209); but the latter's list must be used with caution since not all his examples are equally valid. For a list of Aramaisms, some of them rather far-fetched, see Marshall, *HDB,* I, 268.

[5] These three texts have been designated tentatively as Pseudo-Daniel *a, b,* and *c.*

Origin of the Stories

Raising the question here of where the tales of Bel and the Snake originated is really asking the prior question of where the stories in Daniel 1-6 originated, for the stories in Daniel 14 are typologically identical with those in Daniel 1-6. In both groups of narratives the following holds true: (1) the hero is, with only one exception, Daniel; and he is always introduced in the third person (the visions [chs. 7-12], however, are told in the first person); (2) the most important personage and the one with whom the hero must deal in each story is the then-reigning king; (3) the hero, by virtue of remaining true to the demands of his religion, always finds himself in a degrading or dangerous situation; (4) the hero's faithfulness is always rewarded by his being vindicated by his God, who thereby proves his mighty power and faithfulness to those who trust in him; (5) the enemies of the hero always get their just deserts; and (6) at the end of each story the king acknowledges, in effect, that the God of the hero is the mightiest, the God of gods.

While scholars generally date the compilation of the Book of Daniel itself to ca. 167-163 B.C., they usually date the stories themselves to the third century B.C., regarding them as being originally separate and independent tales circulating in the Persian period.[6]

And what is true of the stories in Daniel 1-6 seems to be true also of "Bel and the Snake." It is evident that the Bel narrative was originally separate and independent of what now precedes it (whether what preceded it was Daniel 12, as in ☉; or "Susanna," as in the LXX and Vulgate) because in vs. 2 of the LXX its ancient author felt it necessary to introduce Daniel formally and fully to his readers, i.e. it was as if his readers had no previous knowledge of who Daniel was (nor is it at all certain that the Daniel initially mentioned in the Snake narrative was *the* Daniel [see NOTE on "more honored than all his friends" in vs. 2]). As for "Bel and the Snake" consisting of two separate entities at an earlier time, all that connects the two stories now, apart from their being converse to one another in theme, is that in the Snake narrative in vs. 23 of the LXX we have the phrase "in that place," referring to Babylon, and in vs. 28 a passing allusion to the Bel incident.

Even the Snake narrative itself seems to be a composite of several originally separate tales, namely: (1) the destruction of the Snake (vss. 23-28); (2) Daniel's seven-day stay in the Lions' Pit (vss. 29-32,40-42), which is reminiscent of the earlier story of Daniel in the lions' den in

---

[6] For excellent but brief introductions to the many puzzling problems of the Book of Daniel, see Eissfeldt, pp. 512-529; and R. H. Pfeiffer, *Introduction to the Old Testament,* rev. ed. (New York: Harper, 1948), pp. 748-781.

Daniel 6 (see COMMENT II, pp. 147-149); and (3) the Habakkuk episode (vss. 33-39), which virtually all scholars regard as being a later addition (see below). In passing, one should note that for the Bel narrative as
well as for the three "mini" tales of the Snake narrative there is evidence
of their having been at one time in Aramaic or Hebrew (see NOTES *passim*), just like the stories in Daniel 1-6.

While "Bel and the Snake," like the stories in Daniel 1-6, also purports
to be factual, very few scholars today would say that these two stories are
literally true as they stand currently—which is not to deny that there may
be a kernel of truth in them. They do have, however, certain historical
improbabilities, if not impossibilities, about them. For example, according
to vs. 22, Daniel himself was responsible for the destruction of Bel and his
temple, whereas, Herodotus, Strabo, and Arrian (respectively fifth century
B.C., 63 B.C.?-?A.D. 24, and the second century A.D.) all agree that the
Persian king Xerxes I bears responsibility for that awesome act (see NOTE
on "destroyed the idol and its temple" in vs. 22). Contrary to vs. 1 of ☉,
Cyrus of Persia did not succeed Astyages (see NOTE ON "succeeded him"
in vs. 1); and as for Cyrus and the prophet Habakkuk being contem-
poraries, that too poses problems (see NOTE on vs. 33). It is believable
that, just as an Ebedmelech kept a Jeremiah from perishing in a cistern
(cf. Jeremiah 38), so a Habakkuk could have played some role in keeping
a Daniel from being devoured by lions; but scholars today find it hard to
believe that Habakkuk had a one-day, round-trip visit from Judea to
Babylon, via an angel carrying him by the hair of his head. Evidently Saint
Jerome did not believe the story either; for in his *Preface to Daniel* he referred to the stories in "Bel and the Snake" as fables.

Once scholars no longer viewed "Bel and the Snake" as historical fact,
then new theories sprang up as to the origin of these tales. One of the
earliest modern theories,[7] and still by far the most probable explanation, is
that these tales are pure Jewish fiction, being popular or priestly anecdotes
of haggadah inspired by several verses in one chapter of Jeremiah:

> Jer 51:34-35 "Nebuchadrezzar the king of Babylon has devoured
> me, he has crushed me; he has made me an empty ves-
> sel, he has swallowed me like a monster; he has filled
> his belly with my delicacies, he has rinsed me out. The
> violence done to me and to my kinsmen be upon Baby-
> lon," let the inhabitants of Zion say. "My blood be
> upon the inhabitants of Chaldea," let Jerusalem say.
>
> vs. 44 And I [i.e. God] will punish Bel in Babylon, and take
> out of his mouth what he has swallowed. The nations
> shall no longer flow to him; the wall of Babylon has
> fallen.

---

[7] The theory was first advanced by Brüll (*JJGL* 8 [1887], 28) and Ball (p. 346).

Between the verses above in Jeremiah 51 and "Bel and the Snake" there are, admittedly, no extant texts illustrating any intermediate stage in the evolution of our two narratives; but the *process* of midrashic elaboration and embellishment is clearly seen in what has subsequently happened to "Bel and the Snake." To take just one phrase as an example (admittedly a very important one), consider what later Jewish interpreters did with a simple detail of fact in vs. 27, namely, that Daniel killed the snake with a concoction of "pitch, fat, and hair": Daniel's concoction concealed pointed nails (*B'reshith Rabbah*); iron combs with very sharp tines (*Josephus ben Gorion*); or iron hatchets (*Chronicles of Jerahmeel*); and according to *Jerusalem Nedarim 37d,* the snake was fed stuffed camel skins, which concealed hot coals! Midrashic elaboration of biblical and non-canonical texts is an indisputable fact (for the same process working in "Susanna," see pp. 85-86);[8] and it is certainly valid to assume that that same process created some of our biblical books, including "Bel and the Snake."

A second theory, and one which had much greater popularity in the early part of this century than now,[9] is that "Bel and the Snake" represents a "judaized" version, or faint demythicized echo, of the most exciting incident in the famous *Enuma Elish,* or Babylonian New Year Creation Epic, namely, the titanic battle between Marduk, the tutelary god of Babylon, and Tiamat, the primordial goddess of salt water:

"Stand thou [Tiamat] up, that I [Marduk] and thou meet in
single combat!"
When Tiamat heard this,
She was like one possessed; she took leave of her senses.
In fury Tiamat cried out aloud.
To the roots her legs shook both together.
She recites a charm, keeps casting her spell,
While the gods of battle sharpen their weapons.
They joined issue Tiamat and Marduk, wisest of gods.
They strove in single combat, locked in battle.
The lord spread out his net to enfold her,
The Evil Wind, which followed behind, he let loose in her face.
When Tiamat opened her mouth to consume him,
He drove in the Evil Wind that she close not her lips.
As the fierce winds charged her belly,
Her body was distended and her mouth was wide open.

---

[8] For stories of Bel and the Snake in later Jewish literature, see also Louis Ginzberg, *Legends of the Jews*, V, VI, *passim.*

[9] The strongest proponent of the theory was Hermann Gunkel (*Schöpfung und Chaos in Urzeit und Endzeit* [Göttingen, 1895], pp. 320-323), whose views were accepted with varying degrees of conviction by Ball (p. 346), Marshall (*HDB*, I, 267), Toy (*The Jewish Encyclopaedia*, II, 650), and others.

He released the arrow, it tore her belly,
It cut through her insides, splitting the heart.
Having thus subdued her, he extinguished her life.
He cast down her carcass to stand upon it.
After he had slain Tiamat, the leader,
Her band was shattered, her troupe broken up;

. . . .

He made them captives and he smashed their weapons
                    ANET², p. 67, lines 86-106, 111

There can be little doubt, of course, that ancient Jews were familiar with this cosmogonic myth or a Syro-Palestinian version of it, because in the Old Testament itself there are clear echoes of a primordial struggle between God and a draconic monster called by many names, including Rahab (Job 9:13, 26:12; Ps 89:10), Leviathan (Ps 74:14; Isa 27:1), and Yam (Job 7:12). For an ancient pictorial representation of an Assyrian god, armed with sword and lightning fork, fighting a winged monster, see Plate 2. Moreover, the din of the battle between Marduk and Tiamat *may* be ever so faintly heard in the ingredients which Daniel concocted and fed to the snake (see NOTE on "pitch, fat, and hair" in vs. 27).

Nonetheless, critics of the theory that "Bel and the Snake" is a judaized version of the Marduk-Tiamat confrontation have been quick to point out that Tiamat was envisioned by the Babylonians as a female dragon, not a snake (for details, see Davies, pp. 653-654). Moreover, the critics have insisted, and rightly so, that there is no evidence of the Babylonians worshiping *living* snakes. To be sure, Simon Landersdorfer,[10] was able to establish from his study of Mesopotamian stelae, reliefs, and seals that snake worship was a part of the Neo-Babylonian religion, and that a snake cult did exist at the Temple of Der; but though he thought it quite probable that living snakes were also worshiped there, he conceded that he could offer no proof of it.

Recently, a new theory has been advanced by Wolfgang M. W. Roth (*CBQ* 37 [1975], 21-47, esp. pp. 42-43), who argues that the oral and literary genre known as the "idol parody," which was created by Babylonian Jews in the exilic period, indirectly underwent a historicization in "Bel and the Snake." As "a Daniel confrontation it [i.e. 'Bel and the Snake'] sought to ground the rejection of idol worship, typically formulated in the inherited parodies, in the historical act of a well known hero of the faith in the period . . . in which it [the idol parody] appeared as a recognizable oral genre" (p. 43). According to Roth, "Bel and the Snake" was written to counteract the appeal of idolatry and, especially, zoolatry (cf. Wisd 15:18-19; Letter of Aristeas 138) to Egyptian Jews of the first century

---

[10] "Der Drache von Babylon," *BZ* 11 (1913), 1-4.

B.C.[11] The principal weakness of Roth's theory is that it assumes that "Bel and the Snake" was originally a Greek composition rather than a translation from Aramaic or Hebrew.

A few words should be said about the origins of the third story in "Bel and the Snake," namely, the Habakkuk episode in vss. 33-39. Regardless of whether or not the Habakkuk mentioned in the earliest form of the story was *the* Habakkuk (see NOTE on vs. 33), in ⊖ he is clearly the famous prophet of that name. The episode had a Semitic *Vorlage,* as evidenced by the LXX's use of *kai egeneto* (vs. 33) and the presence of the phrase "in a gust of wind" (see NOTE on vs. 36). That this episode is secondary, i.e. that it was added later to "Bel and the Snake," is clear from two different lines of evidence: (1) there is far greater verbatim agreement between the LXX and ⊖ in the Habakkuk episode than there is between the LXX and ⊖ in vss. 23-32 or 40-42; (2) whereas, from the point of view of literary-form analysis, vss. 23-27 and 28-32 have identical and detailed schematic agreement with one another, vss. 33-39 evidence irregularities and variations in that schematic pattern (see COMMENT I, p. 147). Exactly where and when this episode was added is impossible to say with any precision; but assuming a Semitic original, we would suggest Babylon or, more likely, Palestine as its place of origin. Jewish tradition is filled with stories about Habakkuk; for examples, see Louis Ginzberg, *Legends of the Jews,* IV, 278, 348; VI, 55, 57, 314, 346, 373, 387, and 432.

Canonicity

If "Bel and the Snake" was originally in either Aramaic or Hebrew and was at one time a part of what is now called the Book of Daniel, then why is it not part of the Jewish canon as established by the Council of Jamnia ca. A.D. 90? There is no certain answer to that question. Of course, if "Bel and the Snake" was a Greek composition, as used to be thought by most scholars and is still so regarded by a few, then the answer is obvious: it never was part of the Palestinian canon. A somewhat more likely explanation is that "Bel and the Snake" was composed, or, better, was added to the Book of Daniel, after the Council of Jamnia. The weakness of that theory is that there is no perceptible difference in the Greek of canonical Daniel and any of its Additions (see pp. 29), and it is generally assumed that the Greek translation of Daniel was made no later than the very beginning of the first century B.C.

---

[11] By then Egypt had had a long history of snake worship; Apophis, the wicked enemy of Re, was depicted as a snake, as was Buto, the snake goddess of Lower Egypt.

The most probable answer to the question is that "Bel and the Snake," coming where it does now (either after Daniel 12, as in ⊙; or after "Susanna," as in the LXX and Vulgate), was a later yet pre-Jamnia addition to the Palestinian version of Daniel, and that the Council of Jamnia either preferred an older and more venerated text of the Book of Daniel, one without "Bel and the Snake," or it could literally see that "Bel and the Snake" was an addition, i.e. the visions (chs. 7-12) were mostly in Hebrew (so 8:1 - 12:13) while "Bel and the Snake" might have been in Aramaic.

Why would anyone have wanted to add "Bel and the Snake" to the vision section of Daniel? Taking a clue from Cyrus H. Gordon,[12] who suggested that the language sequence of Hebrew-Aramaic-Hebrew in canonical Daniel represents a conscious effort by its ancient author to follow a long-established literary convention, namely, the ABA scheme,[13] we suggest that a later Palestinian author may have tried to "improve" on Daniel by duplicating the ABA pattern *in terms of literary genre*, i.e. by his adding "Bel and the Snake" (possibly preceding them with "Susanna") to the canonical Daniel, he had the prologue and epilogue consisting of stories and the middle part of visions.

In any event, in the West "Bel and the Snake" was canonical among Alexandrian Jews and then among the Christians. The Church Fathers did not, however, mention "Bel and the Snake" by name in their lists of canonical books, it being regarded simply as part of Daniel. That it was canonical, nonetheless, is clear from its being quoted as scripture by Irenaeus of Lyons (140-?202) in his *contra Haereses* IV 5, 2 and IV 26, 3; Clement of Alexandria (d. before 215) in *Stromata* I 21; Tertullian of Carthage (160?-220) in *de idololatria* xviii; Cyprian of Carthage (d. 258) in *ad Fortunatum* ii, and by others.[14] It was always the text of ⊙ that was used, never the LXX.

Religious Ideas of "Bel and the Snake"

However, "Bel and the Snake" was by no means referred to as often by the Church Fathers as the other Additions to Daniel. "Bel and the Snake" was evidently either somewhat irrelevant for the purposes of the Fathers

---

[12] *Introduction to Old Testament Times* (Ventnor, N.J.: Ventnor Press, 1953), pp. 72f.

[13] The ABA pattern is found, for instance, in the Code of Hammurapi (1728-1686 B.C.), where the prologue and epilogue are written in a semipoetic style while the body of the code, i.e. the laws themselves, is prose. The Hebrew Book of Job also has the ABA scheme, except that the prologue and epilogue are prose (chs. 1-2, 42:7-17), and the dialogues, or debate, are poetry.

[14] For the most exhaustive list of citations of "Bel and the Snake" by the Church Fathers, see Caspar Julius, *BSt* 6 (1903), 1-183.

(after all, Bel was essentially a detective story, celebrating the cleverness of Daniel, while the snake story was repetitious of Daniel 6 and yet not nearly as dramatic or well told) or, more likely, the Church Fathers found the two stories somewhat lacking in religious or literary value.

Nor have modern commentators been wildly enthusiastic about "Bel and the Snake," as exemplified by the judgments of Pfeiffer ("Jewish fiction of little literary and no religious significance" [p. 456]) and Metzger ("the motifs of these yarns, grotesque and preposterous as they appear to us today" [p. 119]). While the views of both these scholars may be unduly harsh, it cannot be denied that once the two stories in "Bel and the Snake" are no longer regarded as literally true, then they lose their raison d'être, which was to mock idolatry, first by having Daniel himself destroy mighty Bel and the large snake and, secondly, by having God protect Daniel from his enemies who, trusting in false gods as they did, ultimately perished.

The religious ideas of the Bel narrative are confined to two affirmations by Daniel, the one about God and the other about Bel: "I do not revere man-made idols, but the living God who created the heavens and the earth and has authority over all mankind" (vs. 5), and "for it [Bel] is just clay on the inside, and bronze outside. He has never eaten or drunk anything!" (vs. 7). These expressions of Daniel's monotheistic faith were not just pious sentiments, for he was willing to wager his life on them. And the same religious ideas were expressed by Daniel in the Snake narrative: "I will worship the Lord my God, for he is a living God. But with your permission, Your Majesty, I will kill the snake without sword or stick" (vss. 25b-26). The Snake narrative, however, does have two additional features: (1) the king himself ended up acknowledging that God alone exists ("You are great, Lord God of Daniel, there is no other beside you" [vs. 41]); and (2) God vindicated Daniel's confidence in him by saving him in the Lions' Pit.

Nonetheless, "Bel and the Snake" is clearly lacking something, namely, any mention, apart from the intrusive Habakkuk episode, of distinctive Jewish beliefs and practices. In fact, not until five verses from the end of the second story is it even said that Daniel prayed to God (vs. 38)—and by then he had already been in the Lions' Pit for six days! Certainly, without the Habakkuk incident, Daniel rather than God is glorified.

Purpose of "Bel and the Snake"

Its primary purpose was, unquestionably, to ridicule paganism. The only question is: Before whose eyes? Was the intended audience Gentiles living in Babylon or elsewhere? Or, Jews of the Eastern or Western Diaspora, or possibly for Jews in Palestine itself? For a variety of reasons scholars have never advocated strongly that the intended audience was Gentile. But since zoolatry was, undeniably, a real temptation for some Jews living in Egypt (cf. Wisd 15:18-19; Letter of Aristeas 138), whereas, there is no evidence of a snake cult centering around a live snake in Babylon (see p. 124), scholars as far removed from one another as Fritzsche and Roth (*CBQ* 37 [1975], 42-43) have argued for an Egyptian Jewish audience. On the other hand, scholars who believe that Bel and the Snake narratives had Semitic originals look for the intended audience among Jews living in Babylon or Palestine.

Place and Date of Composition

A distinction must be made between the date of the Bel and the Snake narratives, the date when they assumed their "final" form as "Bel and the Snake," and their translation into Greek. The *terminus a quo* for the Bel and the Snake narratives is either the same as that for the stories in canonical Daniel, i.e. the third century B.C., or, quite possibly, somewhat later. In any event, there is nothing in the two narratives to preclude their having originated as haggadic elaborations of Jer 51:34-35,44 some time during the Persian period. (Certainly there is nothing distinctively Greek about the narratives themselves.)

Inasmuch as "Bel and the Snake" was not part of canonical Daniel as determined by the Council of Jamnia, it is quite likely that the two narratives assumed their "present" form and were added to the Semitic text of Daniel several decades after 163 B.C., that year being the approximate date of canonical Daniel. Certainly the reign of the Seleucid king Antiochus VII, Sidetes (138-129 B.C.), who in 135 invaded Judea and razed a portion of the walls of the Holy City and generally gave the Jewish believers a difficult time, would have provided an appropriate *Sitz im Leben* for "Bel and the Snake." The *terminus ad quem* for "Bel and the Snake" is the late second or early first century B.C., that being the date for the Greek translation of Daniel.[15]

As for the place where "Bel and the Snake" was composed, in the past each major area of Jewish settlement has had its advocates: Babylon (Bissell, Oesterley), Egypt (Fritzsche), and Palestine (Brüll, Davies). Given the recent discoveries of Pseudo-Daniel at Qumran, a late second- or early first-century B.C. Palestinian provenance for "Bel and the Snake" is far more tempting and likely than ever before.

---

[15] That the Alexandrian translator of I Maccabees used the LXX of Daniel is clear from a comparison of I Macc 1:54 with Dan 11:31 and 12:11 of the LXX; see also I Macc 2:59-60 of the LXX.

Ancient Versions

LXX and ⊙

In "Bel and the Snake" the ⊙ differs from the LXX in both style and content (see NOTES *passim*), occupying in this regard a middle position with respect to the other Additions to Daniel, i.e. the two Greek versions agree with one another more in "Bel and the Snake" than in "Susanna," and less than in "The Prayer of Azariah and the Hymn of the Three Young Men."[16] The LXX of "Bel and the Snake" is the better Greek translation in that it usually avoids clumsy Semiticisms, while ⊙ abounds in them (see Introduction, pp. 33*f*). As noted earlier, these two Greek versions are separate translations of two different Semitic texts which may not have been in the same Semitic language.

Other Versions

With the exception of the Syro-Hexaplar which slavishly follows the LXX,[17] all the ancient versions were based upon ⊙. Although the versions are very literalistic in their rendering of ⊙, when they do depart from it, it is usually to substitute the personal name or proper name for ⊙'s personal or possessive pronoun (see textual notes *passim*). So literalistic are the versions that the most "expansive" is the Peshitta (Syriac), with its additions in vss. 6 ("Bel is alive"), 14 ("and with Daniel's signet"), and 16 ("and they went there"). The Vulgate, which follows ⊙ very closely, does append to vs. 42 a doxology like that in Dan 6:26-27 (see textual note *ⁿ*). The OL, which consists only of fragments, the Ethiopic, and Bohairic add virtually nothing to our understanding of ⊙. The Arabic version is very literal and quite late (ninth century).

---

[16] This fact was first established by Bludau and has been reaffirmed recently by the very specialized studies of Schmitt (p. 101) and Schüpphaus (*ZAW* 83 [1971], 50).

[17] The only substantive departure of the SyrH. from the LXX is in vs. 3, where the SyrH. has, with ⊙, forty sheep (not four) and wine (not oil).

VII. BEL: A "LIVING" GOD WHO COULD NOT EAT

(Vss. 1-22 [ch. 13 in ⊕; ch. 14 in LXX and Vulgate])

1 When King Astyages was gathered to his ancestors, Cyrus of Persia succeeded him. 2 Daniel was a confidant of the king and more honored than all his[a] friends. 3 Now the Babylonians had an idol called Bel, and every day they provided him with twelve bushels of the finest flour, forty[b] sheep, and fifty-some gallons of wine. 4 The king revered him and every day would go and worship him, but Daniel would worship his own God. 5 So the king said to him, "Why do you not worship Bel?"

"Because," he[c] answered, "I do not revere man-made idols, but the living God who created the heavens and the earth and has authority over all mankind."

6 "You don't think," said the king to him, "that Bel is a living god? Don't you see how much he eats and drinks every day?"

7 Then Daniel chuckled. "Don't be misled, Your Majesty," he said, "for it is just clay on the inside, and bronze outside. He has never eaten or drunk anything!"

8 Incensed, the king summoned Bel's[d] priests and said to them, "If you cannot tell me who is eating these provisions, you shall die! 9 If you can prove that Bel eats these things, then Daniel shall die, because he has blasphemed Bel!"

10 Now there were seventy priests of Bel, not including their wives and children. The king went with Daniel into the temple of Bel. 11 "Look, we'll step outside," said the priests of Bel, "but you, Your

[a] Syriac "the king's"; see NOTE.
[b] "Four" in LXX and Bohairic.
[c] "Daniel" in LXX and most versions.
[d] So Syriac and Ethiopic; ⊕ has "his."

Majesty, set the food out and mix the wine and leave it; then shut the door and seal it with your signet. 12 *e*And when you come back in the morning if you do not find everything has been eaten by Bel, then let us be put to death; otherwise, Daniel, who slanders us." 13 (They were unconcerned because they had made under the table a secret entrance through which they would regularly enter and get it all.) 14 So when these had gone, the king set out the food for Bel. And Daniel ordered his servants to bring ashes, and in just the king's presence they scattered them throughout the whole temple. After going outside, they shut the door, sealed it with the king's signet*f*, and left. 15 During the night the priests came as usual, with their wives and children, and ate and drank up everything.

16 *g*The king got up early the next morning, and Daniel with him.*h*

17 "Daniel," said *i*the king*i*, "are the seals intact?"

"Intact, Your Majesty," he replied.

18 As soon as he had opened the doors, the king spied the table and cried aloud, "You are great, Bel! There's no deception in you at all!"

19 Then Daniel chuckled, and holding the king back from going in, he said, "Look at the floor and observe whose footprints these are!"

20 "I see," said the king, "the footprints of men, women, and children!"

21 Infuriated, the king arrested the priests and their wives and children; and they showed him the hidden doors through which they would enter and consume the stuff on the table. 22 So the king put them to death and handed the Bel over to Daniel, who destroyed *j*the idol*j* and its temple*k*.

---

e Verses 12-13 not in LXX.
f Syriac adds "and with Daniel's signet"; cf. Dan 6:17.
g Verses 16-17 not in LXX.
h Syriac adds "and they went there."
i-i Only ⊕B and Armenian have "he."
j-j Greek "him."
k Gr. *ieron;* some Greek MSS (and Bohairic and Syriac) have *naon;* see NOTE.

NOTES

1. *King Astyages.* Mandane, the daughter of this Median king, married Cambyses I of Persia and had Cyrus by him (Herodotus I 107).

Cyrus of Persia. I.e. Cyrus the Great (550-530 B.C.), the founder of the Achaemenian dynasty and the Persian empire. Cyrus is mentioned also in Dan 1:21 and 10:1. In the Bible, Cyrus is remembered as the one who conquered

Babylon in 539 B.C., and then issued the Edict of 538 B.C., which allowed the Jews to return to Jerusalem to rebuild their temple. For details on Cyrus, see A. T. Olmstead, *HPE*, 34-58; and M. J. Dresden, *IDB*, I, s.v. "Cyrus."

succeeded him. Literally "received [Gr. *parelabe*] his kingdom." Actually, Cyrus did not inherit his grandfather's kingdom: he had to take it from Astyages by force (so Herodotus I 130), although some ancient historians maintained, probably erroneously, that Cyrus took it from a successor of Astyages (see Ball, p. 351). In any case, F. Zimmermann (*VT* 8 [1958], 440) is probably correct in regarding the verb *parelabe* as an Aramaism, the same Greek verb being used by Θ in Dan 6:1 and 7:18 to translate the Aram. *qabbēl*, "succeeded."

The LXX has a Superscription while Θ does not (but see the addition to Sus 64 in the Vulgate): "From the prophecy of Habakkuk son of Joshua of the tribe of Levi." Presumably the Habakkuk mentioned in the Superscription and in vss. 33-39 of the Greek is the same as the minor prophet who had a canonical book named after him, although as long ago as Epiphanius (315-403) this identification has been questioned. The reasons for uncertainty in this matter are threefold: we know neither the name nor the tribe of the canonical Habakkuk; nor are we sure of his date, although a very late pre-exilic date seems most likely. (I Esd 5:58 does mention a post-exilic Levite named Joshua who had several sons, but unfortunately, their names are not given.) We should understand from this Superscription, not that Habakkuk wrote the Bel and Dragon narratives, but that it came from a book about Habakkuk (so A. Bludau, *BSt* 2 [1897], 191-192).

2. *Daniel.* This name, meaning "God has judged," was given to many Jews, including a son of David (I Chron 3:1), a post-exilic priest (Ezra 8:2; Neh 10:6), and Enoch's father-in-law (Jub 4:20). A most ancient Canaanite name, going back at least to the days of Ugarit (1550-1350 B.C.), when a king Dnil figured in the Aqht Legend (see *ANET²*, 149-152), Daniel was a most illustrious name, symbolic of righteousness and wisdom (cf. Ezek 14:14, 28:3). By the intertestamental period, in some quarters at least, just as the once-human Enoch had become an angel (cf. III Enoch 4:2), so had the Wisdom-figure of Daniel, albeit a fallen angel (cf. Enoch 6:7, 69:2).

a confidant [sumbiōtēs] of the king. Literally "one who lives with the king." With the exception of vs. 1 of Θ, the name of the king is nowhere mentioned in the entire chapter; according to the Book of Daniel, the prophet Daniel was held in high esteem by both Nebuchadnezzar (1:20) and Darius (6:3).

In any event, Daniel's relationship to the king was so close that Daniel could presume to chuckle at the king (vss. 7 and 19), and even lay a restraining hand on him (vs. 19), all of which suggests a relationship that was the product of time and intimacy. Thus, the Bel narrative properly comes at the end of the Book of Daniel, i.e. at the end of a long career characterized by confidence in God and success against his enemies.

more honored than [endoxos uper] all his friends. The antecedent of "his" is evidently Daniel. However, the NEB, perhaps taking its clue from the Syriac, understood "his" to refer to the king and so rendered the phrase "the most honoured of all the King's Friends," thereby making Daniel a member of some special group or established council.

The corresponding verse in the LXX is different and is riddled with problems: "There was a certain man, a priest called Daniel son of Abal, who was a confidant of the king of Babylonia." Scholars ancient and modern, including Epiphanius and Bissell, doubt that the Daniel mentioned originally in the Bel narrative is to be identified with the prophet Daniel. They rightly pointed out that whereas the Daniel in the Theodotion version of Bel is obviously well known to his readers, here in vs. 2 of the LXX the man Daniel had to be formally and fully introduced to the readers, i.e. it was as if the readers were not already familiar with him! This "superfluous" introduction to the hero suggests, at the very least, that the Semitic *Vorlage* of Bel (and the Snake) was originally independent of the canonical Daniel.

Doubts as to whether the Daniel of the Bel narrative should have been identified with the canonical Daniel are based, primarily, upon the fact that the biblical Daniel was a prophet of the tribe of Judah (so Dan 1:6), not a priest of Levi; moreover, there actually was a post-exilic priest named Daniel (Ezra 8:2; Neh 10:6). Unfortunately, we do not know the name of Daniel's father. The Book of Daniel does not mention it; and later traditions are contradictory: Jerome (*Preface to Daniel*) said Daniel's father was Abda, while Epiphanius (*Adversus Haereses* 55,3) said it was Sabaan (=*šy'yn* or *šm'yn*). Nor are modern scholars in any more agreement over the name of Daniel's father in the Bel narrative: Is it Abal (=*Hebel*, so Rothstein and Swete), *Abiēl* (=Heb. *'by'l*, so Fritzsche and Ball), or *Habal* (so Plöger)?

Readily conceding that the prophet Daniel was not a priest, A. Bludau, (*BSt* 2 [1897], 192) argued that in the Bel narrative the Gr. *iereus*, "priest," represents a mistranslation of the Heb. *kōhēn*, which, while usually meaning "priest," can also designate a high secular official, as in II Sam 8:18. Regardless of whom the Semitic *Vorlage* of the LXX may have had in mind originally, it is clear that ⊖ would now have us understand that the Daniel of the Bel narrative and the Daniel of the canonical book were one and the same.

3. *an idol* [*eidōlon*]. Except for vs. 7 where the idol is said to consist of clay, covered with bronze, nowhere in the story do we have a description of it, either of its size or "decorations," whether it was overlaid or cast. Possibly, the author of the tale did not know such "vital" facts; but, more likely, not wanting to shift his reader's interest from Daniel to Bel even for a minute, he chose to say nothing. Presumably Herodotus was speaking of this same idol when he wrote: "In the time of Cyrus there was likewise in this temple the figure of a man, eighteen feet high, *entirely of solid gold* [italics added]. I myself did not see this figure. . . . Xerxes, however, the son of Darius, killed the priest who had forbidden him to move the statue, and took it away" (ɪ 183). On the various idols mentioned in the Old Testament and the various Hebrew words for idols, see J. Gray, *IDB*, II, 673-675.

Bel [*bēl*]. Bel (Akk. *belu*, "He who rules") was the title of the great tutelary god of Babylon, Marduk, or Merodach as the Jews called him (Jer 50:2). Scathingly ridiculed in Isa 46:1-2, Marduk was, since the days of Hammurapi (1728-1686 B.C.), regarded by the Babylonians as the creator of the universe, having fashioned heaven and earth out of the defeated goddess Tiamat, and mankind out of her slain consort Kingu (for details on *Enuma Elish*, or the Babylonian Epic of Creation, see *ANET*², 60-72). Clearly, Daniel had chosen to insult no minor deity!

twelve bushels. Literally "twelve *artabas*." The *artabē*, a Persian dry measure (cf. Herodotus I 192), was used in Isa 5:10 to translate the Heb. *homer,* the latter being ca. 134 liters.

fifty-some gallons. Literally "six *metrētai.*" The *metrētēs,* a common Athenian liquid measure, was equivalent to about nine gallons. In the Greek Old Testament, *metrētēs* was used to render the Heb. *sᵉ'āh* (I Kings 18:32) as well as the Heb. *bath* (II Chron 4:5), these two Hebrew measures being of very different capacities.

Although the present-day American can, after some head-scratching and "higher math," compute with precision the exact relation of miles to kilometers, yards to meters, quarts to liters, or Fahrenheit to Centigrade, biblical scholars are confronted by far greater difficulties in trying to establish the precise weights and measures of capacity, length, and areas of the Hebrews, not to mention those of other ancient Near Eastern peoples (for details, see O. R. Sellers, "Weights and Measures," *IDB,* IV, 828-839).

If the modern American equivalents in the translation are even the roughest approximations of the actual measures which the *artabē* and *metrētēs* represented, then for our purposes they suffice; for all the ancient author of the Bel narrative was trying to convey was an impression of the great quantity and quality of food supplied Bel every day. That being the case, the ancient author might not have totally disapproved of the inflated portions given in the Bel narrative of Jerahmeel: "The daily order of the offerings consisted of 1 bullock, 10 rams, 10 sheep, 100 doves, 70 loaves of bread, and 10 barrels of wine, for the table of the god" (Gaster, *Chronicles of Jerahmeel,* 200).

That the Babylonians really did lavish great quantities and varieties of food on their god Bel is well illustrated by the Philipps Cylinder of Nebuchadnezzar: "When Marduk, mighty lord, to the lordship of the land raised me. . . . To Marduk . . . I bowed the neck; his rich oblation, his splendid freewill offerings, above the former amount I increased. For one day an ox . . . fish, fowl, spices . . . honey, curd, milk, the best of oil, sweet wine, wine of Izallam, of Tuimmu, of Cimmini . . . like the waters of a river, numberless, in the chalices of Marduk . . . I made to abound" (1 R. 65, col. 1,8). Clearly, Bel had a well-balanced diet! But brief though the list of offerings is, in our Bel story it does nonetheless include, from a Jewish point of view, the three basic kinds of offerings: cereal, meat, and libation. For an overview of this very broad and complicated subject, see T. H. Gaster, "Sacrifices and Offerings, OT," *IDB,* IV, 147-159.

The corresponding verse in the LXX is not too different: "Now there was an idol, Bel, which the Babylonians worshiped. Every day they lavished on him twelve bushels of the finest flour, four sheep, and fifty-some gallons of oil." Interestingly enough, the SyrH., instead of agreeing as it usually does with the LXX, agrees with ⊚ by having *forty* sheep, and *wine* instead of oil. Inasmuch as oil is nowhere else mentioned in the story while wine is later mentioned by ⊚ (vss. 10,11) *and* the LXX (vss. 11,15,21), in the original Bel narrative wine was probably used also in this verse. After all, tasty though oil is on a salad, who would want to drink gallons of it!

4. *revered him and . . . would . . . worship.* Whether or not our story of Bel is true, it is a historical fact that Cyrus of Persia did worship, at least outwardly, the Babylonian Marduk, as he himself tells us in one of his inscriptions: "Marduk . . . ordered him (i.e. Cyrus) to march against his city

Babylon. . . . He delivered into his (i.e. Cyrus') hands Nabonidus, the king who did not worship him (i.e. Marduk). . . . *I am Cyrus . . . whose rule Bel and Nebo love,* whom they want as king to please their hearts. When I entered Babylon, . . . Marduk, the great lord, [induced] the magnanimous inhabitants of Babylon . . . [to love me], *and I was daily endeavouring to worship him.* . . . Marduk, the great lord, was well pleased with my deeds and sent friendly blessings to myself, *Cyrus, the king who worships him.* . . . May all the gods whom I have resettled in their sacred cities *ask daily Bel and Nebo for a long life for me and may they recommend me (to him); to Marduk, my lord, they may say this: 'Cyrus, the king who worships you, . . .'"* [*ANET*², 315-316; italics added].

worship [*proskunein*] *him.* Literally "to prostrate oneself before." Possibly the word "worship" is a bit too strong here; for in Esther 3:2 of the LXX, it was Mordecai's refusal to bow down (*ou prosekunei*) to a mortal (Haman) that resulted in Haman's initiating a pogrom against the Jews (Esther 3:5-14).

For this verse the LXX has "The king revered him, and every day the king would go and worship him; but Daniel would pray [*proseucheto*] to the Lord [*pros kurion*]." In the Greek the absence of the definite article before *kurion,* "Lord," suggests that the Semitic *Vorlage* of Bel had the tetragrammaton (*yhwh*), which was deferentially read aloud as *'dny,* "the Lord."

5. *the living God.* Cf. Dan 6:20 and 26. In vs. 24 the king will make the same assertion about his snake deity. In both cases, such an epithet had to be justified, not just asserted.

authority. The Greek word *kurieia,* which is used in Daniel to translate the Heb. *mmšl* and *mšl* (11:3,4,5) and the Aram. *šlṭn* (4:19[23 of LXX] and 6:27 ☉), was used most frequently from the first century on (so LSJ, 1,013).

over all mankind. Literally "over all flesh," meaning "over all humans" (as in Gen 6:12 and Joel 2:28[3:1]), not the JB's "over all living creatures." The LXX has "So the king said to Daniel, 'Why do you not worship Bel?' And Daniel answered the king, 'I revere no one except the Lord God who created the heavens and the earth and has authority over all mankind!'" The "I" here is more emphatic in both form and position than in the ☉. Daniel was clearly courting trouble with such a response.

6. *how much he eats and drinks.* "There is something intensely ironical in the proof alleged for Bel's real existence. . . . A necessity of eating is proof not of divinity but of mortality" (Ball, p. 353). Bel could not eat and therefore was not a god; the Snake ate too much and died (vs. 27), thereby proving he was not a god, either. Contrary to what the ancients may have thought, the "fact" of eating was not an adequate criterion for establishing claims to divinity. As the prophet had argued in his biting satire on Bel and Nebo (Isa 46:1-4), and as Daniel himself would later prove in our narrative, a real God can protect himself and his interests (vss. 15,21-22) as well as those of his followers (vss. 34-39).

The LXX has for the verse "The king said to him, 'This, then, is not a god? Don't you see how much they spend on him every day?'" The thrust of the king's argument here is less clear than in ☉, i.e. from what the king says in the LXX one might infer more about the great devotion of Bel's followers than about Bel's existence.

7. *Daniel chuckled* [*gelasas*]. Cf. vs. 19. Since *gellō* properly means "laugh"

or "sneer at," possibly "chuckled" is too weak here, although the Vulgate has "smiled." But Daniel would have had to have felt very secure, indeed, "to laugh at" the king, although the king's very angry response (vss. 8-9) may best be explained by just such an interpretation.

Your Majesty [*basileu*]. Daubney (p. 205) argued that the presence of the vocative here points in the direction of an Aramaic *Vorlage* for the Bel narrative, inasmuch as the vocative, "Your Majesty," occurs a number of times in the Aramaic portion of Daniel (*malkā'*, e.g. in 2:29, 3:10, 5:10, 6:8) but never in the Hebrew sections (1:1 - 2:4a and 8:1 - 12:13). While Daubney's "detail of fact" is true enough, his conclusion is hardly inevitable. The story of Bel may very well have been written in Aramaic, but Daubney's argument does nothing to increase the likelihood of it.

For this verse the LXX has " 'Not at all!' replied Daniel. 'Don't let anybody fool you, for inside it's of clay, and outside of bronze. I swear to you by the Lord God of gods that this idol [literally "one"] has never eaten anything at all!' " For the phrase "God of gods," see Dan 2:47, 11:36; Deut 10:17; and Ps 136:2.

8-9. The LXX has "Incensed, the king summoned those who administered the temple and said to them, 'Produce the one who eats the things provided for Bel. If not, you shall die; or Daniel who alleges that these things are not eaten by him [i.e. Bel].' They answered, 'It is Bel himself who eats these things!' Daniel said to the king, 'So be it! If I cannot show that it is not Bel who eats these things, I shall die, together with all my friends ["all the men with me"].' "

Up to this point vss. 1-9 of the ⊖ and the LXX have been in substantial agreement, but from here on the two Greek versions increasingly differ from one another.

10. For this verse the LXX has "Now the priests of Bel were seventy (apart from their wives and children). They conducted the king to the idol's temple [*eis to eidōleion*]." Typically for the Greek versions of the Additions to Daniel, the LXX here translated its Semitic *Vorlage* which must have had something like *lbyt bl*, "to the house of Bel," into good, classical Greek, *eis to eidōleion*, "to the idol's temple" (cf. I Esd 2:7; I Macc 1:47; I Cor 8:10), whereas ⊖ rendered it quite literally as "the house [*oikou*] of Bel" (cf. II Kings 19:37).

11. *mix the wine.* Possibly by diluting it with water, as in II Macc 15:39 (but see Isa 1:22), but more likely by adding spices to give the wine a more pungent taste (Isa 5:22) or a better bouquet (Song of Songs 8:2). Mixed with myrrh, wine could lessen pain (Matt 27:34); but too much wine could cause great pain (Prov 23:29-35). Metaphorically, a cup of mixed wine could symbolize divine punishment (Ps 75:8[9]; Rev 18:6). On the many different aspects of wine and wine-making, see J. F. Ross, "Wine," *IDB*, IV, 849-852.

The LXX has "Then, in the presence of the king and Daniel, the food was set out and the wine, having been mixed, was brought and set down before Bel. Daniel said, 'You yourself see, Your Majesty, that these things are arranged. You, therefore, seal the bolts of the temple when it is shut.' This advice pleased the king."

For some unknown reason, in the last two verses the roles of Daniel and the priests are reversed in the two Greek versions, i.e. in the LXX it is the priests who took the king to the temple (vs. 10) and Daniel who suggested the procedures and precautions to be taken (vs. 11), whereas in ⊕ it is Daniel who took the king to the temple (vs. 10) and the priests who suggested the procedures and precautions (vs. 11).

13. *get [anēloun] it all.* Literally "they used it up." Some of the food they may have eaten then and there, but obviously some of it was taken back home (cf. vs. 21 of LXX). Whether the Bel story is true or not, such shenanigans did go on in some pagan temples (so Chrysostom *Homily on Peter and Helicon*). For a similar incident in the Temple of Asclepius at Epidaurus, see Aristophanes *Plutus* iii 2.

14. *So [kai egeneto].* Cf. also vss. 18 and 28 of ⊕, and 15 and 33 of LXX. This verse, beginning with a common Hebraism (=Heb. *wyhy*, "and it happened that"), abounds in others, including eight *kai* (=Heb. *wa*, "and").

temple. The Gr. *naos* here designates just the temple building (Heb. *hykl*), and not the temple complex or enclosing structures.

sealed it with [en] the king's signet. An obvious Hebraism; cf. Esther 8:8.

For this verse the LXX has "Then Daniel ordered those with him, after having ushered all the others out of the temple, to scatter the whole temple with ashes without any of those outside knowing it. Then he ordered them to seal it with the king's signet and the signets of certain illustrious priests. And it was done."

15. LXX has "So [kai egeneto] the next morning they returned there. (But the priests of Bel had come in through the false doors to eat everything that had been set before Bel and had drunk the wine.) Daniel said, 'You priests, examine your seals whether they remain unbroken. And you, Your Majesty, see that nothing is out of order.' And they found the seal was intact, and they broke the seal."

16. As in vss. 10-11, so here too the sequence of described events is reversed in the two Greek versions: according to the LXX, Daniel and the others arrived at the temple the next morning (vs. 15a), the priests having already removed the offerings to Bel (15b), whereas in ⊕ the priests removed the offerings during the night (vs. 15), and then the next morning Daniel and everyone else arrived at the temple (vs. 16). From a literary point of view ⊕'s account is certainly preferable. Not only is ⊕'s sequence of described events chronologically more accurate and precise (the LXX does not specify when the pilfering occurred), but in the LXX only one seal has to be broken for them to enter the temple, this despite the fact that in vs. 14 of the LXX several seals were involved!

18. *As soon [kai egeneto] as.* Inasmuch as this Hebraism here and in vs. 14 of ⊕ is missing in the LXX, how else can one explain its presence except by saying that it represents either a "correction" or a translation of a now-lost Hebrew *Vorlage?*

You are great, Bel! The greater literary effectiveness of ⊕, as compared to the LXX, is the result of many small differences, including ⊕'s preference here for speaking *to* rather than *about* the deity.

at all [oude eis]! A very awkward Greek expression meaning "there is not one," the phrase probably is a Hebraism, rendering the Heb. *'n 'ḥd*, which may, in turn, represent a still earlier corruption of *'n kḥd*, "there is no deception" (so Brüll, *JJGL* 8 [1887], 29).

The LXX has "Having opened the doors, they saw that everything set out had been consumed and that the tables were empty. The king was elated and said to Daniel, 'Bel is great! There is no deception in him!'"

19. *floor* [*edaphos*]. Daubey's suggestion (pp. 206-207) that ⊕'s *edaphos* represents a misreading of Aram. *šqr'*, "the deception," for *šqp'*, "the threshold," is possible but unnecessary because, not only does "floor" make eminently good sense here, but there is no manuscript support for "deception" in either the manuscripts of ⊕ or ancient versions based upon ⊕.

The LXX has "Then Daniel laughed heartily and said to the king, 'Come see the deception of the priests! Your Majesty,' said Daniel, 'whose footprints are these?'"

20. Here, as in most other verses of "Bel," the LXX is briefer and less precise: "'Of men, women, and children,' said the king."

21. In the LXX the "details of fact" are quite different from ⊕'s: "Then he went to the building where the priests were living, and he found Bel's food and wine. Then Daniel showed the king the false doors through which the priests would enter to consume the things prepared for Bel." As a result of these differences in details of fact, Daniel himself is seen, morally speaking, in a somewhat more favorable light in ⊕'s account, i.e. in the LXX Daniel relentlessly spells out the details of the crime, whereas, in ⊕ it is the king, having now been alerted to the fact of the ruse, who eagerly prosecutes the matter.

22. *destroyed the idol and its temple*. If the unnamed king of the LXX version of the Bel narrative was actually Cyrus the Great (so vs. 1 of ⊕), then this statement in vs. 22 is untrue, or, as Zöckler rightly put it, it is "haggadic boasting without a historical core" (p. 221). Not only was the historical Cyrus' attitude toward Bel/Marduk tolerant and even reverential (see NOTE on vs. 4), but it was actually Xerxes I (486-465 B.C.) who plundered Bel's great temple of Esagila in Babylon (so Herodotus I 183) and probably destroyed it (so Strabo XVI 1,5; and Arrian *Expedition of Alexander* VII 17), melting its eighteen-foot-high statue of Marduk into eight hundred pounds of gold bullion!

its temple [*ieron*]. In the Bel narrative five different Greek words for "temple" are used: *o oikos*, "the house" (vs. 10 ⊕; see NOTE); *to eidōleion*, "the idol's temple" (vs. 10 LXX); *o naos*, "the temple" (vs. 11 LXX; see NOTE on vs. 14); *to ieron*, "the holy building" (vss. 8 LXX; 22 ⊕); and *to bēleion*, "Bel's temple" (vs. 22 LXX). As one might easily predict, granted the prior impression that the LXX was more paraphrastic and less literal than the ⊕ in translating its Semitic *Vorlage*, the LXX shows the greater variety, using four of the five terms while ⊕ uses only three.

For this verse the LXX had "So the king brought them out of Bel's temple [*tou bēleiou*] and handed them over to Daniel. Bel's provisions he also gave to Daniel, but the Bel he destroyed." Again in ⊕, Daniel is more central, i.e. in the LXX *the king* destroyed the Bel; but in ⊕ it was Daniel who destroyed the Bel *and* its temple!

COMMENT

Although it is impossible to know why the early Christian Church ultimately preferred Theodotion's version of Daniel to the Septuagint's, one can well imagine that the Bel narrative played a contributing role in the Church's decision.

From a literary point of view, for instance, the story of Bel is told far more effectively in Θ. While there are, inevitably, some very subjective reasons why one version of a given story "sounds" better than another, there are nonetheless some distinctive features which make the Θ of "Bel" more readable. The Bel narrative in Θ is better edited; the story itself, for instance, is far better integrated into the canonical Book of Daniel and raises few questions in the minds of its readers (cf vss. 1-2 of the Greek versions). Then too, Θ evidences a greater use of emotive words ("Daniel *chuckled* and said" [vs. 7]; *"Infuriated, the king . . ."* [vs. 21]); and its direct quotations, Θ shows a preference for having its characters speak *to* the deity rather than *about* him (vs. 18). Most important of all, Θ has greater precision and specificity; for example, the king's name was Cyrus (vs. 1); the terms of the wager are spelled out more clearly (vss. 8-9, 12) and Θ's chronology is more correct and precise (vss. 15-16).

A distinction should be made here, however, with regard to the literary merits of the two versions *as translations*. In this respect, the LXX is probably the more "literary." Θ seems to have more Hebraisms, including *kai egeneto* (see NOTE on vs. 14), "there is not one" (see NOTE on *at all* in vs. 18), and eight *kai* (=Heb. *wa,* "and") in vs. 14, as compared to three *kai* in the corresponding verse of the LXX. Moreover, the LXX evidences a slightly greater variety in its vocabulary, as best exemplified by its use of four different Greek words to designate Bel's temple (see NOTE on vs. 22). The Greek texts of the LXX and Θ are conveniently printed side by side for purposes of comparison in Scholz, pp. cxxiv-cxxviii.

From a religious or moral point of view, the story of Bel as presented in Θ is again preferable. For, on the one hand, Daniel is made to seem less deliberately relentless in his prosecution of his enemies in Θ (vs. 21); on the other hand, he is also more conspicuously successful in his struggles against idolatry, in that it was Daniel himself who destroyed Bel and its temple (vs. 22).

VIII. THE SNAKE: A LIVING "GOD" WHO ATE AND DIED

(Vss. 23-42)

23 There was also a large snake*a*, which the Babylonians revered. 24 The king said to Daniel, "*b*You cannot say that this is not a living god, so worship him."

25 *c*Daniel answered, "I will worship the Lord my God, for he is a living God. 26 But with your permission, Your Majesty, I will kill the snake without sword or stick."

"You have my permission," said the king.

27 Then Daniel took pitch, fat, and hair, and he brewed them together and made patties and fed them to the snake. The snake *d*swallowed them and*d* burst open. Then he*e* said, "Look at what you were worshiping!"

28 Now when the Babylonians heard about it, they became very upset and rallied themselves against the king, saying, "The king has become a Jew! He has destroyed Bel, killed the snake, and slaughtered the priests!" 29 *f*So they went to the king and said, "Hand Daniel over to us or else we will kill you and your family!" 30 When the king perceived that they were pressing him hard, out of necessity he handed Daniel over to them. 31 They threw him into the Lion Pit, and he was there for six days. 32 There were seven lions in the pit, and they were fed two human bodies and two sheep every day, but now nothing was given them so that they would devour Daniel.

33 Now the prophet Habakkuk was in Judea; and he had made a stew and had crumbled bread in a bowl and was going into the field to take it to those harvesting, 34 when an angel of the Lord said to

---

a Most MSS and versions add, with LXX, "in that place"; see NOTE.
b Most MSS and versions add, with LXX, "You will not say he is bronze; See, he's alive! He eats and drinks!"
c Verse not in LXX.
d-d Many MSS and versions omit.
e "Daniel" in Syriac, Bohairic, and Ethiopic.
f Verse not in LXX.

Habakkuk, "Take the meal, which you're holding, to Babylon for Daniel in the Lion Pit."

35 "Sir," replied Habakkuk, "I have never seen Babylon, nor do I know *where the pit is*!" 36 So the angel *of the Lord* grabbed *the crown of his head*, and lifting him by the hair of his head, in a gust of wind deposited him in Babylon right above the pit. 37 Habakkuk called out, saying, "Daniel! Daniel! Take the meal that God has sent you!"

38 "You have remembered me, God!" said Daniel, "You have not deserted those who love you!" 39 So Daniel got up and ate, while the angel of God immediately returned Habakkuk to his homeland*.

40 On the seventh day the king went to mourn for Daniel, and he came to the pit and peered inside—and there sat Daniel!* 41 And the king* shouted loudly, "You are great, Lord God of Daniel, there is no other beside you." 42 He hauled him up and tossed into the pit those who had plotted Daniel's* destruction, and they were instantly devoured before his eyes.*

g-g So most MSS and versions; LXX^B has "the pit."
h-h LXX^A and many MSS omit; see NOTE.
i-i Greek "his crown"; LXX^A "his hand."
j Greek "own place."
k Vulgate adds "among the lions."
l So most MSS and versions; LXX^B has "he."
m Greek "his."
n Vulgate adds, "Then the king said, 'Let all the inhabitants in the whole world fear the God of Daniel because he is the savior, working signs and wonders in the earth, who has delivered Daniel from the lions' pit.'" Cf. Dan 6:26-27.

NOTES

23. *a large snake* [*drakōn*]. Apart from being characterized as large and living (vs. 25), our *drakōn*, unfortunately, is nowhere described, probably for the same reason that Bel was not described in the first story (see NOTE on vs. 3, *an idol*). In the Septuagint *drakōn* is used to translate a wide variety of Hebrew words denoting various kinds of terrifying animals, including terrestrial animals, such as the wolf (Micah 1:8), snake (Exod 32:33), and large reptiles (Job 40:20[25]), as well as marine animals, such as actual sea creatures (Ps 103[104]:26) and mythological ones like Rahab (Job 26:13), Leviathan (Ps 74:13) and Yam (Job 7:12). In apocalyptic literature the *drakōn* was often symbolic of evil (cf. Rev 12:3, 20:2; II Bar 29:3-8; II Esd 6:52). While modern English translations still prefer to translate *drakōn* in our verse as "dragon" (with all the awesomeness, mystery, and eerie nuances that that word

may have), it is nonetheless better to render it as "snake," since candidates for our sacred *drakōn* must be limited to the ranks of actual living creatures. Besides, although the standard Greek word for "snake" is *ophis*, since the days of Homer *drakōn* has sometimes been used as a synonym for *ophis*. Live snakes were kept at the shrine of Asclepius, the Greek god of healing, at Epidaurus, Greece; but, unfortunately, there is no extrabiblical evidence of a Babylonian cult centering around a living snake.

For this verse the LXX has "There was also in that place a snake [*drakōn*] which the Babylonians revered." The phrase "in that place," which helps to unite the originally separate and independent Snake narrative to the Bel narrative, cannot refer in the present text to the temple of Bel, as Bludau suggested, but must refer to the city of Babylon, because Bel's temple had already been destroyed (cf. vs. 22).

24. As ℗ currently stands, i.e. without emendation (see textual note *b*), the LXX offers the clearer statement of the king's argument: "The king said to Daniel, 'You will not say he is bronze! See, he's alive! He eats and drinks, so worship him.' "

25. *I will worship the Lord.* Apart from Daniel's exclusive worship of Yahweh as affirmed here and in vss. 5 and 41, not one of the distinctive features of post-exilic Judaism is evidenced in "Bel and the Snake," i.e. no strong emphasis on the Law, *kašrût*, sacrifice, etc. A possible exception to this generalization is the mention of the angel in the Habakkuk incident. (vss. 33-39), but that episode almost certainly is secondary (see COMMENT).

26. *with your permission . . . I will kill.* Literally "give me the authority . . . and [*kai*] I will kill." The use of *kai* here instead of *ina*, "so that," is a Hebraism.

The LXX has "And Daniel said, 'Your Majesty, with your permission I will destroy the snake without sword or stick.' The king cooperated with him and said to him, 'Permission granted.' "

27. *Then* [*kai*]. A Hebraism; the Gr. *kai* occurs eight times in this verse, serving the same functions as the Heb. *wa*, i.e. as an adverb, a coordinating and a subordinating conjunction, etc.

pitch, fat, and hair. This curious concoction, while neither explosive in itself nor poisonous to snakes (though hardly nutritious), has occasioned much speculation, with interpreters taking one of two tacks: either they regard the food as a "cover" or bait for some other lethal element, or they argue that a mistranslation of the Semitic *Vorlage* is involved.

Ancient and modern Jewish commentators evidently preferred a naturalistic explanation. In the *B'reshith Rabbah* 68, dating from no later than the thirteenth century A.D. and probably hundreds of years earlier, we read, "He took straw, and hid nails in the midst thereof; then he cast it before it, and the nails pierced its intestines" (English translation, together with original Hebrew text, in A. Neubauer, *The Book of Tobit*, Oxford at the Clarendon Press [1879], xcii, 43). In a medieval manuscript whose text some scholars think is quite ancient (see M. Gaster, *Chronicles of Jerahmeel*), we read, "And Daniel went and took pitch and fat and flax and hair, and rolled them into one lump, and he made unto himself iron hatchets, and rolled all that round and round the hatchets, and he threw it into the dragon's mouth" (p. 92). And according to the Hebrew text of Joseph ben Gorion, dating from the tenth century and quoted by Jerahmeel, "Making iron instruments like combs, he joined them together back to back, with the points outward. . . . This he rolled in all manner of poisonous fat and grease and other fatty substances, and beneath it he placed pitch and brimstone, until the points of the brass and the other piercing metals were concealed. Then, making it in the shape of an oblation, Daniel cast it into the dragon's mouth. . . . It died on the morrow" (pp. 221-222). For still other ingenious explanations by ancient and medieval Jewish interpreters, see F. Zimmermann, *VT* 8 (1958), 439.

Inasmuch as many modern scholars have regarded the Snake narrative as a judaized "version," or faint echo, of the famous Babylonian story of Marduk killing the primordial goddess Tiamat, it should not surprise us that a few scholars have seen some ingredient in Daniel's concoction as a mistranslation of an element in the Marduk-Tiamat tale. The relevant passage in *Enuma Elish* describes the titanic battle between Marduk and Tiamat.

> *The Evil Wind*, which followed behind, he [Marduk] let loose
>   in her face.
> When Tiamat opened her mouth to consume him,
> *He drove in the Evil Wind that she close not her lips.*
> *As the fierce winds charged her belly,*
> Her body was distended and her mouth was wide open.
> He released the arrow, it tore her belly,
> It cut through her insides, splitting the heart.
> Having thus subdued her, he extinguished her life.
>   *ANET²*, 67, lines 96-103, italics added.

In light of the above passage, Marshall (*HDB*, I, 267) argued that the "pitch" in the Daniel story represents an early confusion of Aram. *wêpi'*, "pitch," for Aram. *wa'api'*, "south wind," the latter being part of the arsenal of Marduk in his battle with Tiamat. F. Zimmermann also believes that the original confusion concerned wind used by Marduk against Tiamat. The Bab. *sâru*, "wind," has an Aramaic cognate *s'r'* or *s'rt'*, meaning "storm" or "whirlwind," but the same consonants in Aramaic can also be read as "barley"; hence, the later introduction, he argues, of patties into the story. The Greek translator then compounded the error by rendering the Aram. *s'rt'* as *trix*, "hair." Although Zimmermann saw all this as an indication that our Snake narrative had an Aramaic *Vorlage*, there is no reason, a priori, why this "error" in translation could not have happened if the Greek translator were working from a Hebrew text; for Hebrew has *śa'ar*, "storm, tempest," and *śē'ār*, "hair," as well as *śe'ārāh*, "storm," *śa'arāh*, "hair," and *śe'ōrāh*, "barley."

For the corresponding verse the LXX has "Then Daniel took thirty-some [thirty *minas*] of pitch, fat, and hair, and brewed them together and made a loaf which ["and"] he tossed into the snake's mouth. The snake swallowed it and burst open. Then he showed it to the king, saying, 'Weren't you worshiping this, Your Majesty?' " From a literary point of view, the LXX once again seems to have the superior reading. Not only is the weight of Daniel's concoction given, suggesting, incidentally, that the snake must have been either a python or a boa constrictor to eat so much (the Mesopotamian *mina* ranged in weight from 1.1 to 2.32 lbs.), but Daniel's rhetorical question is also more pointed and stinging!

28. *Now* [*kai egeneto*]. A Hebraism; see NOTE on vs. 14, *So*.

The king has become a Jew! Such a charge need not have been true to have been effective and very threatening to the king. After all, Cyrus himself had been preferred by the Babylonians to their legitimate king, Nabonidus, because the latter had been guilty of apostasy against Bel by preferring the moon god Sin of Harran (for text of the Cyrus Cylinder, see *ANET²*, 315-316; and for a discussion of the problem, see A. L. Oppenheim, "Nabonidus," *IDB*, III, 493-495). Pagans may have converted occasionally to Judaism (or so Esther 8:17 would have us to understand), but it is not likely that great kings would have done so, as suggested here of King Cyrus or of Antiochus IV (Epiphanes) in II Macc 9:17.

He has destroyed. I.e. the king. Technically, in the Θ it was Daniel who destroyed the Bel and its temple (vs. 22b) and the king who had the priests put to death (vs. 22a), whereas, in the LXX it was the king who destroyed the Bel (vs. 22b) and Daniel who killed the priests (vs. 22a). In any event, the Babylonians held the king ultimately responsible for all of it.

For this verse, 28, the LXX has "Then all the inhabitants of the country were united against Daniel and said, 'The king has become a Jew! He has overthrown Bel and killed the snake!' "

29. *we will kill you and your family!* It is quite beside the point to argue, as some scholars have done, that such an ultimatum is highly improbable because conquered people "just don't talk that way" to their conquerors. Of course they don't—unless, as here, the literary demands of the plot require it, i.e. in the face of Daniel's two stunning victories the king *had to have* a very compelling reason to toss Daniel into the lions' pit.

30. The LXX has for the verse "When the king saw that the people [*o ochlos*] from the country were united against him, he summoned his advisers and said, 'I'm handing Daniel over [I'm giving Daniel for destruction].' "

31. *the Lion Pit.* The lion (*Panthera leo persica*), the largest and mightiest carnivore of the ancient Near East (see Plate 3), has a long history in Mesopotamian and Palestinian art and literature but was rarely given religious significance, although in late apocalyptic literature the lion image does appear (cf. Ezek 1:10; Dan 7:1-4; Rev 4:7, 9:8,17 [see W. S. McCullough and F. S. Bodenheimer, "Lion," *IDB*, III, 136-137]). The symbol of royalty, especially in the Neo-Assyrian and Neo-Babylonian periods, the lions in our tale were probably kept for hunting purposes, lion hunting being the sport of kings then, although one cannot dismiss the "deterrent values" of having these ferocious beasts serve as royal executioners, as asserted in vs. 31 of LXX.

six days. Cf. Dan 6:19, where Daniel had spent only one night in the lions' den; for a more detailed comparison of these two lion accounts, see COMMENT I.

32. *human bodies* [*sōmata*]. Since in the Septuagint *sōma*, "body," can refer to either a corpse (Tobit 1:18; Sir 38:16) or a living person (Gen 36:6), especially a slave (Tobit 10:10; Rev 18:13), the translation covers both meanings. After all, it mattered little to the king whether the lions' food was alive or not.

would devour Daniel. Such a death was abhorrent to ancient man, be he Egyptian, Babylonian, or Jew; for not only was the manner of dying terrible in itself, but the final result was even worse, i.e., no proper burial of the body (cf. II Macc 9:15, 13:7-8; see W. L. Reed, "Burial," *IDB*, I, 474-476).

Verses 31-32 of the LXX have "There was a pit in which seven lions were kept, and the conspirators of the king were given to them. Every day they were provided with two people [*sōmata*] condemned to death. The rabble [*oi ochloi*] tossed Daniel into the lions' pit so that he might be eaten up and have no burial. Now, Daniel was in the pit for six days." It is a tossup here whether the LXX or ⊗ is the more interesting and dramatic; for the LXX expressly states that Daniel would not have a proper burial, but ⊗ makes the lions more ravenous.

33. *the prophet Habakkuk.* As far as ⊗ is concerned, there can be no doubt that the individual in question here was *the* Habakkuk. It should be noted, however, that in the corresponding verse of the LXX, he is not identified as a prophet, although in the Superscription of "Bel and the Snake," the LXX does say, "From the prophecy of Habakkuk . . ." But as indicated in a Note on vs. 1 of the LXX, there is considerable doubt as to whether *the* Habakkuk was originally intended in the earliest form of the Snake narrative. Certainly Davies is justified in saying of the Habakkuk narrative in vss. 33-39 that it "has no vital connection with the rest of the narrative, and is certainly a later interpolation" (p. 663).

made a stew. Cf. Gen 25:29 and II Kings 4:38 of the LXX.

The LXX has for this verse "Now [*kai egeneto*] it was on the sixth day that Habakkuk, who had a bowl of soup with dumplings and a jug of mixed wine, was going into the field to those harvesting." Curiously, the ⊗ has no mention of the wine.

34. *an angel of the Lord.* See Sus 42 of the LXX, where an angel is also necessary to activate a mortal into saving a doomed person.

For vss. 34-35 the LXX has "When an angel of the Lord spoke to Habakkuk, saying 'Thus the Lord God says to you: Take the meal which you have to Daniel in the Lion Pit in Babylon.' And Habakkuk replied, 'Lord God, I have never seen Babylon, nor do I know where the pit is!' "

36. *the angel* [*o aggelos*]. The presence of the definite article here where most Greek manuscripts omit "of the Lord" (see textual note *h-h*) and the omission of the definite article in vs. 34 (*"an* angel of the Lord") in a context where one would ordinarily expect the Greek to have it, are both Hebraisms.

lifting him by the hair of his head. This rather hair-raising means of travel is patterned evidently after that in Ezekiel (Ezek 8:3, 3:12,14).

in a gust [*roizō*] *of wind.* A most baffling phrase for all translators (in fact, the entire verse is puzzling to scholars). Perhaps the most plausible of all explanations is that of M. Gaster (*PSBA* 17 [1895], 87). His ancient Aramaic text of "Bel and the Snake" has *kd tb rwhyh* ("when he recovered his breath"), which, says Gaster, was misread as *brth rwhyh* ("in a fury of wind"). The latter phrase was then translated into Greek as *en tō roizō tou pneumatos* and erroneously taken with the end of vs. 36, instead of at the beginning of vs. 37.

For this verse the LXX has "Grabbing Habakkuk by the hair of his head, the angel of the Lord deposited him above the pit in Babylon." Of the two Greek versions, the LXX is once again clearer and simpler, there being in the LXX neither a doublet nor an Aramaism.

37. The LXX has "Habakkuk said to Daniel, 'Get up and eat the meal that

the Lord God has sent you!'" In the Habakkuk narrative the verbatim agreement between the LXX and ⊕ seems closer than in the preceding materials in the Snake narrative (see COMMENT I).

38-39. The LXX has "Daniel said, 'The Lord God, who does not desert those who love him, has remembered me!' Then Daniel ate, and that same day the angel of the Lord returned Habakkuk to the place from which he had taken him. So the Lord remembered Daniel."

40. *and there [kai idou] sat Daniel!* Kai idou (=Heb. *whnh*) is another Hebraism. While probably too paraphrastic, the translation of JB nicely captures the psychological impact for the king: "and there was Daniel, quite unperturbed."

For this verse the LXX has, "Later ["after these things"] the king came to mourn for Daniel, and peeking into the pit he saw him—sitting there!" The LXX, it should be noted, is less precise as to how much time has elapsed.

41. The LXX has, "The king shouted, 'The Lord God is great, and there is no other beside him!'" The ⊕ is probably more effective by having the king speak directly to the Lord, instead of, as in the LXX, about him.

42. *those who had plotted Daniel's destruction.* Literally "those guilty of his destruction."

they were instantly devoured. Cf. Dan 6:24: "and before they reached the bottom of the den the lions overpowered them and broke all their bones in pieces."

The LXX has "The king brought [*exēgagen*] Daniel out of the pit, and in Daniel's presence tossed into the pit those who had plotted his destruction, and they were devoured." Here, the LXX is far more clear and precise than ⊕, the latter using the third person singular personal pronoun or pronominal adjective four times, with their antecedents not clear half the time, i.e. "his destruction" and "his eyes." That the LXX used the verb *exēgagen* in a positive sense here but in a negative sense in vs. 22 probably argues for it being used to render two different Semitic words, presumably Heb. *yṣ'*, "go out," and *'lh*, "go up" (so Daubney, p. 208).

COMMENT I

When the Greek texts of ⊕ and the LXX are printed side by side for purposes of comparison (as in Scholz, pp. cxxviii-cxxxi), then the differences between the two versions are quite evident. Obvious at a glance is LXX's omission of vss. 25 and 29; but the most significant feature is the very pronounced *lack of verbatim agreement* between the two versions. Sometimes it is variations in "details of fact" which make the difference (cf., for example, vss. 32 and 36); but more often it is a matter of slightly differing wording, or syntax, of essentially the same substantive material. Only the introductory verses (vss. 23-24) show substantial (i.e. about 75 per cent) verbatim agreement between the two versions.

It is noteworthy that vss. 28-32 and 40-42 have very little identical agreement, whereas there is a very pronounced verbatim agreement in vss. 33-39, i.e. in the Habakkuk episode. This close agreement in the Habakkuk material suggests, at the very least, that the Habakkuk episode was originally a separate and probably later element in the Semitic *Vorlage* of the Snake narrative. This conclusion is independently supported by the literary-form analysis of A. K. Fenz (*SEÅ* 35 [1970], 5-16), who found identical and detailed form agreement (or schematic pattern) in vss. 23-27 and vss. 28-32, but not in vss. 33-39, i.e. the latter verses evidenced some irregularities and variations in schematic pattern. The introduction later on of a human intermediary (Habakkuk), who would provide food for Daniel, was necessitated by the fact that Daniel had to stay in the lions' pit *for six whole days* (so Fenz, pp. 14-16).

Two other differences between the Greek versions should be noted. First, and not at all surprising, ⊙ has the greater number of Hebraisms (see NOTES on "Then" in vss. 26,27; on "Now" in 28; on "the angel" in 36; and on "and there" in 40); the LXX has only one Hebraism (*kai egeneto* in vs. 33). Second, and quite surprising, the LXX seems to be the better narrative, i.e. the more effectively told. The LXX is better edited (see e.g. the LXX's "in that place" in vs. 23), and is more simple and precise in its content (see NOTES on the LXX text of vss. 24, 27, 36, and 42). The literary "superiority" of the LXX here is in sharp contrast to its literary inferiority to ⊙ in the Bel narrative (see COMMENT, p. 139), and undoubtedly reflects differences in their respective Semitic *Vorlagen*, i.e. the Bel and the Snake narratives were originally separate and independent Semitic tales in which the Bel narrative was told more effectively in the Semitic *Vorlage* of ⊙, and the Snake narrative in the Semitic *Vorlage* of the LXX.

In addition to the Semiticisms already alluded to in the preceding paragraph, attention should also be called to those possibilities noted at vs. 27 (see NOTE on "pitch, fat, and hair") and vs. 37 (see NOTE on "in a gust of wind"). On the basis of all these Semiticisms, one might be tempted to say that in the Snake narrative ⊙ had a Hebrew *Vorlage* while the LXX had an Aramaic one; but the difficulty with that generalization is that the only ancient Semitic text we have of the Snake narrative is in Aramaic and it closely resembles ⊙, not the LXX (see M. Gaster, *PSBA* 17 [1895], 75-94). Thus, it is a moot question whether the Semitic *Vorlagen* for the Snake narrative of the LXX and ⊙ were both originally in Hebrew, in Aramaic, or one in each.

COMMENT II

Scholars have frequently observed that the Bel and the Snake narratives of Daniel 14 are very reminiscent of two earlier stories in the Book of Daniel, namely, the Three Youths in the Fiery Furnace (ch. 3) and Daniel in the Lions' Den (ch. 6). A priori, the stories in Daniel 14 could be doublets of Daniel 3 and 6, especially since they currently seem out of place, coming as they do after the long vision section (chs. 7-12) of canonical Daniel. Moreover, it can be said that the Bel and the Snake narratives, like the stories of the

Three Youths in ch. 3 and of Daniel and the Lions in ch. 6, are "confrontation stories" *but with a reverse twist,* i.e. whereas in chs. 3 and 6 the heroes found themselves inevitably caught up in a perilous situation, on both occasions in ch. 14 Daniel actively courted danger.

Certainly, a quick reading of the English version of the Snake narrative raises the question of whether it is a variant, or doublet, of the lions' tale in Daniel 6. But as soon as one compares *the wording* of the Greek texts of Dan (both LXX and ⊕) with our narrative (LXX and ⊕), it becomes quite clear that, apart from an occasional word or phrase, there is virtually no similarity between the two stories.

Moreover, when plot and details of fact are taken into consideration, then the differences between Daniel 6 and the Snake narrative are even more pronounced; for according to Daniel 6, Daniel was put in a lions' den because he had deliberately *violated the king's thirty-day interdict,* which prohibited everyone from petitioning any god or person other than the king himself. King *Darius* half-expected Daniel to survive his ordeal in the den; but to preclude any trickery or charge of it, the king had the den *covered with a stone,* and he himself sealed it with his own signet and the signets of top-ranking officials. Arriving at the den early *the next day,* King Darius learned that Daniel was alive and unharmed, because God (acting through an angel, according to ⊕) had kept the mouths of the lions tightly shut. Daniel was immediately released; and his accusers, *together with their wives and children,* were thrown into the den, where they were torn to pieces even before their bodies touched the ground.

Fenz, using a quite different type of approach from the one above, came to similar conclusions. In his detailed literary-form analysis of the canonical and deuterocanonical lion tales, Fenz (*SEÅ* 35 [1970] 6-13), concluded that they cannot possibly be doublets and that, at most, they are two independent stories containing legendary embellishments of a *possibly* common historical core which now cannot be more narrowly defined or precisely described than by key words, such as Daniel, king, lions' den, and angel.

Though often asserted, the claim that the stories of Bel and the Three Youths in the Fiery Furnace are reminiscent of one another has very little merit to it, as the following summary makes clear. In the plain of Dura in the province of Babylon, Nebuchadnezzar had set up a gold image (Gr. *eikōn*), which all his subjects were to bow down to and worship. When the Jewish youths Shadrach, Meshach, and Abednego refused to do so, they were immediately thrown into a fiery furnace, which was so hot that those who were to throw them in were consumed by its heat even as they approached it! However, in the fiery furnace the three young men experienced no discomfort, for they were protected by an angel of God. When Nebuchadnezzar saw that not even their hair was singed in the terrible blaze, he released them; and he effusively praised them and their God.

Although it is true that the story above and the Bel narrative both feature a Babylonian idol and both have the enemies of the heroes destroyed, the similarities end there. The narratives have different kings, different heroes, and vastly dissimilar plots. Nor is there any significant correspondence in the Greek wording of the two stories. In fact, the great dissimilarity of the two stories is symbolized by the fact that two different Greek words are used to describe the false god: in ch. 3 he is called an *eikōn*, "image," and in the Bel narrative, an *eidōlon*, "idol."

How, then, could some scholars think that these two narratives were reminiscent of one another? It was probably a matter of their not seeing the forest for the trees. For, unquestionably, certain features in Daniel 3 and 6 *were* appropriated by the writer of ch. 14, notably, the door of Bel's temple was sealed with the signet of the king (and with the signets of the illustrious priests, according to the LXX) in 14:14, just as earlier the stone covering the mouth of the lions' den had been sealed with the signets of the king and his top-ranking officials (6:17); and the king's withholding from the lions their daily food allotment so as to whet their appetite for Daniel (14:32) seems but a variation of Nebuchadnezzar's strategy of heating the furnace seven times hotter than usual so as to assure that the fires would consume Shadrach, Meshach, and Abednego (3:19). Such similarities in details are, however, little more than literary influences or contaminations, hardly doublets or variants.

THE ADDITIONS TO ESTHER

INTRODUCTION

A Brief Description of Additions

The Greek version of Esther includes six extended passages (107 verses) which have no counterpart in the Hebrew text. Identified in the present volume as the "Additions," they vary from one another—as well as from the canonical portions—in purpose, content, and style.[1] In Addition A, vss. 1-11 contain the dream of Mordecai which foreshadows the events of the story; and vss. 12-17 tell of how Mordecai uncovered a conspiracy against the king. Additions B and E purport to be verbatim copies of the royal edicts dictated by Haman and Mordecai, respectively, which were only summarized in the MT (Esth 3:13 and 8:11-12). Addition C contains the prayers of Mordecai (vss. 1-11) and Esther (vss. 12-30), uttered prior to her going unsummoned to the king, while Addition D is a very dramatic and expanded account of that audience described so briefly in 5:1-2 of the MT. And finally, Addition F provides a detailed explanation of Mordecai's dream described in A 1-11.

While these Additions make the events and personages of the Hebrew story more believable and increase the story's dramatic appeal (especially D), they are primarily intended to strengthen the book's religious character (so A, C, and F) and authenticity (so B and E), the absence of religious elements and questionable historicity being the principal "deficiencies" of the Hebrew version.

Their Secondary Character

Although some of these extended passages are survivals, i.e. witnesses to no longer extant Semitic originals, they are all still properly called "additions"; for both the external and internal evidence indisputably indicate that they were not originally a part of the Esther story but were added later.

As for the external evidence, none of the standard Semitic translations based on the Hebrew text has them, i.e. neither the Talmud, Targums, nor

---

[1] Following the practice in the critical Greek editions by Swete, then by Brooke, McLean, and Thackeray, and most recently by Hanhart, these six Additions are designated as A, B, C, D, E, and F, this system of designation being simpler than Rahlfs' and more logical than the Vulgate's.

the Syriac translation has these particular additions.[2] (There does exist a Hebrew version of a portion of the Additions, but it was made in the Middle Ages.[3]) Although not mentioning Additions A, D, and F in this connection, Origen (185?-?254) did note in his *Epistle of Africanus* iii, that neither the prayers of Esther and Mordecai nor the royal letters dictated by Haman and Mordecai appeared in the Hebrew texts current in his own day.[4] (To conclude from Origen's remarks that Additions A, D, and F *did* exist in the Hebrew Bibles of his day is an argument based on silence; but his remark is nonetheless curious.) Jerome (340?-420), after his Latin translation of Esth 10:3 noted that because those passages which we call "Additions" were not in the Hebrew text current in his day, in his Latin translation he removed them from their place corresponding to the Septuagint's and put them at the end of the canonical portion of his own translation. Nor are Additions A and F present in Josephus' paraphrase of Esther in his *Jewish Antiquities,* although this fact may not mean that they did not exist then, ca. A.D. 93-94 (see Introduction, p. 166, n. 33). Neither the Additions nor even canonical portions of Esther are found in Aquila, Symmachus, or Theodotion (see Roberts, *OTTV,* pp. 120-127), unless the AT or the "LXX" is really Theodotion.

Internal evidence also confirms the view that these passages are secondary. The account in Hebrew is an intelligible and consistent whole, and the Additions contradict the MT at a number of points (see NOTES and COMMENTS *passim*). Moreover, virtually all modern scholars agree that the two royal letters (Additions B and E) are much too florid and rhetorical in character to be anything but Greek in origin (see e.g. F. X. Roiron, *RSR* [1916], 8-9).

---

[2] Conversely, the versions having these additions are those which are recognized universally for the Old Testament as a whole as being translations of the LXX rather than the Hebrew, namely, the Old Latin, Coptic, and Ethiopic.

[3] Fragments of the Additions in Hebrew (Mordecai's dream and the prayers of Mordecai and Esther) are to be found in *Sefer Josippon,* a tenth-century work by an Italian Jew, Josephus ben Gorion, sometimes called "Pseudo-Josephus." Written in comparatively "pure" Biblical Hebrew, the work is a history of the Jews from the fall of the first temple in 586 B.C., to the fall of the second one in A.D. 70. Drawing upon biblical, Judaic, and classical sources, *Josippon* abounds in historical errors and misconceptions. Experts on *Josippon* regard the fragments of the Esther Additions as a Hebrew translation of the Greek Additions appearing in Josephus' *Jewish Antiquities.* Aramaic fragments of Additions A (Mordecai's dream) and C (the prayers of Mordecai and Esther) occur in a few late medieval manuscripts (I. B. de Rossi, *Specimen varr. lectionum sacri textus et Chaldaica Estheris additamenta* [Tübingen, 1784] 122*f;* Joannes Theodorus Beelen, *Chrestomathica Rabbinica et Chaldaica,* I [*pars posterior*], 13 [de Rossi's text of Mordecai and Esther's prayers]), but seem not to be directly based on the Greek Additions (so Fuller, p. 363).

[4] The relevant portion of Origen's statement (in Greek) may be found in H. B. Swete, *IOTG,* p. 257, n. 3; for the passage in its entirety, see J. P. Migne, *Patrologiae Graeca,* IX, col. 53.

Original Languages of Additions

All six of the Additions to Esther are secondary, i.e. they were supplied after the Book of Esther had been written. But that is not to say that some of them were not a part of a Semitic text of the Book of Esther *at a later point*. As a matter of fact, Additions A, C, D, and F give clear internal evidence of having a Semitic *Vorlage,* and Additions B and E are unquestionably Greek compositions (see NOTES *passim;* for a more detailed discussion of these matters, see C. A. Moore, *JBL* 92 [1973], 382-393). These findings concerning Semitic origins of Additions A, C, D, and F (as well as the Greek origins of Additions B and E) were confirmed in an independent study by R. A. Martin, who isolated seventeen syntactical features as criteria for judging whether a particular Greek passage is "translation-Greek" or "Greek-original" (*JBL* 94 [1975], 65-72). Why and how were these passages added to the Esther story? The answers to these questions are rooted in Esther's highly contested canonical status.

The Canonicity of the Book of Esther

Disagreement over the canonical status of the Additions has existed among Christians of the West only since the days of the Protestant Reformation. Following the lead of Martin Luther,[5] Protestants have rejected them, calling the Additions "apocryphal"; and on those occasions when Protestants have printed them, they have usually relegated them to a separate place in the Protestant Bibles, usually between the Old and New Testaments. Roman Catholics, following the decrees of the Council of Trent (A.D. 1546), have called them "deuterocanonical" and, after the fashion

[5] Luther voiced the sentiments of many Protestants when he said, "I am so hostile to this book [II Maccabees] and to Esther that I could wish they did not exist at all; for they judaize too greatly and have much pagan impropriety" (*Tischreden,* I [Weimar Edition, 1912], 208). There is today little justification to H. H. Howorth's charge (*PSBA* 31 [May 1909], 163) that scholarly discussions of problems such as the origin and value of the Additions have been too often predetermined by prior theological commitments of Christian scholars, i.e., Catholic scholars have been bound since 1546 by the decrees of the Council of Trent to affirm the inspiration of the books of the Deutero-Canon while Protestants want to accept as true and genuine only those OT books found in the MT. Speaking of his church's doctrinal position concerning the Deutero-Canon, the Roman Catholic biblical scholar L. Soubigou (pp. 581-582, 597) notes that while a Catholic scholar must accept as doctrinally true *the inspiration* of the Additions to Esther, he need not subscribe to the view that the Additions were an original part of the Esther story, the distinction here being that the provenance and original language of the "Additions" is a matter for literary and linguistic analysis, not doctrinal pronouncement.

of Jerome, have printed them immediately after the canonical version of Esther.

But whereas disagreement over the canonicity of the Additions is a relatively "recent" matter, the debate centering on the canonicity of the book itself is not. Among both Jews and Christians the canonical status of Esther was a debatable matter for centuries. The Jewish community at Qumran, dating from the second century B.C. to A.D. 68, evidently did not include Esther among their sacred writings, or at least so we may infer from the fact that thus far no copy of Esther has been found there and, more importantly, none of the liturgical calendars at Qumran include the festival of Purim. In any case, some Jews did reject Esther as late as the third or fourth century A.D. (For a detailed treatment of the canonicity of Esther, see AB 7B.)[6] A number of Eastern Church Fathers also denied the book canonical status, including Melito of Sardis, Athanasius, Gregory of Nazianzus, Theodore of Mopsuestia, Junilius, Leontius, and Nicephorous (for their dates, see Appendix I, p. 359).

Even after the book had been accepted as canonical by all, its religious merits continued to be a matter of dispute, with Jews tending to love the book (as its many extant copies from the Middle Ages attest) and Christians often ignoring or even disliking it. There are, for instance, no allusions to the book in the New Testament, and rarely do Church Fathers so much as even allude to it, let alone quote it. A complete commentary was not written on it until that of Rhabanus Maurus in the ninth century.

In the absence of sufficient evidence one can only theorize on why the book was so long denied canonical status by some Jews and many Christians. But as the treatment of the Greek version here (see NOTES and COMMENTS *passim*) and the much more detailed treatment of the Hebrew in AB 7B (XXXII-XLIX) will show, there were three quite legitimate grounds for at least questioning, if not denying, canonical status to the original Hebrew version: (1) there seems to be a distinct absence of religious elements in the Hebrew text; (2) the historicity of the events narrated in the Hebrew version seems quite questionable; and (3) Purim may have originally been a non-Jewish festival.

In the Greek version, the Additions attempt to correct, with varying degrees of success, the first two "weaknesses"; and, as for the third "weakness," Purim itself is much less stressed (see below, NOTES and COMMENTS *passim*).

---

[6] AB 7B is the abbreviation used in the present work for the writer's Anchor Bible volume on the Hebrew text, *Esther: Introduction, Translation, and Notes* (AB, vol. 7B, 1971). Many considerations concerning the Hebrew version which are touched upon only briefly in the present volume are treated more thoroughly there, a detailed discussion of the canonicity of Esther being a case in point (see AB 7B, pp. XXI-XXXI).

On the Absence of Religious Elements
in the Masoretic Text

Although the Persian king is mentioned 190 times in 167 verses of Esther, the Lord God of Israel is not mentioned once, nor are such basic OT themes as Law or Covenant. Also missing from the MT are such key Jewish concepts as prayer, election, salvation, Jerusalem, temple, kašrût,[7] and the like. In fact, fasting is the only religious practice mentioned (see NOTE: on 4:16 and 9:31).

Has this always been the case, or have all of these religious elements been deliberately edited out of the Hebrew (so F. Kauler, G. Jahn, and A. Barucq) because of the joyous, almost abandoned, way in which Purim was to be celebrated? The word "abandoned" is used advisedly since, according to the Mishnah, while celebrating Purim Jews were to drink wine until they were unable to distinguish between "Blessed be Mordecai" and "Cursed be Haman" (*Megillah 7b*). Such a ruling is undoubtedly the reason for no mention of the Deity, especially since several passages in the MT either contain surrogates for the Deity (see NOTE on 4:14, *from another quarter*) or presuppose the power or providence of God (see AB 7B, 66-67).

The Mishnaic ruling, however, does not suffice for explaining the omission of *all* the other religious elements as well. The explanation of this particular phenomenon doubtless lies in the fact that Esther is a *"historicized wisdom tale. . . . and enactment of standard 'Wisdom' motifs."*[8] Just as the usual elements of Jewish piety—faith in the transcendent God who answers prayer, observance of dietary laws, belief in sacrifice, the covenant, and the like—are virtually ignored in such books of the Wisdom school as Proverbs, Job, and Qoheleth, so these things are completely ignored in Esther. The authors of the Additions, however, tried to rectify this situation.

---

[7] I.e. laws concerning ceremonial, ritual, or dietary "cleanness." In the Old Testament, foods were either clean or unclean. For example, among the meats, quadrupeds with cloven hooves and which chewed their cuds, and fish with fins and scales were clean (see Lev 11:2-12), while other meats were unclean, including pork, certain birds and insects, all reptiles (see Lev 11:13-44). For a brief discussion of dietary laws in the Old Testament and more technical aspects of kašrût, see L. E. Toombs, *IDB*, I, s.v. "Clean and unclean."

[8] Shemaryahu Talmon, *VT* 13 (1963), 426. Barucq (pp. 83-84) has also called attention to some jointly shared Wisdom motifs in Esther and the Wisdom of Solomon, the latter dating from the second half of the first century B.C.

Religious Elements in the Greek Version

The most striking addition in the Greek text is, of course, God himself, the word or his name occurring over fifty times. Nor is the explicit mention of the Deity confined to the Additions; for in the canonical portions of Esther the Greek has the following:

"to fear God and obey his commandments" (2:20)
"call upon the Lord" (4:8)
"but God shall be their help and salvation" (4:14 of the AT)
"propose a service and earnestly beg God" (4:16 of the AT)
"and the Lord drove the sleep from the king that night" (6:1)
"for God is with him" (6:13)
"Esther was uneasy about speaking because the enemy was right in front of her, but God gave her the courage for the challenge" (7:2 of the AT).

Given the fact that the MT implicitly recognizes the power and presence of God (see above, p. 157), one cannot categorically assert that all of these very brief clauses mentioning God in the canonical portions of the Greek are additions rather than survivals from a Semitic original; but probably most, if not all, originated in the Greek. In any case, it is in the Additions that their authors most compensate for the religious "deficiencies" of the MT. In Addition C, for instance, the author could express his theological concerns as he wished (for details, see COMMENT, p. 213). Taking the Additions together, one may say that their clearly articulated concerns are God's providential care of his people (Additions A and F), God's miraculous intervention in a specific moment of history (see especially D 8, and COMMENT); an anti-Gentile attitude (A 6, C 26,28, F 5,8, and COMMENTS); the efficacy of prayer and fasting (see C, and COMMENT); concern for kašrût in both food and marriage (C 26-28); and the importance of cult and temple (C 20). With the exception of fasting, none of the above is mentioned expressly in the MT, all of which is another indication of the Additions being of a later date, i.e. in the Hellenistic period.

Barucq is not quite accurate when he writes, "The Additions of the Greek text, therefore, do not make a secular book a religious book: they express that which the Hebrew author had left to infer" (p. 87); for the presence of the Additions do significantly change the emphases in the Greek version. First, Esther and Mordecai were the heroes of the story in the MT; but in the Greek version, God is (see Soubigou, p. 583). Second, whereas the author of the Hebrew text was primarily interested in providing the "historical" background for cultic considerations, i.e. for establishing the historical basis for celebrating Purim, the authors of the Additions concentrated more on the religious aspects, i.e. on God's concern for his people and his deliverance of them (see NOTE on D 8). But the LXX's shift of emphasis from the establishment of the Purim festival to God's saving act in D 8 still did not make the book very appealing to Christian writers. The NT writers ignored the book completely, and the patristic writers virtually so, the one real exception being Augustine who in two separate works[9] briefly treated the king's miraculous change of attitude in D 8.

Historicity of Esther and the Greek Version

To what extent the ancients were concerned about the historicity of the Esther story is unknown. Just because modern scholars have difficulty in accepting it as essentially historical is no reason to think that the ancients felt the same way.[10] (The colophon in F 11 [see COMMENT] *may* be a faint echo of ancient misgivings as to the veracity of the details, if not the entire story.) If the Purim festival was suspected by some of being a pagan celebration in origin, then that would have created grave misgivings as to the historicity of the Jewish account.

One thing is certain: Additions B and E deepened for the Greek reader the impression of the story's historicity and authenticity by supplying verbatim copies of those royal edicts composed by Haman and Mordecai, respectively, the line of argument being "who would dare to invent such edicts?" Under the logic of "they wouldn't dare print it if it weren't true," many unsophisticated people even in this day and age will believe something if they see it in print, boldly stated.

But even as formal and impersonal as Addition E is, its author still used it as a vehicle for expressing his own religious concerns, as the following excerpts indicate:

> "They . . . even assume that they will escape the evil-hating justice of God, who always sees everything" (E 4)
> "Jews . . . are governed by very just laws, and are sons of the living God, most high, most great, who has directed the kingdom for us and our forefathers in the most successful way" (E 15-16)

---

[9] *City of God*, XVIII 36; and *Christ's Grace and Original Sin*, I 24.

[10] Like the pearl which consists of a hard, solid core over which successive layers of a colorful foreign substance have been added, the Book of Esther consists of a solid core of truth (the story of Mordecai and Haman—and possibly even the story of Esther) to which were added legendary and fictional elements, notably the story of Vashti (ch. 1), the search for a successor to Vashti (ch. 2), the second day of fighting in Susa (9:11-19), and a few other details (*passim*).

Haman and his family have been hanged, "an appropriate sentence which the omnipotent God promptly passed on him" (E 18)

"For the omnipotent God has made this a day of joy for his chosen people instead of their day of destruction" (E 21).

The Additions are both a symptom and a result of Esther's questionable status, i.e. the Additions were invented to strengthen the book's deficiencies, but only a book with questionable canonical status permitted such "presumptuous" tampering with the text.

Purim in the Hebrew and Greek Versions

Although Purim is emphasized in the Hebrew version—in fact, its institution as a Jewish festival is the raison d'être of the Hebrew text in its final form—Purim is actually de-emphasized in the Greek version. In large part, the very presence of the Additions, not to mention their theological content, shifts the focus from the cultic to the "religious," from the military deliverance by the people themselves on a certain date to God's miraculous deliverance of Esther, the latter event being the climax in the Greek version. But Purim is given less emphasis even in the canonical portions of the Greek version, especially in ch. 9 of both the LXX and the AT.[11] This playing down of Purim may reflect some reservations about, if not rejection of, Purim as a Jewish religious festival. As noted earlier, the Jews of Qumran did not include Purim in their religious calendar, possibly because they thought, with just cause, the festival was pagan in origin.[12]

Likely though it is that some, if not all, of the Additions were products of Jewish rather than Christian editors (else why the distinctive Jewish piety of Addition C or the anti-Gentile spirit of Additions A and F?), still the Esther story with the Additions would have been somewhat more palatable to Christians.[13] After all, the raison d'être of the Hebrew version was the establishment of Purim, a Jewish festival which, unlike Passover or Pentecost, had no counterpart in the Christian calendar. On the other hand, even with the Additions the Greek version still stressed Purim enough and was sufficiently nationalistic and anti-Gentile in spirit as to be virtually ignored by the Christian Church for the first eight centuries.

[11] According to Torrey (*HTR* 37 [1944], 16-17) the Semitic text underlying the AT ended with ch. 7, and a later editor added to the AT a brief summary based on text of the LXX.

[12] It may well be that Purim was a pagan, Persian(?) festival in origin, and that the name itself is secondary, *purim*, "lots," being a later folk etymology supplied by Babylonian Jews. For a fuller discussion of the probable non-Jewish origins of Purim, see AB 7B, XLVI-XLIX.

[13] Especially C and D, which emphasize God's concern for those who serve him as well as the efficacy of faith and prayer.

The Greek Version in General

Before discussing the date, provenance, and authorship of the Additions, we must first answer certain questions about the Greek translation in general.

Date, Place, and Author of Translation

The *terminus a quo,* or earliest date, must be the date of the "final"[14] form of the Hebrew version which, on the basis of the literary evidence, was the early Hellenistic period, although earlier versions may have gone back to the late Persian period.[15] The *terminus ad quem* is ca. A.D. 93-94; for that is when the Greek version of Esther, with its Additions, was paraphrased by Josephus in his *Jewish Antiquities.* The most probable date, however, is over a century earlier, being either 78 B.C., or, more likely, 114 B.C., assuming that Esther's colophon[16] is genuine (see NOTES and COMMENT on F 11). Such a date is quite compatible with Esther's Greek literary style.

There is no reason to reject, as Jacob did,[17] the colophon's claim that the Greek translation was made in Jerusalem by one Lysimachus the son of Ptolemy; it even appears that all the Additions were translated by him except B and E (see COMMENTS *passim*).

[14] By "final" is meant that stage where the book had assumed its essential shape, with most of its present elements existing. Naturally, in the process of manuscripts being copied one from another some changes in the text occurred after that "final" stage.

[15] The literary style of the Hebrew version of Esther has little in common with the first- and second-century B.C. Hebrew of Qumran, nor does the MT evidence any Greek influences. Moreover, its language and style most resemble the Hebrew of Chronicles and Ecclesiastes, books whose date of composition are being increasingly placed by scholars in the fourth or fifth centuries B.C. Then too, the book's very sympathetic attitude toward a "Gentile" king suggests a date much earlier than the Maccabean period (167-135 B.C.). For more on the date of composition, see AB 7B, LVII-LX.

[16] "An inscription placed at the end of a book or manuscript, often containing facts relative to its production, as the scribe's, illuminator's, or printer's name, the place and date of publication, etc.; as, from title page to *colophon.* . . ." *Webster's New International Dictionary,* 2d ed., s.v. "colophon. 2."

[17] Jacob (*ZAW* 10 [1890], 280-287) argued that an Egyptian provenance for the translation is indicated by a number of Greek renderings, including *ethronisthē* for *ks' mlkwtw* (1:2), *prostagma tou basileōs* for *dbr hmlk* (2:8), *philoi* for *śrym* (1:3, 3:1), and *sōmatophulakes* for *mšmry hsp* (2:21). One can accept Jacob's arguments for the Egyptian influence, however, without rejecting the claims of the colophon since, as the colophon itself implies, the translator had some sort of Egyptian background since Lysimachus' father had an Egyptian name, Ptolemy.

The Nature of the Greek Translation of Esther

Two things immediately strike one on reading the Greek version for the first time. First, the Septuagint, typified by LXX[B], is conspicuous not only for the Additions but also for its "omissions," there being scarcely a verse where the LXX[B] does not omit a word, phrase, or clause of the MT.[18] The full extent of these omissions can best be seen by examining the hexaplaric "corrections" in LXX (see final NOTE on F 11), and in the manuscripts designated *f, k,* and *z* in the larger Cambridge Septuagint of Esther, these manuscripts being Septuagint manuscripts which have also been "corrected" by the Hexapla.[19] Secondly, there is an appreciable difference between the Septuagint (or LXX[B]) and the AT, the significance of which will be discussed later.

The Septuagint, or B-text

Apart from a few Hebraisms which may very well be later intrusions,[20] the translation is "literary," having very few places that are so labored or unclear as to remind the reader that it is a translation. The translator was not concerned with preserving the Hebrew word order or with giving consistent, mechanical one-for-one translations of the Hebrew.[21] The Greek translator, who was quite well versed in Hebrew, translated verse by verse the content but not the exact wording of the text before him. His translation is free rather than literal and, on occasion, quite paraphrastic[22]; for example, he translated "about Esther's well-being and progress" in 2:11 as "what shall happen to Esther"; "what this was and why it was" in 4:5 as "the full particulars"; and "who fills his heart" in 7:5 as "who has dared" (for further examples, see textual notes and NOTES *passim*). A sophis-

---

[18] The LXX differs sufficiently from the MT that C. C. Torrey felt justified in writing: "Why is there no Greek translation of the Hebrew text? Every other book of the Hebrew Bible, whatever its nature has its faithful rendering (at least one, often several) in Greek. For the canonical Esther, on the contrary, no such version is extant" (*HTR* 37 [1944], 1).

[19] For details, see Moore, "The Origenic Recension of the Book of Esther," in *GTE*, pp. 23-54.

[20] E.g. *ēmeran ex ēmeras* for *mywm lywm* (3:7); *pesōn pesē* for *npwl tpwl* (6:13); *kata chōran kai chōran* for *mdynh wmdynh* (8:9); *kata genean kai genean* for *dwr wdwr* (9:28)—all of these are such obvious Hebraisms that it is improbable that a stylist as sophisticated as the Greek translator of Esther would have made them. It is far more likely that they are later contaminations from the Hexapla, especially since virtually no manuscript families from antiquity have escaped Hexaplaric contamination (for details, see Moore, *GTE*, pp. 54-71).

[21] *Dbr* is rendered *rēmata* (1:17), *ta lechthenta* (1:18), *logous* (4:9), *rēma* (5:14); *byt: oikiais* (1:22), *ta idia* (5:10), *osa upērchen Aman* (8:1), *epi panton tōn Aman* (8:2), and *ta uparchonta* (8:7); *śrym: philoi* (1:3,3:1) and *archontes* (1:14,16,21); and *'bdym: ethnē* (1:3), *dunameis* (2:18), and *oi en* (3:2). For other examples, see textual notes and NOTES *passim*.

[22] So paraphrastic is the translation that B. Jacob concluded, not without some justice, that LXX[B] is "more or less worthless as a critical witness of the original Hebrew text" (*ZAW* 10 [1890], 270).

1. A view of the city of Babylon and its justly famous ziggurat, in the days of the Neo-Babylonian empire.

2. Ancient relief depicting a Mesopotamian deity pursuing a winged monster.

3. A ferocious lioness mauling an Ethiopian; eighth century B.C., from Nimrud.

4. Natural and mythical animals, on colored tiles, decorate the southeastern pillars of Babylon's Ishtar Gate; sixth century B.C.

5. Gold foundation plaque of Darius I (522–486 B.C.), telling the details of the *apadana's* construction.

6. An ancient document (a marriage contract in Aramaic) written in 449 B.C.: papyrus, rolled, tied, and sealed.

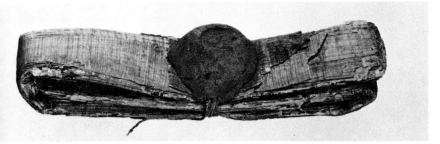

7. A synagogal mural at Dura-Europos, depicting Esther and Xerxes receiving a message (cf. Esther 9:11); third century A.D.

8. View of a procession entering Babylon's famous Ishtar Gate (for close-up of a portion of the gate, see Plate 4).

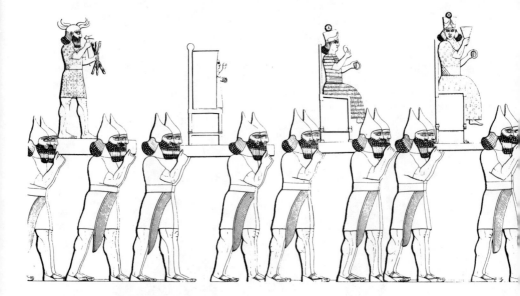

9. Line drawing of a relief depicting soldiers of Tiglath-pileser III (745–727 B.C.) carrying on their shoulders captured idols.

10. Seated Canaanite god in bronze, covered with gold leaf, dating to ca. 1350–1100 B.C.

11. Syrian god in bronze with silver overleaf, dating to 1600–1400 B.C.

12. Nude, winged Babylonian goddess on the Burney Plaque; early second millennium B.C.

13. Dead Sea scroll fragment of vs. 44 of the Epistle of Jeremiah, from Cave VII, dating to the first century B.C.

ticated stylist[23] who disliked the frequent repetitions and redundancies of the Hebrew version, the Greek translator deliberately omitted many of them (see textual notes *passim;* but especially the manuscripts "corrected" by the Hexapla; cf. p. 162, n. 19). That his Hebrew text was substantially like the MT is highly probable, but in the absence of any Hebrew manuscript of Esther earlier than the eleventh-century Ben Asher text (*Leningrad MS. B. 19*[A]) impossible to prove, although the Septuagint manuscripts "corrected" by the Hexapla, such as LXX[N], *f, k,* and *z,* increase the likelihood of our assumption.

The AT, or A-Text

The AT of Esther is considerably shorter than the LXX, despite the presence of a few "additions" (see NOTES *passim*).[24] Its brevity is due to: (1) its numerous "omissions" of personal names, numbers, dates, and repetitious elements present in LXX;[25] and (2) its frequent "abbreviations," e.g. while 2:12-14 is lacking in the AT, it is summed up in 3:17 of the AT with "when the king had carefully examined all the maidens"; and while the LXX has in 5:3: "What do you want, Esther, and what is your request up to half of my kingdom? And it shall be yours," which agrees with the MT, the AT simply has, "What is it, Esther? Tell me, and I shall do it"; and while in 5:11 the LXX has "and he indicated to them his wealth and the honor which the king had conferred upon him, and how he [the king] had made him to be first and to be leader of the realm," the AT simply has "He boasted, saying."[26]

In the paragraph above the words "additions," "omissions," and "abbreviations" were put in quotes because, in contrast to most scholars,[27] the

---

[23] Jacob's characterization of the translation as "a readable prose" (p. 274) is unduly severe, especially since the Hebrew version is hardly a literary masterpiece, at least, not as far as its vocabulary and style are concerned (see AB 7B, LIV-LVII).

[24] A number of the "additions," "omissions," and "abbreviations" of the AT will be found in the notes of the present volume; but for an exhaustive list of these and other peculiarities of the AT, Moore, *GTE,* pp. 128-173.

[25] See Notes *passim,* and Moore, *GTE,* pp. 141-146. According to Herbert J. Cook *ZAW* 81 [1969], 369-376), the A-text also deliberately omitted "irrational elements" of the Esther story so as to produce a more "reasonable" story.

[26] For other examples, see Moore, *GTE,* pp. 16-63.

[27] Most modern scholars, following Paul A. de Lagarde and Frederic Field, regard the AT of Esther as "the Lucianic recension" of the Septuagint (see AB 7B, LXII), the one major exception being C. C. Torrey who argued that the AT is based upon an Aramaic text quite different from the Aramaic text upon which the LXX(!) was based (see *HTR* 37 [1947], 1-40). Earlier, H. H. Howorth had asserted, without citing any supporting evidence, "that the Book of Esther with its so-called additions was originally written in Aramaic . . . and was translated from Aramaic into Greek by 'the Seventy'; and so having had the so-called additions excised was then translated into Hebrew by the doctors at Jamnia, who issued the Ur-text of the Bible" (*PSBA* 31 [May 1909], 157). That such a far-fetched proposal could have arisen testifies almost as much to the complexity and seemingly insoluble Lower Criticism problems pervading the Book of Esther, especially the relation of the LXX and the AT to the MT, as it does to the unbridled imagination of some scholars.

present writer does not regard most of the variants in the AT as additions, omissions, or abbreviations of the LXX; but, as shown in some detail elsewhere,[28] the AT of Esther is not the Lucianic recension of the Septuagint but a separate translation of the Hebrew.

The principal reasons for regarding the AT as a separate translation of the Hebrew and not a recension of the LXX are as follows: (1) the presence of a number of passages that are translated quite differently in the AT and the LXX and yet seem to presuppose the same Hebrew *Vorlage,* or original, for instance, the Hebrew of 2:4 *whn'rh 'šr tyṭb b'yny hmlk tmlk tḥt wšty* is rendered in the LXX as *kai ē gunē ē an aresē tō basilei basileusei anti astin,* and in the AT as *kai ē pais ē ean aresē tō basilei katastathēsetai anti ouastin* (for other examples, cf. the AT and the LXX in 1:10, 3:1, 6:6, and 7:9); (2) the very low incidence of *verbatim agreement* between the AT and the LXX, namely, of the 163 verses in the canonical portion of the LXX, only 45 of them have some phrase preserved by the AT[29]; (3) the presence of Hebraisms and infelicities of phrase in the AT, e.g. the Hebrew of 1:21 *wyyṭb hdbr b'yny hmlk whśrym wy'š hmlk kdbr mmwkn* is in the LXX as *kai ēresen o logos tō basilei kai tois archousi kai epoiēsen o basileus katha elalēsen o mouchaios,* and in the AT as *kai agathos o logos en kardia tou basileōs kai epoiēsen etomiōs kata ton logon touton* (cf. the LXX and the AT also in 1:2,14, 3:11); and (4) the abundance of synonyms in the AT, some of which agree with Josephus or the MT.[30]

Evidently the Hebrew text behind the AT was at points quite different from the one presupposed by the LXX as well as from the one from which the MT descended; for many of the so-called additions, omissions, and abbreviations of the AT reflect a different Hebrew *Vorlage* rather than editorial treatment by the Greek translators.[31]

Only if one ignores the witness of the AT can one agree with Bardtke (p. 267) that the MT is essentially identical with the Hebrew as it left the hands of its Jewish author. Whether the existence of three such different Hebrew texts as those in the MT and as presupposed by the LXX and the AT is the cause or the result of Esther's questionable canonical status is difficult to say, although the latter is more likely. In any case, interesting or relevant readings from the AT are to be found in the present volume.

---

[28] C. A. Moore, *ZAW* 79 (1967), 351-358. Using a different type of linguistic and literary analysis, H. J. Cook (*ZAW* 81 [1969], 369-376) confirmed Moore's findings, and then went on to argue that the Semitic text of the A-text of Esther ended with Esther 8:5, and that 8:17-21 of the A-text may have had a Semitic *Vorlage* but 8:33-38 of the A-text definitely did not.

[29] For details, see Moore, *GTE,* pp. 150-154.

[30] Ibid., pp. 156-160.

[31] For a brief defense of this view, see the writer's article in *ZAW* 79 (1967), 355-358; see also H. J. Cook, *ZAW* 81 (1969), 369-376.

On Additions in the AT

The AT and the LXX disagree with one another much less in the Additions than in their canonical portions, a fact best explained by theorizing that one text borrowed its Additions from the other. Certainly Addition E was not at first a part of the AT but was borrowed from the LXX, since Addition E has a different place in the AT (8:22-32) and repeats in expanded form the content of 8:35-37 of the AT, the latter being the AT's original version of the second royal letter. Moreover, since in the other Additions the OL agrees much more frequently with the LXX and since the LXX also usually provides the preferred reading (see textual notes *passim*), it is probable that the AT borrowed all its Additions from the LXX rather than the reverse (although one cannot ignore the possibility that each version contributed some Additions to the other). All this being the case, only the more important or interesting variants of the AT will be noted in the present volume.[32]

Date of Additions

It is highly unlikely that the Greek translator composed any of the Additions. For there are the inconsistencies and contradictions which a translator who had labored over a Hebrew text would presumably have noted (see COMMENT, p. 179); moreover, the author of Additions B and E was a very sophisticated stylist who would never have made such literal Greek renderings of the Hebrew as those noted in the canonical portions (but see p. 191). It is not likely he would have been content to render the other Additions so simply and prosaically. Recognizing the cogency of these observations, some scholars, such as Soubigou (p. 588), believe that Lysimachus translated everything except the two royal edicts which Lysimachus inserted just as they were into his Greek translation, since they were part of the court archives. In any case, just how soon after 114 B.C. (see p. 161) Additions B and E were composed is impossible to say.

Additions B, C, D, and E were in existence at least by A.D. 93-94, for they were paraphrased by Josephus in his *Jewish Antiquities*. Whether A and F (the dream and its interpretation) were lacking in the particular text Josephus used or whether he deliberately omitted them from his paraphrase is unknown, although the latter possibility seems the more proba-

---

[32] Since the AT seems to be more associated with the Eastern than the Western Church Fathers, it may be that men in the East denied Esther's canonicity more often because many of them knew the Greek version without the "redeeming" features of the Additions (see Schildenberger, p. 22). An English translation of the Additions of the AT may be found in Bissell.

ble.[33] In any case, they existed by Origen's day (185?-?254), although, curiously enough, Origen does not expressly state (as he did for Additions B, C, and E) that Additions A, F (and D) were lacking in the Hebrew Bible of his day.

That the Additions were not all composed at the same time is suggested by the fact that both Josephus and the OL lack A 12-17 and C 17-23, presumably because these passages were lacking in their Greek texts. The oldest Additions could easily have been composed in the second century B.C. A priori, there is no difficulty in accepting Mordecai's dream as a creation of the second century B.C., especially since the dream sounds like those recorded in Daniel, a work completed in the same century. Certainly the theology of the Additions and their anti-Gentile spirit (especially A 6, C 26,28, F 5,8) are quite compatible with a second-century B.C. date. Then too, the spirit and details of Additions C and D are similar to those in the Book of Judith, a Hebrew work composed in the same century (see COMMENT II, pp. 220-222).

Provenance and Authorship of Additions

Given the distinctive Greek character of Additions B and E (see NOTES passim), they may very well have originated in some sophisticated non-Palestinian Jewish center such as Alexandria, Egypt (see NOTE on "their immediate subordinates" in B 1). Schildenberger (p. 20) is undoubtedly correct in saying that, from the point of view of subject matter and style, the same individual composed Additions B and E; but that they should be attributed to Lysimachus (so Torrey, HTR 37 [1944], 27-28) is quite unacceptable. One can scarcely imagine the same man being capable of keeping two such radically different Greek styles quite separate from one another, i.e. keeping the simple, unpretentious style of the canonical portions uncontaminated by the flowery rhetoric so obviously enjoyed by the author of Additions B and E.

The other Additions may very well have originated in Palestine (but see Schildenberger, p. 39). At least such is the inference to be drawn from the colophon, which comes after the interpretation of the dream (F 1-10). Hence its claim would have applied to A 1-11 as well as F 1-10. Then too, Additions C and D each gives evidence of having a Semitic *Vorlage* by having a phrase which, though translated differently by the LXX and the

---

[33] To Josephus, who was concerned with telling the Romans the story of Esther and Mordecai, the inclusion of Mordecai's dream and its interpretation might have seemed irrelevant, if not openly offensive to his readers, given its pronounced anti-Gentile spirit. Moreover, as Nöldeke long ago observed, the absence of Additions A and F from Josephus' Greek text need not mean that they "were necessarily lacking in all the other MSS. of the same period" (*Encyclopaedia Biblica* [1901], col. II, 1406).

AT, presupposes the same Aramaic phrase (see NOTES on "out of arrogance" in C 7 and "full of graciousness" in D 14). The theological content of these Additions is quite compatible with Palestinian Judaism as we know it in books such as Daniel, Judith, and the sectarian literature of Qumran. The anti-Gentile spirit of A and F is certainly appropriate enough to the situation in second-century B.C. Palestine. The author/s of A and F need not be responsible for C and D, especially since part of C (vss. 17-23) is lacking attestation in Josephus and the OL. In sum, Additions A, C, D, and F were missing from the Hebrew text used by the Syriac and Jerome because they were secondary, not because they were "Greek" creations.

The Additions, then, are products of the imagination of their authors and are without any factual basis. Nevertheless, they do shed interesting additional light on Jewish thought and practice in the second and first centuries B.C.

Other Versions of Esther

Speaking of the ancient versions of Esther, Barucq observed that ancient translators had taken in their translations of the Hebrew "a liberty which astonishes us" (p. 78) and suggests, not without some justice, that this indicates that they regarded Esther less as a historical document than a book of edification and treated it as such. In any case, the OL, Coptic (Sahidic dialect), and Ethiopic versions of Esther are based on the LXX,[34] although the OL does have a striking number of readings agreeing with the AT.[35] The Syriac and Vulgate are based on the Hebrew text, the Syriac being quite faithful to it.

Given Jerome's claim for the Vulgate's very literal faithfulness to the Hebrew,[36] one might be surprised that the Vulgate is not nearly as close to the MT as one might expect, but is sometimes quite paraphrastic (see NOTES passim). Because Jerome translated the Additions even more freely than the canonical portions of Esther, his version is of little help in "correcting" the Additions.

Esther's two targumim (Aramaic translations dating from not earlier than the eighth and ninth centuries) are quite faithful to the Hebrew but

---

[34] The same may be said of these versions for the other books of the Bible as well; see Roberts, OTTV, pp. 227-235. For further details on the Coptic, Ethiopic, and OL versions of Esther, see Moore, GTE, 17-20, 20-22, and 96-127, respectively.

[35] According to Schildenberger (pp. 12-20), the OL is not a conflated or contaminated text but an accurate Latin translation of "the inspired Greek" version (p. v), a Greek text which was quite different from either the LXX or the AT.

[36] "What is found in the Hebrew," wrote Jerome after Esther 10:3, "I have expressed with complete fidelity. However, the material which follows is found in the Common Edition, which is expressed in the language and script of the Greeks."

include so much haggadic material that I Targum is more than twice as long as the MT, and II Targum is twice as long as I Targum.[37] Unfortunately, only for the Greek and Vulgate are there what might properly be called "critical editions" (see BIBLIO II, pp. 171-172).

Brief yet very helpful descriptions of the various early Midrashes, i.e. Jewish commentaries containing haggadic and halakhic traditions of Esther, including even dreams and prayers of Mordecai and Esther, may be found conveniently in Paton (pp. 101-104). His conclusion in 1908 that these Jewish commentaries have virtually no material to support the thesis that the LXX Additions are translations of a Semitic *Vorlage* is still shared by nearly all scholars.

In Defense of Procedure

It is a serious mistake to read the Additions out of context, i.e. either *after* reading the canonical portion (as in the Vulgate) or *without* any canonical text at all (as in most "Protestant" Bibles, e.g. KJ, RSV, NEB, *et alia*). Therefore, in order to provide the reader with some context for the Additions as well as to remind him of how very different in style and spirit they are from the canonical Hebrew text, in the present commentary the Additions will be placed within the context of our English translation of the Hebrew text. (To have put them within the Greek version would not have been as illuminating to the reader, since in the Greek version the canonical parts and the Additions are harmonized and leveled through, the many differences and contradictions between the Hebrew version and the Greek Additions being minimized.[38]

This admittedly unorthodox procedure was decided upon by the present writer only after considerable inner debate, but he could think of no more simple and effective way of providing, simultaneously, the reader context *and contrast* and can only hope the reader will withhold judgment on this procedure until after its fruits have been tasted. Needless to say, even in the canonical portion of this translation, i.e. in the MT, important omissions, or modifications in the Greek versions will be pointed out in the commentary.

[37] For a short but excellent introduction to the subject of I and II Targums, as well as a topical listing of haggadic materials included in each, see Paton, pp. 18-24. Translations of the Targums (and Midrashes) are almost all publications in either Latin or German, but not English. Fuller is the one scholar who has incorporated into his commentary a selective but considerable amount of this material in English.

[38] For example, wherever the MT has "Mordecai sat at the gate of the king," the LXX has "Mordecai served in the court of the king." This change from "at the gate of" to "in the court of" is clearly an inner-Greek development (see NOTE on A 2).

BIBLIOGRAPHY II

Commentaries

Bardtke, Hans. *Das Buch Esther*, Kommentar zum Alten Testament. Gütersloh: Mohn, 1963. *Cited as* Bardtke.

————— "Zusätze zu Esther," in *Historische und legendarische Erzählungen, Jüdische Schriften aus hellenistisch-römischer Zeit*, ed. Werner Georg Kümmel et al., I, 1. Gütersloh: Mohn, 1973.

Barucq, André. *Judith, Esther*, 2d ed., La Sainte Bible. Paris: Cerf, 1959. *Cited as* Barucq.

Bertheau, Ernst, and rev. by Victor Ryssel. *Die Bücher Ezra, Nehemia und Esther*, 2d. ed., Kurzgefasstes exegetisches Handbuch zum Alten Testament. Leipzig: Hirzel, 1887.

Bissell, E. C. *The Apocrypha of the Old Testament, with Historical Introductions and Notes and Explanatory*. New York, 1880. *Cited as* Bissell.

Fritzsche, Otto. *Zusätzen zum Buch Esther*, Kurzgefasstes exegetisches Handbuch zu den Apokryphen des Alten Testaments, eds. O. Fritzsche and C. Grimm, I. Leipzig: Hirzel, 1851. *Cited as* Fritzsche.

Fuerst, W. J. "The Rest of the Chapters of the Book of Esther," in *The Shorter Books of the Apocrypha*, ed. J. C. Dancy. The Cambridge Bible Commentary, 1972.

Fuller, J. M. "The Rest of the Chapters of the Book of Esther," in *Apocrypha of the Speaker's Commentary*, ed. Henry Wace, I. London: John Murray, 1888. *Cited as* Fuller.

Gerleman, Gillis. *Esther*, Biblischer Kommentar Altes Testament, XXI/1-2. Neukirchen-Vluyn: Neukirchener Verlag, 1970-73.

Girbau, B. M. *Esther*, La Biblia. Montserrat: Montserrat, 1960.

Gregg, J. A. F. *The Additions to Esther*, in *APOT*, I, 665-684. *Cited as* Gregg.

Haupt, Paul. "Critical Notes on Esther," *AJSL* 24 (1907-8), 97-186. Reprinted as "The Book of Esther: Critical Edition of the Hebrew Text with Notes," in *Old Testament and Semitic Studies in Memory of William Rainey Harper*, eds. R. F. Harper, Francis Brown, and George F. Moore, I. The University of Chicago Press, 1911. *Article cited as* Haupt.

Jahn, Gustav. *Das Buch Esther nach der Septuaginta hergestellt, übergestellt, übersetzt und kritisch erklärt*. Leiden, 1901.

Langen, Joseph. *Die deuterocanonischen Stücke des Buches Esther*. Freiburg im Breisgau, 1862.

Moore, Carey A. *Esther: Introduction, Translation, and Notes*, The Anchor Bible, eds. W. F. Albright and D. N. Freedman, vol. 7B. New York: Doubleday, 1971. *Cited as* AB 7B.

Paton, Lewis B. *A Critical and Exegetical Commentary on the Book of Esther,* International Critical Commentary. New York: Scribner, 1908. *Cited as* Paton.

Ringgren, K. V. H., and A. Weiser, *Das Hohe Lied, Klagelieder, Das Buch Esther,* Das Alte Testament Deutsch, XVI. Göttingen: Vandenhoeck und Ruprecht, 1958. *Cited as* Ringgren.

Ryssel, Victor. *Zusätzen zum Buch Esther,* Die Apokryphen und Pseudepigraphen des Alten Testament, ed. E. F. Kautzsch. Tübingen: Mohr, 1900. *Cited as* Kautzsch-Ryssel.

Schildenberger, Johannes B. *Das Buch Esther,* Die Heilige Schrift des Alten Testaments. Bonn: Peter Hanstein Verlag, 1941. *Cited as* Schildenberger.

Scholz, Anton. *Commentar über das Buch Esther mit zeinen Zusätzen und über Susanna.* Würzburg-Wien: Verlag Leo Woerl, 1892.

Soubigou, L. *Esther traduit et commente,* 2d ed., La Sainte Bible—Bible de Jérusalem. Paris: Cerf, 1952. *Cited as* Soubigou.

Other Books

André, L. E. T. *Les apocryphes de l'Ancien Testament.* Florence, 1903.

Beelen, Joannes Theodorus. *Chrestomathica Rabbinica et Chaldaica cum Notis Grammaticus, Historicis, Theologicis, Glossario et Lexico.* 2 vols. Lovanii, Vanlenthout et Vandenzande, 1841.

Eissfeldt, Otto. *The Old Testament: An Introduction, including the Apocrypha and Pseudepigrapha, and also the works of similar type from Qumran,* tr. from the 3d Ger. ed. by Peter R. Ackroyd. New York: Harper & Row, 1965. *Cited as* Eissfeldt.

Hoschander, Jacob. *The Book of Esther in the Light of History.* Philadelphia: Dropsie College, 1923. *Cited as* Hoschander.

Kauler, Franz. *Einleitung in die Heilige Schrift Alten und Neuen Testaments,* Theologische Bibliothek. Freiburg im Breisgau: Herdersche, 1890.

Moore, Carey A. *The Greek Text of Esther* (abbr. *GTE*), a Johns Hopkins University dissertation, 1965. Microfilm-Xerox reprint, no. 65-6880. Ann Arbor, 1965.

Oesterley, W. O. E. *An Introduction to the Books of the Apocrypha.* New York: Macmillan, 1935. *Cited as* Oesterley.

Pfeiffer, Robert H. *History of the New Testament Times with an Introduction to the Apocrypha.* New York: Harper, 1949. *Cited as* Pfeiffer.

Roberts, B. J. *The Old Testament Text and Versions: The Hebrew Text in Transmission and the History of the Ancient Versions* (abbr. *OTTV*).

Torrey, Charles C. *The Apocryphal Literature.* Yale University Press, 1945. *Cited as* Torrey.

Articles

Bickerman, E. J., "Notes on the Greek Book of Esther," *PAAJR* 20 (1950), 101-133.

——— "The Colophon of the Greek Book of Esther," *JBL* 63 (1944), 339-362.

Brownlee, W. H., "Le Livre grec d'Esther et la royauté divine. Corrections orthodoxes au livre d'Esther," *RB* 73 (1966), 161-185.

Cook, Herbert J., "The *A*-text of the Greek Versions of the Book of Esther," *ZAW* 81 (1969), 369-376.

Ehrlich, Ernst, "Der Traum des Mardochai," *ZRGG* 7 (1955), 69-74.

Gordis, Robert, "Studies in the Esther Narrative," *JBL* 95 (1976), 43-58.

Horn, S. H., "Mordecai, a Historical Problem," *BR* 9 (1964), 22-25.

Howorth, Henry H., "Some Unconventional Views on the Text of the Bible. VIII. The Prayer of Manasses and the Book of Esther," *PSBA* 31 (May 1909), 89-99, 156-168.

Jacob, Benno, "Das Buch Esther bei dem LXX," *ZAW* 10 (1890), 241-298.

Jones, Bruce W., "Two Misconceptions about the Book of Esther," *CBQ* 39 (1977).

Langen, Joseph, "Die beiden griechischen Texte des Buches Esther," *TQ* (1860), 244-272.

Marcus, Ralph, "Dositheus, Priest, and Levite," *JBL* 64 (1945), 269-271.

Martin, Raymond A., "Syntax Criticism of the LXX Additions to the Book of Esther," *JBL* 94 (1975), 65-72.

Moore, Carey A., "A Greek Witness to a Different Hebrew Text of Esther," *ZAW* 79 (1967), 351-358.

—— "Archaeology and the Book of Esther," *BA* 38 (1975), 62-79.

—— "On the Origins of the LXX Additions to the Book of Esther," *JBL* 92 (1973), 382-393.

Roiron, F. X., "Les parties deuterocanoniques du Livre d'Esther," *RSR* (1916), 3-16.

Striedl, Hans, "Untersuchung zur Syntax und Stilistik des hebräischen Buches Esther," *ZAW* 55 (1937), 73-108.

Talmon, Shemaryahu "Wisdom in the Book of Esther," *VT* 13 (1963), 419-455.

Torrey, C. C., "The Older Book of Esther," *HTR* 37 (1944), 1-40.

Versions of Esther and the Additions

Brooke, A. E., Norman McLean, and H. St. John Thackeray, eds. *Esther, Judith, Tobit*. The Old Testament in Greek, III, Part 1. Cambridge University Press, 1940.

Geissen, Angelo. *Der Septuaginta-Text des Buches Daniel: Kap. 5-12, zusammen mit Susanna, Bel et Draco, sowie Esther Kap. 1,1a-2,15, nach dem Kölner Teil des Papyrus 967*, Papyrologische Texte und Abhandlungen, V. Bonn: Rudolf Habelt, 1968.

Hanhart, Robert. *Esther*. Septuaginta. Vetus Testamentum Graecum auctoritate Societatis Gottingensis editum, ed. J. Ziegler, III. Göttingen, 1966.

Kenyon, F. G., ed. *Ezekiel, Daniel, and Esther*. The Chester Beatty Biblical Papyri [of the Greek Bible], fasc. VII. London: Emery Walker, 1937.

de Lagarde, Paul A., ed. *Targum Rishon*. Hagiographa Chaldaice. Leipsig, 1873.

—— *Targum Sheni*. Hagiographa Chaldaice. Berlin, 1873.

Libre Hester et Job. Biblia Sacra iuxta Latinam Vulgatam versionem, ed. Ordinis Sancti Benedicti. Rome: Trypsis Polyglottis Vaticanis, 1951.

Pereira, Esteves, ed. *Le livre d'Esther, version éthiopiene.* Patrologia Orientalis, ed. R. Graffin, IX. Paris, 1913.

Thompson, H. F., ed. *A Coptic Palimpsest in British Museum containing Joshua, Judges, Ruth, Judith, and Esther in the Sahidic Dialect.* Oxford University Press, 1911.

I. ADDITION A:

MORDECAI HAS A DREAM AND UNCOVERS A CONSPIRACY
(A 1-17; AT 1-18; Vulg. 11:2-12:6)

A ¹ In the second year of the reign of Artaxerxes the Great*ᵃ*, on the first day of Nisan*ᵇ*, Mordecai the son of Jair, son of Shimei, son of Kish, a Benjaminite, had a dream. ² He was a Jew living in the city of Susa, a prominent man who served in the king's court*ᶜ*. ³ He was one of the prisoners whom Nebuchadnezzar, king of Babylon, had brought down from Jerusalem with Jeconiah, king of Judah. ⁴ And this was his dream:

> *ᵈ*Cries and clamoring*ᵉ*, thundering and earthquake, and confusion upon the earth!
>
> ⁵ And two great dragons advanced, both of them ready for battle; *ᶠ*and they roared loudly*ᶠ*. ⁶ *ᵍ*And at their roaring every nation got itself ready for battle that it might fight against the righteous nation.
>
> ⁷ A day of gloom and darkness, affliction and distress, oppression and great confusion upon the earth! ⁸ And the entire righteous nation was alarmed, dreading their ill-fate; and they were prepared to die*ʰ*; ⁹ and they cried out to God. And from their crying there arose, as though from a tiny spring, a mighty river, a

---

ᵃ Only LXXᴮ and OL add "king."
ᵇ AT "Adar-Nisan, which is Dystrus-Xanthicus"; see NOTE.
ᶜ AT and OL summarize all of vs. 2 with "a great man."
ᵈ Here and at the beginning of vss. 5 and 7, Greek has "And behold!" See NOTE.
ᵉ AT "And behold! Crying and clamorous shrieking."
ᶠ⁻ᶠ Literally "and their cry was great"; Vulgate omits.
ᵍ For vss. 6-8, AT is briefer; see NOTE.
ʰ For this verse OL has simply "and they were afraid."

veritable flood! 10 Light and sun arose; *and the humble were exalted and devoured the eminent*.

11 Now when Mordecai, who had seen this dream and what God
had resolved to do, awoke, he puzzled over it all day and wanted to
understand it in every detail.

12 And Mordecai was dozing in the court with Gabatha and Tharra,
two of the king's eunuchs who kept watch in the court; 13 he overheard their discussion, and investigated their nervousness, and learned
that they were preparing to assassinate King Artaxerxes. So he informed the king about them. 14 The king then interrogated the two
eunuchs;ʲ and after they had confessed, they were executed. 15 The
king wrote a memorandum of these thingsᵏ. 16 The king ordered Mordecai to serve in the courtˡ, and rewarded him for these things. 17 But
Haman son of Hammedatha, *a Bougaion*, enjoyed great favor with
the king, and he sought to do harm to Mordecai and his people because *of the two eunuchs of the king*.

ⁱ⁻ⁱ AT "and the rivers flooded and swallowed up the eminent."
ʲ AT adds "and he confirmed the words of Mordecai."
ᵏ AT "And Mordecai was written up in a memorandum in the king's diary."
ˡ AT adds "of the king and to guard visibly every door."
ᵐ⁻ᵐ AT "a Macedonian"; see NOTE.
ⁿ⁻ⁿ AT "he had spoken to the king about the eunuchs so that they were killed." Vulgate adds to LXX *qui fuerant interfecti.*

NOTES

A 1. In the Vulgate, the dream, which is missing from Josephus (see p. 165,
n. 33), comes after its interpretation because Jerome took all of Addition A,
as well as Additions B, C, D, and E, which he quite rightly regarded as not
being part of the original Hebrew text (see Introduction, pp. 153-155; see also
Ernst Ehrlich, *ZRGG* 7 [1955], 69-74), and put them after the canonical portion.

second year. The dream takes place one year earlier than the opening scene
of the MT (cf. 1:3), and five years before Esther became queen (cf. 2:16 and
19); whether or not this is a discrepancy depends upon one's interpretation of
A 12 (see NOTE on "was dozing" in vs. 12).

Artaxerxes. So the LXX and Josephus identify *ᵃḥašwērôš* of the MT. The
Hebrew name is transliterated by the AT (*assuēros*), the OL (*assuerus*), and
the Vulg. (*asuerus*). Although the linguistic and archeological evidence make it
clear that *'hšwrwš* is Xerxes and not Artaxerxes (see NOTES on "Xerxes" in 1:1
of AB 7B), "Artaxerxes" is retained in the Additions because, in addition to
being the only possible translation of the LXX, it also serves to remind the

reader of the difference between the Additions and the canonical Esther, where "Ahasuerus" is used.

Nisan. Nisan is the post-exilic equivalent of the pre-exilic Abib, the first month of the Jewish year. The AT has "Adar-Nisan, which is Dystrus-Xanthicus," the latter two names being the Macedonian equivalents of the former. For Dystrus (March), see Josephus *Ant.* xi 6:13; for Xanthicus (April), see II Macc 11:30,33,38.

Mordecai. Handicapped though the Greek alphabet is in transliterating Hebrew personal names because of its lack of equivalents for certain sibilant and guttural sounds of the Hebrew (see Roberts, *OTTV*, pp. 108-110), the LXX occasionally preserves an older and more accurate form of foreign names, "Mordecai" being a case in point. Since the name is theophorous, containing the name of the Babylonian god Marduk (see NOTE on 3:5 of AB 7B), the Septuagint's *mardochaios* (so also AT, Josephus, OL, and Vulgate) is more accurate than the MT's *mordᵃkay;* but the conventional masoretic spelling has been retained here for the sake of convenience.

the son of Jair, son of . . . Benjaminite. This being the first mention of Mordecai in the book, it is appropriate to give his genealogy; but then, it is unnecessary to repeat it, as does the Greek in 2:5. The implications of this duplication are, however, quite clear: the genealogy in 2:5 of the LXX represents the Greek translation of the Hebrew text while Addition A is secondary and, since Mordecai is first mentioned there, his genealogy logically must be given there; hence the repetition (but see Soubigou, p. 676).

2. *a prominent man.* In the MT there is no express statement that Mordecai was a prominent man until 8:2, where he is obviously such by virtue of being made prime minister, although, as S. H. Horn has pointed out, such an appointment would hardly have gone to one who had no previous standing. That Jews could and did attain positions of prominence and great wealth in the days of Artaxerxes I and Darius II is clear from the archives of the Murashû sons of Nippur, bankers and brokers of that day (for names and details, see S. H. Horn, "Mordecai, a Historical Problem," *BR* 9 [1964], 22-25).

served in the king's court. Throughout the Greek where the MT has "sat at the King's Gate" (2:19,21, 3:2, 5:9, 6:10,12), the Greek has "served in the king's court." This erroneous translation originated in the Greek where an early copyist read *aulē*, "court," instead of *pulē*, "gate," the uncial *a* and *p* (Greek capital letters) being easily confused.

3. *one of the prisoners [aichmalōsias].* See Judith 2:9; I Macc 9:70-72. Concerning the obvious chronological difficulties with respect to Mordecai's age if he was one of the prisoners of Nebuchadnezzar and yet was still living in the time of Artaxerxes, see NOTE on 2:6 of AB 7B.

4. The images of vss. 4,5, and 7 are each introduced in the Greek by *kai idou* ("and behold!"); but instead of translating *kai idou,* its meaning has been expressed here by the use of punctuation, namely, by making vss. 5 and 7 new paragraphs. A *kai idou* serves to introduce three of the four "scenes" of Mordecai's dream, which are, according to Ehrlich (*ZRGG* 7 [1955], 71), chaos upon the earth, the battle of the dragons, the endangered nation, and divine deliverance.

More importantly, *kai idou* presupposes the Heb. *wᵉhinneh* (or Aram. *waʾᵃrû*), a word used in the MT to introduce a dream in general (cf. Gen 37:7 and 9) or various components within the same dream (cf. Gen 41:2,3, and 5; Dan 7:2,5,6, and 7). Another Hebraism in Mordecai's dream is the frequent use of "and" [Heb. *wa*] at the beginning of a sentence, namely in A 4, 5b,6,8, and 9.

Just as Joseph's dreams (Gen 37:7 and 9) provided the hero and the reader with hints as to Joseph's future success, so does Mordecai's dream (or as the editors of the JB put it, "This dream outlines the story in advance in enigmatic and apocalyptic terms" [p. 641, n. c]). This, then, is another example of the influence of the Joseph story on the Book of Esther (see NOTE on "robe" in 6:8).

Cries and clamoring . . . confusion. Sources of inspiration for the imagery are difficult to identify. Ehrlich (p. 72, nn. 23 and 24) hears echoes of a mythological motif (cf. Ps 74:12-14), while Schildenberger (p. 52) is reminded of the theophany of Sinai (Exod 19:16,18-19, 20:18) and the judgment spoken of by the prophets (Isa 22:5, 24:18-20; Jer 30:5).

5. *two great dragons.* Whether "dragon" is the best word to use here is debatable inasmuch as these particular *drakontes* are not described in sufficient detail. *Josippon* (see p. 154, n. 3) has the Heb. *tnyn,* which in non-mythological passages means "sea monster" (cf. Gen 1:21; Ps 148:7; Job 7:12). In the LXX, *drakōn* includes a wide range of terrifying beasts, from dangerous land animals like the wolf (Jer 9:11[10]; Micah 1:8) and snake (Deut 32:33; Ps 90[91]:13) through the large land reptiles (Job 40:20[25]) and sea creatures (Ps 103[104]:26), to "magic" serpents (Exod 7:9), "divine" snakes ("Bel and the Snake," vs. 23), and mythical creatures like Rahab (Job 26:13), Leviathan (Ps 74:13; Isa 27:1), and Yam (Job 7:12). A dragon is sometimes the symbol for a pagan ruler (Ezek 29:1*f*, 32:1-16; Ps of Sol 2:25). In apocalyptic literature a *drakōn* is a major figure and is symbolic of evil rather than good (cf. Rev 12:3, 13:2, 20:2; II Bar 29:3-8; and II Esd 6:52). For relevant books and articles on "dragon," see Ehrlich (p. 71, n. 13). Whether the dragons involved in this verse are terrestrial or marine is impossible to say; they are in either case, large, ferocious, and awesome to watch. Moreover, they symbolize Mordecai and Haman (so F 4) whose personal struggles foreshadow the wider struggles of the 13th and 14th of Adar (cf. Esth 9:1-19).

6. For vss. 6-8, the AT is brief: "Calling to witness all the peoples. A day of gloom and darkness, and confusion of battle! And every nation was prepared to fight." Unhappy with both the LXX and the AT, and in keeping with his view that the OL best reflects the oldest and most original form of the Greek version, Schildenberger (p. 54) substitutes the reading of the OL for vss. 6b-8: "And they waged a great battle between them and tried to subdue one another. And the people assembled themselves on the dark and evil day, and there was great confusion among the inhabitants of the earth. And they feared defeat."

to fight against the righteous [dikaion] nation. I.e. Israel (so F 4). The Jews are called *dikaioi* in the Wisdom of Solomon (16:23, 18:7), but also "Saints," *osioi* (Wisd 18:1,5 and 9) and "holy people," *laon osion* (Wisd 10:15; cf. also *laō agiō* in Dan 7:27 of LXX; *dēmon agiōn* in Dan 8:24

[*laon agion* in LXX]; and *ton agion sou laon* in II Macc 15:24). For a similar convening of the nations against Israel, see Joel 3[4]:2, and Zech 14:2.

7. *gloom and darkness, affliction.* In contrast to the imagery in vs. 4, the biblical source for this imagery is quite clear: Joel 2:2,10-11; Zeph 1:15 (see also Matt 24:29). The eschatological cast of this verse (so Ehrlich, *ZRGG* 7 [1955], 71) substantially helps to transform the character of the Greek version of Esther, i.e. the transformation from a historical novel of court intrigue in the Hebrew to an eschatological struggle in the Greek version.

9. *God.* The AT has "Lord," the stock Greek translation for Yahweh. The explicit mention of the Deity here, as well as forty-one times elsewhere in the Additions, constitutes the most conspicuous theological difference between the Greek and Hebrew Esther (see Introduction, p. 157).

tiny spring. I.e. Esther (so F 3).

mighty river. Possibly symbolizing irresistible power, as in Astyages' dream in Herodotus *History* I 107.

a veritable flood! Literally "much water."

10. *Light and sun.* Used here as symbols of happiness; cf. Wisd 5:6. Ehrlich (p. 72, n. 24) regards this phrase as meaning "the morning," which is, he says, symbolic of the time of deliverance (cf. Isa 33:2; Pss 30:5[6H], 46:5[6H], 112:4).

eminent. Although the Greek form is plural, Haman is primarily intended; cf. A 17.

11. *puzzled over it all day.* Literally "held it in his heart until the evening." Ehrlich's suggestion (p. 70, n. 6) that "until the evening" may mean "until the *following* evening," at which time Mordecai hoped for a second and more informative dream, seems a somewhat strained interpretation.

For vss. 11-13 of the LXX, the AT has instead "and when Mordecai rose from his sleep, he puzzled intently upon what the dream meant and what the Almighty was planning to do. And his dream had been hidden in his heart, and at every opportunity he was examining it. The meaning of it was given to him on the day when Mordecai fell asleep in the court of the king with Astaus and Thedeutus, two of the king's eunuchs, and heard their words and slanders as they were planning to attack King Assuerus, to destroy him." Like Daniel (cf. Dan 7:28), and unlike Joseph (Gen 37:5,9), Mordecai told no one of his dream, possibly because he believed that only God could interpret it (cf. Gen 41:15-16; Dan 2:26-28). Schildenberger (p. 55), again rejecting the LXX and the AT in his preference for the OL, reads the OL in place of vss. 11-17, namely, "And Mordecai, who had seen the dream, stood up and said, 'What does God intend to do?' And the vision was kept in his heart until it was revealed."

to understand it in every detail. Mordecai understood the general import of the dream, namely, that although the Jews would be threatened by their enemies (vs. 8), God would deliver them (vs. 9). The specifics, however, eluded him—who or what were the two dragons? the tiny spring? Not until Addition F is the reader told.

12. *was dozing.* Literally "was at rest." If, as certainly seems to be the case, there is less than twenty-four hours separating Mordecai's dream (vss. 1-11)

from his discovery of the plot against the king (vss. 12-17), then this is another contradiction between Addition A and the MT; for in Addition A the discovery of the plot occurred in the second year of the king, not the seventh (so 2:21 of the MT). Whether the editor of the AT recognized this contradiction or not, the AT avoided the problem by saying that Mordecai puzzled over the dream "until the day when" (See NOTE on C 11). Jerome avoided the difficulty somewhat by making vs. 12 of the LXX the first verse of a new chapter (i.e. of ch. 12 of the Vulgate), while the OL avoids the problem entirely by not having any of vss. 12-17. (That Josephus and the OL have none of vss. 12-17 may indicate that these verses were not an original part of Addition A.)

Gabatha and Tharra. Cf. 2:21 of the MT: *bigtān, tereš.* The AT has *astaou* and *thedeutou* (Josephus *theodestou*), the *d* of *thedeutou* probably being a misreading of the *r* of *tereš,* although the reverse may be the case; in any event, letters *r* and *d* in the Hebrew script are easily confused.

13. *their nervousness.* Literally "the anxious thoughts."

he informed. Another contradiction of the Hebrew version; in the MT, Esther did it in Mordecai's name (cf. 2:22).

14. *they were executed.* Literally "they were led away." The Vulgate preserves the sense with its *duci iussit ad mortem.*

15. *wrote a memorandum.* Literally "wrote as a memorial"; cf. 2:23 and 6:1 of the MT. In some such record Xerxes noted the names of those who had served him well and deserved a reward (cf. Herodotus VII 100, VIII 85, 90).

16. *rewarded him.* Literally "gave to him." In sharp contrast to the MT (6:1-11), here Mordecai is immediately rewarded for foiling the plot against the king; see, however, Gregg (p. 673) who, following the Vulg.'s *pro delatione,* argues that the phrase "for these things" refers to "services rendered" rather than "on account of the eunuchs."

17. *a Bougaion.* Cf. 3:1, where the LXX renders the MT's *hā'ᵃgāgî,* "the Agagite," as *bougaion.* (For *bougaios* in A 17, Vulgate has *bugeus,* but in 3:11 it has "he was of the tribe of Agag.") Although the origin and meaning of *bougaion* are unknown (for possible explanations, see NOTE on 3:1 in AB 7B), the substitution of "Macedonian" for *bougaion* by the AT here and by the LXX in 9:24 and E 10 (see NOTE) suggests that *bougaion,* like "Macedonian," was an updated term of reproach, i.e. the once opprobrious but now innocuous term *bougaion* was now replaced by "Macedonian," the latter term being far more meaningful to Greek-reading Jews who knew well the reputation of the Macedonians. Thus, just as the MT (3:1) used "Agagite" (Josephus *amalekiten*) as a name representing the implacable arch enemy of the Israelites, so Greek editors of Esther used equally meaningful contemporary terms for their Hellenistic readers, first Bougaion, and later, Macedonian. Fuller (p. 378), however, believes that "Macedonian" refers to Haman's political sympathies, not his ethnic origins.

enjoyed great favor with the king [*endoxos enōpion tou basileōs*]. A Hebraism, *enōpion* presupposes the Heb. *lipnê.*

because of the two eunuchs. Another inconsistency between the Additions and the MT: here Haman is hostile because of Mordecai's informing on the conspirators with whom Haman was presumably in league; in the MT, however, Haman's enmity was rooted in Mordecai's refusal to bow down to him (cf. 3:6). Fuller (p. 373) thought that the LXX spoke of two separate conspiracies; thus the conspirators mentioned here are not the same as those in 2:21-23, his reason being the names of the conspirators in 2:21-23 of the LXX are omitted (ergo, unknown [!]), and that they have different responsibilities, i.e. the plotters in 2:21 "guarded the threshhold" rather than "kept watch in the court" (A 12). Against this is the simple fact that the AT, Josephus, and the OL speak of only one conspiracy, the AT telling of the plot of Astaus and Thedeutus in Addition A, and Josephus and the OL of the conspiracy of Bartageus and Thedestes in the place corresponding to 2:21-23. Different though the names are, they certainly represent the men referred to in the MT as Bigtan and Teresh.

COMMENT

Brief though Addition A is, it still vividly points up two basic characteristic differences between the Greek and Hebrew versions of Esther: (1) the explicitly acknowledged activity of God; and (2) some obvious contradictions to the MT. In striking contrast to the Hebrew account (see NOTES [esp. on 4:14 and 16] and COMMENT [esp. on 6:1-6] in AB 7B), the Greek version stresses the crucial role played by God in all the events of Esther: in Addition A, for instance, God indicates in a cryptic dream what he intends to do (vss. 4-10); the people of Israel will cry to God for help (vs. 9); God's providential care is explicitly acknowledged by the phrase "what God had resolved to do" (vs. 11). To be sure, the Greek version does not confine its acknowledgment of God's activity to the Additions, explicit mention of the Deity being found even in the canonical portions of the Greek Esther: "to fear God and obey his commandments" (2:20); "call upon the Lord" (4:8); "and the Lord drove sleep from the king that night" (6:1); and "for the living God is with him" (6:13). For additional references to God in the AT only, see 4:14,16, and 7:2.

Inconsistencies and contradictions between the Greek and Hebrew versions abound in Addition A, but in the setting (vss. 1-3 and 11-17) rather than in the dream itself (vss. 4-10). In contrast to the MT where Mordecai "sits at the king's gate" (2:21) and is not promoted until after Haman's death (7:10 - 8:2), in A 2 Mordecai is already "a prominent man who served in the king's court" (see also A 12). According to A 13, Mordecai himself informed the king of the plot and was immediately rewarded, while in 2:22 of the MT Esther informed the king in Mordecai's name and Mordecai was not rewarded until much later (6:11). Haman's hostility toward Mordecai was rooted in the latter's informing on the conspirators (so A 17), not because Mordecai refused to bow down to Haman (3:5). For contradictions elsewhere, see NOTES on C 7,23,26,28; E 14 and 18. Since these contradictions and inconsistencies in Addition A are so obvious to us, it is not unlikely that later Greek editors were responsible for many of them, since the original translator would, more likely, have tried harder to reconcile his "facts."

There can be no doubt that Addition A is secondary. Its contradictions to the

MT as well as its explicitly stated religious concerns indicate that A 1-17 was not an original part of the Esther story. Whether it is Semitic or Greek in origin is more problematical, and scholars have been found on both sides of the question. The Addition, which naturally divides itself into two distinct sections, the dream [vss. 1-11] and the plot [vss. 12-17], is certainly the work of different authors. The primary external evidence for thinking that vss. 12-17 were not a part of Addition A even as late as the second century A.D. is that vss. 12-17 are missing from the OL. As for the internal evidence, there is no reason to think that vss. 12-17 represent a survival, especially since these verses contradict the MT (see above), and because they are superfluous and redundant, repeating in expanded form the LXX material of 2:21-23, the latter obviously being a translation of the Hebrew (see also Jacob, ZAW 10 [1890], 297-298).

On the other hand, the dream itself is probably a separate entity and a survival, i.e. is Semitic in origin. Some of the Additions appearing in *Josippon's* Hebrew version (see p. 154, n. 3) may very well be based upon his translation of Josephus' *Antiquities*. Such, however, can not be said of Mordecai's dream, for it is not present in *Antiquities*. One may agree with A. A. Newman (*JQR* 43 [1952/53], 1ff) that *Josippon* also used the LXX. One indication of there being a Semitic *Vorlage* for the dream in vss. 4-10 is that vss. 1-3 and 11-17 are in far "better" Greek, vs. 1 beginning, for example, with a genitive absolute construction, and vs. 11 with subordinate clauses and phrases. Then too, from the colophon one would assume that the dream was in the Hebrew text used by Lysimachus (see COMMENT, p. 251); and in terms of literary style (see NOTE on vs. 4) and theological content, the dream is sufficiently simple and representative of OT dreams to be Semitic in origin. (Detailed analysis of the dream must be reserved for § XIV, pp. 245-249.) Of considerable relevance here is the work of R. A. Martin. Using his seventeen syntactical features as the criteria for determining whether a particular Greek passage is "original Greek" or "translation Greek," Martin (*JBL* 94 [1975], 65-72) concluded that Addition A clearly had a Semitic *Vorlage*.

Not surprisingly, scholars who expect to find an Egyptian provenance for Addition A can point, with Grotius, to "Egyptian" elements in the dream—the river, like the Nile, is the emblem of life and the source of all other blessings; the sun can typify the pharaoh and the god Re, the source of life and joy. But thanks to the compactness and vagueness of the poetry, one can just as easily detect "Persian" influence and coloring—the themes of light and strife are reminiscent of the struggle between the fire god Ahura Mazda and the evil Ahriman (the latter often represented by a dragon) while the river reminds us of the Persian water goddess Anahita (see Fuller, pp. 376-377). Or, one could argue for Babylonian influence, pointing to Marduk's battle with the sea goddess Tiamatu in *Enuma Elish* (for the Babylonian story in English translation, see *ANET²*, pp. 60-72). Roiron (*RSR* [1916], 3-16), for instance, believes that the dream and its interpretation were part of Mordecai's "first" letter, the one mentioned in 9:20-23. Either Egyptian or Mesopotamian provenance is possible, but neither is necessary. For Palestinians also knew the power and importance of a swollen stream, and the appropriateness of light and sun as symbols of joy. In any case, the images themselves are quite biblical (so

Ehrlich, *ZRGG* 7 [1955], 71-72), being drawn either from mythological allu-sions or eschatology.

But even if one could be absolutely certain of the provenance of the dream— be it Egypt, Mesopotamia, or Palestine—certainty concerning the dream's meaning would still be denied him. Even if the dream is not textually corrupt (which it probably is), it is still quite terse and imprecise, possibly because it is poetry rather than prose. Finally, in their approach to dream analysis, many psychoanalysts today have insisted that the same dream-symbol can have quite different meanings in different dreams, and that even within the same dream a particular symbol may have several levels of meaning, some of them mutually contradictory.

The dream's imagery and literary style are not unlike second-century B.C. vi-sions such as those found in Daniel. The discrepancies in the content and inter-pretation of the dream (see COMMENT on Addition F, pp. 248-249) may very well indicate that the dream was originally independent of the Esther story and was later imperfectly adapted to it.

Two points are yet to be made. First, it should be noted that the great hero in Addition A, as in the rest of the Greek version, is Esther, symbolized by the mighty river, not Mordecai, one of the great dragons. Second, although implicit here (see especially vs. 6), it is not clear until the dream's interpretation (see COMMENT on Addition F, pp. 248-249) that what in the MT was essentially a court intrigue, or at most the result of historical antipathy between Jew and Amalekite, has been changed in the Greek into something much worse: a uni-versal antagonism between Jew and non-Jew. In the Greek, possibly under the influence of the apocalyptic passages of Joel 3:2; Zeph 1:15; and Zech 14:2 (see also NOTE on vs. 7), the struggle between the Jews and their enemies is on a universal, cosmic level, where *all* men are enemies of the Jews, all are anti-Semitic. That being the case, small wonder God is invoked in the Greek ver-sion!

II. VASHTI IS DEPOSED, AND ESTHER BECOMES QUEEN

(1:1 - 2:18)

1 [1] It was*ª* in the days of Ahasuerus*ᵇ* (the Ahasuerus who used to reign from India to Ethiopia over a hundred and twenty-seven provinces), [2] at that time when King Ahasuerus sat on his royal throne in the acropolis*ᶜ* of Susa; [3] he gave a banquet in the third year of his reign for all his officials and courtiers: *ᵈ*the officers of*ᵈ* the army of Persia and Media, the nobles, and the rulers of the provinces who were present, [4] and displayed the great wealth of his empire and the glorious splendor of his majesty for many days (for half a year).

[5] Now when all that was over, the king gave a *ᵉ*week-long*ᵉ* party for all the men staying in the acropolis of Susa, for both the important and the unimportant alike, in the courtyard of the king's pavilion. [6] The courtyard was decorated with white and violet cotton curtains, which were fastened by linen and purple cords to silver rings and marble columns; and couches of gold and silver were on a mosaic pavement of porphyry, marble, mother-of-pearl, and colored stones. [7] And the drinks were served in gold goblets, with no two alike; and there was plenty of royal wine, as befitted a king. [8] The drinking, however, was not*ᶠ* according to the law: no one was constraining, for the king had ordered all the palace waiters to serve each guest as he wished. [9] Queen Vashti, too, gave a party for the women in the royal house of King Ahasuerus.

[10] On the seventh day, when the king was feeling high from the wine, he ordered Mehuman, Biztha, Harbona, Bigtha, Abagtha, Zethar, and Carcas, the seven eunuchs who personally served King Ahasuerus, [11] to bring Queen Vashti, wearing the royal turban, before

---

ª Greek adds "after these things," i.e. after the dream and the conspiracy (A 1-17).
ᵇ MT *'ḥšwrwš;* see NOTE on *Artaxerxes* in A 1.
ᶜ LXX *tē polei,* "the city"; see NOTE.
ᵈ-ᵈ MT omits; see NOTE.
ᵉ-ᵉ LXX "for six days."
ᶠ So LXX; see NOTE.

the king so that he might show off her beauty to the guests and the officials; for she was very beautiful.

12 Queen Vashti, however, refused to come at the king's order conveyed by the eunuchs. The king became very angry at this, and he was quite incensed. 13 The king immediately conferred with the experts, who knew the laws*g* (for that was the king's practice in the presence of all those who knew law and government; 14 and those next to him were *h*Charshena, Shethar, Admatha, Tarshish, Meres, Marsena, and Memukan*h*, the seven princes of Persia and Media who could personally converse with the king and who sat first in the kingdom) 15 as to what should be done, from a legal point of view, to Queen Vashti for not obeying King Ahasuerus' order brought by the eunuchs.

16 Memukan then observed in the presence of the king and the princes, "It is not only the king whom Queen Vashti has wronged but also all the officials and people in all the provinces of King Ahasuerus. 17 When all the women hear the rumor about the queen, they will look down on their husbands (when it is said, 'King Ahasuerus ordered Queen Vashti to be brought before him, and she would not come!').*i* 18 So this same day those ladies of the Persians and Medes who have heard about the queen's conduct *j*shall show themselves obstinate*j* to all the king's officials, and there will be contempt and anger to spare!

19 "If it please the king, let him issue a royal edict, and let it be recorded among the laws of the Persians and Medes so that it cannot be revoked, that Vashti shall never again appear before King Ahasuerus; and let the king confer her royal post on a woman who is better than she. 20 Then, when the king's decree, which he has proclaimed, is heard throughout his kingdom (extensive as it is), all women, regardless of their status, shall show proper respect to their husbands."

21 This suggestion pleased the king and the princes. So the king followed Memukan's advice, 22 and sent dispatches to all the royal provinces, to each province in its own script,*k* and to each people in its own language, to the effect that every man should be master in his own home and say *l*whatever suited him*l*.

---

g Reading *dtym*, instead of *'tym*, "time."
h-h LXX lists only three: *arkesaios*, *sarsathaios*, and *malēsear*; AT, none.
i AT omits verse; LXX omits "King Ahasuerus ordered . . . would not come!"
j-j Reading *tamreynâ*, instead of *tō'marnâ*.
k AT omits verse; LXX omits "in its own script."
l-l Reading *kl šwh 'mw*, instead of *klšwn 'mw*; Greek omits.

2 ¹ Sometime later, when King Ahasuerus' anger had subsided, he remembered^m Vashti, and what she had done and what had been decreed against her. ² So the king's pages said, "Let beautiful young virgins be selected for the king, ³ and let the king appoint commissioners in all the provinces of his kingdom to gather together every beautiful young virgin to the acropolis of Susa, to the harem under the authority of Hegai, the king's eunuch who is in charge of the women; and let him give them their beauty treatment. ⁴ Then, let the girl who most pleases the king be queen in place of Vashti." This advice appealed to the king so he followed it.

⁵ Now there was in the acropolis of Susa a Jew whose name was Mordecai the son of Jair, son of Shimei, son of Kish, a Benjaminite; ⁶ he had been carried away from Jerusalem with the exiles who had been deported with Jeconiah king of Judah, whom Nebuchadnezzar king of Babylon had taken into exile. ⁷ And he had reared his cousin^n Hadassah (Esther, that is) since she had neither father nor mother. The girl was shapely and had a beautiful face. After her father and mother had died, ᵒMordecai adopted herᵒ.

⁸ Later on, when the king's edict was promulgated and when many young girls were brought to the acropolis of Susa and placed in Hegai's custody, Esther was also taken to the palace and was entrusted to Hegai, who had charge of the women. ⁹ The girl pleased him and gained his support so that he promptly gave her her beauty treatment and her delicacies, and he provided her with the seven special maids from the palace and transferred her and her maids to the best quarters of the harem. ¹⁰ ᵖEsther had not said anything about her origins because Mordecai had forbidden her to do so, ¹¹ and every day Mordecai used to walk about in front of the court of the harem so as to find out about Esther's well-being and progress.

¹² Now when the turn came for each girl to go in to King Ahasuerus, after having been treated according to the regimen for women for twelve months (for this was the prescribed length for their treatment: six months' treatment with oil of myrrh, and six months' fumigation with other cosmetics for women), ¹³ when the girl was to go in to the king, she was given whatever she wanted to take with her when she left the harem for the king's apartment. ¹⁴ She went in in the eve-

---

^m LXX adds "no longer"; see NOTE.
^n OL and Vulgate "niece." LXX adds "daughter of Ameinadab," the name appearing in 2:15 and 9:29 of the LXX where MT has 'byḥyl.
ᵒ-ᵒ LXX "he took her as a wife"; see NOTE.
ᵖ AT omits vss. 10-13.

ning; and the next morning she returned to the second harem to the custody of Shaashgaz^q, the king's eunuch who had charge of the concubines. She never again went to the king unless the king desired her especially, and she was summoned by name.

15 Now, when the turn came for Esther, the daughter of Abihail the uncle of Mordecai ^{r}(who had adopted her as his own daughter)^r to go to the king, she asked for nothing beyond that which Hegai, the king's eunuch in charge of the women, had advised. Esther had charmed all who saw her; 16 so when Esther was taken to King Ahasuerus, to his royal apartment, that is, ^{s}in the tenth month, which is Tebeth^s, in the seventh year of his reign, 17 the king loved Esther more than all his other wives; and more than all the other girls she won his favor and devotion so that he placed the royal turban on her head and made her queen in place of Vashti. 18 Then the king gave a great banquet for all his officials and courtiers (it was a banquet in honor of Esther) and proclaimed a holiday for the provinces and distributed gifts worthy of a king.

^{q} LXX "Gai," as in vs. 8; LXX$^{\aleph}$ "Sasgaios."
$^{r-r}$ LXX omits; possibly a gloss from vs. 7.
$^{s-s}$ LXX "in the twelfth month, which is Adar."

NOTES

1:1. *Ahasuerus.* In the MT the king is clearly Xerxes (see NOTE on *Xerxes* in 1:1 of AB 7B); but Hoschander (pp. 30-41, 77-79, 118-138), following the lead of the LXX and Josephus, translates *'ḥšwrwš* as "Artaxerxes," and argues that the literary and archaeological evidence indicate that this particular *'ḥšwrwš* was Artaxerxes II (404-358 B.C.).

For some photographs and diagrams relevant to the Esther story, see Plates 5, 6, and 7, as well as the plates between pages 22 and 23 in AB 7B; but best of all, see the superb photographs in Roman Ghirshman, *The Arts of Ancient Iran from Its Origins to the Time of Alexander the Great,* tr. by Stuart Gilbert and James Emmons, in the Arts of Mankind Series, eds. André Malraux and Georges Salles (New York: Golden Press, 1964), pp. 155-209. For the light that archaeology has shed on various aspects of the Esther story, see the present writer's "Archaeology and the Book of Esther," *BA* 38 (1975), 62-79.

2. *sat.* Seeing a clue in the LXX's *ethronisthē,* which suggests the idea of enthronement (so Jacob, p. 281), many scholars understand the word as meaning "when he sat *securely,*" thereby alluding to Xerxes' having had to put down uprisings in Egypt and Babylon in the early years of his reign.

acropolis [*habbîrâ*]. The LXX now has "the city" (*tē polei*), but earlier transliterated the Hebrew, as the OL's *thebari* clearly indicates.

3. *the officers of.* The phrase is missing from the MT. The reading adopted here sees the LXX's *kai tois loipois,* "and the rest of," as the translation of *wš'r,* which was, in turn, a corruption of *wśry,* "officers of," a view held by many scholars.

5. *all that.* Literally "these days," to which the LXX adds *tou gamou,* "of the marriage," which is, in all likelihood, a corruption of *tou potou, potos* being the Greek word in Esther for the Heb. *mišteh,* "banquet."

6. A difficult verse, filled with technical and rare terms. The Greek shows, however, how doublets result from a misreading of the Hebrew. The Heb. *wdr wšḥrt,* "mother-of-pearl and colored stones," was read by the Greek as *wrdy šḥrt,* "and roses in a circle." The AT has "woven with flowers," which is a doublet with "caught up with linen cords," *'ḥwz bḥbslt* having been misread for *'ḥwz bḥbly bwṣ.*

7. *as befitted* [*kyd*] *a king.* Literally "according to the hand of the king," which the LXX translated as "which the king himself drinks."

8. The adopted reading follows the interpretation of the LXX, with its inclusion of the word "not," and after Haupt (p. 106), understands the verb *'ns* to mean "constrain," i.e. in the sense of urge to *or* from an action.

2:1. *remembered Vashti.* Failing to see the three phrases ("he remembered Vashti," and "what she had done," and "what had been decreed against her") as parallel to one another, the Greek translator understood the latter two phrases as explanations of the first, thus concluding that the king "remembered Vashti *no longer.*"

7. *Hadassah.* The name is missing from all versions based on the LXX.

adopted her. Literally "took her to himself for a daughter," which makes perfectly good sense since only virgins would have been taken to the king's harem (2:2,8). Both the LXX and *Megillah* 13a have "he took her to himself for a wife." Probably the LXX's translator read *lbt,* "for a daughter," as *lbyt,* since in the Talmud the latter can mean either "for a house" or "for a wife" (so Haupt, p. 116).

8. *Esther was also taken.* In sharp contrast to C 25-30, the MT gives no hint of Esther going to Susa with any reluctance. In the MT her selection as a candidate was a stroke of "good luck"; but according to F 1 and 3, it was part of the Divine Plan.

9. *and her delicacies.* Presumably some of this food was not kosher. That Esther could have concealed her Jewishness, that is, her adherence to the Jewish religion, so successfully, certainly argues that she did not observe all the Jewish laws, the claims of II Targum and C 28 notwithstanding.

12. *turn.* "Turn" is not to be understood here in the sense of a king's many wives "taking turns" sleeping with him (as, for instance, the wives of the False Smerdis in Herodotus III 69); the LXX correctly expresses the meaning of the Heb. *tōr* by rendering it with *kairos,* "the critical moment," or "the opportune time."

15. *the daughter of Abihail.* *'byḥyl* is corrupted (?) to *ameinadab* in the extant Septuagint manuscripts; but the OL's *abiel* attests to the one-time existence of a Greek transliteration reminiscent of the Hebrew. (This assertion is based on the universally accepted view that the OL of Esther is a translation of the Greek, and the Vulgate primarily of the Hebrew.)

III. EVENTS LEADING UP TO THE EDICT AGAINST THE JEWS

(2:19 - 3:13)

2[a] 19 [b]Now when various virgins were being gathered together and[b] Mordecai was sitting at the King's Gate 20 (Esther had not revealed her ethnic origins because Mordecai had so instructed her, for Esther still obeyed Mordecai just as she had when she was being raised by him), 21 at that time when Mordecai was sitting at the King's Gate, Bigtan and Teresh, two of the king's eunuchs who guarded the threshold, were angry with the king, and so they planned to assassinate King Ahasuerus. 22 The plot, however, became known to Mordecai, who disclosed it to Queen Esther who, in turn, informed the king in Mordecai's name. 23 When the plot was investigated and its existence confirmed, the two conspirators were hanged on the gallows; and the whole affair was recorded in the daily record in the king's presence.

3 1 [c]Some time later on King Ahasuerus promoted Haman the son of Hammedatha, the Agagite, advancing him and making him the prime minister. 2 So all the king's servants at the King's Gate used to bow down and prostrate themselves before Haman, for that is what the king had commanded to be done to him.

Mordecai, however, would never bow down and prostrate himself. 3 So the king's servants at the King's Gate said to Mordecai, "Why do you disobey the king's command?" 4 Finally, when they had spoken to him day after day and he had not listened to them, they informed Haman in order to see whether Mordecai's conduct would be tolerated. (For he had confided to them that he was a Jew.) 5 When Haman had seen for himself that Mordecai did not bow down or prostrate himself before him, he was furious. 6 However, he hated to kill just Mordecai (for they had told him who Mordecai's people were), and so Haman sought to wipe out all the Jews throughout the whole kingdom of Ahasuerus, [d]along with[d] Mordecai.

---

[a] AT and Jos. omit vss. 19-23.
[b-b] LXX omits; see NOTE.
[c] AT and OL add "And it happened that," presupposing Heb. *wyhy.*
[d-d] Reading *'im*, instead of *'am*, "the people of."

7 In the first month, which is the month of Nisan, of the twelfth year of King Ahasuerus, the *pur* (that is, the lot) was cast in Haman's presence to determine the day and the month; *and the lot indicated the thirteenth[f] day of the twelfth month[e], which is the month of Adar. 8 Then Haman said to King Ahasuerus, "There is a certain people scattered, yet unassimilated, among the peoples throughout the provinces of your kingdom whose statutes are different from every other people's. They do not observe even the king's statutes! Therefore, it is not appropriate for the king to tolerate them. 9 If it please the king, let it be recorded that they are to be destroyed; and I shall pay ten thousand silver talents to the proper officials to deposit in the king's treasury." 10 So the king took his signet ring from off his hand and gave it to Haman son of Hammedatha, the Agagite, the enemy of the Jews.

11 "Well, it's your money," said the king to Haman, "do what you like with the people."

12 Then the king's secretaries were summoned on the thirteenth day of the first month; and the edict was written exactly as Haman had dictated to the king's satraps, the governors of every province, and the officials of every people (it was written to each province in its own script and to each people in its own language) in the name of King Ahasuerus, and was sealed with the royal signet ring. 13 Dispatches were sent out by couriers to all the king's provinces, to wipe out, slaughter, and annihilate all the Jews—men and boys, women and children—in a single day, on the thirteenth day of the twelfth month, which is the month of Adar, and to plunder their possessions.

e-e So LXX; lacking in MT by haplography.
f So AT; see NOTE.

NOTES

2:19. *various [šnwt] virgins.* Significantly, the LXX omits this very confusing matter of the virgins and has for vs. 19 simply "and Mordecai was serving in the king's court."

20. *Mordecai had so instructed her.* The LXX piously and characteristically amplifies the meaning by adding "to fear God and to do his commandments" and "she did not change her way of life," i.e. she continued to observe *kašrût* (see C 28).

22. *The plot . . . became known.* The MT does not say how this came about. Ancient sources theorized that Mordecai had either overheard the conspirators while serving in the court (so A 12), thanks to his knowledge of seventy lan-

guages (I Targum), to a holy spirit (II Targum), or to Barnabazos, a Jewish slave of Teresh, one of the two conspirators (Josephus *Ant.* XI 207).

3:2. *would never bow down.* Mordecai's refusal to do obeisance to Haman is explained in C 7 by his unwillingness to give to a mortal that homage due only to God, and in the Targums and Midrashes by the presence of an idol worn on Haman's chest, both explanations being mere speculations.

7. *the* pur . . . *was cast.* It is unclear whether Haman was determining the most propitious day for presenting his proposal to the king (so Paton) or the best date for his pogrom (so 4:7 of the AT and most commentators).

the thirteenth. So the AT; the LXX has "fourteenth" here and in B 6, but elsewhere "the thirteenth" (8:12, 9:1 of the LXX).

8. *scattered, yet unassimilated.* The LXX may be in error here by treating these two participles as needlessly repetitious synonyms and rendering them with one word, "distributed." The first participle can emphasize the fact that the Jews were scattered throughout the provinces of the empire, and the second, that their separateness was self-imposed, a practice which helped them to preserve their separate ethnic and religious identity.

11. *"Well, it's your money."* Literally "the silver is given to you." This passage is usually misunderstood by scholars; the king is not really refusing Haman's offer of money here but, as the LXX suggests by its translation ("Keep the money!"), he is actually engaged in Near Eastern bargaining, determining the amount of *bakshish* Haman will give (for details, see NOTE on 3:11 of AB 7B).

12. *to each province in its own script . . . in its own language.* For an example of an official document written in Aramaic on papyrus, rolled and sealed, dating to the fifth century B.C., see Plate 6.

IV. Addition B:

TEXT OF THE FIRST ROYAL LETTER
(B 1-7; AT 4:14-18; Vulg. 13:1-7)

B 1 The text of the dispatch was as follows:

The great king Artaxerxes writes these things to the governors of the one hundred and twenty-seven provinces from India to Ethiopia, and to their immediate subordinates.

2 After I had become ruler of many nations and had conquered the whole world, I was determined—not out of any power-madness but always acting with restraint and gentleness—to see to it that my subjects lived untroubled lives; by making the kingdom more civilized*ᵃ* and by ensuring unhampered travel throughout the entire land, *ᵇ*I was determined*ᵇ* to restore that peace which all men want.

3 When I asked my advisers how this end might be accomplished, Haman, who is conspicuous among us for his balanced judgment and is recognized for his consistent*ᶜ* kindness and unwavering devotion and has attained next to the highest rank in the kingdom*ᵈ*, 4 informed us that there is scattered among the nations of the world a certain antagonistic people, whose laws make it hostile to every nation and who habitually ignore the royal ordinances, *ᵉ*so that that government, demanded by us with the best of intentions, cannot be achieved*ᵉ*.

5 Realizing, therefore, that this nation, and it alone, consistently stands in opposition to all men, perverting society with its own laws, and that it is hostile to our interests*ᶠ*, and does all the harm it can*ᵍ* *ʰ*so that the well-being of the land is threatened*ʰ*,

---

ᵃ Ēmeron; many MSS have ēremon, "quiet."
ᵇ⁻ᵇ Lacking in Greek; see NOTE.
ᶜ Reading with AT and Kautzsch-Ryssel, aparallatō, instead of aparallatōs.
ᵈ Basileiōn; see NOTE.
ᵉ⁻ᵉ AT "so that the stability of the kingdom is not established."
ᶠ Pragmasin; AT prostagmasin, "orders."
ᵍ Greek has "can and."
ʰ⁻ʰ AT "so that our sovereignty is never established, as directed by us."

⁶ we have, therefore, commanded that those designated to you in the communications of Haman, who is the one responsible in this matter and is a second father to us, shall all—wives and children included—be completely wiped out by the swords of their enemies, without pity or restraint, on the thirteenth* day of the twelfth month *of Adar, in the present year*, ⁷ so that they who have always been hostile may on a single day go violently down into Hades,* thereby making our government* secure and untroubled for the future.

---

* Greek "fourteenth"; see NOTE.
*ʲ AT "this is the month of Adar (which is Dystrus), to kill all the Jews and to seize the children."
* AT concludes verse with "that thereafter they may be quiet and never again disturb our government."
* *Pragmata;* LXX^A *prostagmata.*

NOTES

B 1. Addition B, which appears between what would be verses 13 and 14 of the MT, is very florid and rhetorical in its literary style and, unlike A, C, D, and F, must be regarded as composed originally in Greek. Compare it, for example, with other Persian letters and decrees in the Bible such as in Ezra 1:2-4, 4:17-22, 6:3-12, and 7:11-28. It is far more instructive, however, to compare Addition B with King Ptolemy Philopator's letter in III Macc 3:12-29, since Ptolemy's letter is strikingly similar, being as bombastic, artificial, and convoluted as Addition B (see COMMENT II, p. 197). Recognizing some similarity in the literary styles of Addition B and III Macc 3:12-29, Schildenberger (p. 76) has suggested that Addition B could still be genuine since, according to Esth 3:12, the edict "was written to each province in its own script and to each people in its own language"; but his argument has little cogency.

The great king. In the Behistun Inscription, Xerxes describes himself as "the great king, the only king (lit. king of kings)"; see *ANET²*, pp. 316-317.

their immediate subordinates. Literally "to the *toparchs* who are subject to them." A *toparch* was the governor of a district, especially in Egypt; cf. Gen 41:34 and Dan 3:2 of the LXX. The occurrence of the word here suggests to some scholars that the provenance of Addition B is Egypt.

2. *not out of any power-madness.* Literally "not being lifted up by the presumptuousness of authority." He is, claims the king, motivated by his concern for his people's welfare and not by a love of power.

unhampered travel . . . land. Literally "traversable to the frontiers." The real measure of an empire's strength included its ability to keep the distant border situations safe and secure.

I was determined. Although *ēboulēthēn* occurs but once in the verse, the

Greek is so diffuse and verbose that for the sake of clarity English requires that
"I was determined" be repeated.

3. *When I asked my advisers.* Not necessarily just those advisers listed in
1:13-15, where Haman's name is not even mentioned (although it does erroneously [?] appear in the list of the seven eunuchs in 1:10 of the LXX). The
king received advice from a variety of quarters, even from his pages (cf. 2:2).
The Greek clause here is quite elegant, being among other things a genitive absolute construction.

balanced judgment [*sōphrosunē*]. Literally "moderation." The MT attributes
no such quality to Haman; but since the king had made Haman his prime
minister, he must have thought Haman possessed this quality as well as "consistent kindness and unwavering devotion" (vs. 3). Moreover, as Schildenberger
(p. 77) has pointed out, the pogrom becomes more sensible and less ruthless as
a proposal when the readers of the harsh edict know the type of man responsible for it, namely, the kind and noble Haman. The reader of the Esther story
sees all these exemplary attributes of Haman as an expression of Haman's vanity inasmuch as the reader knows that Haman himself had actually dictated the
edict.

next to the highest rank. Literally "the second rank," i.e. immediately after
the king.

kingdom. Basileiōn may be translated either as "kingdom" or "palace,"
depending upon where one places the accent. (The most ancient Greek manu-
scriptions were written only in capital letters [uncials], with no accent marks or
separation between words.)

4. *whose laws make it hostile.* Literally "whose laws are contrary to," i.e. its
Mosaic laws. Haman's criticism of the laws is not that they are different but
that they, in effect, separate and alienate the Jews from others, thus creating
suspicion and antagonism. These same laws, however, enabled the Jews to
preserve their cultural and religious identity, especially in the second and first
centuries B.C., when the Additions were probably written (see Introduction, pp.
165-166). Verse 4 is a restatement of charges in 3:8 of the MT.

5. *in opposition.* A military metaphor; cf. I Macc 13:20.

perverting society with its own laws [*diagōgēn nomōn xenizousan parallas-
son*]. The Greek is probably corrupt. In any time or place this is always an
effective charge to level against one's enemies. Tacitus, for instance, mentions
similar charges against the Christians in his *Annals* xv 44.

6. *second father.* Cf. E 11 and Gen 45:8. The Vulgate's "whom we honor as
our father" represents the correct sense, if not literal rendering.

be completely wiped out. Literally "to destroy, with root and branch"; but
many manuscripts, the OL, and Vulgate have here the passive. The well-
established tolerance of Achaemenian kings for Jews (so Barucq), not to mention the inherent improbability of any sensible king having an entire people
within his empire so treated, makes the proposed pogrom highly improbable.

thirteenth. Both the LXX and the AT have "fourteenth," but "thirteenth"
elsewhere (3:12, 8:12, 9:1; and E 20), so unless one argues here that "fourteenth" is a reflection of the uncertain tradition concerning the dates of Purim
(so Fritzsche, Ryssel-Kautzsch, and others), we must regard "fourteenth" here
as a copyist's error. Such an error is quite understandable, since in several

Greek manuscripts, including the oldest (a Chester Beatty papyrus), the easily misread alphabetic equivalent of the number (*iota delta*) was used instead of spelling the number out.

7. *always.* Literally "long ago and now."

Recognizing the abruptness of the letter in its present form, Schildenberger (p. 78) has tried to correct this by adding a reading from the OL: "But whoever shall hide the Jewish race shall be without a place to live, not only among men but also among birds, and he shall be consumed by holy fire, and his possessions shall revert to the State. Farewell!" Unfortunately, there is no support for this reading from the other versions. However, in spirit, if not in specifics, the ending in the OL is comparable to the ending of Addition E (vs. 24), both of which are very reminiscent of Ptolemy Philopator's concluding words in his letter to the soldiers in III Macc 3:27-29: "And whoever shall harbor any Jew, old man or child or very suckling, shall with all his house be tortured to death with the most horrible torments. . . . And every place where a Jew shall be detected at all in concealment shall be made a waste and burnt with fire, and shall become entirely useless to any mortal creature for all time."

COMMENT I

Neither the king's self-characterization (vs. 2) nor his description of Haman (see NOTE on vs. 3) corresponds to the characterization in the MT. However, the disparity between the two accounts would not in itself be an argument against the genuineness or veracity of Addition B. After all, rare is the ruler who sees himself in exactly the same light as do his subjects, nor should one expect that a rascal like Haman would be seen in the same light from above and below, i.e. by the king and the Jews, respectively. Then too, according to 3:11-12, it was not the king who dictated the royal edict but Haman himself; thus as Soubigou has sarcastically observed: "The eulogy of Haman was by Haman" (p. 680).

But the literary style of Addition B does rule out the possibility that Addition B is a translation of a Semitic passage which has not survived in the MT (see COMMENT II, below). The Greek of Addition B is exceedingly florid and diffuse, so much so that while the Greek phrases within a verse are clear enough in meaning, one sometimes finds it difficult to translate the entire sentence sequentially into English, i.e. one has problems determining which phrases should come first, and which should be subordinate in an English translation. The same cannot be said for Additions A, C, D, or F, whose literary style is so simple and straightforward that they are almost certainly Greek translations of a now-lost Hebrew or Aramaic original; but no such possibility exists for Addition B. Its literary style clearly indicates it was composed in Greek. This conclusion has been independently confirmed by R. A. Martin (*JBL* 94 [1975], 65-72) in his syntactical analyses of Addition B.

If the material in the letter were genuine and originally a part of the Hebrew version, then one is hard-pressed to explain why it was ultimately omitted by the MT. For instance, one cannot argue (as one can in the case of Additions A, C, D, and F) that the mention of God was the reason for this material being deleted from the MT, i.e. that the rowdy and uninhibited celebration of Purim required that all religious elements be omitted from the book lest they be profaned.

One final note: in spite of the abundance of textual footnotes for Addition B (see p. 190), the agreement between the LXX and the AT is still much greater in this Addition than in the canonical portions of Esther (see COMMENT, § X, p. 230f) a clear indication that the one Greek version borrowed the Addition from the other (see Introduction, p. 165). The same thing may be claimed for Addition E.

Relying primarily upon his own imagination for the contents of the letter, the author of Addition B did utilize some of the phraseology of the Greek translation of the Hebrew, as the following examples illustrate:

> B 1 basileus megas artaxerxēs tois apo tēs indikēs eōs tēs aithiopias ekaton eikosi epta chōrōn archousi kai toparchais upotetagmenois
>
> 1:1 outos o artaxerxēs apo tēs indikēs ekaton eikosi epta chōrōn ekratēsen
>
> 3:12 kai tois archousin kata pasan chōran apo indikēs eōs tēs aithiopias tais ekaton eikosi epta chōrais tois te archousi tōn ethnōn
>
> 8:9 tois oikonomois kai tois archousin tōn satrapōn apo tēs indikēs eōs tēs aithiopias ekaton eikosi epta satrapais kata chōran kai chōran
>
> B 4 en pasais kata tēn oikoumenēn phulais enamemichthai dusmenē laon tina tois nomois antitheton pros pan ethnos ta tē tōn basileōn parapempontas diēnekōs prostagmata
>
> 3:8 uparchei ethnos diesparmenon en tois ethnesin en pasē tē basileia sou, oi de nomoi autōn exalloi para panta ta ethnē tōn de nomōn tou basileōs parakouousin
>
> B 6 pantas sun gunaixi kai teknois apolesai ollorrizei tais tōn echthrōn machairais aneu pantos oiktou kai pheidous tē tessareskaidekatē tou dōdekatou mēnos adar tou enestōtos etous
>
> 3:13 aphanisai to genos tōn ioudaiōn en ēmera mia mēnos dōdekatou os estin adar kai diarpasai ta uparchonta autōn

Whether based on the author's imagination or his personal experience with anti-Semitism, this letter is a cleverly constructed piece of propaganda which, feeding as it does on the fears and greed of men, well illustrates the scapegoat mechanism. Nobly wishing to make the lives of his subjects untroubled by restoring peace (vs. 2), the king learned through a most able and "impartial" adviser (vs. 3) that *the one and only* obstacle to the realization of all his selfless aims for his subjects was a certain people (vss. 4-6). This people was characterized as antagonistic, uncooperative, and disobedient (vs. 4), so much so that they were deliberately—and successfully—perverting all of society (vs. 5). The king's prescription was as simple as his diagnosis: "Wipe them out!" No crass words were written concerning the inevitable spoils; but Persians, like everyone else, could be trusted to read between the lines.

COMMENT II

There can be no doubt that Addition B was originally composed in Greek rather than translated from Hebrew/Aramaic. One way to illustrate the striking difference between a letter conceived in Hebrew/Aramaic from one composed originally in Greek is to give an example of each. In II Targum we have an Aramaic version of Haman's letter which is quite Semitic in character, being very simple, graphic, and straightforward in its literary style:

> Ahasuerus the king to all peoples, nations, and languages that dwell in my kingdom, greeting. This is to make known that we have met with a man, not of our place or province, who hath made a league with us to destroy our enemies. This man's name is Haman. He is the descendant of King Agag, the son of Amalek the Great, the son of Ruel, the son of Eliphaz, the eldest son of Esau; the descendant therefore of a wealthy and celebrated people. Haman hath addressed to us a petition on a trifling and insignificant matter, and hath represented to us the blameworthy customs and practices of the Jews. He hath told me that when Jews came out of Egypt they were 600,000 strong; and he hath offered me 600,000 talents of silver, a talent per head, to give up to him this people for destruction. I have accepted this offer gladly. I have taken the money and have sold this people to be murdered. Therefore do ye also eat and drink and rejoice, as I eat, drink and rejoice. Whosoever of you understands the use of the bow, let him seize his bow; or of the sword, let him grip his sword. Be strong on the 14th and 15th days of the month called Adar in our language. Spare not the prince or lord or child, but slaughter them and seize upon their possessions, each one for himself. Further, I, King Ahasuerus, command all peoples, nations, languages, tribes, families, and cities, that wherever there be found Jewish man-servant or maid-servant there shall be the owners of the same executed at the gate of their city, because they have not obeyed my command that no Jew be met with in the territory of my kingdom. (English translation is by Fuller, p. 382.)

Though there are some similar elements between this and Addition B, dependency of one upon the other or even upon a common source is, by common scholarly consent, out of the question.

Of all the many versions purporting to offer the text of the king's letter, including the Targums and the Midrashes, the text which most resembles the literary style of Addition B is Ptolemy Philopator's letter in III Macc 3:12-29, a clear indication that Addition B, like III Maccabees, is a first-century B.C. Greek composition, not a translation. (III Maccabees is an apocryphal work composed originally in Greek somewhere between 100 and 30 B.C., probably by an Alexandrian Jew [see C. W. Emmet's treatment in *APOT*, I, 155-162; Eissfeldt, pp. 581-582; and W. H. Brownlee, *IDB*, III, 210-212].) Emmet's translation of III Macc 3:11-30 is as follows:

11 So the king, puffed up by his present prosperity, and regarding not the power of the most high God, but supposing that he himself would always hold firmly to the same purpose, wrote this letter against them.

12 King Ptolemy Philopator to his generals and soldiers in Egypt and every place greeting and prosperity. 13 I myself and our affairs prosper. 14 Our expedition into Asia, of which you yourselves are aware, having been brought to an expected conclusion by the help of the gods granted us deliberately, 15 we thought, not by force of arms, but by kindness and much benevolence to foster the peoples of Coele-Syria and Phoenicia, bestowing benefits upon them with all readiness.

16 And having granted large revenues to the temples in the cities, we came to Jerusalem as well, going up thither to show honour to the temple of the accursed people who never cease from their folly. 17 Seemingly they welcomed our presence, but their welcome was insincere; for when we were eager to enter their shrine and to honour it with magnificent and beautiful offerings, 18 carried away by their ancient pride they prevented us from going in, being left unhurt by our power on account of the benevolence we have to all. 19 But they show plainly their ill-will towards us, and standing alone among nations in their stiff-necked resistance to kings and their own benefactors, they refuse to take anything in a proper spirit.

20 We accommodated ourselves to their folly, and returning victoriously to Egypt, and treating all nations with kindness, have acted as was right. 21 And under these circumstances, making known to all our ready forgiveness of their fellow-countrymen, on account of their alliance, and the numerous matters which have been freely entrusted to them from of old, we have ventured to make a change, and have made up our mind to hold them worthy even of Alexandrian citizenship, and to give them a share in our religious rites from time to time. 22 But they taking this in the opposite spirit and rejecting the good offer with their inborn ill-feeling, and continually inclining to evil, 23 not only refused the invaluable citizenship, but also show their contempt silently and by words for the few among them who have behaved properly towards us, in every case secretly expecting that through their infamous behavior we should speedily alter our policy.

24 Therefore having good proof of our persuasion that they are evilly disposed towards us in every way, and taking precautions lest when some sudden tumult is raised against us hereafter we should have these impious people behind our backs as traitors and barbarous foes, 25 we give order that, as soon as this epistle reaches you, you shall at once send to us with harsh and violent treatment those who dwell among you with women and children, binding them fast in every way with iron chains, to meet a terrible and ignominious death, as befits traitors. 26 For we believe that when they have been punished together, our estate will be established for the future in the surest and best condition. 27 And whoever shall harbour any Jew, old man or child or very suckling, shall with all his house be tortured to death with the most horrible torments. 28 Information may be given by any one; the informer to receive the estate of the guilty party, with two thousand drachmae from the royal treasury, and to be honoured with freedom. 29 And every place where a Jew shall be detected at all in conceal-

ment shall be made a waste and burnt with fire, and shall become entirely useless to any mortal creature for all time. Thus ran the letter.

Ptolemy's letter is, it should be noted, of one piece with the rest of III Maccabees. Speaking of the style of III Maccabees in general, C. W. Emmet wrote: "The book is a product of Alexandrian literature, exemplifying in its extremest form the pseudo-Classicalism of the Atticists. . . . its artificiality and extravagance make it hardly worthy of the name of literature. . . . obscure and bombastic. . . . His sentences are full of repetitions and awkwardly constructed . . . (*APOT*, I, 161). Such a description applies equally well to the literary style of Additions B and E. Compare, for example, the bombastic and tortuous literary style of B 2 with III Macc 3:14, or of B 3-4 with 3:21.

As for similarity of content, consider the following:

Esther	*III Maccabees*
B 2a After I had become ruler of many nations and had conquered the whole world	3:14 Our expedition into Asia, of which your yourselves are aware, having been brought to an expected conclusion by the help of the gods granted us deliberately
B 2b I was determined—not out of any power-madness but always acting with restraint and gentleness—to see to it that my subjects lived untroubled lives; by making the kingdom more civilized and by ensuring unhampered travel throughout the entire land, I was determined to restore that peace which all men want.	3:15 We thought, not by force of arms, but by kindness and much benevolence to foster the peoples of Coele-Syria and Phoenicia, bestowing benefits upon them with all readiness.
B 4 There is scattered among the nations of the world a certain antagonistic people, whose laws make it hostile to every nation and who habitually ignore the royal ordinances	3:19 But they show plainly their ill-will towards us, and standing among nations in their stiff-necked resistance to kings and their own benefactors, they refuse to take anything in a proper spirit.
B 5 This nation, and it alone, consistently stands in opposition to all men, perverting society with its own laws, and that it is hostile to our interests, and does all the harm it can so that the well-being of the land is threatened.	3:22-24 They taking this in the opposite spirit and rejecting the good offer with their inborn ill-feeling, and continually inclining to evil, not only refused the invaluable citizenship, but also show their contempt silently and by words. . . . they are evilly disposed towards us in every way . . . impious people . . . traitors and barbarous foes

Esther

B 6 We have, therefore, commanded that those designated to you in the communications of Haman . . . shall all—wives and children included—be completely wiped out by the sword of their enemies, without pity or restraint

B 7 So that they who have always been hostile may on a single day go violently down into Hades, thereby making our government secure and untroubled for the future.

III Maccabees

3:25 We give order that, as soon as this epistle reaches you, you shall at once send to us with harsh and violent treatment those who dwell among you with women and children, binding them fast in every way with iron chains, to meet a terrible and ignominious death as befits traitors.

3:26 For we believe that when they have been punished together, our estate will be established for the future in the surest and best condition.

The reader may have noticed that these parallels between Addition B and III Maccabees 3:11-30 retain even their respective sequences, i.e.

Esther	III Maccabees
B 2a =	3:14
B 2b =	3:15
B 4 =	3:19
B 5 =	3:22-24
B 6 =	3:25
B 7 =	3:26

Interestingly enough, the similarities between III Maccabees and the Book of Esther are not confined to Esther's Greek version. Both books tell stories of how "disloyal" Jews would have been wiped out in royally sanctioned pogroms had not the Jews been miraculously delivered by their God (III Macc 6:16-29; for justification of the word "miraculously" as applied to the Hebrew version of Esther, see COMMENTS in AB 7B, 52, 66-67). Moreover, in both books the proposed pogrom was first announced in a letter by the king (III Macc 3:11-30; Esth 3:13-14), only to be revoked in his second letter (III Macc 7:1-9; Esth 8:10-13). Also, after the Jews had defeated their enemies (i.e. Jewish informers and apostates in the case of III Macc 7:10-15; the hostile Gentiles in Esther), the victorious Jews commemorated the day by instituting a joyous festival (III Macc 7:15,19-20; Esth 9:1-32). However, W. H. Brownlee's observation that "The conspiracy of Theodotus (1:2) recalls that of the chamberlains of Esth. 2:21-23; and Dositheus saves the king's life (III Macc. 1:3), as does Mordecai (Esth 6:2)" (*IDB*, III, 211) seems rather strained and unconvincing.

Barucq may have somewhat exceeded the evidence when he wrote: "III Maccabees seems to be a Hellenistic imitation of Esther" (p. 84); but if there was any general influence or inspiration of one book upon the other, the precedence must naturally be given to the Book of Esther, which clearly antedates III Maccabees. To say this, however, does not rule out the possibility of III Maccabees later influencing some portion of the Greek Esther, i.e. Addition B could have been inspired by III Maccabees 12-29, especially since the latter is, by universal scholarly consent, a Greek composition and not a translation of a Semitic text.

V. ESTHER CONSENTS TO GO
UNSUMMONED TO THE KING

(3:14 - 4:17)

3 14 The contents of the document were to be promulgated in each province, to be published to all people, namely, to be ready for that day. 15 At the king's command the couriers went out quickly, and the edict was published in the acropolis of Susa. Then the King and Haman sat down to drink, but the city of Susa was thrown into confusion.

4 1 When Mordecai learned of everything that had been done, Mordecai tore his clothes and put on sackcloth and ashes. Then he went out into the midst of the city and wailed *bitterly*, 2 and then he came as far as the King's Gate (for no one in sackcloth was allowed to enter the King's Gate). 3 And in every province where the king's command was heard there was loud mourning among the Jews, with fasting and weeping and wailing; most of them were lying in sackcloth and ashes.

4 When Esther's maids and eunuchs came and told her, the queen was quite shocked; and she sent clothing for Mordecai to wear so that he could take off his sackcloth, but he would not accept it. 5 So Esther summoned Hatak, one of the royal eunuchs whom the king had appointed to wait on her, and ordered him to go to Mordecai to learn the full particulars. 6 So Hatak went out to Mordecai in the city square which was in front of the King's Gate. 7 Mordecai then informed him of everything that had happened to him, and also of the exact amount of money that Haman had promised to pay to the royal treasury for the extermination of the Jews. 8 Mordecai also gave him a copy of the written decree which had been posted in Susa concerning their destruction so that he might show it to Esther and report to her, and that he might instruct her to go to the king to intercede and beg with him for her people.

9 So Hatak went and told Esther everything*b* Mordecai had said. 10 Then Esther talked to Hatak and gave him this message for Mor-

---

a-a LXX "An innocent people is condemned to death!"
b So LXX and Vulgate; MT omits; see NOTE.

decai: 11 "All the king's courtiers, and even the people of the king's provinces, are well aware that there is one penalty for every man or woman who approaches the king inside the inner court without having been summoned: to be put to death, the one exception being that person to whom the king extends the gold scepter so that he may live. And I have not been summoned to come to the king for the past thirty days!"

12 When ᵉHatak had conveyedᵉ to Mordecai allᵈ Esther's words, 13 then Mordecai said to reply to Esther, "Don't think that because you're in the king's house you'll be safer than the rest of the Jews! 14 For if you persist in keeping silent at a time like this, ᵉrelief and deliverance will appear for the Jews from another quarterᵉ; but you and your family will perish. It's possible that you came to the throne for just such a time as this."

15 Thereupon Esther said to reply to Mordecai, 16 ᶠ"Go and gather all the Jews now in Susa, and fast for me. Don't eat or drink for three days, either day or nightᶠ; and I, with my maids, will fast as you do. In this condition I'll go to the king, even though it's against the law. And if I perish, I perish!" 17 Mordecai then left and carried out all Esther's instructions.

ᶜ⁻ᶜ Reading with LXX and OL, *wayyagēd hᵃtāk* instead of *wayyagîdû*.
ᵈ So LXX.
ᵉ⁻ᵉ AT "but God shall be their help and salvation"; see NOTE.
ᶠ⁻ᶠ AT "Propose a service and earnestly beg God."

NOTES

3:14-15. Schildenberger (pp. 78-79) follows here neither the Hebrew nor the Greek but instead substitutes a 176-word addition found only in the OL, telling of the reaction of the Jews to the edict and giving a version of their prayer for deliverance.

4:1. *put on sackcloth and ashes.* Was Mordecai's conduct a natural expression of his grief over the fate of his people (so the LXX; see textual noteᵃ⁻ᵃ), a quick and certain way of gaining Esther's attention, or an expression of self-reproach for bringing all this misfortune upon his people? The MT does not say. Typical of his procedures elsewhere, the Jewish author of Esther describes what happens, without explaining the why or how (see "The Author's Intent," AB 7B, LIII).

4. *quite shocked.* The LXX adds "When she heard what had happened," i.e. that Mordecai was in sackcloth. *Wtthlhl*, the Hithpalpal of *hyl*, occurs only

here in the Old Testament, and should conceivably be translated as "was per-
plexed," since the Greek translates it with *etarachthē*, the verb also used in
translating *nābôkâ* (3:15) and *nib'at* (7:6).

8. The Greek versions have an extended and theologically significant addition
to this verse: "Remembering your humble station when you were supported by
my hand because Haman, who is second to the king, has sentenced us to death.
Call upon the Lord, and speak to the king about us, and save us from death."

10. *gave him this message.* Literally "she charged him to Mordecai." The
LXX has direct address ("Go to Mordecai and say"), which is free but not incorrect inasmuch as she was sending back a message and not just a messenger.

11. *the past thirty days!* The AT, as well as the OL and Vulgate, adds "and
how can I go to the king without being summoned?"

14. *from another quarter.* The AT (textual note *e-e*), Josephus, and I and II
Targums are completely justified in seeing in the Hebrew a veiled allusion to
God, just as "mercy" is a veiled allusion to God in I Macc 16:3, and as "the
kingdom of heaven" is a surrogate for "the kingdom of God" in Matthew (for
further details, see AB 7B, 50).

16. *Go and gather* [*lk knws*]. The AT's "Propose a service" ignores the literal
meaning of the Hebrew but does express well the deeper implications of intent
behind the Hebrew.

fast for me. In effect, Esther was asking for the Jewish community to intercede with God on her behalf (see NOTE on "fast for me" in AB 7B, 51), even
as the AT expressly states: "Propose a service and earnestly beg God."

17. At this point the OL has a fifty-word addition which begins in a most
significant way: "He announced a healthiness [*sanitatem*]; the grooms shall go
out from their bridal chambers and the brides from their pastures [*pas-
cuis*]. . . ." Neither "healthiness" nor "pastures" makes good sense. But as B.
Jacob (*ZAW* 10 [1890], 257) pointed out, *sanitatem* presupposes the Greek
word *therapeian*, which can be read either as "healthiness" or "worship service"
(cf. Joel 2:15: *agiasate nēsteian kēruxate therapeian* [Heb. *' aṣārâ*]); and "from
their pastures" presupposes a Greek word which misread the Heb. (or Aram.)
mēḥedrêhen, "from their bridal chambers," as *mē'edrêhen*, "from their pastures." Thus the OL attests to a now-lost Greek passage which, in turn, was
based on either a Hebrew or Aramaic passage. Of some possible relevance is
the fact that the OL here preserves two additional readings (*boves et pecores
non pascantur tribus diebus* [vs. 16], and *boves et pecora praecepit ut tribus
diebus et tribus noctibus non pascerentur* [vs. 17]) which are roughly parallel
to Esther's words in II Targum: "Let neither man nor beast, herd nor flock
taste anything." Apparently the Greek passage presupposed by the OL as well
as the Aramaic passage in II Targum go back ultimately to a common Semitic
ancestor.

VI. Addition C:

THE PRAYER OF MORDECAI
(C 1-11; AT 5:12-17; Vulg. 13:8-18)

C 1 *a*Then, remembering all the deeds of the Lord, Mordecai prayed to the Lord, 2 *b*saying,

*c*Lord, Lord, King who rules over all, the universe is subject to you*c*. There is no one who can oppose you when you desire to save*d* Israel, 3 for you have made heaven and earth and every marvelous thing under heaven. 4 *e*And you are Lord of all, and there is no one who can resist you who are the Lord*e*.

5 You know all things*f*; you know, Lord, that it was not because of insolence *g*or arrogance*g* or vanity that I did this: that I did not bow down before arrogant*h* Haman; 6 for I would have been quite willing to kiss the soles of his feet for *i*Israel's sake*i*. 7 *j*But I did it in order that I might not put the glory of a man above the glory of God*j*, nor will I bow down to anyone except you who are my Lord, nor will I do this out of arrogance.

8 And now, Lord *k*God and King, the God*k* of Abraham, spare your people! For they *l*are plotting*l* our ruin, and they desire to destroy*m* your ancient heritage. 9 Do not neglect your portion

a For vs. 1, OL has instead "Mordecai tore his clothes and spread out sackcloth and fell on his face to the earth, and so did the elders of the people, from morning until evening."

b For vss. 2-4, OL has, "And they said, 'Blessed are you, the God of Abraham, the God of Isaac, and the God of Jacob!' "

c-c AT "Master, Almighty, by whose power all things exist."

d AT adds "the house of."

e-e AT "You are master of all."

f AT adds "and the people of Israel."

g-g AT omits.

h AT "uncircumcised."

i-i So AT; LXX "the salvation of Israel."

j-j AT "I acted so that I should not assign your glory, Lord, nor bow down to any except you, who are true; and I shall not do it when tempted."

k-k Many MSS have "O King," while AT and Vulgate have "who made a covenant with."

l-l AT "are applying themselves to."

m AT adds "and to abolish."

which you ransomed for yourself from the land of Egypt. [10] Hear
my prayer and be merciful to your inheritance[n], and turn our
mourning into feasting[o] that we may live to sing praises to your
name, Lord, and [p]do not stifle[p] the mouths of those who praise
you.

[11] [q]And all Israel cried out as loud as they could because their end
was near.

[n] AT "heritage."
[o] AT "good cheer."
[p-p] Literally "do not blot out."
[q] AT omits verse through haplography, *kai*, "and," beginning both vss. 11 and 12 in
LXX.

NOTES

C 2. *the universe*. Not just heaven and earth as in vs. 3, but the entire universe; cf. Sira 42:17 and 43:27.

5. *not because of insolence . . . that I did this*. Cf. C 25–29 where Esther
also protests her innocence, as does the Psalmist in Ps 18:21–24.

6. *kiss the soles of his feet*. Apparently the ultimate form of homage in Persia, possibly reserved for kings; cf. Xenophon *Cyropaedia* VII 5.32; Judith
10:23; see also Ps 72:7–9 and Isa 49:23.

7. *glory of a man*. Cf. Dan 3:18 and II Macc 7:2. Unlike the MT where
Mordecai's reason for refusing to bow down to Haman is somewhat obscure
(see NOTE on 3:2), the reason in C 3–5 is quite clear: Mordecai refuses to bow
to any mortal, reserving such honor for God alone. (No mention is even made
here about Haman being either a Bougaion [A 17], Macedonian [A 17 of the
AT], or an Amalekite [Josephus and the MT].) While Mordecai's rationale
may reflect the personal preference and religious scrupulousness of the author's
Judaism, it does not reflect the actual practice in either the Persian or Hellenistic periods, inasmuch as Jews, like everyone else then, did obeisance (see NOTES
on 3:2 and 4 in AB 7B).

out of arrogance [*en hyperēphania*]. AT has *en peirasmō*, "in rivalry"; both
words are legitimate translations of the same Aramaic word *b'ithnassā'ah* (so
C. C. Torrey, *HTR* 37 [1944], 8).

8. *plotting our ruin*. Literally they are "looking upon us for destruction."
ancient. Literally "from the beginning."
heritage. For Israel as God's own possession, see Pss 28:9 and 94:5.

9. Verse is reminiscent of Deut 9:26 and 29 of the LXX.

10. *inheritance* [*klērō*]. Along with *klēronomia*, "heritage" (vs. 8), and
meris, "portion" (vs. 9), *klēros* emphasizes God's ownership of his people.

11. *as loud as they could*. Literally "from their strength." Cf. Dan 3:4, 4:11;
Isa 42:13.
their end was near. Literally "their death was in the eyes."

COMMENT

Although one can identify this or that phrase in the prayer as reminiscent of some phrase in the MT (see NOTES *passim*), this or that petition as reminiscent of some prayer (e.g. II Chron 20:5-12; II Macc 1:24-29; Sira 36:1-19), Mordecai's prayer is not an artless mosaic of biblical phrases. Rather, it is a beautiful and appropriate prayer whose contents accurately reflect the needs of Mordecai and his fellow Jews.

In this short prayer one word stands out above all the rest, namely, *kurios*, "Lord," occurring eight times in the prayer itself and twice in the preface to the prayer (see vss. 1,2,4,5,7,8, and 10). When speaking about God, Mordecai may use *theos*, "God" (vss. 2 and 8), or *basileus*, "king" (vss. 3 and 8); but when speaking *to* God, he distinctly prefers the more intimate *kurios*, the Greek translation of Yahweh, God's personal name. Mordecai's prayer is a balanced mixture of praise (vss. 2-4), "confession" (vss. 5-7), intercession and petition (vss. 8-10). "Confession" is put in quotes because behind Mordecai's assertion of a clear conscience in the whole matter there seems to be a hint of defensiveness, e.g. "it was not because of insolence or arrogance or vanity that I did this" (vs. 5). Justified though Mordecai's actions may have seemed to him at the time, they might not have seemed so had he known then what evil they would bring upon his people. For Mordecai, God's deliverance of his people (vss. 8-10) can be the justification of Mordecai's conduct in this matter (so Schildenberger).

As noted earlier (p. 154, n. 3), there exist in the Vatican Library several manuscripts containing an Aramaic version of Mordecai's prayer. The extent to which that version agrees with C 2-11 the reader may judge for himself by reading an English translation of it (Fuller, p. 385):

> O God, Lord of all ages, my heart is not hid from Thee. It is not from pride of spirit or exaltation of heart that I have done this, and not bowed before Haman, this Amalekite. From fear of Thee have I acted. I was stirred up against him that I should not bow down to him, for I feared Thee, O God of ages, and would not give the glory due to Thee to any son of man made of flesh and blood. Wherefore I refused to bend the knee to this uncircumcised, unclean man; (I can) only (worship) Thy Name, the great and holy (Name) named over us. For what am I and my house that I should not bow to man in order to procure the redemption of Israel, and (seek) his help; yea, even to lick the dust of Haman's feet wheresoever he may set the sole of his foot? Surely in Thy word doth our soul hope, for Thou only art for us and our fathers. And now, O God, deliver us from his hand, and let him fall into the pit which he hath digged, and let him be taken in the snare which he hath hid and set for the feet of Thy saints. So shall all nations know that Thou hast not forgotten the covenant which Thou didst make with our fathers, and that Thou didst not deliver us into

captivity, as on this day, because Thy hands were feeble: but on account of our sins were we sold (into captivity), and on account of our iniquities were we led away captives, for we have sinned against Thee. And now, O God, mighty to save, save us from his hand, and deliver us from his wicked devices. We are in trouble before Thee, deliver us! To Thee we flee to be raised up. Thou only canst establish the right hand of the poor, and deliver us from those who rise up against us. Remember that we are Thy portion from days of old, and that we are Thy beloved amongst the nations. In the divisions of men hast Thou separated us to be Thy lot, and among nations to be Thy beloved; and Thou has sanctified us by Thy Name as (a mark of) separation from all people. And now, O God, wherefore should our oppressors say, "Surely they have no God to save them"? They will open their mouths to devour us Thine inheritance, and to praise their graven images and their idols (vanities), saying, "By these have we subdued this people." I pray Thee, O our God, deliver us from their hands. Let the nations be ashamed of their graven images and their temples, and their false gods; and let them put their hands to their mouths when they see Thy deliverance, O Lord. Have compassion upon Thy people and Thine inheritance. Let not the mouths of them who praise Thee be stopped, who continually, evening and morning, magnify Thy Name. Turn our sorrow into joy and praise. So shall we live and praise Thee for the good deliverance which Thou hast wrought for us.

When one compares the Aramaic prayer with the LXX, certain phrases or ideas seem to resemble one another:

"It is not from pride of spirit or exaltation of heart that I have done this, and not bowed before Haman, this Amalekite."

　　　C　5: "It was not because of insolence or arrogance or vanity that I did this: that I did not bow down before arrogant Haman."

"I would not give the glory due to Thee to any son of man made of flesh and blood"

　　　C　7: "But I did it in order that I might not put the glory of a man above the glory of God, nor will I bow down to anyone except you."

"For what am I . . . that I should not . . . to procure the redemption of Israel . . . lick the dust of Haman's feet?"

　　　C　6: "For I would have been quite willing to kiss the soles of his feet for Israel's sake."

"Have compassion upon Thy people and Thine inheritance. Let not the mouths of them who praise Thee be stopped, who continually, evening and morning, magnify Thy Name. Turn our sorrow into joy and praise. So shall we live and praise Thee for the good deliverance"

　　　C 10: "Hear my prayer and be merciful to your inheritance, and turn our mourning into feasting, that we may live to sing praises to your name, Lord, and do not stifle the mouth of those who praise you."

Even more significant, these similar passages are *in almost identical sequence,* i.e. the phrases taken in order out of the Aramaic version parallel those in C 5,7,6, and 10. This fact is exceedingly important since were it otherwise, one might argue that separate authors, starting with the essential circumstances of Mordecai, could independently have arrived at similar ideas and phrases, especially since some of these ideas (like C 7 and 10) are so common in the Old Testament that they can hardly be regarded as the unique possession of the Book of Esther. The very close agreement of verse sequence, however, precludes such an argument.

On the other hand, it seems unlikely that either version is dependent upon the other. There is no reason to think that the Greek constitutes a summation or condensation of a prayer now preserved in the Aramaic. The logic, style, and theological content of C 2-11 seem to be too consistent and integrated for that to be the case. The Aramaic version could, like the Targums, include biblical material and expansions of it; but this is probably not the case here, else how can one explain the omission of C 2-4,8-9 in the Aramaic version? If there is any genealogical relationship between the two versions—and the almost identical sequence in parallel ideas suggests that there may be—then both the Aramaic and the Greek are related to one another by being descendants of either the same Hebrew *Vorlage* or oral tradition, a situation that a priori seems quite possible, given the style, theology, and probable date of Addition C (on its date, see p. 165). R. A. Martin, it will be remembered, has found that the syntax of Addition C clearly indicates a Semitic *Vorlage* for it (*JBL* 94 [1975], 65-72).

VII. Addition C, continued:

THE PRAYER OF QUEEN ESTHER
(C 12-30; AT 5:18-29; Vulg. 14:1-19)

C 12 Queen Esther was terrified and sought refuge in the Lord.
13 She took off her stately robes*a* and put on clothes appropriate for
distress and mourning, and instead of extravagant perfumes she
covered her head with ashes and dung. She debased her body completely, and *b*she covered with her disheveled hair*b* those parts which
she ordinarily loved to adorn. 14 *c*Then she prayed to the Lord God of
Israel*c* and said,

> *d*My Lord, only you are our king*d*! Help me who am alone*e* and
> have no helper except you, 15 for I am risking my life. 16 All my
> life I have heard *f*in my family's tribe*f* that you, Lord, chose*g* Is-
> rael from all the nations, and our fathers from all their prede-
> cessors, for a perpetual inheritance; and you treated them just as
> you had promised*h*.
>
> 17 *i*But now we have sinned against you, and you have handed
> us over to our enemies 18 because we extolled their gods. You
> were in the right, Lord. 19 Nevertheless, they are not satisfied that
> we are in galling slavery; but *j*they have made an agreement with
> their gods*j* 20 to nullify the promise you made, to blot out your in-
> heritance, to silence the lips of those who praise you, to quench
> the glory of your house and altar, 21 to open the mouths of the

a AT adds "and every sign of her magnificence."
b-b AT "she clothed her lovely hair with humility"; see NOTE.
c-c AT "she prayed to the Lord"; OL omits.
d-d AT "Lord, King, you are my only ally"; OL "the God of Abraham and the God
of Isaac and the God of Jacob."
e AT "insignificant."
f-f AT "from my father's book"; see NOTE.
g Elabes; AT "redeemed" (*elutrōsō*).
h AT adds "you provided them as much as they asked."
i Jos. and OL omit vss. 17-23; see COMMENT I, pp. 213-214.
j-j Reading, with most MSS, AT, and Vulgate, "they placed their hands on the hands
of their idols"; see NOTE.

*k*pagans*k* for the praise of idols, and to idolize for ever a mere mortal king. 22 Do not relinquish your scepter, Lord, *l*to non-existent gods*l*. And do not let them laugh*m* at our downfall. Frustrate their plot and make an example of him who started it all! 23 Remember*n*, Lord, reveal yourself in this time of our afflictions! *o*Give me courage*o*, King of the gods and Lord of all governments!

24 Make me persuasive *p*before the lion and*q* dispose*p* him to hate the one who fights against us so that there may be an end of him and of those agreeing with him. 25 Rescue us by your hand and help me *r*who am alone and have no one except you, Lord*r*.

You know everything 26 so you know that I hate the pomp of the wicked, and I loathe*s* the bed of the uncircumcised—*t*and of any foreigner*t*. 27 You know my "duty": that I loathe*s* that symbol of my exalted position which is upon my head*u*. When I appear at court—I loathe it like a menstruous rag—I do not wear it when I am not at court. 28 Your maid servant has not dined at *v*Haman's table*v*, nor have I extolled a royal party nor drunk the wine of libations. 29 From the day I arrived here until now, your maid servant has not delighted in anything except you, *w*Lord, the God of Abraham*w*. 30 *x*God, whose might prevails over all*x*, hear the voice of the despairing, and save us from the hands of the wicked! *y*And, Lord, protect me from my fears*y*!

---

k-k *Ethnōn;* AT *echtrōn,* "enemies."

l-l *Mē ousin;* see NOTE.

m AT "be delighted."

n AT "Appear to us."

o-o *Eme tharsunon,* which AT renders as *mē thrausēs ēmas,* "do not crush us," omitting the rest of the verse.

p-p AT "and make my words pleasing before the king and turn."

q OL adds "make me most attractive before him."

r-r AT omits.

s-s LXX*A* omits by haplography everything from the first *bdelussomai,* "I loathe," through the first *bdelussomai* in vs. 27.

t-t AT and OL omit.

u OL omits the rest of verse.

v-v AT "their tables."

w-w AT omits; OL "Lord."

x-x AT "And now, you who are mighty over all."

y-y Literally "and save me from my fear"; AT concludes with "take me, Lord, from the grip of my fear."

NOTES

C 12. *was terrified.* Literally "being seized in the agony of death"; cf. Luke 22:44. Frightened by the threats of Mordecai (see NOTES on "think" and "your family will perish" in 5:13 and 14, respectively, in AB 7B) and afraid of the king, Esther was acutely aware of the risk—and of her own sense of helplessness and isolation (cf. C 14-15 and 30).

13. *stately robes.* Literally "clothes of glory," including her crown (cf. C 27).
put on clothes appropriate for distress. I.e. sackcloth; cf. Judith 8:5 and 9:1. The Greek editor has drawn an inference from 5:1 of the MT, where it was stated that Esther put on "stately robes," the implication being that she had previously been dressed in clothes appropriate for distress and mourning.

covered her head with ashes and dung. To use ashes was standard practice (see Lam 4:5; Isa 3:24; Judith 9:1), the use of dung was a more extreme gesture (see Mal 2:3).

those parts. Apparently her neck and shoulders, unless we are to understand that in her anguish Esther literally cut or tore her hair out by the roots, letting it fall everywhere (cf. Amos 8:10; Isa 22:12; Jer 7:29, 48:37; Ezek 27:30-31; Micah 1:16; and Ezra 9:3). The Greek in this verse is probably corrupt.

14. *My Lord.* Soubigou (p. 682) notes that just as Mordecai used "Lord" (*kurios*) seven times in his prayer, so does Esther in hers. Such an assertion, however, requires deleting two "Lords" in C 14-30; for as the text stands, "Lord" appears nine times (vss. 14,16,18,22,23 [twice], 25,29, and 30).

only [monos] you are our king! Only (*monos*) God can help Esther who is alone (*monē*). Despite Artaxerxes' claim to being "the great king" (see B 1), Esther knows better: only YHWH is king.

15. *I am risking my life.* Cf. Judg 12:3; I Sam 28:21; Job 13:14; Ps 119:109. Literally "for my danger is in my hand."

16. *All my life.* Literally "from the moment of my birth."
I have heard in my family's tribe. Whether Esther is thinking here of the informal learning of everyday living (so the LXX) or readings from the Old Testament (so the AT's "from my father's book"), one can easily imagine some of the stories involved, e.g. Deut 32:7-14 and Ps 44:1-3. Leaving nothing, however, to the reader's imagination, the OL in a 134-word addition cites the Lord's support of Noah (cf. Genesis 6*ff*), Abraham (Gen 14:13*ff*), Jonah 2, Daniel (Dan 6 and 14:27*f*), Hananiah, Mishael, Azariah (Daniel 3); Hezekiah (II Kings 20:1*ff* [Isaiah 38]), and Hannah (I Sam 1:2-2:10). This OL passage may, as Schildenberger has suggested (pp. 89-90), be a witness to the oldest Greek version of Esther; but it is not, as some have suggested a witness to a Semitic *Vorlage*, their argument being that in the place corresponding to C 17, we read in II Targum: "As you [God] did save Hananiah, Mishael, and Azariah out of the burning furnace, and Daniel out of the lion's den." For if the three youths (Hananiah, Mishael, and Azariah) are counted as one

example, then Esther has cited here in the OL *seven* case studies of those
delivered by the Lord; and the citing of seven examples was clearly a recognized literary device in apocryphal literature, e.g. in the Wisdom of Solomon
(10:1 - 11:4) the author alludes to seven well-known biblical figures whom
Wisdom had delivered (Adam, Cain, Noah, Lot, Jacob, Joseph, and Moses);
and in the Prayer of Eleazar in III Macc 6:4-8 seven case studies are cited,
namely, Pharaoh, Sennacherib, Daniel and his three friends, and Jonah. Finally, in I Macc 2:52-61, the dying Mattathias recalls the heroic examples set
by Abraham, Joseph, Phinehas, Joshua, Caleb, David, Elijah, Daniel and his
three friends.

chose. Literally "took"; cf. Deut 4:20,34, 26:5; and Josh 2:4.

inheritance. Cf. Gen 12:1; Deut 21:5, 32:9; Josh 24:2.

18. *extolled their gods.* Referring probably to Israel's pre-exilic behavior
which resulted in her Babylonian Captivity (see II Kings 17:10-16,29-41,
21:7,21; and Isa 40:1-2), rather than to some subsequent relapse into idolatry
(so Kautzsch-Ryssel) in the exilic or post-exilic period.

You were in the right. Literally "you were righteous." Esther is acknowledging here the justness of God's decision, not his character.

19. *they have made an agreement with their gods.* Literally "they placed their
hands on the hands of their idols" (see textual note *j-j*). For possible parallels
where someone places his hands on idols as an act of sealing an agreement, see
II Kings 10:15; Lam 5:6; and I Macc 6:58; see also Prov 11:21 of the LXX.
The Vulgate has "they attribute the strength of their own hands to the power of
their idols," a perceptive insight perhaps, but still a misleading translation.

20. *nullify the promise you made.* Literally "abolish the decree (*orismon*) of
your mouth." Cf. Dan 6:7,8,12 and 15. As Gregg (p. 677) has observed, "If
the *orismoi* of the Medes and Persians were unchangeable, what an impiety to
seek to overthrow those of the living God!"

to silence the lips. Literally "to stop the mouth."

house and altar. I.e. the temple of Jerusalem. Although the concern shown
here for Jerusalem and its temple and cult is absent in the Hebrew version,
such concern was quite justified in the Hellenistic period (cf. II Macc 14:33
and III Macc 5:43).

21. *idols.* Literally "the vain things"; cf. Lev 17:7 of the LXX.

idolize for ever. I.e. idolize as the mortal who destroyed the devotees of the
one, immortal God.

22. *scepter [skēptron].* Here it is the symbol of an earthly king's power and
authority (cf. Gen 49:10; Num 24:17; but see Schildenberger [p. 90] who
notes the *skēptron* is also the Greek translation for *šbṭ*, "tribe," in I Sam 2:28
and 9:21). Thus, if God does not save his people from destruction, he has, in
effect, surrendered his divine power and authority to mortal men and helpless
"gods."

to non-existent gods [tois mē ousin]. Literally "to them who are not"; cf. Wisd
13:10-19, 14:13; I Cor 8:10. The AT has the fascinating reading *tois misousi
se ethrois,* "to the enemies hating you," where *misousi se,* "hating you," represents a corruption of LXX's *mē ousin,* while *ethrois,* "enemies," is a later
doublet of *misousi se.*

Frustrate their plot. Literally "turn back their plot upon them," which emphasizes the biblical idea of retributive justice.

started it all! Literally "who began against us," i.e. Haman.

23. Up to this point (vss. 12-22), Esther has been interceding for her people. Now she petitions for herself, pointing out how her religious scruples (vss. 26-29) have made her royal office repugnant to her. Her attitude here conflicts with the MT where no hint is given of any such reluctance to be queen. The editors of JB have observed quite rightly: "The prayers of Mordecai and Esther are rich in O.T. piety, but they betray an introspective interest and a concern with self-justification that is not found in the older texts" (p. 645, note e). For another prayer of protested innocence, see Tobit 3:13-15.

King of the gods. Cf. Ps 95:3: "The Lord is . . . a great king above all gods"; see also "God of gods and Lord of lords" in Deut 10:17; Ps 136:2-3.

24. *Make me persuasive.* Literally "put a pleasing word in my mouth."

lion. I.e. the king, "lion" symbolizing here either the king's terrible anger (cf. Prov 19:12), his strength (Jer 49:19), his ferocity (Prov 20:2; Sira 28:23), or inescapable judgment (Amos 5:19).

dispose him. Literally "change his heart."

26. *I loathe.* This is Esther's justification for violating Judaism's prohibition against mixed marriages (cf. Deut 7:3-4; Ezra 10:2; and Neh 13:23-27); her attitude here is in sharp contrast with the MT, where apparently no such rationalization for her marriage was felt necessary.

In this verse, as in others (C 19-21,26,28), the enemy whom Esther really fears and hates are the Gentiles and their religion rather than Haman himself who is mentioned by name only once (C 28) and alluded to twice (C 22,24). Again, this emphasis would be especially meaningful to Diaspora Jews.

27. *my "duty."* Literally "my necessity"; she must wear the crown she detests —or else!

at court . . . not at court. Literally "in the days of my appearing . . . in the days of my leisure."

menstruous rag. Cf. Isa 64:6[5]. Given the Jewish taboos on menstruation (cf. Lev 15:19-24), one can hardly imagine a stronger expression of Esther's abhorrence for her royal turban. For details on menstruation and other taboos in the Old Testament, see L. E. Toombs, *IDB,* I, s.v. "Clean and Unclean," especially p. 644.

28. In contrast to the MT, where Esther apparently ate the delicacies from the king's cuisine (2:9), here she avoids eating the king's food, some of which was certainly not kosher. But even here her abstinence is not as total as Daniel's (cf. Dan 1:8,13, and 15).

royal party. Literally "feast of the king"; cf. 1:5 and 2:18.

libations. While the Persians were notorious for their lavish drinking parties (see NOTE on "the drinks" in AB 7B, 7), Esther is not alluding to that custom but to their toasts (cf. Daniel 1-14) and libations to the gods (cf. Deut 32:38; see also G. G. Cameron, *The Persepolis Treasury Tablets* [University of Chicago Press, 1948], p. 9).

30. *voice of the despairing.* Cf. Judith 9:11.

COMMENT I

Not surprisingly, Esther's prayer is almost twice as long as Mordecai's. For at the time Esther was in much the greater danger. Mordecai's death was possibly a year away and, in any case, he could do nothing about it; she on the other hand was courting death right now.

Although by statistical fact the first person singular pronoun (I, me, my) predominates in the prayer, appearing more than twice as often as the plural (we, us, our), Esther's prayer is not a self-centered prayer in which her personal safety is primary and her people's secondary. It is a tribute to Esther's character, or better, to the author of the prayer, that she first prayed extensively for her people (vss. 16-22), *and then* prayed at lesser length for herself (vss. 26-29), vss. 23-25 being transitional and containing petitions for both.

Queen Esther voices strong feelings here on two matters not even alluded to in the MT: the temple at Jerusalem (see NOTE on vs. 20) and *kašrût* (see p. 157, n. 7). So devout a Jewess is Esther and so strong are her religious scruples that her role as queen and its social obligations are very distasteful to her (cf. vss. 26-29); yet in the MT there is no hint of any reluctance or reservation on her part.

The special interests and concerns of the author of the Addition are easily seen. For him Yahweh is the omnipotent (vss. 2,4,23, and 30), omniscient (vss. 5,26, and 27), righteous (vs. 18), yet merciful (vs. 10) Creator (vs. 3), the only true God (vs. 14). The God of Abraham (vss. 8 and 29), Yahweh chose Israel for himself (vss. 9 and 16), and redeemed her from Egypt (vs. 9). Jealous of his honor (vss. 7,8,20,22, and 28-29), Yahweh punishes sin (vss. 17 and 22), but is ever ready to help those in need (vss. 14,24,25, and 30). God expects his followers to be humble (vs. 26), to delight only in him (vs. 29), and to refrain from mixed marriages (vs. 26), from food which is not kosher (vs. 28), and from wine libations (vs. 28).

Since all these concepts occur frequently in the Bible, the question of the source of the author's ideas is gratuitous. How could anyone who knew the Old Testament possibly escape them! A far cry from the sophisticated thinking of an Egyptian Philo, these concepts are sufficiently simple and unsophisticated to express the views of pious, orthodox Jews anywhere, but especially in the Maccabean period as its spirit is reflected in the final form of Daniel and in other Hellenistic Jewish writings. For a brief treatment of prayer as a reflection of the concept of God in this period, see Norman B. Johnson, *Prayer in the Apocrypha and Pseudepigrapha, JBL* Monograph Series, II (1948), 76.

The absence of vss. 17-23 from both Josephus and the OL deserves some comment. Their absence in the OL not only suggests that these seven verses were missing in the OL's Greek *Vorlage* of the second century but also that they were missing in the Greek text of the first century used by Josephus, rather than that Josephus chose to omit them for fear of offending his Roman readers. In terms of their content, these verses seem neither to add nor detract from the theological content of the prayer, especially since all the elements in vss. 17-23 find parallel expression in concept, if not in wording, elsewhere in the Greek Esther. Since they really add nothing new, it seems more likely that these verses were added early rather than late, that is, possibly before Josephus' day rather than afterward. In any case, these verses were not originally a part of Addition C.

COMMENT II

Efforts to find a Semitic *Vorlage* for Esther's prayer have met with virtually no success to date. One can find "parallels," and two of them are instructive to examine.

First, not a few scholars have observed that Esther's prayer is reminiscent of Daniel's prayer in Dan 9:3-19. The setting for the two prayers is certainly similar:

> Dan 9:3   Then I turned my face to the Lord God, seeking him by prayer and supplications with fasting and sackcloth and ashes (RSV).
>
> C 13   She took off her stately robes and put on clothes appropriate for distress and mourning, and instead of extravagant perfumes she covered her head with ashes and dung.

There are also similar ideas and theology:

> Dan 9:4-5   I prayed to the Lord my God and made confession, saying, "O Lord, the great and terrible God, who keepest covenant and steadfast love with those who love him and keep his commandments, we have sinned and done wrong and acted wickedly and rebelled . . ." (RSV).
>
> C 14-17   Then she prayed to the Lord God of Israel and said, "My Lord, only you are our king! Help me who am alone and have no helper except you, for I am risking my life. All my life I have heard in my family's tribe that you, Lord, chose Israel from all the nations, and our fathers from all their predecessors, for a perpetual inheritance; and you treated them just as you had promised. But now we have sinned against you, and you have handed us over to our enemies."

But the similarity between the two prayers is one of spirit and theology, not of phraseology—at least not in the Greek. In the Greek there are virtually no linguistic parallels, or even similarities, between the two prayers. There is no evidence that either prayer was derived from the other, although one may assume that the prayer in Daniel antedates the one in Esther. In all likelihood, similarity of phrases and ideas grow out of a common past (the heritage of the Old Testament) and a similar historical setting.

Although the contents of I and II Targum are too dissimilar to those of C

12-30 to suggest any dependence of one upon the other, or of all three upon a common source, there is another Aramaic text which is worth mentioning here since it contains Esther's prayer and bears some similarity to C 12-30. This text, first published by de Rossi in 1784, contains most of the ideas of the Greek version, but is three times as long. For example, whereas the LXX has

> All my life I have heard in my family's tribe that you, Lord, chose Israel from all the nations, and our fathers from all their predecessors, for a perpetual inheritance; and you treated them just as you had promised. But now we have sinned against you, and you have handed us over to our enemies (C 16-17)

this particular Aramaic text reads as follows:

> I have heard from my fathers, and I myself have understood, how Thou didst lead our fathers from the midst of the peoples, and didst bring them out of Egypt, and didst slay all the first-born of Egypt on account of them. Thou didst lead Thy people from among them, and didst shew Thy mighty hand and uplifted arm to the Egyptians on account of Thy people. Thou didst make them to go through the wilderness, as a horse passeth through the desert, and cattle in the valley. Thou didst give them bread from heaven (to satisfy) their hunger; and when they were thirsty, Thou didst bring water out of the hardest rock. (Thou didst give them) fleshmeat and fowls of the air to satisfy them, and water out of the great rock at their desire. Thou didst feed them forty years in the desert, (in) a land without inhabitants; and Thou didst wipe out before them kings great and mighty. Thou didst cause them to possess the land, and in great goodness didst give them a notable land, a good possession. And when our fathers sinned against Thy great name, Thou didst deliver them into the hand of those who led them away captive; and lo! they are in exile this day.

For an English translation of the entire prayer, including the section above, see Fuller (pp. 390-391). If there is a Semitic *Vorlage* for Esther's prayer, de Rossi's Aramaic text is certainly not a witness to it. The consensus of the experts is that this Aramaic text was based on Josippon's Hebrew text (see p. 154, n. 3), and then greatly elaborated.

VIII. Addition D:

ESTHER APPEARS UNSUMMONED
BEFORE THE KING

(D 1-16; AT 6:1-12; Vulg. 15:4-19)

D 1 On the third day, when she had finished praying, she took off the clothing of a suppliant^a and ^{b}dressed herself in splendid attire^b. 2 After she had called upon the ^{c}all-seeing^c God and savior, she, looking absolutely radiant, took two maids, 3 leaning daintily on the one, 4 while the other followed carrying her train. 5 She was radiant, in the prime of her beauty, and her face was assured as one who knows she is loved, but her heart was pounding ^{d}with fear^d.

6 When she had passed through all^e the doors, ^{f}she stood before the king. He was seated on his royal throne, arrayed in all his splendid attire, all covered with gold and precious stones—a most formidable sight^f! 7 ^{g}Raising his face, flushed with color, he looked at her^h in fiercest anger.^{g} The queen stumbled^i, turned pale and fainted, keeling over on the maid who went before her.

8 But God^j changed the king's spirit^k to gentleness. ^{l}The king leaped down^l from his throne in alarm and took her up in his arms ^{m}until she revived. He comforted her with reassuring words^m, 9 saying

---

^{a} OL adds "and washed her body with water and applied cosmetics"; see NOTE.
$^{b\text{-}b}$ LXX "she put on her glory"; AT "she put on stately robes"; (cf. C 13).
$^{c\text{-}c}$ AT "all-knowing."
$^{d\text{-}d}$ AT omits; OL adds "and fearing the Lord, in the terror of death, because death was before her eyes."
^{e} LXX^A and AT omit "all."
$^{f\text{-}f}$ OL "she entered the inner hall and found King Artaxerxes sitting on his glorious throne, and he was dressed in purple and precious stones and had a gold scepter in his hand."
$^{g\text{-}g}$ OL "Looking with his eyes, he saw her as a bull at the peak of his anger, and he considered killing her; but he was uncertain, and calling out, he said, 'Who dares to enter unsummoned into the court?' "
^{h} AT adds "like a bull."
^{i} AT "was afraid."
^{j} OL inserts "of the Jews and the Lord of all creatures."
^{k} AT adds "and altered his anger."
$^{l\text{-}l}$ So AT; LXX "He sprang."
$^{m\text{-}m}$ AT "and comforted her."

to her, "What's the matter, Esther? I'm your brother. Relax. 10 You're not going to die! This practice applies only to our subjects. 11 Come here[n]!"

12 Then he raised his gold scepter and tapped her neck; he hugged her and said, "Talk to me!"

13 o"My lord[o]," she said, "I saw you like an angel of God, and [p]I was upset[p] by [q]your awesome appearance[q]. 14 [r]For you are wonderful, my lord, and your face is full of graciousness."

15 And as she spoke, she sagged with relief. 16 The king was upset, and all his court tried to reassure her.

[n] Vulgate adds "and touch the scepter," while AT adds "and the threat does not apply to you." Then AT and OL add, "See, the scepter is in your hand!"
[o-o] AT omits.
[p-p] Literally "my heart was disturbed (*etarachthē;* AT *etakē,* 'melted')."
[q-q] AT "the glory of your anger, Lord."
[r] For vss. 14-15, AT has only "And there was perspiration on her face"; see NOTE.

NOTES

D 1. Addition D is an imaginative and highly dramatic expansion of 5:1-2 of the MT, the latter simply being:

> So it was that on the third day Esther put on her royal robes and stopped in the inner court of the palace, opposite the royal apartment. The king was seated on his royal throne in the throne room, facing the building's entrance. Finally, when the king noticed Esther standing in the court, she won his favor; and the king extended to Esther the gold scepter that he was holding. Then Esther came up and touched the tip of the scepter.

In contrast to the prayers of Addition C, Addition D is fully paraphrased by Josephus who, always willing to tell a good story, gives the details of Esther's audience with obvious relish and embellishment. (For a brief statement on the importance of Josephus for biblical studies in general and for the Book of Esther in particular, see AB 7B, XXII-XXIII, n. 10.)

clothing of a suppliant. Literally "clothes of service" (Ethiopic "of lamentation"; Coptic "humiliation"; cf. also 2:12) which refers to the clothes she had worn while serving the Lord with her fasting (cf. 4:16) and prayer (C 12-30). Fritzsche rightly emends Vulgate's *vestimenta ornatus* to *vestimenta oratus.*

2. *looking absolutely radiant.* Literally "having become conspicuous," which Jerome translated as *regio fulgeret habitu,* "she gleamed in her regal attire," while Josephus has "she adorned herself as became a queen."

two maids [abras]. Cf. 2:9; Gen 24:61; Judith 8:33 and 10:5.

3. *daintily.* Not "languishingly," as some translators have suggested, but daintily, in keeping with the day's conception of the delicate, well-bred woman of the harem. Since Esther had been fasting for three days, she may very well have felt somewhat unsteady on her feet; but she was nonetheless relying on her beauty (vs. 5) rather than upon the king's pity.

5. *was assured as . . . loved.* Literally "happy as a beloved"; Esther's cheerful, confident air successfully disguised her true feelings.

pounding with fear. Literally "being in anguish from fear."

6. *splendid attire.* Literally "clothing of manifestation (*epiphaneias*)." This Greek word is often used for the appearance of a divine being, especially in II Maccabees (2:21, 3:24, 5:4, 12:22, 14:15, 15:27); see NOTE on vs. 13, and W. H. Brownlee, *RB* 73 (1966), 161-185.

a most formidable sight! Literally "and he was very terrible." For an impressive wall relief depicting King Darius sitting on his throne, holding his scepter and giving audience, see photograph opposite p. 22 in AB 7B; see also Herodotus' description of Xerxes in *History* VII 187.

7. *flushed with color.* Literally "flamed with glory." The reason for the king's anger is expressly given only in the OL (see textual note *g-g*).

turned pale and fainted. Esther's conduct need not be seen as "just an act," designed to elicit the king's sympathy. His openly hostile reaction to her, following as it did her fasting and the terrifying prospect of appearing unsummoned before him, had been too much for her.

keeling over on. Literally "she bent down on the head of." Esther fell down here in fear and not, as in 8:3, in obeisance.

8. *God changed the king's spirit.* This may well be "the culminating point" and "La l'unique miracle" of the Greek version (so Brownlee, *RB* 73 [1966], 182), but it is certainly not the climax of the Hebrew version, where the establishment of Purim in ch. 9 is the main consideration. The phrase "God changed the king's spirit" involved two important and dramatic elements: God himself, and a dramatic change in the king's initially hostile attitude. Neither element is found in 5:2 of the MT (but see Prov 20:2). Nor is there much tension in the Hebrew version of her unannounced audience with the king: Esther simply stands in the inner court until the king looks up, whereupon he immediately extends his gold scepter and, without any obvious emotional stress, she makes her request.

reassuring words. Literally "peaceable words"; cf. Deut 2:26; Micah 7:3; and Sira 4:8. The phrase is common in I Maccabees, occurring seven times (1:30, 5:48, 7:10,15,27, 10:3,47).

What's the matter? . . . Relax. The translation here may strike some readers as sounding too colloquial and, thus, in poor taste for a biblical translation. But it must be remembered that the king was quite surprised and concerned; the Greek itself, in keeping with the abruptness and informality of the scene, is certainly terse and informal, and anything but stilted and "proper." This should not be too surprising: in the emergencies of life "good" or "correct" grammar and etiquette are not of the highest priority.

brother. A term of endearment here, this word, which expresses the king's intimate and tender feelings for his queen, has sometimes been cited as proof for an Egyptian provenance of Addition D (see Gregg, p. 679); but similar terminology is found in Palestinian works, e.g. the word "sister" in Song of Songs 4:9-10 and 5:1-2.

10. *This practice . . . subjects.* Literally "for our order is public," referring to the practice of executing those who appeared unsummoned before the king (cf. 4:11). Esther, says the king, is an exception.

13. *like an angel of God.* Cf. I Sam 29:9; II Sam 14:17,20, and 19:27, where David was so described; so also Mephibosheth in II Sam 19:27. If this phrase represents only flattery on Esther's part, then it is quite unconscionable, if not blasphemous, for one with the scruples of the Greek Esther (cf. C 26-29). Interestingly enough, the phrase is in neither Josephus nor the Midrash. On the other hand, Walther Eichrodt (*Theology of the Old Testament*, tr. J. A. Baker, I [Philadelphia: Westminster Press, 1961], 448) and W. H. Brownlee (*RB* 73 [1966], 172) argue that the title is an expression of "the divine royalty," and not just a flattering phrase.

14. *full of graciousness [chariton meston].* Cf. Ps 45:2. According to C. C. Torrey (*HTR* 37 [1944], 8), the LXX presupposes the Aram. *ml' r't'*, since the AT (see textual note *r*) has in the "corresponding" place *metron idrotos* (Aram. *ml' d't'*), the *r* easily being confused with *d* in the Aramaic script. On the basis of syntax criticism, R. A. Martin (*JBL* 94 [1975], 65-72) has argued for a Semitic *Vorlage* for Addition D.

15. *sagged with relief [epesen apo ekluseos].* Cf. D 7. Literally "she fell from release."

16. *court [therapeia].* Cf. *pharao kai e therapeia autou* in Gen 45:16 of the LXX. The story of the patriarch Joseph affected the Esther account (see AB 7B, LII, n. 8).

COMMENT I

Unquestionably, Addition D is the dramatic climax of the Greek Esther (but see NOTE on vs. 8). Esther's appearance before the king was certainly the high point in her own life: she had taken extensive precautions, fasting and praying to God (C 12-30), and then dressing up in her finest (D 1-5). But although Esther had steeled herself for the terrible moment of truth—so much so that her outward appearance gave no hint of her inner fears (vs. 5)—when the terrible moment came and the awesome king glared at her, Esther failed completely: she fainted dead away (vss. 6-7). She was inadequate for the test. But God was not: he changed the king's mood to gentleness (vs. 8), thereby bringing victory out of her defeat. It was God's power, not Esther's courage or charms, that saved the day. God, not Esther, is the hero of Addition D.

Reassured by the solicitous king (vss. 8-11), Esther realizes that all her anxieties had been groundless and that, by virtue of being queen, she was exempt from any restrictions with respect to approaching the throne (vs. 10). (But of such ignorance—and courage—is great drama made!) Rather than admit she had fainted out of fear for her life, Esther tried to justify her conduct by explaining how she had been overwhelmed by the king's appearance which was "like an angel of God," a phrase which may have been more than just flattery (see NOTE on vs. 13). It had been a harrowing experience for her; small wonder she had sagged with relief (vs. 15), and that, as the AT adds, "there was perspiration on her face." Esther's problems, however, were not over. Not to be summarily killed by the king was one thing: to have him grant her wish was another matter.

COMMENT II

The combined effect of Additions C and D is to alter appreciably the image of Queen Esther from that presented in the MT, where it is more asserted by the Jewish writer than felt by his readers that she was good and courageous (2:20 and 4:16 notwithstanding). In the Hebrew version, Mordecai is the greater hero, mapping out the strategy while Esther merely follows his orders; even her audience with the king (5:1-2) is rather cut and dried. (One has the feeling that Esther showed her courage more in coming to her decision than in carrying it out.)

Additions C and D change all that! Esther's prayer in C, which is twice as long as Mordecai's, makes her a more flesh-and-blood human being, revealing as it does her faith and fears. In her dramatic audience with the king in D, she steals the spotlight from Mordecai whose moment of triumph in 6:11-12 seems almost unimportant by comparison. It is no coincidence that Christians, who knew the story with the Additions, always called the book "Esther," while Jews frequently referred to it as the "Scroll" (*Megillah*). In line with this, it should be remembered that in the earliest allusion to the events of Esther outside the book itself, i.e. in II Macc 15:36, the fourteenth of Adar was known as "the day *of Mordecai*" (italics added), not "the day of Esther."

Again, it is the presence of Additions C and D which makes the Book of Judith come to our minds, even as it did to the early Church Fathers, evidence of this fact being that the three earliest Christian allusions to Esther also mention Judith in the same breath,[1] and that in a number of lists of canonical books the one is mentioned immediately after the other.[2] The similarity of the stories goes far beyond their common theme of how a beautiful and God-fearing woman saved her people from destruction through her courage and cunning. A brief summary of the relevant features of the Book of Judith are given below, including some quotations (RSV) from the book itself.

Before going to the camp of General Holofernes and just as the evening sacrifice was being offered in the temple at Jerusalem, the lovely widow Judith, in sackcloth and ashes, prayed to the Lord (9:1). She asked God to destroy the Assyrians who wanted to defile his sanctuary, pollute the tabernacle, and cast down the horns of his altar where his glorious name was (9:8). She stressed in her prayer that the Lord was "God of the lowly, helper of the oppressed,

---

[1] I Clement LV, dating from the first century; *Stromata* IV 19 of Clement of Alexandria, who died before 215; and the *Constitutions of the Holy Apostles* V iii 20 (ca. 380).

[2] For example, the lists of Augustine, Innocent I, Pseudo-Gelasius, Cassiodorus, Isidorus, the Cheltenham, the Council of Carthage in 397, as well as LXX[A] [B].

upholder of the weak, protector of the forlorn, savior of those without hope [9:11]. . . . God of the inheritance of Israel, Lord of heaven and earth, Creator of the waters, King of all . . ." (9:12), and that the "whole nation and every tribe" knew and understood that he was "God, the God of all power and might, and that there is no other who protects the people of Israel" (9:14) but him alone.

When Judith had finished praying, "she removed the sackcloth which she had been wearing, and took off her widow's garments, and bathed her body with water, and anointed herself with precious ointment, and combed her hair and put on a tiara, and arrayed herself in her gayest apparel . . . [10:3]; and she gave her maid a bottle of wine and a flask of oil, and filled a bag with parched grain and a cake of dried fruit and fine bread; and she wrapped up all her vessels and gave them to her to carry" (10:5) with them to the camp of the enemy.

At the camp Judith won the approval of all the men who saw her (10:14), so much so that a hundred of them were escorting her to Holofernes, encouraging her and saying, "Some of us will escort you and hand you over to him. And when you stand before him, do not be afraid in your heart, but tell him just what you have said, and he will treat you well" (10:15-16).

"And when Judith came into the presence of Holofernes and his servants, they all marveled at the beauty of her face; and she prostrated herself and made obeisance to him, and his slaves raised her up [10:23]. Then Holofernes said to her, 'Take courage, woman, and do not be afraid in your heart, for I have never hurt any one who chose to serve Nebuchadnezzar, the king of all the earth [11:1]. . . . Have courage; you will live, tonight and from now on. No one will hurt you, but all will treat you well . . .'" (11:4).

Judith, in turn, assured Holofernes that God would deliver the Jews into his hands because they had sinned: they "have determined to use all that God by his laws had forbidden them to eat. They have decided to consume the first fruits of the grain and the tithes of the wine and oil, which they had consecrated and set aside for the priests . . ." (11:12-13) at Jerusalem. Although she would willingly remain in Holofernes' camp, Judith did ask him that each evening she be permitted to go out into the valley to learn from her God when Holofernes should attack the Jews (11:17-18).

When Holofernes "ordered them to set a table for her with some of his own food and to serve her with his own wine . . . Judith said, 'I cannot eat it, lest it be an offense; but I will be provided from the things I have brought with me'" (12:1-2). When, on the fourth day, she was invited by Holofernes to a small, intimate party, "she got up and arrayed herself in all her woman's finery, . . ." (12:15). Then Judith took "and ate and drank before him what her maid had prepared. And Holofernes was greatly pleased with her, and drank a great quantity of wine, much more than he had ever drunk in one day since he was born" (12:19-20).

Later that night, when Judith and Holofernes were alone, she cut off Holofernes' head with his own sword (13:9), and then carried it off in a sack to her countrymen. The Jews, inspired by Judith's courageous example and strengthened by their God, "with one accord . . . fell upon the enemy . . ." (15:5); and "the rest of the people of Bethulia fell upon the Assyrian camp and plundered it, and were greatly enriched. And the Israelites, when they returned from the slaughter, took possession of what remained, and the villages and towns in the hill country and in the plain got a great amount of booty, for there was a vast quantity of it" (15:6-7).

Small wonder the Church Fathers frequently associated Esther and Judith in their own minds! Similarities in theme, plot, and even details[3] between the stories of Judith and Esther are striking, especially as the latter is enlarged and altered in the Greek by Additions C and D.

Esther's claims to canonicity were certainly not strengthened by its frequent association with the Book of Judith, although why the latter was denied canonical status is not known. Despite the fact that no Hebrew text of Judith is extant, there is every reason to believe the book was originally composed in Hebrew, sometime in the first half of the second century B.C.[4] Judith's omission from the Jewish canon is to be explained either by Jewish recognition of its fictional or unhistorical character,[5] or, more likely, by later Jewish disapproval of the book's fanatical nationalism which, although quite understandable in terms of the book's probable date of composition and historical context, was nonetheless untempered by the ethical and moral considerations so characteristic of Judaism. For a balanced assessment of the religious and ethical strengths and weaknesses of the book, see Pfeiffer, pp. 301-303, and Oesterley, pp. 175-176.

[3] But not of wording, at least, not in the Greek versions, even if the English translations seem to suggest that such is the case. In their present form the Greek vocabulary and style are sufficiently dissimilar so that the question of whether one Greek version affected the other does not cogently arise. If there was any influence of one upon the other, it was in the Semitic stage, not the Greek.

[4] For a translation and notes, see The Book of Judith, ed. A. E. Cowley, in APOT, I, 248-267; see also the articles on the book itself by P. Winter in IDB, II, 1,023-1,026; Eissfeldt, pp. 585-587; and Pfeiffer, pp. 285-303.

[5] But see Claus Schedl, who argues for a core of historicity to Judith in the days of Darius, "Nabuchodonosor, Arpakšad, und Darius," ZDMG 115 (1965), 242-254.

IX. HAMAN IS "HONORED," THEN MORTIFIED, AND FINALLY EXECUTED

(5:3-7:10)

5 ³ The king then said to her, "What do you want, Queen Esther? What is your petition? Even if it be half of my kingdom, you may have it."

⁴ "If it please the king," said Esther, "let the king come with Haman^a today to a dinner that I have prepared for him."

⁵ "Bring Haman right away," said the king, "so that we may do as Esther wants."

So the king and Haman came to the dinner that Esther had arranged. ⁶ While they were drinking, the king said, "What's your request? It shall be given you. What's your petition? ^{b}Even if it be half the kingdom^b, it shall be done!"

⁷ So Esther answered, saying, ^{c}"All right^c. ⁸ If I have found favor with the king and if it please the king to grant my request and to fulfill my petition, then let the king and Haman come tomorrow^d to a dinner which I shall give for them; and tomorrow I will do as the king has said."

⁹ So that day Haman left joyful and exuberant. But when Haman noticed Mordecai at the King's Gate, and that he neither stood up nor trembled in his presence, Haman was infuriated with Mordecai. ¹⁰ Nevertheless, Haman restrained himself, went home, and assembled^e his friends and his wife Zeresh; ¹¹ and Haman recounted to them the extent of his wealth, his large number of sons, every instance where the king had honored him, and now he had advanced him beyond the officials and courtiers.

¹² "Besides all that," said Haman, "Queen Esther invited only me to

^{a} AT and OL add "your friend."
$^{b\text{-}b}$ LXX now omits; but AT and Josephus have it.
$^{c\text{-}c}$ All ancient versions have "my request and my petition"; see NOTE.
^{d} So LXX; see NOTE.
^{e} So the Greek; see NOTE.

attend the dinner she gave for the king. And along with the king, I have been invited by her again tomorrow. 13 But all this fails to satisfy me whenever I see Mordecai the Jew sitting at the King's Gate."

14 So his wife Zeresh and all his friends advised him, "Have them make a gallows seventy-five feet high; and tomorrow morning speak to the king and have them hang Mordecai on it. Then, in good spirits accompany the king to the dinner." This advice appealed to Haman, so he had the gallows erected.

6 1 The king could not sleep that night so he gave orders to bring the record book, the daily record; and it was read to him. 2 And it was found recorded there that Mordecai had given information about ⸒Bigtan and Teresh⸒, the two royal eunuchs who had guarded the threshold and who had plotted to assassinate King Ahasuerus.ᵍ 3 Whereupon the king asked, ʰ"What great honorʰ was conferred on Mordecai for this?"

Then replied the king's servants who were waiting on him, "Nothing has been done for him."

4 "Who is in the court?" asked the king.

Now Haman had just entered the outer court of the king's apartment to ask the king about hanging Mordecai on the gallows he had prepared for him. 5 So the king's servants told him, "Haman is waiting in the court."

"Let him enter!" said the king.

6 When Haman entered, the king said to him, "What should be done for the man whom the king especially wants to honor?"

Now Haman reasoned to himself, "Whom would the king especially want to honor besides me!" 7 So Haman said to the king, ⁱ"All right!ⁱ 8 Have them bring a royal robe which the king has worn and a horse the king has ridden, one with a royal crown on its head. 9 Then have them hand over the robe and the horse to one of the king's most noble princes and have him robe the man whom the king especially wants to honor, and have the prince lead him on horseback through the city square, proclaiming before him, 'This is what is done for the man whom the king especially wants to honor!' "

10 "Hurry up," said the king to Haman, "and take the robe and the

---

ᶠ⁻ᶠ Possibly a gloss; Greek omits.

ᵍ AT and OL then have the king observe: "Mordecai is a faithful man for protecting my life. Since he has kept me alive until now and I sit on my throne and I did nothing for him, I have not acted justly."

ʰ⁻ʰ MT "What honor and dignity"; hendiadys.

ⁱ⁻ⁱ All ancient versions have "the man whom the king especially wants to honor"; see NOTE.

horse, and do exactly as you have advised to Mordecai the Jew who sits at the King's Gate. Do not omit a single detail that you have suggested!"

11 So Haman took the robe and the horse; and he robed Mordecai, and led Mordecai through the city square, proclaiming before him, "This is what is done for the man whom the king especially wants to honor." 12 Mordecai then returned to the King's Gate, and Haman hurried home, despondent and with his head covered. 13 When Haman had recounted to his wife Zeresh and all his friends everything that had just happened to him, then his advisers and his wife Zeresh advised him, "If this Mordecai before whom you have started to fall is Jewish, you won't succeed against him but will undoubtedly fail^j."

14 While they were still talking with him, the king's eunuchs arrived; and they hurried to bring Haman to the banquet that Esther had prepared. 7 1 When the king and Haman were there at Queen Esther's party 2 on the second day, the king again asked Esther while they were drinking, "What do you want, Queen Esther? It shall be granted you! What's your petition? Even if half the kingdom, it shall be done for you!"

3 Then Queen Esther answered, saying, "If I have obtained your favor, Your Majesty, and if it please the king, let my life be granted me as my request. And my people's as my petition! 4 For we've been sold, I and my people, for destruction! For slaughter and annihilation! If we had just been sold as slaves and servant girls, I would have kept quiet; ^{k}for our problem would not have been worth bothering the king.^{k}"

5 "Who is it?" ^{l}exclaimed King Ahasuerus to Queen Esther^l. ^{m}"Where is he?^{m} who has the nerve to do this?"

6 "An enemy! An adversary!" said Esther, "this wicked Haman here!"

Haman was dumbfounded before the king and queen; 7 but when the king ^{n}arose in anger from his wine and went out into the pavilion garden^n, Haman remained behind to beg Queen Esther for his life. For he saw ^{o}that the king had decided to punish him^o. 8 As the king came back from the pavilion garden to the banquet hall, Haman was

---

^{j} Greek, OL, Ethiopic, and Coptic add "for God is with him."
$^{k-k}$ AT "but I did not want to announce it lest I should distress my lord"; see NOTE.
$^{l-l}$ So LXX; see NOTE.
$^{m-m}$ Greek omits.
$^{n-n}$ So LXX rightly translates the ellipsis of the MT: "he arose from his wine in anger into the garden."
$^{o-o}$ LXX "himself to be in trouble."

prostrate on the couch where Esther was; so the king exclaimed, "Would he actually violate the queen while I'm in the building?"

As soon as these words were uttered, they covered Haman's face. 9 Then observed Harbonah[p], one of the eunuchs in attendance on the king, "Then too, there is the gallows at Haman's house which he made for Mordecai who saved the king's life. Seventy-five feet high!"

"Hang him on that!" said the king.

10 Haman was hanged on the same gallows that he had erected for Mordecai. Then the king's anger abated.

[p] LXX *Bougathan.*

NOTES

5:4. *with Haman.* The AT and the OL add "your friend," the phrase being intended perhaps to arouse the king's resentment against Haman because the latter was regarded in Esther's eyes as almost the king's equal.

7. *All right.* Literally "my request and my petition," which in Hebrew is a circumlocution for "yes," and not an anacoluthon, as is often argued (see NOTES on "All right" in vs. 7 and 6:7 in AB 7B).

8. *tomorrow to a dinner . . . and tomorrow I will.* The first "tomorrow" (*māḥār*) is now missing from the MT by haplography, that is, as the LXX indicates, it immediately preceded the second *māḥār,* and an early Jewish copyist omitted it.

10. *assembled.* So the Greek, which rightly regards the MT's "sent and brought" as hendiadys. The custom implied is that of having slaves bring the guest to a banquet (cf. 5:12, 6:14).

6:1. *king could not sleep.* The LXX, AT, Jos., and the OL give an explicit reason for the king's insomnia: God prevented him from sleeping.

7. *All right.* See textual note [t-t], and then NOTE on 5:7, above.

8. *robe.* The LXX adds "linen" (Heb. *šēš*), while Josephus adds "a gold necklace" (Heb. *rᵉbîd hazzāhāb*), both additions having been made under the influence of Gen 41:42-43, where Joseph was elevated by Pharaoh (see L. A. Rosenthal, "Die Josephsgeschichte mit den Büchern Ester und Daniel vergleichen," *ZAW* 15 [1895], 278-284; 16 [1896], 182; and Moshe Gan, "The Book of Esther in the Light of the Story of Joseph in Egypt" [in Hebrew], *Tarbiẓ* 31 [1961-62], 144-149). But whereas Rosenthal and Gan saw in Esther only literary and stylistic influences of the Joseph narrative, Gillis Gerleman argues that the influence of the sojourn in Egypt extended *to even the most minor details* of the Esther story (G. Gerleman, *Esther,* 11-23). For a discussion of Gerleman's thesis, see this writer's review of Gerleman's book (*JBL* 94 [1975], 293-296).

11. While the AT has an addition here which purports to give an account of what happened between Haman and Mordecai ("And Haman said to Mordecai, 'Take off the sackcloth!' And Mordecai was troubled as one who is dying, and in distress he took off the sackcloth. But then he put on the splendid garments, and he thought he saw an omen, and he trusted [literally "his heart was to"] the Lord; and he was speechless"), the MT left the entire encounter to the reader's imagination, telling only the sequel (vs. 12).

13. *friends.* So LXX; MT "wise men."

you . . . will undoubtedly fail. Literally "you . . . will utterly fall before him." Unlike the ancient versions (see textual note *j*), the author of Esther tells his story without offering explicit theological explanations, letting the events speak for themselves.

7:2. *for you!* Unlike the MT, the AT has God change the hearts of both the king (so D 8) and Esther; for the AT adds here "Esther was uneasy about speaking because the enemy was right in front of her, but God gave her the courage for the challenge."

4. *for our problem . . . the king.* The adopted reading, which agrees in substance with the AT (see textual note *k-k*), understands Esther to say that if the Jews had only been sold into slavery, she would have kept quiet since she would not have bothered the king with their "petty" problems (for details, see NOTE on 7:4 in AB 7B, 70). The LXX's "for the slander is not worthy of the king's court" represents a rendering of *'yn ḥḥsr šwh bmzyq hmlk* (so Hoschander).

5. The AT underscores Esther's outward calm by adding, "But when the queen saw that it seemed terrible to the king and that he hated the evil, she said, 'Don't be angry, my lord! It's enough that I have your support. Enjoy yourself, my king. Tomorrow I shall do as you have commanded.' But the king urged her to tell him who had behaved so arrogantly as to do this, and with an oath he promised to do for her whatever she should ask."

8. *was prostrate.* In an expression of humility and contrition, Haman apparently either seized Esther's feet (so the AT) or even kissed them.

they covered Haman's face. The LXX has "he was confounded in the face," which means that its Greek translator must have read either *hāpērû*, "his face grew red" (so Felix Perles, *Analekten*, p. 32), or *hāwērû*, "his face became pale" (Wilhelm Rudolph, "Text-Kritisches zum Estherbuch," *VT* 4 [1954], 90).

X. THE KING BEGINS TO UNDO
THE EVIL OF HAMAN
(8:1-12)

8 ¹ That same day King Ahasuerus gave Queen Esther the entire estate of Haman, the enemy of the Jews; and when Mordecai was presented to the king (for Esther had disclosed to him their relationship), ² the king took off the signet ring which he had recovered from Haman and presented it to Mordecai; and Esther appointed Mordecai over Haman's estate. ³ Then Esther again spoke to the king, collapsing at his feet and crying and begging him to frustrate the evil intention of Haman, the Agagite, and the scheme which he had devised against the Jews.

⁴ When the king extended his gold scepter to Esther, Esther arose and stood before the king, ⁵ and said, "If it please the king, and if I have found his favor, and the request is proper in the king's opinion, and if he really likes me, let a decree be written to revoke the letters— ᵃthe scheme of Haman son of Hammedatha, the Agagiteᵃ—which he dictated for the extermination of the Jews in all the king's provinces. ⁶ How can I bear to see this calamity overtake my people? How can I bear to see the destruction of my own relatives?"

⁷ "Well," said King Ahasuerus to Queen Esther ᵇand Mordecai the Jewᵇ, "I have given Haman's estate to Esther, and he has been hanged on the gallows because he attacked the Jews. ⁸ But you yourselves write in the king's name whatever you want concerning the Jews; then seal it with the royal signet." (For an edict written in the king's name and sealed with the royal signet cannot be revoked.)

⁹ So the king's secretaries were summoned on the twenty-third day of the ᶜthird month (which is the month of Sivan)ᶜ; and the edict concerningᵈ the Jews was written exactly as Mordecai had dictated, to the satraps, governors, and officials of the provinces from India to

---

ᵃ⁻ᵃ LXX omits; see Note.
ᵇ⁻ᵇ The Greek, Josephus, OL, and Ethiopic omit; see Note.
ᶜ⁻ᶜ LXX "first month, which is Nisan."
ᵈ Reading 'l, instead of 'l, "to."

Ethiopia, one hundred and twenty-seven provinces, each province in its script, each people in its own language, including the Jews, in their own script and language. 10 He wrote in the name of King Ahasuerus and sealed it with the royal signet, and he sent the dispatches by mounted couriers riding *on swift horses, the royal coursers bred from the mares*, 11 to the effect that the king had given permission to the Jews in every single city to organize themselves and to defend themselves, to wipe out, slaughter, and annihilate every armed force of any people or province that was hostile to them, along with their children, and women, and to plunder their personal property 12 on one day in all King Ahasuerus' provinces, namely, on the thirteenth day of the twelfth month, which is the month of Adar.

e-e LXX omits: see NOTE.

NOTES

8:2. *the signet ring which he . . . presented . . . to Mordecai.* That the king is investing Mordecai with the powers previously held by Haman (3:10) is explicitly stated by the AT in 8:17: "and the king entrusted to him the affairs of the kingdom."

5. *and the request is proper . . . really likes me.* A number of scholars, with the LXX, delete this phrase as being needlessly repetitious.

the scheme . . . Agagite. Some scholars, with the LXX, erroneously delete this phrase; but then they are forced to posit a "Haman."

6. Esther's request in the AT is brief and brutal: "Grant me to deter my enemies by means of a massacre."

my own relatives [môladtî]. Misunderstanding the Hebrew, the LXX understood Esther to be referring to her own destruction and, thus, rendered it as "and how shall I be able to survive in the destruction of my father's house?"

7. *and Mordecai the Jew.* Many scholars, following the ancient versions, have deleted this phrase, but its retention here is indispensable for a correct understanding of vss. 1-8 (for details, see the NOTE in AB 7B, 79). That the Vulgate does have this phrase is proof that the phrase was current in the Hebrew text of Jerome's day (see p. 167).

"Well" [hinneh]. Unlike the LXX which adds "and I have shown favor to you . . . what more do you seek?" sounding very much like a rebuke by the king, in the MT the king actually seems to be encouraging Esther to ask more of him.

he has been hanged on the gallows. The AT has "and Queen Esther also conferred with the king about the children of Haman, that even they might die with their father."

9. *concerning ['l] the Jews.* Because the LXX read 'l, "to," instead of 'l, it omitted altogether the later phrase in the verse: "including the Jews in their script and language." The LXX also omits "exactly as Mordecai had dictated."

10. *on swift horses . . . from the mares.* The LXX omits the obscure, technical terms (for details, see NOTE in AB 7B, 80), although some manuscripts "corrected" by the Hexapla erroneously(?) transliterated *hārammākîm* as *ramacheim* or *rachein.*

11. *to the effect that . . .* The LXX has here "he commanded them to observe their own laws in every city, and to assist them, and to pursue their adversaries and the ones opposing them as they wished," while the AT has "Let a copy of the letter be posted in every place: for the Jews to practice their own laws, and to strengthen them so that in the time of oppression they may defend themselves against those who attack them" (8:29).

COMMENT

As noted earlier, the translator of the LXX seems to have translated the Hebrew text of Esther rather freely (see Introduction, p. 162), while the translator of the AT not only made his own Greek translation but also had a Hebrew text differing significantly from the MT (see p. 164). These differences between the LXX and the AT in a canonical portion of Esther are clearly seen by comparing 7:9b - 8:8 of the LXX with the corresponding passage in the AT, 8:13-20.

LXX   7: 9b "Let him be crucified [*straurōthētō*] on it!" said the king.
10 And Haman was hanged [*ekemasthē*] on the gallows that had been prepared for Mordecai. And then the king's anger abated.
8: 1 And the same day King Artaxerxes presented Esther with what had belonged to Haman, the slanderer. Then Mordecai was summoned by the king (for Esther had informed [him] that he was related to her), 2 and the king took the signet ring which he had taken back from Haman and gave it to Mordecai; and Esther appointed Mordecai over all of Haman's things. 3 And again, she spoke to the king and fell at his feet and asked him to remove the evil of Haman and as much as he had done to the Jews. 4 The king extended to Esther the gold scepter; Esther arose to speak to the king.
5 "If it seems good to you and I have found favor," said Esther, "let letters be sent to turn back the things sent out by Haman, which were written to destroy the Jews who are in your kingdom. 6 For how shall I be able to see the calamity of my people? And how shall I be able to survive in the destruction of my father's house?"
7 And the king said to Esther, "If I have given (you) all the property of Haman and have shown favor to you and I have hanged him on the gallows because he laid hands on the Jews, what more do you seek? 8 But you write in my name, as it seems good to

you, and seal it with my signet ring; for what is written when commanded by the king and sealed by my signet ring cannot be contradicted."

9 And the secretaries were summoned in the first month, which is the month of Nisan, on the twenty-third day of that year, and there was written to the Jews just what he commanded, also to the administrators and the rulers of the satraps from India to Ethiopia, a hundred and twenty-seven provinces, to each province, according to its own language. 10 It was written in the king's name and sealed with his signet ring, and they sent out the letters by couriers. 11 Thus he commanded them to observe their own laws in every city, and to assist them, and to pursue their adversaries and the ones opposing them as they wished 12 on one day in all the kingdom of Artaxerxes, on the thirteenth day of the twelfth month, which is the month of Adar. (Addition E is introduced at this point in the LXX.)

AT 8: 13 "Let him be hanged [*kremasthētō*] on it!" said the king. And the king removed the signet ring from his hand, and his life [i.e. Haman's fate] was sealed with it.

14 Then said the king to Esther, "Did he intend to hang even Mordecai, the one who had saved me from the hand of the eunuchs? Did he not know that Esther and Mordecai are related on their fathers' side [literally "that his paternal race is Esther"]?"

15 The king then summoned Mordecai and bestowed on him everything that had been Haman's 16 and said to him, "What do you want? I shall do it."

"That you revoke Haman's letter," said Mordecai.

17 And the king entrusted to him the things concerning the kingdom. 18 Whereupon Esther then said to the king, "Grant me to deter my enemies by means of a massacre."

19 And Queen Esther also conferred with the king about the children of Haman, that even they might die with their father.

"Let it be done!" said the king.

20 And he killed the enemy in great numbers. 21 The king made an agreement with the queen for the men in Susa itself to be killed, and said, "I allow you to hang them." And thus it was done. (Addition E is introduced at this point in the AT.)

When one compares the LXX with the MT, one sees that the LXX is more free, following the MT verse by verse but often omitting repetitious elements or needless details (see NOTES and textual notes). On the other hand, it is clear that the AT differs from the LXX (and the MT) by having additional (see 8:13b and 14a of the AT) as well as contradictory material (cf. 8:2b with 8:15a of the AT, and 8:3 with 8:16b of the AT). These differences between the LXX and the AT are a major argument in C. C. Torrey's interesting but ultimately unconvincing view that the original text of Esther ended with ch. 7, and that the LXX and the AT are Greek translations of two quite different Aramaic(!) texts (see his treatment in *HTR* 37 [1944], especially pp. 16-17).

XI. ADDITION E:
TEXT OF THE SECOND
ROYAL LETTER
(E 1-24; AT 8:22-32; Vulg. 16:1-24)

E 1 The text of the dispatch was as follows:

"The great king Artaxerxes to the governors of the one hundred and twenty-seven provinces*a* from India to Ethiopia and to our loyal subjects, greetings!

2 "Honored excessively by the very great generosity of their benefactors, many men become more arrogant. 3 Unable to bear success, they not only endeavor to injure our subjects, but they even resort to scheming against their own benefactors! 4 Puffed up by flattery of the foolish, they not only deprive men of gratitude but *b*even assume that they will escape the evil-hating justice of God, who always sees everything*b*. 5 And often many of those who are in positions of authority have been made accomplices in the shedding of innocent blood by the persuasiveness of 'friends' who, having been entrusted with the administration of public affairs, *c*have involved*c* them in irremediable misfortune, 6 beguiling*d* the good faith of their rulers by malicious equivocation.

7 "Now all this can be seen, not so much from the ancient records *e*that we have received*e*, as from an examination of what has recently been perpetrated by the *f*destructive behavior*f* of unworthy officials. 8 (In the future we will make every effort to make the kingdom quiet and peaceful for all men, 9 both *g*by paying no attention to slanders*g*, and by *h*always judging with a more con-

---

a LXX*B* adds "satrapies"; LXX*A* and AT add "satraps."
b-b AT "outwitted by the praise of the foolish, they thought to escape the just judge who hates evil and who holds sway over all ('who . . . all,' so also Ethiopic)."
c-c Periebalon (so AT); LXX periebale; see NOTE.
d Emending paralogisamenōn to paralogisamenoi of AT.
e-e AT "which have come down to us," see NOTE.
f-f Loimotēti; AT ōmotēti, "cruelty."
g-g So AT; see NOTE.

sidered attention[h] the matters which are presented to us.) 10 For Haman son of Hammedatha, [i]a Macedonian[i]—without any Persian blood and quite devoid of our goodness—was treated by us as a guest; 11 he enjoyed the benevolence which we have for every nation, to the extent that he was called in public 'our father' and that all the people bowed down to him as second only to the king. 12 Unable, however, to contain his arrogance, he schemed to deprive us of both empire and life. 13 By involved deceptions and arguments[j] he sought the destruction of both Mordecai, our savior and constant benefactor, and Esther, our blameless partner in the kingdom, as well as all their nation. 14 For by this strategy he thought he would leave us helpless[k] and could transfer the hegemony of the Persians to the Macedonians.

15 "We, however, find that the Jews who were consigned for destruction by this blackguard are not criminals, but are governed by very just laws 16 and are sons of [l]the living God, most high, most great[l], who has directed the kingdom for us [m]and our forefathers[m] in the most successful way.

17 "You are well advised, therefore, not to act upon the letters sent by Haman son of Hammedatha 18 since he who contrived these things has been hanged at the gates of Susa [n]with all his family (an appropriate sentence which the omnipotent God promptly passed on him[n]).

19 "Post a copy of this dispatch in every public place, and allow the Jews to observe their own customs, 20 and support them so that [o]on that same day (the thirteenth of the twelfth month Adar)[o] in the hour of trial they may defend themselves against those who attack them. 21 [p](For the omnipotent God has made this a day of joy for his chosen people instead of their day of destruction.[p] 22 [q]Therefore, you must joyously celebrate it as a

---

[h-h] AT "treating with fairness."

[i-i] AT "the Bougaion"; see NOTE.

[j] Reading, with AT, *methodeiais*, instead of *methodōn*.

[k] AT adds "in alienation"; OL *desertos nos accipiens in alienationem.*

[l-l] AT "the one, true God."

[m-m] AT "until now."

[n-n] AT "the judge, who always sees everything, gave him the deserved punishment"; see NOTE.

[o-o] AT "and it was decreed by the Jews throughout the kingdom to celebrate the fourteenth of the month which is Adar, and to observe also the fifteenth," an obvious gloss.

[p-p] AT "For in those days the Almighty provided them with deliverance and rejoicing."

[q] AT and Josephus omit verse; see NOTE.

special day among your commemorative festivals [23] so that both now and in the future it may represent deliverance for you[r] and sympathetic[s] Persians but a reminder of destruction for your enemies.) [24] Every city or province, without exception, which does not act according to the above, shall be furiously devastated by spear and fire; it shall be made not only inaccessible to men [t]forever, but also most[t] hateful to wild animals and birds."

[r] Reading, with some Greek MSS., *umin*, instead of *ēmin*, "us."
[s] AT "obedient."
[t-t] LXX[A] and AT omit.

NOTES

E This Addition, purporting to be a copy of the king's letter mentioned in 8:9 of the MT, was rather fully paraphrased by Josephus. As to be expected, the Targums and Midrashes give extended versions of the king's second royal letter. The interested reader will find extensive portions of this material translated by Fuller (pp. 400-402).

1. *loyal subjects*. Literally "those heeding our affairs." In contrast to Addition B, this royal letter is addressed to everyone in the empire, not just the officials.

2. *excessively*. Literally "too much."

benefactors [*euergetountōn*]. The king has himself in mind. Ptolemy III of Egypt actually bore the title Euergetes, "The Benefactor." Herodotus mentions several individuals who bore the title, bestowed on them by Darius or Xerxes (III 140, VI 30, VIII 85,90).

many men. An indirect reference to Haman (cf. vss. 10-12).

3. *success* [*koron*]. Literally "satiety." In this connection, Kautzsch-Ryssel appropriately quotes a Greek proverb: "Satiety [*koros*] is shown in insolence [*ubrin*]."

scheming against their own benefactors! Cf. A 17, where Haman seems to have been, at the very least, sympathetic toward the would-be assassins of the king; see also 7:8, where the king thought Haman had compromised the queen.

4. *Puffed . . . foolish* [*tois tōn apeiragathōn kompois eparthentes*]. A difficult phrase, but OL's *avidorum praesumptionibus inflammti* is far closer to the Greek than the Vulgate's *humanitatis in se iura violare*. "Foolish" probably refers to sycophants and opportunists of the court and the streets.

evil-hating justice of God. In the AT (see textual note [b-b]) "evil-hating" modifies God rather than his justice; cf. II Macc 3:1, 4:49, and 8:4.

5. *And often many* [*pollakis de kai pollous*]. This phrase and *paralogismō paralogisamenōn* (vs. 6) are intentional alliteration, according to Soubigou; but see NOTE on vs. 6.

accomplices in the shedding of. Literally "sharers of." The king is not protesting the fact but insisting on the innocent intent of rulers such as himself.

'friends.' In a sarcastic rather than the technical sense of "high officials" (cf. I Macc 2:18; see, however, Benno Jacob, *ZAW* 10 [1890], 283); the word emphasizes the ingratitude of men like Haman. The king tries to absolve himself of all guilt in the matter of the pogrom on the grounds that he had been duped by a trusted adviser and friend.

have involved [periebalon]. Reading the plural (so the AT), instead of the singular, with "friends" as the subject since "persuasiveness" *(paramuthia)* is read here as a dative instead of a nominative.

6. *by malicious equivocation.* Literally "by the deceptive fallacy (*tō tēs pseudei paralogismō*) of maliciousness (*kakoētheias;* LXX^A "sincerity" [*alētheias*], AT "evil doing" [*kakopoiias*])." Although the precise meaning of the accusation is not clear in the LXX, the patent seriousness of it is quite evident. The absence of *paralogismō,* "fallacy," in the AT may mean that *paralogismō* is a dittography for *paralogisamenōn,* "beguiling," the two words being side by side in the LXX. Evidently the king had in mind, among other things, Haman's charges in 3:8.

7. *ancient records . . . received.* The king is not referring, as some scholars have argued, to private records of former kings, i.e. to records comparable to those mentioned in 2:23 and 6:1; for chronicles such as these would have been inaccessible to all but a few officials. Rather, he is referring to public monuments, such as those at Naqsh-i-Rustam and the Behistun Inscription, the latter giving, for instance, an account of the rebellion of Gaumata against Artaxerxes' grandfather, Darius Hystaspes. (This fascinating story has been known to Western man for over twenty-four hundred years, thanks to Herodotus III 61-79; for details, see *HPE,* 105-110, 116-118, esp. n. 39.)

recently. Literally "by your feet"; Josephus "before our eyes." Paton's "in your presence" and the NEB's "in your familiar experience" are somewhat misleading, the former being too spatial and the latter too paraphrastic. The incident which is so recent will be spelled out by the king in vss. 10-14.

8. *In the future.* So also in vs. 23; literally "after these things."

9. *by paying no attention to slanders.* So the AT. LXX^B has "by paying attention to changing purposes," to which many Greek manuscripts, the OL, Vulgate, and Coptic prefix the word "not."

more considered attention. Literally "a more moderate encountering." The verse, but especially this particular phrase, would hardly appear in a genuine royal edict, since it would have been tantamount to the king's admitting that he had been negligent in his duties and that the pogrom against the Jews was more his fault than Haman's.

which are presented to us. Literally "which come by the face."

10. *a Macedonian.* A term of reproach which stamps Haman as a mortal enemy of all good Persians. The Vulgate's "and in spirit and race a Macedonian" suggests that *bougaion* of the AT is also a term of reproach (see NOTE on A 17).

without any. Literally "an alien of"; Haman could not claim his privileges by virtue of birth, all of which makes his crime the more heinous.

treated . . . as a guest. This emphasizes the king's generosity as well as Haman's ingratitude.

11. *'our father.'* A title of respect; cf. B 6; Gen 45:8; and II Kings 5:13.

second only to the king. Cf. 3:1 and B 3. Literally "the second of the royal throne"; see also II Chron 28:7 and I Esd 3:7.

13. *savior.* Such an honorific title for Mordecai may seem excessive to the Christian reader for whom the word "savior" has strong Christological over-tones, but it should be remembered that Hellenistic kings called themselves just that, namely, Antiochus I, Soter (280-261 B.C.) and Ptolemy VIII, Soter II (117-108 B.C.).

14. *For by this strategy.* So the OL rightly translates the literal Greek "by these means."

us. The plural of majesty; the king is referring to himself.

transfer. A 17 notwithstanding, the reason offered here for Haman's duplicity remains unconvincing, for as Prime Minister Haman had little to gain and much to lose by conspiring with foreign powers. The more plausible explana-tion for his conduct is found in 3:5 of the MT, i.e. Haman's personal hatred for Mordecai and his people's hostility to the Jews.

to the Macedonians. Great caution should be exercised so as not to read too much into this phrase. From the point of view of the Hebrew version any mention of the Macedonians in this context would be anachronistic. On the other hand, the phrase is crucial in suggesting a Macedonian/Hasmonean (not Persian) date *only for* Addition E, i.e. such an allusion does not necessarily suggest a Maccabean/Hasmonean date for the other Additions as well.

15. *blackguard.* Literally "triple-dyed"; the same epithet was given in II Macc 8:34 and 15:3 to Nicanor, one of the generals of Antiochus Epiphanes.

criminals. Literally "evil-doers." Evidently the king had in mind here Haman's description of the Jews (3:8) as well as "his" own description of them (cf. B 4).

16. *the living God . . . who has directed . . . successful way.* Although a Persian king could have uttered such an expression of monotheistic faith (for examples of actual sayings of Persian kings, see Olmstead, *HPE,* 195-199), as indeed the Bible itself suggests (see Ezra 1:2, 6:10; Isa 45:1-7), and although a Persian king could have referred to the Jews as "sons of the living God," it is far more likely that the faith of the Jewish writer is expressing itself here, espe-cially since the phrase "sons of the living God" occurs in Hosea 1:10 and 2:1 of the LXX and since the attribution of monotheistic-sounding speeches is sometimes found in highly improbable circumstances (cf. Nebuchadnezzar's paean of praise in Dan 4:34-37).

17. *You are well advised.* Literally "you shall do well."

18. *has been hanged at the gates of Susa with all his family.* This phrase con-tradicts the MT at two points: according to 7:9, Haman was hanged on the gallows at his home; and according to 9:12-14, Haman's sons were killed on the thirteenth of Adar and their corpses exposed on the fourteenth, i.e. *months* after the king's second royal letter. The Hellenistic author, however, was not concerned here with establishing where and when each male of Haman's family died but rather with emphasizing that all shared the same evil but richly de-served fate. Retributive justice, not precise chronology, was the author's con-cern here.

19. *and allow . . . their own customs [nomimois].* Many Greek manuscripts (including LXX^A), the OL, and Josephus read *nomois,* "laws." In either case,

the reference is to the Jews' distinctive religious laws and customs. Ezra received a similar carte blanche from Artaxerxes (see 7:25*f*). Brief though the verse is, it is the most important one in Addition E (see COMMENT).

20. *hour* [*kairō*]. Literally "time," in either the critical or opportune sense.

21. *his chosen people.* Appropriate enough for a Jew to use (see I Kings 3:8; I Chron 16:13; Ps 105:6; and Isa 43:20), this phrase would hardly have been applied by a Persian king to non-Persians (but see Soubigou, p. 695). Either the Jewish author of Addition E has unintentionally shown his hand here or, more likely, vs. 21, like vs. 22, is secondary.

22. The verse is rightly omitted by the AT and Josephus, since it, being addressed *only* to the Jews, may represent a faint echo of the pagan origins of the Festival of Purim. (For the view that Purim was originally a pagan festival adopted and adapted by the Jews, see "The Non-Jewish Origins of Purim" in AB 7B, XLVI-XLIX.)

24. *according to the above.* Literally "according to these things."

furiously devastated. Literally "be destroyed with anger."

inaccessible . . . hateful. Cf. Jer 32:43, 51:62; Ezek 25:13; and 32:13. If the king had actually been as emphatic as this in the MT, it is unlikely that as many as seventy-five thousand non-Jews (so 9:16) would have perished on the thirteenth of Adar.

Somewhat parallel to E 24 in both tone and imagery is the concluding sentence in Ptolemy Philopator's letter in III Macc 3:29: "And every place where a Jew shall be detected at all in concealment shall be made a waste and burned with fire, and shall become entirely useless to any mortal creature for all time." The spirit in E 24 and III Macc 3:29 is the same; but those threatened are different.

COMMENT

Even more florid and rhetorical in its literary style than Addition B, this Addition is incontestably a letter originally composed in Greek, most probably by the author of Addition B. Certainly no Persian king, let alone an edict composed in Aramaic or Hebrew (see NOTE on B 1), would produce such a convoluted letter as this, filled as it is with constructions typical of Pseudo-Classicalism, namely, participles, infinitives, and the definite article separated from its noun by adjectives and phrases. Moreover, one can hardly imagine a Persian king uttering such effusive praise of non-Persians as that found in vss. 16 and 18, let alone such self-incriminating sentiments as those found in vss. 8-9. All this being the case, the contents of E must be regarded as fiction, composed originally in Greek and designed primarily to increase the reader's interest and to underscore the historicity of the Esther story in general.

Then too, the central message of Addition E is far more appealing and appropriate for Greek-speaking Jews of the Diaspora than for Jews living in Palestine. As Schildenberger (p. 37) has pointed out, the main point of the edict as given in 8:11 of the MT ("to the effect that the king had given permission to the Jews . . . to wipe out, slaughter, and annihilate every armed force of any people or province that was hostile to them, along with their children and women, and to plunder their property") was not really a live option for Diaspora Jews who, no matter how numerous, were still a distinct and relatively defenseless minority among their Gentile neighbors. However, the central portion of the Greek version of the letter as recorded in E 19b ("and allow the Jews to observe their own customs"), appealed to the deepest hopes and desires of the Diaspora.

In addition to being diffuse and florid in style, Addition E is quite corrupt: emendations are necessary (see textual notes *passim*); and there is greater disagreement between the LXX and the AT than in any other Additions. Moreover, the fact that vss. 1-24 of the OL are very corrupt probably attests to the LXX's corrupt state in the second century A.D., when the *Vetus Latina* was made.

Although the stated intent of the king's letter (see 8:8 and 11) was to neutralize the pogrom proposed in the first royal letter (Addition B), most of the space in Addition E is devoted to a scathing attack on Haman, who is mentioned in fourteen of the twenty-four verses, either explicitly (vss. 10-14,17-18) or by implication (vss. 2-7 and 9). By contrast, the Jews are mentioned in only six verses (vss. 13,15-16,19-20, and 21), and Mordecai and Esther only in vs. 13. Either the king, the author, or both were venting here their hatred for Haman—the author because Haman was "the enemy of the Jews," and the king because Haman had betrayed both his office and the king's friendship by involving the latter in a most embarrassing and unjust situation. The king's explanation for Haman's conduct may sound unconvincing to the reader (see NOTE on "transfer" in E 14), but for public consumption rulers have often found the charges of treason a good cover-up for their own failures.

Haman was false (vss. 10-14), and so were his charges against the Jews (vss. 15-16). That being the case, the real purpose of the king's letter is stated at last, briefly and to the point: "You are well advised not to act upon the letter sent by Haman" (vs. 17); rather the Persians are to leave the Jews alone in their community life (vs. 19), and are even to support them on the day the Jews are attacked by their enemies (cf. vs. 24).

Haman had done his worst; Esther and Mordecai, their best. Now the king had finally tried to do justice. But as Addition F will insist, it was all in the hands of God from the very beginning!

XII. PURIM: ITS ORIGINS AND
LATER OBSERVANCE
(8:13 - 9:32)

8 13 The contents of the edict were to be promulgated in each province, to be published to all peoples, that the Jews were to be ready on that day to take revenge on their enemies. 14 So, urged on by the king's command, the couriers riding on swift horses, the royal coursers, galloped away. Meanwhile, the decree had been published in the acropolis of Susa. 15 When Mordecai left the king's presence in a royal robe of violet and white, wearing a big gold turban and cloak of fine linen and purple, then the city of Susa cheered and was happy.

16 For the Jews there was light and joy, rejoicing and honor. 17 Likewise, in every province and in every city wherever the king's command and edict reached, the Jews had joy and gladness, feast and holiday. Moreover, many of the pagans*a* professed themselves Jews, for they were afraid of the Jews.

9 1 On the thirteenth day of the twelfth month, which is the month of Adar, when the king's command and edict were about to be enforced (on that day when the enemies of the Jews had hoped to destroy them, the opposite happened: the Jews destroyed their enemies), 2 the Jews had gathered in their cities throughout King Ahasuerus' provinces to kill those who sought their ruin. No one, however, was successful against them since everyone feared them. 3 Moreover, all the provincial officials, satraps, governors, and those who conduct the king's affairs aided the Jews; for they feared Mordecai. 4 For Mordecai was very influential in the royal house, and his reputation spread to all the provinces as the man Mordecai grew more and more powerful. 5 *b* So the Jews defeated all their enemies, slaughtering and annihilating them, and treating their enemies as they pleased. 6 The Jews slaughtered five hundred men in the acropolis of Susa itself. 7 They also killed Pharshandatha, Dalphon, Aspatha, 8 Poratha, Adalia,

---

a LXX and OL add "were circumcised and"; in the AT this phrase replaces MT's "professed themselves Jews."

b LXX omits vs. 5 (see NOTE); OL omits vss. 6-19.

Aridatha, 9 Parmashta, Arisai, Aridai, and Vaizatha, 10 the ten sons of Haman son of Hammedatha*c*, the enemy of the Jews; they did not*d*, however, lay a hand on any plunder.

11 That same day the number of those killed in the acropolis of Susa was reported to the king, 12 and the king said to Queen Esther, "In the acropolis of Susa alone the Jews have slaughtered five hundred men, as well as Haman's ten sons. What, then, must they have done in the rest of the king's provinces! But, what do you still want? It will be granted you! What is your petition? It will be done!"

13 *e*"If it please the king," said Esther, "allow the Jews in Susa to act again tomorrow according to the terms of today's edict. And let Haman's ten sons be exposed on the gallows!"*e*

14 So the king commanded this to be done: a decree was issued in Susa, and Haman's ten sons were exposed.

15 So the Jews in Susa reorganized themselves again on the fourteenth of Adar and killed three hundred men in Susa, but they did not lay a hand on any plunder. 16 Now the rest of the Jews in the king's provinces had organized and defended themselves, gaining relief from their enemies and killing seventy-five thousand of those who hated them (they did not, however, lay a hand on any plunder) 17 on the thirteenth of the month of Adar. Thus, they rested on the fourteenth day, making it a day of feasting*f* and rejoicing. 18 But the Jews in Susa had organized themselves on both the thirteenth and the fourteenth; and so they rested on the fifteenth, making it a day of feasting and rejoicing. 19 (This is why the Jewish villagers who are living in unwalled towns celebrate the fourteenth day of the month of Adar as an occasion for rejoicing and feasting, for holiday-making and exchanging delicacies.)

20 Then Mordecai recorded these things*g*, and sent letters to all the Jews throughout the king's provinces, regardless of distance, 21 enjoining them to continue to celebrate annually both the fourteenth and the fifteenth of the month of Adar 22 as the days when the Jews got relief from their enemies and as the month which had been changed for them from sorrow to joy and from mourning to a holiday, and that they should make them days of feasting and rejoicing, and for sending delicacies to one another as well as alms to the poor. 23 *h*So the Jews

---

c Greek adds "the Bougaion"; see NOTE on *Macedonian* in E 10.
d Greek "they *did* plunder"; see NOTE on 9:15.
e-e AT is more brutal and brief: "And Esther said to the king, 'Permit the Jews to destroy whomever they wish and to plunder!' And he consented."
f Here and in vs. 18, LXX has "pleasure."
g Greek adds "in a book."
h AT omits vss. 23-26; OL omits vss. 24-27; see NOTE.

made customary what they had started doing, just as Mordecai had written to them.

24 For Haman son of Hammedatha, *the Agagite*, the enemy of all the Jews, had plotted against the Jews to destroy them and had cast *pur* (the lot, that is) to discomfort and destroy them. 25 But when Queen Esther came before the king, the king gave orders in writing that the wicked scheme which Haman had devised against the Jews should come upon his own head, and that he and his sons should be hanged on the gallows. 26 That is why these days are called "Purim," from the word *pur*.

Therefore, because of all that was written in this letter and because of all that they had experienced and because of what had happened to them, 27 the Jews agreed and made it customary for themselves, their descendants, and all future converts to continue to celebrate annually, without fail, these two days, as specified in their letter and on the proper dates; 28 that these days should be remembered and celebrated by every single generation, family, province, and city; that these days of Purim should never be abrogated among the Jews; and that the memory of them should never die among their descendants.

29 Also Queen Esther, the daughter of Abihail, along with Mordecai the Jew, wrote with full authority, thereby ratifying this second letter of Purim. 30 Friendly and sincere letters were sent to all the Jews throughout the one hundred and twenty-seven provinces of Ahasuerus' kingdom 31 to establish these days of Purim on their proper date, just as Mordecai the Jew*j* had enjoined them and as they had agreed for themselves and their descendants, *k*with respect to their fasting and lamentations*k*. 32 So Esther's word fixed these practices for Purim, and it was preserved in writing.

i-i LXX "the Macedonian."
j MT adds "and Queen Esther"; see NOTE in AB 7B, 96.
k-k LXX "concerning their health and their plan"; see NOTE.

NOTES

8:13. *take revenge.* The LXX's "fight against" conveniently eliminates the embarrassing element of revenge.

9:2. *was successful against them.* Literally "stood before them." This phrase was misunderstood by the LXX which rendered it "for no one resisted them." Obviously thousands *did* resist them (see 9:16). See Plate 7.

5. The LXX omits the verse, possibly because the MT's patent delight in such bloodshed was ethically offensive to the Greek translator.

7. *Pharshandatha.* This name is an excellent example of the vagaries experienced by a personal name as it goes from one language to another. Regardless of its original form in Persian(?), the MT has *pharšandātā'*, which was rendered as follows in the Greek: *pharsannestain* (LXX^ℵ); *pharanestan* (LXX^A); *pharsan* (AT). LXX^B treated the name as two names (*pharsan* and *nestain*), while the AT included it as one of the five hanged *in addition to* the ten unnamed sons of Haman. It is omitted in Josephus and the OL, along with the names of Haman's other sons. Predictably, the Vulgate agrees with the MT, except that the Latin, having no real equivalent to the Heb. *š*, rendered it as *pharsandatha.*

13. *exposed.* It is Esther's request for the exposure of Haman's sons and for another day of fighting in Susa, coupled with her "unwillingness" to intercede for Haman in 7:9, that has been the basis for her reputation of being a sophisticated Jael, i.e. for being a deceitful and bloodthirsty woman (see Judg 4:17-22). Moreover, the AT reinforces such an impression (see textual note *e-e*). But unless one is willing to judge Esther's outward act in complete isolation, without any real knowledge of her inner motives and without full knowledge of the external circumstances, such a judgment must be quite tentative. (For a more detailed "defense" of her request concerning the sons of Haman, see AB 7B, COMMENT on §11.)

15. According to both the MT and the LXX, the Jews did *not* plunder in Susa itself on the fourteenth; but unless the Greek in 9:10 has accidentally lost its negative (which may very well be the case), the Greek translator maintained that the Jews did plunder in the acropolis on the first day.

16. Verses 16-19, which are a brief restatement of the preceding events and "facts," are omitted by the AT.

seventy-five thousand. An enormous casualty figure, which was later reduced to 15,000 in the LXX, and to 10,107 in the AT, but probably not before ca. A.D. 93, inasmuch as Josephus has 70,000.

19. The LXX draws a valid inference from the MT and adds "and those living in the metropolitan centers [walled cities] celebrate also the fifteenth of Adar with good cheer, sending out gifts to the poor."

24. Briefly summarizing the events of chs. 3-7, the content of vss. 24-26 differs enough in detail from those chapters to be regarded as being earlier (so Hoschander), later (Haupt), or at least independent (Paton) of that material. Although the extended lacunae in the AT and the OL (see textual note *b*) support Haupt's view, Bardtke (p. 393) argues convincingly that the summary character of these verses accounts for their contradictions, not their being taken from a different source.

28. In this verse the LXX is not so painstakingly explicit as in the MT, for the LXX has "These days of Purim should be observed for all times, and their meaning should not be omitted from the generations" (for the LXX's position on Purim, see Introduction, p. 160).

29. Verses 29-32 are either a variant tradition or, more likely, a later addition to ch. 9, since they lack the support of the AT for vss. 28-32 and the OL for vss. 30-32, while the LXX is also somewhat different; but some scholars, including Striedl and Ringgren, defend their authenticity.

this second [hz't hšnyt] letter. A perplexing phrase which, with the LXX and the Syriac, many scholars delete. Roiron (*RSR* [1916], 3-16), however, understands it to be our present Hebrew version of Esther, the first letter being the message of Mordecai (cf. 9:20-23), which contained, says Roiron, Mordecai's dream and its interpretation (Additions A and F), a brief summary of Haman's intrigues and of the events which brought about his ruin, and the institution of the commemorative festival of Purim.

31. *with respect to their fasting and lamentations.* Since in the MT this phrase seems semantically and syntactically unrelated to what precedes it and since the element of a memorial fast is also missing from the LXX, AT, Josephus, and the OL, this phrase is undoubtedly a later feature or tradition, introduced into the MT at some point after the letter's translation into Greek. Such a view seems all the more likely since the LXX's reading (see textual note [k-k]) presupposes in Heb. *dbry šlwm w'mt k'ṣtm* (so Hoschander, p. 286, n. 61).

XIII. THE CONCLUSION OF THE
HEBREW VERSION
(10:1-3)

10 ¹Now King Ahasuerus levied*ᵃ* taxes on both the mainland and the islands; ²but as for all the achievements *ᵇ*and might of King Ahasuerus*ᵇ*, *ᶜ*as well as for an exact account of the influence of Mordecai whom the king had promoted*ᶜ*, is not all this recorded in the *Annals of the Kings of Media and Persia?* ³For Mordecai the Jew ranked next to King Ahasuerus and was influential among the Jews and acceptable to the mass of his own countrymen. He sought the best interests of his people and was concerned for the welfare of his kinsmen.

ᵃ Greek "wrote."
ᵇ⁻ᵇ MT "and his might"; see *ᶜ⁻ᶜ*.
ᶜ⁻ᶜ Greek "wealth and glory of his kingdom"; in the Greek Mordecai is not even mentioned.

XIV. ADDITION F:

THE INTERPRETATION OF
MORDECAI'S DREAM

(F 1-10; AT 8:53-58; Vulg. 10:4-13)

F 1 "This is God's doing," said Mordecai, 2 "for *ᵃI remember*ᵃ the dream *ᵇI had about these things. None of it is unfulfilled*ᵇ—3 the tiny spring which became a river, *ᶜas well as the*ᶜ light and sun and veritable flood:

> The river represents Esther, whom the king married and made queen.*ᵈ*
> 4 The two dragons represent me and Haman.
> 5 The nations represent those who gathered to destroy the name of the Jews.*ᵉ*
> 6 And my nation—this is Israel who cried out to God and was saved.

The Lord has saved his people. The Lord has rescued us from all these evils. God has worked great signs and wonders, such as had never before occurred among the pagans.*ᶠ*

7 He*ᵍ* made two lots, one for the people of God and the other for all*ʰ* the nations;*ⁱ* 8 and these two lots came*ʲ* to the appointed time, *ᵏto the day of the trial before God and*ᵏ among all the nations. 9 And God

---

ᵃ⁻ᵃ AT and OL "he remembered."
ᵇ⁻ᵇ AT "he had, and it was fulfilled. And he said."
ᶜ⁻ᶜ Literally "and there was"; see NOTE.
ᵈ For vs. 3, AT and one OL manuscript have simply "The tiny spring represents Esther."
ᵉ For vs. 5, AT and OT have "The river represents the nations which were assembled to destroy the Jews. The sun and light which appeared to the Jews are manifestations of God. This is the judgment." See NOTE.
ᶠ For vs. 6, AT has "And God performed these signs and wonders which had not been done (before) among the nations."
ᵍ So AT; LXX "On account of this, he."
ʰ AT omits "all"; see COMMENT.
ⁱ LXXᴬ omits verse.
ʲ AT and OL add "forward."
ᵏ⁻ᵏ AT "to the day of the Eternal's rule."

remembered his people and acquitted his inheritance.[*l*] [10] Therefore, they shall ever after celebrate these days on the fourteenth [*m*]and the fifteenth[*m*] of the month of Adar by gathering together in joy and gladness before God—throughout all generations among his people Israel."

[*l*] AT adds "and all the people cried in a loud voice and said, 'Blessed are you, Lord, who remembers the covenant with our fathers!' "
[*m-m*] LXX[A] ℵ omit.

NOTES

F 1. *"This is God's doing."* Cf. Ps 118:23[Matt 21:42]. Literally "these things [*tauta*] were from God." Behind *tauta* would seem to be the Heb. *debārîm*, which means either "words" or "things." Thus, the author is referring, not to the words of the dream but, to *all* the events narrated in the Greek Esther, including the Additions. The author of the MT allows his readers to infer for themselves God's extensive involvement.

2. *had.* Literally "saw."

3. As is often the case with poetry, the style of the verse is terse and condensed—unless of course the verse is also corrupt, a not unlikely possibility since the AT and the LXX differ radically in their interpretation of the symbols; but see COMMENT.

light and sun. Since the LXX offers no further explanation of the significance of light and sun, they presumably are to be understood in the sense of 8:16, where "light" (Heb. *'ôrâ*) is a symbol of well-being (cf. Pss 97:11, 139:12; Job 22:28, 30:26) and prosperity (cf. Pss 27:1, 36:9). But according to the AT "the sun and light . . . are manifestations (*epiphaneia*) of God." The phrase "manifestation of God" as an expression of some visible proof or surrogate for God's presence occurs at least three times in II Macc (3:24, 14:15, 15:27).

The river represents Esther. But according to the AT (cf. textual note [*e*]), the river represents the enemies of the Jews; see also COMMENT.

4. *two dragons.* It is uncertain why the dragon-figure was chosen in preference to some other animal. Given the prevalence of the dragon-figure in apocalyptic literature (see NOTE on A 5), it is a highly appropriate symbol for the wicked and powerful Haman—but not for Mordecai (see COMMENT).

me and Haman. Although this sequence of pronouns strikes the English-speaking reader as awkward and unnatural, one is not justified in rendering it as "Haman and myself" (so RSV). Mordecai did not share our polite English convention of having the speaker always put himself last—even when speaking of an arch enemy.

5. *The nations* [*ta ethnē*]. In vs. 5, entire world, not just Haman, was pitted against the Jews. For a similar convening of the enemies of Israel, see

Zech 14:2 and Joel 3:2-3 (it is improbable that the mention of "lots" in the latter passage accounts for the mention of lots in F 7 [see below]).

name. I.e. Israel's existence and, ultimately, even the very memory of her name. For the significance of one's name in the ancient world, see R. Abba, *IDB,* III, 501-505.

6. *cried out.* The author of F was referring not just to a cry of animal fear or pain (cf. 4:1,3), but to Israel's cry of faith (Addition C) and repentance (see NOTES in AB 7B on "from another quarter" in 4:17 and "fast for me" in 4:16; also AB 7B, 50-52).

great signs and wonders. Cf. Ps. 135:9. Presumably the "historical" events of the Esther story, unless the author of the LXX had in mind "the light and sun" of F 3, which the AT regarded as divine surrogates (see textual notes *e*, *f*).

pagans [ethnesin]. Except for vs. 6, where Israel is called a "nation," here in Addition F Mordecai refers to Israel's enemies as *ta ethnē,* "the nations" (Heb. *gwym*), and reserves the warm, emotion-filled word *laos,* "people" (Heb. *'m*) for Israel itself (vss. 6,7,9). In Joel 3[4]:2, which partially, at least, inspired the dream (see NOTES on A 6-7), the distinction between the *gwym* and the *'m* of God is preserved (see also E. J. Hamlin, "Nations," *IDB,* III, 515*f,* and J. A. Wharton, "People of God," *IDB,* III, 727-728).

7. *two lots [klērous duo].* Although no mention of these lots (Heb. *gwrlwt*) was made in Addition A, their appearance here would seem to be appropriate, at least at first glance. After all, the Esther story purports to provide the historical basis for the festival of Purim, *pûrîm* being the hebraized form of the Bab. *pūru,* "lot" (see AB 7B, XLVI-XLIX). On closer examination, however, one sees that the meaning of "lots" in F 7 is quite different from the Hebrew version where it was used in the literal and original sense as a device for deciding or divining the will of the gods, in this case the "propitious" day for Haman's pogrom (see NOTES on 3:7 and 9:26 in AB 7B; but see Soubigou, p. 674). Nor is "lots" used here as in Prov 18:18, where the casting of lots settles a dispute between contenders.

Here in vs. 7 "lots" is used in the figurative sense of "portion" or, better, of "destiny" (cf. Dan 12:13; Isa 17:14; and Jer 13:25). The sense is not unlike the use of "lots" in the Qumran *Manual of Discipline* where "the priests shall bless all the men of God's lot [i.e. the members of the Dead Sea Community at Qumran] who walk perfectly in all his ways [2:2]. . . . Then the Levites shall curse all the men of Belial's lot [2:5]." "Lots," in both the literal and metaphorical sense, played an important role in the community at Qumran, *gorāl* occurring eighteen times in the *War of the Sons of Light and the Sons of Darkness* (including such phrases as *bgwrl bny ḥwšk* [1:1]; *lkwl gwrl bly'l* [1:5]; *'l bly'l wkkwl 'nšy gwrlw* [4:2]), and fourteen times in *The Manual of Discipline.*

This clash between the "two lots" in F 7 is somewhat reminiscent of "the two spirits" of Qumran literature (cf. *Manual of Discipline,* 3:1 - 4:26), and the struggle between good and evil as embodied in the sons of light and the sons of darkness. Significantly, the terrible darkness of Addition A ("a day of gloom and darkness," vs. 7) is not even mentioned in Addition F, only "light and sun" (F 3). This fact, as well as the similarity in the meaning of "lots" here in vs. 7 and in the Dead Sea scrolls, has some relevance for assigning a date and provenance for Addition F.

8. *came to the appointed time.* Literally "came to the hour and moment," i.e. the two groups came to their respective moments of destiny. Unhappy with the LXX as it stands, many scholars have added, with Fritzsche, *tō laō autou,* "for his people," thereby bringing the thought of the verse into better agreement with vs. 9.

before God. A Hebraism; "before" presupposes the Heb. *lipnê.*

all the nations. Even if vs. 8 is corrupt, one thing is clear: unlike the MT where the Jewish author shows a somewhat sympathetic attitude toward the Gentile king, the Greek Esther is anti-Gentile, i.e. in the Greek version this is a struggle between the Jews and all non-Jews.

9. *acquitted.* Literally "he justified"; cf. Deut 25:1 and Sira 13:22.

10. *ever after.* Literally "for eternity." While needlessly repetitious with the phrase "throughout all generations," this phrase underscores the author's concern that Purim be forever observed among the Jews.

COMMENT

In both the Greek and Latin versions, Addition F follows immediately after 10:3 of the MT, except that in the Vulgate Jerome inserted after 10:3 a note concerning his efforts to translate quite literally the canonical portions of Esther (see p. 167, n. 36).

As Mordecai's dream is set forth in A 5-10, the differences in detail between the LXX and the AT are negligible. The same, however, cannot be said for the dream's interpretation in F 2-6. In the LXX, the river represents Esther (so F 3), but according to the AT (and the OL), the enemies of the Jews (see textual note *e*). The AT's interpretation seems somewhat self-contradictory since "the river represents the nations . . . assembled to destroy the Jews" (so F 5 of the AT); yet according to A 10 of the AT, "the rivers flooded and swallowed up the eminent" (see textual note *t-t*, p. 174). Another difference in detail is that in the LXX "light and sun" are evidently symbolic of the Jews' well-being and prosperity (see NOTE on vs. 3); but according to F 5 of the AT, they are visible proofs or surrogates of God's presence.

Given the nature of F's subject matter, i.e. dream interpretation, not to mention the compact literary style of the dream itself in Addition A, the differences listed above between the LXX and the AT may be nothing more than an inner-Greek phenomenon, that is, corruptions originating within the Greek itself.

There is, however, a better explanation for these differences. Since some features of the dream's interpretation are confusing, if not incompatible with the broadest features of the Esther story, and since the dream in its theme, imagery, and literary style does seem to resemble the dreams and visions found in such a second-century B.C. Palestinian book as Daniel, it is more likely that the

dream was originally a separate Hebrew (Aramaic?) entity circulating quite independently of the Esther story and was later adopted and adapted to it.

Surely one would expect a dream originally conceived and designed for the
Esther story to fit better than does the present dream and its interpretation.
Consider the following difficulties: (1) The river is either Esther or the enemies
of the Jews, depending upon whether one reads with the LXX or the AT. (2)
The dragon-figure is quite inappropriate for Mordecai (see NOTES on A 5 and
F 4). (3) As for "the light and sun" of F 3 (cf. also A 10), they seem to be
interpreted differently by the LXX and the AT (see NOTE on vs. 3). (4) The
"veritable flood" of F 3, which apparently corresponds to "the river" of A 10
of the AT and which seems to be waters *quite distinct from* "the tiny spring
which became a river" (F 3 of the LXX), is not mentioned at all in the dream's
interpretation!

The easiest explanation for all this is that the dream was originally a separate
entity and since in broad lines it could be adopted to the Esther story, it was;
however, although some features of the dream were less appropriate than
others (for instance, Mordecai as a dragon-figure), the original features were
nonetheless retained. According to this view, the differences in the interpretation of the dream by the LXX and the AT represent an imperfect adaptation of the dream's details to the particulars of the Esther story.

That the dream was originally in Hebrew (Aramaic?) rather than Greek is
quite likely, especially since the imagery and literary style are similar to dreams
and visions recorded in the Book of Daniel, a second-century B.C. Semitic work.
Certainly nothing in the dream's imagery or literary style lends itself more to a
Greek than a Semitic origin. (In its brevity and imprecision it is the antithesis
of Additions B and E.) Then too, the theme of the Gentile nations united
against the Jews in general and against some Jews in particular, with God
delivering both, is reminiscent not only of the Book of Daniel, but also of the
Book of Judith, another Semitic work of the second century B.C. To be sure,
these lines of argument for a Semitic original for the dream are far from conclusive, but they do have a high degree of plausibility.

Regardless of the dream's origins, its interpretation (F 3-6) dramatically alters the character of the Book of Esther, for what in the MT had been essentially a court intrigue has become in the Greek an eternal, cosmic conflict between Jew and Gentile. It is no longer the traditional antipathy between a
Jewish Mordecai and an Amalekite Haman but rather a strong and irrational
hostility between Jews and all non-Jews (cf. vss. 5 and 8). In other words, the
author of the dream's interpretation in F, in contrast to the author of the
Hebrew story, regarded all Gentiles as his enemy, a view which is quite understandable, given the rampant apocalyptic and eschatological emphases of Jewish
thought at that time, i.e. sometime between ca. 200 B.C. and A.D. 90 (see Introduction, p. 166). Certainly the Palestinian Jews' experience, first with the
Greeks and then with the Romans, did not increase their appreciation of Gentiles. Such a strong anti-Gentile attitude was probably stronger inside Palestine
than out, and suggests a Palestinian provenance for the dream *and its interpretation.* In this connection it should be noted that, on the basis of syntax criticism, R. A. Martin concluded that Addition F could "be either original-Greek
or a very free translation of a Semitic *Vorlage*" (*JBL* 94 [1975], 69).

XV. Addition F, continued:
THE COLOPHON TO THE GREEK VERSION OF ESTHER

(F 11; AT 8:59; Vulg. 11:1)

F [11][a]In the fourth year of the reign of Ptolemy' and Cleopatra, Dositheus, who "said" he was a priest and a Levite, and his son Ptolemy brought the above book of Purim, which they "said" was authentic and had been translated by Lysimachus son of Ptolemy, a member of the Jerusalem community.[b]

[a] Only one AT manuscript has verse; see COMMENT.
[b] LXX[N] adds its own colophon; see final NOTE.

NOTES

F 11. *Ptolemy.* Several Ptolemies fit the description of having a reign of at least four years and a wife named Cleopatra, including Ptolemy the XIIth, ca. 77 B.C. (so E. J. Bickerman, *JBL* 63 [1944], 339-362), and the XIVth, ca. 48 B.C. (so Schildenberger); but the most likely candidate is Ptolemy VIII, Soter II (ca. 114 B.C.; cf. Benno Jacob, *ZAW* 10 [1890], 279*f*, and Soubigou, p. 967); see also P. G. Elgood, *The Ptolemies of Egypt* (London: Arrowsmith, 1938).

Dositheus. A common Hellenistic name, occurring also in II Macc 12:19,24-25 (a captain under Judas Maccabeus), II Macc 12:35 (a cavalryman under Gorgias), and III Macc 1:3 (a general under Ptolemy IV, Philopator).

who "said" [ephē] he was. Ephē, translated twice in this verse as "said," is the most crucial word in the entire Greek version of Esther. In these two places does "said" mean "to certify," i.e. he attested in a routine but formal way as to who he, Dositheus, was and from where the particular translation came; or does "said" mean here "to claim," i.e. he affirmed something in an emphatic way because it was doubted or suspected by the colophonist of being untrue? Although one cannot be dogmatic about it, the present writer subscribes to the second view (hence "said" is placed in quotation marks) for two reasons. First, if the colophonist knew anything about Judaism of that general period, he would have known that it was impossible for Dositheus to be a priest *and* a

Levite (for a brief discussion of the respective roles of priests and Levites in the Bible, see R. Abba, *IDB*, III, s.v. "Priests and Levites"). Second and more probably, the colophonist may have been aware of the strikingly different versions of Esther: not only did the LXX and the AT differ from one another in the canonical portions of Esther, but there may very well have been current Greek versions with or without the Additions. The AT, for instance, may have lacked some of them, notably Addition E and, therefore B (see p. 165). That the colophonist was aware of the striking differences between the MT and the LXX seems to be less likely.

Levite. Bickerman (*JBL* 63 [1944], 348) would read here the personal name Leveites; but see Ralph Marcus' rebuttal (*JBL* 64 [1945], 269-271).

the above book [*tēn prokeimenēn epistolēn*]. I.e. the entire Greek version of Esther and not, as some scholars have suggested, just the letter of Esther and Mordecai referred to in 9:29.

which they "said" was authentic. As suggested above, the phrase implies the colophonist's reservations about either the authenticity or the accuracy of this particular text, possibly because he was aware of another competing Greek translation—be it the AT, or the LXX without some of the Additions included in Lysimachus' translation. Since the colophon comes *after* the dream interpretation, it may be safely assumed that the latter as well as A 1-11 were originally included in Lysimachus' translation.

Lysimachus. Another popular Hellenistic name, borne by, among others, the brother of Menelaus (II Macc 4:29), the latter being the cruel and sacrilegious Jew who had supplanted Jason as high priest in 171 B.C.

For a discussion of the seventh-century colophon appended to the end of F 11 in LXX[N], to the effect that Codex Sinaiticus had been corrected by an ancient manuscript which had, in turn, been corrected by Origen's Hexapla, see Moore, *GTE,* 54; H. B. Swete, *IOTG,* 75-77; and H. J. Milne and T. C. Skeat, *Scribes and Correctors of the Codex Sinaiticus* (British Museum, 1938), 46.

COMMENT

The authenticity of this colophon is of crucial importance because, as the colophon presently stands, it does the following: (1) provides the date of the translation as well as the name and place of the translator; (2) witnesses, coming as it does *after* the dream interpretation, to the presence of at least A 1-10 and F 1-10 in the Hebrew text translated by Lysimachus (but, as Schildenberger [p. 9] has pointed out, not necessarily to the presence of all the Additions, e.g. not to Additions B and E); and (3) implies the existence of another translation claiming to be *the* authentic Greek version, be it the AT or the LXX, with or without some of the Additions.

Regardless of what the colophonist intended to imply (see NOTES on *who "said"* and *which they "said"*), there is no reason to doubt the essential veracity of the colophon itself. Esther, to be sure, is the only book of the Jewish canon having a colophon for its Greek translation, but that very uniqueness and specificity can be used as arguments in favor of its authenticity. Moreover, ancient libraries, such as the one at Alexandria, often appended to their acquisitions colophons like Esther's, especially when the librarian had some reservations about the book's authenticity. For some other colophons from antiquity, see Bickerman, *JBL* 63 (1944), 339-344.

Certainly the specifics of the colophon are believable enough. A date such as 114 B.C. (or even 77 or 48 B.C. [see NOTE on "Ptolemy"]) is quite compatible with the literary style and theological emphases of the Greek Esther. Nor does the name or place of the translator have anything improbable about it. In the colophon it is evidently either the claims of Dositheus or the pedigree of the particular version he brought that is suspect, not the existence or translation skills of one "Lysimachus son of Ptolemy, a member of the Jerusalem community." Ptolemy, the name of Lysimachus' father, suggests that Lysimachus may have had an Egyptian father. Although Lysimachus was living in Jerusalem at the time of the translation, he need not have been born there; he may have moved there from Egypt and had Greek rather than Hebrew as his first language, all of which would help to explain his considerable skills as a translator.

The crux of the matter, then, is not whether the colophon is authentic but rather to which Greek version did it originally apply, since it could not have been appended to both the LXX and the AT, they being independent translations of the Hebrew (see Introduction, p. 164). Inasmuch as all the LXX manuscripts have it (as well as the Ethiopic, Coptic, and Vulgate) while two of the three extant AT manuscripts do not, we are probably justified in concluding that the colophon originally applied to the LXX and that its presence at the end of one of the AT manuscripts is to be explained as contamination. In drawing such a conclusion one runs the risk of being accused of determining the probability of a reading on a purely quantitative basis, a notoriously reprehensible procedure in lower criticism. Still, the colophon probably belongs to the LXX, not to the AT.

THE ADDITIONS TO JEREMIAH

I BARUCH

INTRODUCTION

Reputed Author

Baruch son of Neriah, the reputed author in antiquity of I, II, and III Baruch,[1] was the secretary and confidant of the prophet Jeremiah. Baruch (meaning "Blessed" in Hebrew) came from a very eminent Judean family, his brother Seraiah, for instance, being the chief quartermaster of King Zedekiah (Jer 51:59). It was Baruch who copied and delivered Jeremiah's Oracles of Destruction to King Jehoiakim, which were then burned, section by section, by the irate king, only to have Baruch make a new and expanded copy (Jer 36:1-32). Accused of being a Babylonian sympathizer by Azariah son of Hoshaiah, Baruch was taken to Egypt with Jeremiah and those Jews who survived the assassination of the Jewish governor Gedaliah (Jer 43:1-7). Although the Bible does not say when, where, or how Baruch died, extra-biblical evidence, often quite conflicting in character, abounds.[2]

Although some portions of the Baruch scroll alluded to in Jer 36:27-32 are undoubtedly included in the present Book of Jeremiah,[3] there is no valid reason to regard any of I Baruch as being composed by Baruch son of Neriah. To be sure, some portions of I Baruch do contain concepts and phraseology reminiscent of Jeremiah, notably, the Confession for the Palestinian remnant (I Bar 1:15-2:5) and the Prayers of the exiled community (2:6-3:8); but other sections in I Baruch are almost totally devoid of materials reminiscent of Jeremiah, notably, the Poem in praise of Wisdom (3:9-4:4) and the Psalm of encouragement and hope (4:5-5:9). Granted also that I Baruch contains references to a number of historical persons and events within the exilic period, ranging from the time shortly after the fall of Jerusalem in 597 B.C., to shortly before the fall of Babylon in 539 B.C. (see NOTES passim).

---

[1] II Baruch is The Syriac Apocalypse of Baruch; III Baruch is The Greek Apocalypse of Baruch. For brief descriptions of these pseudepigraphical works, see Eissfeldt, pp. 627-630, 775; and E. Jenni, *IDB*, III, 361-362. For detailed analyses and translations of these two texts, see R. H. Charles, pp. 470-526, and H. M. Hughes, pp. 527-541 in *APOT*, II.

[2] For details, see NOTE on "in Babylon" in 1:1.

[3] See T. H. Robinson, "Baruch's Roll," *ZAW* 42 (1924), 209-221.

Arguments Against Baruchian Authorship

Nonetheless, there are some insurmountable difficulties which prevent our book from being accepted for what it purports to be, namely, a composition by Baruch son of Neriah. In its Introduction (1:1-14), certain imprecisions and errors of fact which are characteristic of very late post-exilic works argue against the authenticity of the book's claims (see COMMENT, p. 275), as do striking parallels between I Baruch and books dating to the late Greek or early Roman period, namely, parallels between I Bar 1:15-2:19 and Dan 9:4-19, and between I Bar 4:36-5:9 and Ps of Sol 11:3-8.[4]

Even though the five major sections of I Baruch presuppose for their setting the exilic period, each differs from the others in a number of crucial ways. Consider, for instance, their moods and attitudes toward the Exile and toward their foreign masters: the Introduction (1:1-14) is resigned and sympathetic, respectively; the Confession for the Palestinian remnant (1:15-2:5) is dispassionate and accepting; the Prayers of the exiled community (2:6-3:8) is deeply chastened yet self-righteous; the Poem in praise of Wisdom (3:9-4:4) is almost indifferent to both, while the Psalm of encouragement (4:5-5:1) is quite hostile towards Babylon and is filled with almost irrepressible expectancy.[5]

Such contrast in thought and mood could be expressed by the same writer, especially if different circumstances and conditions existed at the time of the writing of each composition. But there are other basic difficulties and contradictions, such as the marked theological contrast between the Wisdom approach (3:9-4:4) and the prophetic stance (1:15-3:8; 4:5-5:9), or the contrast between the prose (1:1-3:8) and poetry (3:9-5:9). To be sure, the same individual could have written both the prose and poetry sections; but if he did, then the two sections certainly had different Greek translators,[6] a fact which would also suggest different provenances for the two sections.

Last but not least, I Baruch was excluded ultimately from the Jewish canon (but not until it, like so many other Jewish works, had established itself in the Christian canon, see pp. 261-262), so that by Origen's day (ca. 185?-?254) no Hebrew copies remained, at least not in Palestine (but see pp. 261-262). Properly speaking then, I Baruch is a pseudepigraph rather than an apocryphon.

---

[4] See COMMENT II, pp. 291-293; and COMMENT II, pp. 314-316.
[5] For details, see COMMENTS on each section.
[6] See H. St. John Thackeray, *JTS* 4 (1903), 245-266.

Description of Major Sections

Before any meaningful conclusions can be reached about the book as a whole, certain questions such as to *what, where, why,* and *when* must first be applied to the five major sections.

For the reader's convenience, the salient features of each section have been characterized briefly here, leaving the justification for these characterizations to the subsequent detailed analysis of each section. The first section, Introduction and covering letter to Baruch's message (1:1-14), is imprecise in both style and content, and it abounds in improbabilities and errors of "fact" (see COMMENT, p. 275). That Introduction was originally written in Hebrew can scarcely be denied (see NOTES on "prisoners" in vs. 9, and on "cereal offerings" in vs. 10). That it was written in Hebrew certainly argues for a Palestinian provenance. The author's attitude toward Israel's foreign masters is so docile—almost sympathetic (cf. vss. 11-12)—that it seems most compatible with general Jewish thinking in one of three periods: (1) prior to Israel's confrontation with the Seleucids in the first quarter of the second century (200-175 B.C.); (2) sometime after Pompei's entrance into Jerusalem in 63 B.C.; or (3) after Israel's crushing defeat by Rome in A.D. 70. The author of Introduction must be the compiler of most, if not all, of I Baruch.

The Confession for the Palestinian remnant (1:15-2:5) was originally written in Hebrew (see NOTES, for instance, on "because we have sinned" in 1:17, and "to be an object of reproach and horror" in 2:4). In terms of its general theme (We have been very *justly* punished [cf. 1:21-2:1]) and biblical sources (strongly Jeremianic and Deuteronomistic), Confession is, at face value, compatible with what it purports to be, namely, an exilic work by Baruch the Scribe. Nevertheless, its strong affinities with Daniel 9 (see COMMENT II, pp. 291-293) and its inclusion in a book long regarded as apocryphal argue for a *terminus a quo* not earlier than the third century B.C., while its accepting attitude toward the Diaspora and Israel's masters suggests a *terminus ad quem* late in the Greek period, i.e. prior to the defiant mood of the Hasmonean Revolt in 168 B.C. Since Confession was originally composed in Hebrew, Palestine would presumably have been its provenance.

The Prayers of the exiled community (2:6-3:8) is the section of I Baruch most reminiscent of the Book of Jeremiah, distinctive views and phraseology of Jeremiah occurring in almost every verse. That it was originally composed in Hebrew is incontrovertible (see COMMENT I, p. 291). The perspective of Prayers, while consistently appropriate for those living in the Babylonian Exile (in keeping with the claims of 1:1-14), is equally applicable to all the Jewish communities of the Diaspora. Consequently, Prayers may have originated in Babylon, but need not have. Like Confession (1:15-2:5), Prayers is at numerous points almost identical with Daniel 9 and, like the prayer in Daniel 9, antedates the Hasmonean Revolt of 168 B.C., going back in its earliest form perhaps to a time as early as the late Persian period (see COMMENT II, pp. 291-293).

The Poem in praise of Wisdom (3:9-4:4) differs in many ways from the preceding sections of I Baruch: it is poetry, not prose; it relies primarily on Wisdom literature and virtually ignores the Book of Jeremiah; it has a different name for the Deity. In short, it breathes a different spirit and has a different point of view (see COMMENT, p. 303). Nor, apart from the fact that it is also poetry, does Poem seem compatible or congruous with what follows, namely, Psalm (see COMMENT I, pp. 313-314).

If, as seems most likely, Poem was originally composed in Hebrew (or Aramaic, see COMMENT, p. 303), then it certainly had a translator other than the one who did 1:15-3:8. Poem's strong affinities with concepts and phrases characteristic of such later Jewish literature as the Wisdom of Sira and the Wisdom of Solomon suggest either the second or first century B.C. as the date for its composition. In any case, the Diaspora is depicted in Poem as being a long-standing condition (cf. 3:10-11). In its contents, emphases, and spirit, Poem is incongruous with the material that precedes and follows it; and its only justification for being included in I Baruch is that, like the material which surrounds it, Poem presupposes the situation of the Exile.

The Psalm of encouragement (4:5-5:9), whose message is addressed first to the exiled children (4:5-29) and then to their mother Jerusalem (4:30-5:9), finds its scriptural inspiration primarily in Isaiah 40-55 (see COMMENT I, p. 313). The oft-noted similarity of I Bar 4:36-5:9 to the eleventh chapter of the Psalms of Solomon (a pseudepigraphic work of the first century B.C.) is to be explained in one of two ways. Either I Bar 5:5-9 is based on Ps of Sol 11:3-8 or, more likely, both psalms are derived from a common source (see COMMENT II, pp. 314-316). That Psalm was originally composed in Hebrew is probable but far from certain. Even less certain is the date of its composition, although with the exception of its last stanza (5:5-9), a date between the first half of the second century B.C. and the first half of the first century B.C. seems reasonable (see COMMENT II, p. 316).

Concerning the Book as a Whole

Theme and Religious Ideas

If our characterizations of the major sections are correct, then certain conclusions may be made about the book as a whole. A composite of the

works of several authors, I Baruch consists of poems and prayers, of uneven quality, bound together only by their having the same assumed historical background, i.e. the Exile. While it is possible to detect in the arrangement of the separate sections a certain progression of thought, or thread of
argument,[7] Psalm clearly contradicts a basic attitude expressed in Introduction (cf. 1:11-12 with 4:15,21,33-35; and 1:13c with 4:36-54), and
Poem seems totally incongruous with what precedes and follows it (see
COMMENT, p. 304. (It is possible, of course, that Psalm was a later addition to I Baruch, even as the older Epistle of Jeremiah was a later addition to I Baruch [see p. 325].)

A mosaic of older biblical passages, I Baruch has virtually no new or
original religious ideas. The seriousness of sin, the righteousness and forgiveness of God, the Law as the embodiment of God's Wisdom, God's devotion to his people Israel—these and other religious ideas in I Baruch are
not only worked out in greater detail in certain books of the canon but
often more effectively.

That the composite work contains theolog*ies* rather than a *Theology* is
evident, for instance, in the differences in the Doctrine of God reflected in
the title used for addressing the Deity: the "prophetic" portions preferring
either "Lord," YHWH (1:1-3:8), or "The Eternal" (4:5-5:9), the
Wisdom poem commonly using "God," *theos,* but never the personal
name *kurios* (YHWH). Apart from Poem (3:9-4:4), the God worshiped
in I Baruch is the personal, anthropomorphic God of the Covenant, the
God of Abraham, Isaac, and Jacob, the God described by the prophets
(see COMMENT, p. 304). Whereas in Poem God's transcendence and
omnipotence are emphasized, the other portions stress his righteousness,
justice, compassion, and faithfulness.

Language of Composition

Apart from an ancient and puzzling allusion to the liturgical use of I
Baruch in synagogal services (see Introduction, p. 261), there is little
or no external evidence of I Baruch ever having been in Hebrew. I Baruch
bore the Hexaplaric obelus of Origen (A.D. 185?-?254), which meant that
he knew of no extant Hebrew text, an assertion also made by Jerome,
the translator of the Vulgate. Nor has any trace of I Baruch been found
yet at Qumran. (Fragments of the Greek version of the Epistle of Jeremiah have been found at Qumran [see p. 349], but it is impossible to
say whether they are all that survived of *just* the Epistle of Jeremiah or of
I Baruch (1-6).

The internal evidence, however, suggests otherwise. Abounding in

---

[7] "The theme of the book as a whole is Israel's sin, punishment, and forgiveness,"
Pfeiffer, p. 423. Pfeiffer's work, incidentally, is probably the best over-all treatment
of I Baruch in English, its principal drawback being that the text itself is not included.

Hebraisms and mistranslations (see NOTES *passim*),[8] I Baruch gives every indication of being "translation-Greek," although the possibilities of Greek origins do somewhat increase for the last two sections, especially with Psalm (see NOTES and COMMENTS *passim*). These findings, it should be noted, have been verified essentially by Raymond A. Martin in an unpublished paper in which he used a method of syntactical analysis which he had developed in detail elsewhere for distinguishing "translation-Greek" from "original-Greek."[9]

Date and Place of Compilation

The place and time of the final compilation seem to be Palestine in the early part of the second century B.C., i.e. prior to the defiant Jewish mood of 168 B.C., although again, the final section, Psalm, gives evidence of being an addition of the first century B.C. The external evidence is not very helpful here, except that from Athenagoras' quotation of I Baruch 3:34 in his *Supplication for the Christians* IX, we can establish a *terminus ad quem* of A.D. 177.

If the reader is somewhat frustrated by our tenuousness and hedging regarding the language and date of the final compilation, one can only counter that it is unavoidable, the evidence being too scanty and ambiguous to permit greater precision or certainty. Thus, although the present writer cannot refute the claims of Kneucker (p. 32-37), Whitehouse (pp. 574-576), and others who would date the final form of I Baruch to sometime between A.D. 70 and 135, he sees no cogent argument, based upon the internal evidence, to date I Baruch (with the possible exception of 4:5-5:9) any later than the early part of the second century B.C.

Author

Baruch, the confidant of Jeremiah, was not the author of I Baruch. That is all that may be said with certainty on the matter. The likelihood, however, is that a Palestinian Jew in the early part of the second century B.C. either composed, or possibly modified, what later became Confession (1:15-2:5) and Prayers (2:6-3:8) and a portion of Psalm (4:5-5:4), and then wrote for them the Introduction (1:1-14). It was sometime after this that someone else interpolated Poem (3:9-4:4), and possibly as late as the first century B.C. that someone else added 5:5-9.

Literary Character

Judging the literary merits of a book that is known to us only in translation is a precarious, if not an unfair, thing to do. Inevitably though, im-

---

[8] For examples conveniently assembled in one place, see Harwell, pp. 52-56, and Whitehouse, pp. 571-572. Kneucker (pp. 24-29) has the most exhaustive but uncritical list so it must be used with extreme care.

[9] Martin, pp. 5-38.

pressions are formed and judgments made. Scholars differ in their estimates of the literary merits of I Baruch. Keerl was too harsh when he
wrote, "Every prophet of the Old Testament brings new as well as old out
of his treasure. The worthy Baruch contents himself with transcribing the
older prophecies. In comparing the contents of his book, there comes over
one a feeling as if some incompetent scribbler had wished to do an exer-
cise in the language and style of the Prophets; it reminds one of the rhetorical practice of a feeble schoolboy, who composes an opusculum out of all
sorts of passages" (quoted by Gifford, p. 248).

On the other hand, the book was evidently weighed by the Council of
Jamnia (ca. A.D. 90), and was found wanting. In any case, I Baruch is not
in the Jewish canon; and except for 3:36-38 which was regarded by Greek
and Latin Fathers as predictive of the Incarnation, I Baruch was generally
ignored by Christian writers.

I Baruch generally was bypassed by the Christian Church, not because it
was recognized as a pseudepigraphon but because it did not pass "the test
of time." More specifically, the book's literary style, which is at best uneven in quality, was not sufficiently strong or memorable to compensate for
the book's theological and religious weaknesses, especially in the book's
lack of originality and consistency.

Baruch's Canonical Status

Evidently, I Baruch had never gained acceptance among the Jews (so
Jerome), notwithstanding the assertion in the *Constitutions of the Holy
Apostles* V xx (ca. 380) that the Jews "even now on the tenth day of the
month Gorpiaeus, when they assemble together, read the Lamentations of
Jeremiah . . . and Baruch in whom it is written, 'This is our God; no
other can compare with him. . . . appeared on earth and lived among
men [Bar 3:36,38].' "[10] Possibly I Baruch was denied canonical status
among the Jews of Jamnia because they recognized its pseudepigraphic
character; more likely they recognized the book's literary and theological
inadequacies. After all, other pseudepigraphic works got into the Jewish
canon, as witness the long, hard but ultimately successful debate concerning the canonicity of Ecclesiastes.

There are no indisputable instances of I Baruch being used by the NT
writers.[11] A number of Church Fathers, however, did regard it and the

---

[10] Thackeray, *The Septuagint and Jewish Worship*, 2d ed., pp. 107-111, has taken
this clue and constructed an elaborate argument for I Baruch's being part of Jewish
synagogal liturgy among sixth-century Jews in the area of Edessa, Turkey. For a recent evaluation of Thackeray's argument, see Albert Sundberg, *The Old Testament of
the Early Church*, HTS, XX (Cambridge, Mass., 1958), 74-77.

[11] Cf. Bar 3:29 with John 3:13 (and Wis 18:16; IV Esd 4:8); and cf. Bar 4:7 with
1 Cor 10:20 (and Deut 32:17).

Epistle of Jeremiah as adjuncts, or supplements, to the Book of Jeremiah rather than as separate books.[12] I Baruch was mentioned *by name* as being canonical by several Greek Fathers,[13] but by none of the Latin Fathers, presumably because they, following the logic of Jerome, regarded it as non-canonical. Nevertheless, although the oldest known manuscript of the Vulgate, *Amiatinus,* omits both I Baruch and the Epistle of Jeremiah, these works ultimately found their way into the Vulgate, and at the Council of Trent in 1546 were recognized as part of the Deutero-Canon. Wycliffe (1320?-1384), while noting in the Preface to his translation Jerome's comments on the contents of the Jewish canon, nonetheless included I Baruch in his Bible. However, Luther and the other Reformers either omitted the Apocrypha from their Bibles or relegated it to a lesser place.

Ancient Versions of I Baruch

The Greek

I Baruch is found in a number of ancient Greek manuscripts, including Alexandrinus (LXX^A) and Vaticanus (LXX^B).[14] In I Baruch the differences between these two great uncials are quite negligible, as are the differences between them and the Lucianic recension (LXX^L). Although no Theodotion translation of I Baruch has survived, its one-time existence is attested by the presence of five readings in the Syro-Hexaplar designated as Theodotion (Harwell, pp. 6-7).[15] In most Greek manuscripts I Baruch comes after Jeremiah and before Lamentations.

It would seem that the Semitic text of I Baruch had at least two different Greek translators, namely, the one who did Jeremiah 29-52 through I Bar 3:8, and the one who did I Bar 3:9 - 5:9.[16] That the Greek translations of the Semitic text were fairly literal is best attested by the relative ease and accuracy with which Harwell, for instance, was able to "translate" the Greek back into Hebrew, even to the point of finding three-beat measures in Poem (3:9 - 4:4) and five-beat measures in Psalm (4:5 - 5:9).

---

[12] So Irenaeus (A.D. 140-?202) in Gaul, Clement of Alexandria (d. before 215), and Cyprian of Carthage (d. 258); in many ancient Greek manuscripts, including Vaticanus and Alexandrinus, I Baruch immediately follows Jeremiah. It is not certain whether Origen's mention of the Epistle of Jeremiah as canonical was intended to include or exclude I Baruch.

[13] For example, Athanasius, Cyril of Jerusalem, Epiphanius, and Nicephorus; for details, see Swete, *IOTG,* pp. 203-214, 274-276.

[14] But not Sinaiticus (LXX^ℵ).

[15] On the nature and the history of translations like the Theodotion, and of Septuagint recensions like the Lucianic, see Roberts, *OTTV,* 120-143.

[16] So Thackeray, *JTS* 4 (1903), 245-266. Emanuel Tov agrees with Thackeray that Bar 1:1 - 3:8 was done by the same Greek scribe who did Jeremiah 29-52 except that Tov would call that Greek scribe a "reviser," not a "translator."

Other Versions

The other ancient versions of I Baruch are based upon the Greek. Harwell (pp. 5-9, 10-28) has shown convincingly that the two Syriac versions, the Syro-Hexaplar (SyrH.) and the regular Syriac, are both based upon the Greek. Rarely does either text provide readings preferable to the LXX (see NOTES *passim*). While scholars have debated the origins and relative merits of several ancient Latin texts, there is little doubt that both the *Vetus Latina* (OL) and the Vulgate are based upon the Greek (see Harwell, pp. 29-51); and again, they provide little in the way of preferred readings (see NOTES *passim*).

The *apparatus criticus* of Ziegler's excellent critical text of I Baruch[17] also includes readings from other ancient versions, including the Arabic, Armenian, Bohairic, and Ethiopic, all of which seem to be based upon the Septuagint. Inasmuch as all of these are versions based upon texts which are either very late, mixed, or unscientific, they must be used with great care. Fortunately for our purposes, they cast virtually no new light on the Greek text of I Baruch.

Possibly one more indication of the mixed light in which our book was regarded by the ancients is the book's title in various ancient versions:

> "Baruch" (LXX and SyrH.)
> "The Second Epistle of Baruch" (Syriac)
> "Prophecy of Baruch" (OL and Vulgate)
> "Baruch the Prophet" (Coptic)
> "Epistle of Baruch" (Armenian)

[17] See Bibliography IIIA for full title.

Commentaries

Fritzsche, Otto F. *Das Buch Baruch,* Kurzgefasstes exegetisches Handbuch zu den Apokryphen des Alten Testaments, eds. O. Fritzsche und C. Grimm, I. Leipzig: Hirzel, 1851. *Cited as* Fritzsche.

Gelin, Albert. *Le Livre de Baruch,* 2d ed., La Sainte Bible—Bible de Jérusalem, XXIII. Paris: Cerf, 1959. *Cited as* Gelin.

Gifford, E. H. *Baruch,* Apocrypha of the Speaker's Commentary, ed. Henry Wace, II. London: John Murray, 1888. *Cited as* Gifford.

Gunneweg, A. H. J. "Das Buch Baruch," in *Historische und legendarische Erzählungen,* Judische Schriften aus hellenistisch-römischer Zeit, ed. Werner Georg Kümmel et al., III, 2. Gütersloh: Mohn, 1975.

Hamp, Vincenz. *Baruch,* Die Heilige Schrift in deutscher Übersetzung. Würzburg: Echter Verlag, 1950.

Kalt, Edmund. *Das Buch Baruch,* Die heilige Schrift des Alten Testamentes, eds. F. Feldmann and H. Herkenne, VII/4. Bonn: Peter Hanstein, 1932.

Kneucker, J. J. *Das Buch Baruch, Geschichte und Kritik, Übersetzung und Erklärung.* Leipzig: F. A. Brockhaus, 1879. *Cited as* Kneucker.

Reusch, F. H. *Erklärung des Buches Baruch.* Freiburg: Brisgovi, 1853. *Cited as* Reusch.

Rothstein, Johann W. *Das Buch Baruch,* Die Apokryphen und Pseudepigraphen des Alten Testaments, ed. E. F. Kautzsch, I. Tübingen: Mohr, 1900. *Cited as* Rothstein.

Schneider, Heinrich. *Baruch,* Herders Bibelkommentar. Freiburg im Breisgau: Herder, 1954.

Wambacq, Bernard N. *Jeremias, Klaagliederen, Baruch, Brief van Jeremias,* De Boeken van het Oude Testament. Roermond: Romen & Zonen, 1957.

Whitehouse, O. C. *The Book of Baruch,* APOT, I, 569-595. *Cited as* Whitehouse.

Zöckler, Otto. *Das Buch Baruch,* Die Apokryphen des Alten Testamentes, Kurzgefasstes Kommentar zu den heiligen Schriften des Alten und Neuen Testamentes sowie zu den Apokryphen, eds. O Zöckler and H. Strack, IX. München: Oskar Beck, 1891.

Other Books

Battistone, J. J. "An Examination of the Literary and Theological Background of the Wisdom Passage of the Book of Baruch." Dissertation, Duke University, Durham, N.C., 1968.

Bentzen, Aage. *Introduction to the Old Testament,* I, 6th ed. Copenhagen: G. E. C. Gad, 1961.

Eissfeldt, Otto. *The Old Testament: An Introduction, including the Apocrypha and Pseudepigrapha, and also the works of similar type from Qumran,* tr. from the 3d Ger. ed. by Peter R. Ackroyd. New York: Harper & Row, 1965. *Cited as* Eissfeldt.

Fraenkel, Isaac S. *K⁽ᵉ⁾tûbîm 'aharônîm* (A Hebrew translation of the Apocrypha). Warsaw, 1863.

Harwell, R. R. *The Principal Versions of Baruch.* Yale University Press, 1915. *Cited as* Harwell.

Hoberg, Gottfried H. *Die älteste lateinische Übersetzung des Buches Baruch,* 2d ed. Freiburg im Breisgau, 1902.

Martin, Raymond A. *Syntactical Evidence of Semitic Sources in Greek Documents,* Society of Biblical Literature, Septuagint and Cognate Studies, III. Missoula, Mont.: Scholars Press, 1974. *Cited as* Martin.

Metzger, Bruce. *An Introduction to the Apocrypha.* Oxford University Press, 1957. *Cited as* Metzger.

Oesterley, W. O. E. *The Books of the Apocrypha.* New York: Revell, 1914.

——— *An Introduction to the Books of the Apocrypha.* New York: Macmillan, 1935. *Cited as* Oesterley.

Pfeiffer, Robert H. *History of New Testament Times, with an Introduction to the Apocrypha.* New York: Harper, 1949. *Cited as* Pfeiffer.

Ryle, Herbert E., and Montague R. James. *Psalms of the Pharisees, Commonly Called the Psalms of Solomon.* Cambridge at the University Press, 1891. *Cited as* Ryle and James.

Schürer, Emil. *Geschichte des jüdischen Volkes im Zeitalter Jesu Christi,* 4th ed., III. Leipzig: Hinrichs, 1909. *Cited as* Schürer.

Stoderl, Wenzel. *Zur Echtheitsfrage von Baruch 1-3,8.* Münster: Aschendorffschen, 1922. *Cited as* Stoderl.

Thackeray, H. St. John. *The Septuagint and Jewish Worship,* 2d ed. Oxford University Press, 1923.

——— *Some Aspects of the Greek Old Testament.* London: Allen & Unwin, 1927.

Torrey, Charles C. *The Apocryphal Literature.* Yale University Press, 1945. *Cited as* Torrey.

Tov, Emanuel. *The Book of Baruch Also Called 1 Baruch (Greek and Hebrew):* Edited, Reconstructed and Translated in Texts and Translations, VIII, and Pseudepigrapha, VI, of the Society of Biblical Literature, ed. Robert A. Kraft. Missoula, Mont.: Scholars Press, 1975.

——— "The Relation between the Greek Versions of Baruch and Daniel," in *Armenian and Biblical Studies,* ed. M. E. Stone. Jerusalem: St. James Press, 1976.

——— *The Septuagint Translation of Jeremiah and Baruch: A Discussion of an Early Revision of the LXX of Jeremiah 29-52 and Baruch 1:1 - 3:8,* in Harvard Semitic Museum and Harvard Semitic Monographs, VIII, ed. Frank Moore Cross. Missoula, Mont.: Scholars Press, 1976.

Articles

Bewer, Julius A., "The River Sud in the Book of Baruch," *JBL* 43 (1942), 226-227.

Heinisch, Paul, "Zur Enstehung des Buches Baruch," *Theologie und Glaube* 20 (1928), 696-710.

Marshall, J. T., "The Book of Baruch," *HDB*, I, 251-254.

Moore, Carey A., "Toward the Dating of the Book of Baruch," *CBQ* 36 (1974), 312-320.

Pesch, Wilhelm, "Die Abhängigkeit des 11. salomonischen Psalms vom letzten Kapitel des Buches Baruch," *ZAW* 67 (1955), 251-263.

Thackeray, Henry St. John, "Notes and Studies: The Greek Translators of Jeremiah," *JTS* 4 (1903), 245-266.

Toy, Crawford H., "The Book of Baruch," in *The Jewish Encyclopaedia,* ed. I. Singer (New York: Funk & Wagnalls, 1905), II, 556-557.

Wambacq, Bernard N., "Les prières de Baruch (i 15 - ii 19) et de Danel (ix 5-19)," *Biblica* 40 (1959), 463-475.

———— "L'unité litteraire de Baruch i-iii 8," *Bibliotheca ephemeridum theologicarum Lovaniensium* 12 (1959), 455-460.

———— "L'unité de livre de Baruch," *Biblica* 47 (1966), 574-576.

Versions

Swete, Henry Barclay, ed. *Baruch.* The Old Testament in Greek according to the Septuagint, III. Cambridge University Press, 1894.

Ziegler, Joseph. *Ieremias, Baruch, Threni, Epistula Ieremiae.* Septuaginta. Vetus Testamentum Graecum auctoritate Societatis Gottingensis editum, ed. J. Ziegler, XV. Göttingen, 1957.

I. INTRODUCTION AND COVERING
LETTER TO BARUCH'S MESSAGE
(1:1-14)

1 ¹ And these are the words of the letter which Baruch son of Neriah, the son of Mahseiah son of Zedekiah son of Hasadiah son of Hilkiah, wrote in Babylon ² in the fifth year, on the seventh day of the fifth*ᵃ* month, the date the Chaldeans captured Jerusalem and burned it with fire.

³ And Baruch read aloud the contents of this letter to Jeconiah son of Jehoiakim, king of Judah, and to all the people who had come to hear the letter read, ⁴ and to the nobles and princes and to the elders and to all the people, regardless of their status—all who lived in Babylon by the Ahava*ᵇ* river.

⁵ Then they wept and fasted and *ᶜ*prayed before*ᶜ* the Lord. ⁶ And they raised money, each giving as much as he could, ⁷ and sent it to Jerusalem to the high priest Joakim son of Hilkiah, the son of Shallum, as well as to the priests and all the people that were found with him in Jerusalem ⁸ when he took the vessels of the temple of the Lord which had been taken from the sanctuary to return them to the land of Judah, on the tenth day of Sivan*ᵈ*, the silver vessels which Zedekiah son of Josiah, king of Judah, had made ⁹ after Nebuchadnezzar, king of Babylon, had deported Jeconiah and the nobles and the prisoners*ᵉ*, both the influential and the rank and file, from Jerusalem and brought him*ᶠ* to Babylon. ¹⁰ And they wrote:

ᵃ Missing in LXX and versions; see Note.
ᵇ Emending *soud* (Vulg. *sodi*) to *eoua;* see Note.
ᶜ⁻ᶜ LXXᴬ, many Greek MSS, and ancient versions have "vowed vows to."
ᵈ Syr. *Nisan.*
ᵉ LXXᴸ, Syriae, SyrH. add "and the craftsmen"; see Note.
ᶠ Many MSS and versions read "them."

We are sending you herewith money. Now use the money for burnt offerings *and sin offerings* and incense, and prepare *cereal offerings*; then offer them* on the altar of the Lord our God. 11 And pray for the life of Nebuchadnezzar, king of Babylon, and for the life of his son Belshazzar that their days may be as long as the days of heaven are above the earth. 12 And the Lord will give us strength and will sharpen our vision, and we will live under the protection of Nebuchadnezzar, king of Babylon, and under the protection of his son Belshazzar, and we will serve them for a long while and find their favor. 13 And pray to the Lord our God for us, for we have sinned against the Lord our God, and to date neither the Lord's fury nor his anger has turned away from us. 14 So read aloud this letter which we have sent you when making your confession in the Lord's temple on festival day* and season*.

ᵍ⁻ᵍ LXX "and for sin"; Vulgate omits; OL, Syriac "for sin"; see NOTE.
ʰ⁻ʰ Emending *manna* to *manaa;* see NOTE.
ⁱ Vulgate adds "for sin."
ʲ Many MSS and versions read "days."
ᵏ Syriac "on days of the Lord"; see NOTE.

NOTES

1:1. *the words of the letter* [*oi logoi tou bibliou*]. Cf. vs. 14. See Jer 36[29]:1 where *biblion* [MT *sēpher*] obviously refers to a letter. "The words" refers to I Bar 1:15 - 5:9.

Baruch son of Neriah . . . Hilkiah. Cf. Jer 32[39]:12, 36:4,15[43:4,14]. Baruch was not the only son of Neriah; Baruch had a brother, Seraiah, who was the chief quartermaster, *śar mᵉnūḥâ,* under King Zedekiah and who carried Jeremiah's oracles to the king (cf. Jer 51:59). Joseph characterizes Baruch's family as "very eminent" (*Ant.* x 9.1). Baruch's immediate ancestors bore famous names, but they are not to be identified with the best-known bearers of those particular names; for details, see H. B. MacLean, *IDB,* IV, s.v. "Zedekiah"; *IDB,* II, s.v. "Hasadiah", and B. T. Dahlberg, s.v. "Hilkiah." For a brief biographical sketch of the historical Baruch, see J. M. Ward, *IDB,* I, 361.

in Babylon. According to Jer 43:6-7, after the assassination of Gedaliah (see II Kings 25:22-26), Baruch was taken with Jeremiah to Egypt, a view which is also supported by Josephus *Ant.* x 9.6. Since the MT does not say where Baruch died, it should not be surprising that in this matter conflicting traditions abound. For instance, Jerome, in his commentary on Isa 30:6-7, says Baruch died in Egypt. However, Josephus *Ant.* x 9.7 has been taken by some to mean that after Nebuchadnezzar had conquered Egypt in 568 B.C., Baruch was taken, along with Jeremiah, to Babylon. Baruch's later presence in Babylon is also expressly affirmed in other Jewish sources, including *Seder 'Olam Rabba* 26; *Midrash Rabba* to Song of Songs 5:5; and *Megillah* 16b, the last reference asserting the impossible view, chronologically speaking, that in Babylon Baruch was the teacher of Ezra the Scribe. For further details on Jewish legends concerning Baruch, see Louis Ginzberg, *The Legends of the Jews* (Philadelphia: Jewish Publication Society, 1909), IV, 354-355, VI, 399, 411, and VII, 58.

Tempting though it is, we must reject the Syriac reading "to Babylon" as the alternative to the Greek "in Babylon." For "to Babylon" (*bbl*) reflects either a misreading of *bbbl*, "in Babylon" (so Whitehouse, p. 578), or, more likely, it is to be explained by the Syriac editor's view that, as expressly stated in II Baruch (i.e. the Apocalypse) 77:19, *two* letters were sent by Baruch to the Jews in Babylon, the Apocalypse and our present work (so Harwell, p. 12).

In sum, while the biblical traditions do not preclude a period of Babylonian residency for the scribe Baruch after the defeat of Egypt by Nebuchadnezzar, none of the extra-biblical sources, including the Book of Baruch, cogently argues for its historicity.

2. *in the fifth year . . . fifth month.* The unemended Greek text ("in the fifth year on the seventh day of the month"), which all the ancient versions follow, is very vague and inevitably raises several questions. The fifth year *of what?* Of Jerusalem's capture in 598 B.C. (II Kings 24:12-16) or her destruction in 586 B.C. (II Kings 25:1-13)? The seventh day of *what month?* The reading adopted here follows Kneucker (pp. 10-16) and most scholars who, on the basis of II Kings 25:8 where the armies of Nebuchadnezzar burned the temple and palace of Jerusalem on the seventh day of the fifth month, emend the Greek to read "in the fifth year in the fifth month of the seventh day of the month." Baruch would have written his letter, then, in 581 B.C., five years, *to the day,* after those terrible events. Certainly in terms of what little is known of Baruch's life, it is far more likely that he would have been in Babylon (or better, that the final editor of the Book of I Baruch would have put him there) sometime after the deportation of 586 B.C. rather than the one of 597 B.C. (see NOTE on "in Babylon" above).

Although the emendation proposed above is probably the best solution, it is not without its difficulties. According to Jer 52:12, the temple was burned on the tenth day, not the seventh. In any case, the temple was burned in 586 B.C., not in 597 B.C.; and yet according to 1:7,10,14, and 2:16, the temple is still standing or, more accurately, the cult is still functioning there (but see 2:3, which certainly refers to the conditions of 586 B.C., not 597). It was because of these contradictions between vss. 1-2 and 3-14 that scholars such as Eissfeldt (p. 594) have regarded vss. 3-14 as a later insertion.

the date [*en tō kairō ō*]. Literally "at the season which." Torrey (p. 60) saw this phrase as referring not to a specific day but, as in Deut 16:6 of the LXX, to a process or whole series of events, in this case, to a period extending over a decade, i.e. from 598 to 583 B.C. But more likely, the expression "the seventh day of the fifth month" was proverbial and in its meaning to Jews as self-evident as the expression "December Seventh" is to Americans, or "Bastille Day" is to Frenchmen, in which case the phrase "the Chaldeans captured Jerusalem and burned it with fire" is a gloss.

3. *read aloud . . . to.* Literally "read in the ears of," as in Jer 36[43]:6,10,13, and elsewhere.

Jeconiah. Probably the personal or private name here and in Jer 27:20 for Jehoiachin, king of Judah (598-597 B.C.), the latter being his throne name. In the contemporary cuneiform inscriptions he is called Yaukin. Son (but see Matt 1:11-12) and successor of Jehoiakim, Jehoiachin reigned for only three months before he was carried into exile by Nebuchadnezzar (see II Kings 24:6-17). Jehoiachin's presence in Babylon, however, does not necessarily indicate that Bar 1:2 refers to the fifth year after Jehoiachin's exile in 597 B.C.; for it is clear from II Kings 25:27-30 and Jer 52:31-34 that Jehoiachin was still alive in Babylon long after the destruction of 586 B.C. For further details, see H. G. May, *IDB*, II, s.v. "Jehoiachin."

all the people. Theoretically thousands of Jews could have been present inasmuch as II Kings 24:14 reports that 10,000 accompanied Jehoiachin into exile, although Jer 52:28 puts the figure at only 3,023.

who had come to hear the letter read. Literally "that came to the book." The entire scene and language are reminiscent of II Kings 23:2 and II Chron 34:30.

4. *princes* ["sons of the kings"]. These are the princes of the house of David, not just the sons of Jehoiachin, although LXX^A and some versions read "sons of the king." Jeremiah 22:30 notwithstanding, Jehoiachin did have sons (see I Chron 3:17), as the Babylonian cuneiform inscriptions also attest (see *ANET²*, p. 308).

elders. Cf. Jer 29:1.

regardless of their status. Literally "from small to great," which can refer to social status, age, or size; the translation is intended to include all three. Cf. Esth 1:20.

Ahava [LXX *soud*] *river.* For the many reasonable as well as farfetched explanations for *soud* in the LXX, see Whitehouse, p. 583. The reading adopted here follows the suggestion of J. A. Bewer (*JBL* 43 [1942], 266*f*) that the river intended was the Ahava ('ah^awā' in Ezra 8:15,21,31 of the MT), which is transliterated by the LXX as *aoua, eoue,* and *eoua,* respectively. Thus, *soud* here probably represents a miscopying of *eoua,* in the Greek uncial script the letter *e* being easily confused with *s,* and the *a* with *d.* The entire scene seems inspired by that in Ezra 8:15,21,31. (The only problem is that 4QpJer [a Dead Sea scroll commentary on Jeremiah in Cave IV] has *swr.*)

5. *Lord* [*kurios*]. In I Bar 1:1 - 3:8 the word "Lord" (Heb. *YHWH*) without any modifiers occurs over twenty-five times, not to mention such modified phrases as "the Lord" (2:9,17); "Lord our God" (1:18,22, 2:5, 3:8); and "Lord Almighty, the God of Israel" (3:1,4), and constitutes a basic literary difference between this section and I Bar 3:9 - 4:4 where "God" (*theos*) dominates, and between I Bar 4:5 - 5:4, where "The Eternal" is the favorite term of address for the God of Israel (see NOTE on "The Eternal" in 4:10).

6. *they raised money.* Literally "they collected silver"; cf. II Chron 24:5,11.

each giving . . . as he could. Literally "the hand was able according to each," an obvious Hebraism; cf. Deut 16:10 and 17 of the LXX.

7. *it.* I.e. the money; the pronoun is lacking in the LXX and versions.

the high priest [ton ierea] Joakim. Because the LXX has only "the priest," scholars such as Zöckler and Stoderl, taking their clue from Kneucker (pp. 206-210), regard Joakim, not as the chief priest, but as the second in command as, for example, Pashhur son of Immer (Jer 20:1) or Zephaniah son of Maaseiah (Jer 29:25*f*).

But more likely, "the priest" here means the high priest, as in Num 3:6; I Kings 4:2; II Kings 11:9, 12:8. To be sure, Joakim son of Hilkiah is not mentioned among the chief priests of Baruch's time in the list of I Chron 6:13-15[5:39-41 MT], which names Shallum, Hilkiah, Azariah, Seraiah, and Jehozadak. And only in later sources is a high priest named Joakim mentioned for this period: a Joakim son of Jeshua is mentioned as a contemporary of Nehemiah and Ezra in Neh 12:10,11,26, and Josephus *Ant.* XI 5.1, as well as a Joakim in the time of Nebuchadnezzar in Judith 4:6,14, 15:8, all of which is regarded by some scholars as further evidence of the late date of the Book of Baruch or, at least, the late date of I Bar 1:1-14. I Bar 1:1-14 is of late date, but the mere fact that Joakim son of Hilkiah is not mentioned in I Chron 6:13 is not necessarily proof that Joakim was not high priest, for the dangers in assuming total accuracy and completness in name lists is well known. J. M. Myers' conclusion at the end of his examination of I Chron 6:1-15 is well worth remembering: "That we do not have a full list here is beyond doubt" (*I Chronicles*, AB, vol. 12, 46). Although Myers is probably correct in rejecting the idea that Joakim son of Hilkiah was really a high priest in the period under discussion, he nonetheless recognizes that "the priest" in I Bar 1:7 means "the high priest" (*Ezra · Nehemiah*, AB, vol. 14, 197*f*).

8. *when he took [en tō labein auton].* The antecedent of the pronoun is unclear. Some scholars have suggested that it refers to Joakim of vs. 7, but more likely, it refers to Baruch of vs. 3.

sanctuary [naou]. The *naos*, or holy place, was within the temple ("house") of the Lord; see I Kings 6:3,5.

to return them. Long ago Rothstein (p. 216) rightly characterized the contents of this verse as "doubtful." To be sure, in 594 B.C., Hananiah son of Azzur predicted to King Zedekiah and Jeremiah the return within two years of the sacred vessels taken by Nebuchadnezzar in 597 B.C. (Jer 28:3), but there is no evidence that his prophecy was fulfilled. According to the MT, Nebuchadnezzar carted off many sacred vessels to Babylon in 597 B.C. (II Kings 24:13; II Chron 36:10), and again in 586 B.C. (II Kings 25:13-16; Jer 52:17-19); and these remained in Babylon until 537 B.C., when Sheshbazzar brought 5,469 gold and silver vessels back to Jerusalem (Ezra 1:7-11).

Sivan. Siwān, Hebrew cognate of the Bab. *simanu* (May/June), is the third month of the Jewish year; see Esth 8:9.

silver vessels . . . Zedekiah . . . had made. Another unhistorical assertion, or at least, there is no mention made of this in the MT. Stoderl's argument (p. 19) that after Nebuchadnezzar had carried off the sacred vessels in 597 B.C. new vessels for the temple had to be made and since Israel was now poorer Zedekiah would have made the vessels of silver (as vs. 8 suggests) is quite logical but ultimately unconvincing, especially so, since according to II Kings

25:13-16, in 586 B.C. Nebuchadnezzar carted off to Babylon bronze and gold vessels as well as silver.

Most likely, this entire verse is, as so many commentators have suggested, a gloss, i.e. a marginal note that some later copyist incorporated into his text.

9. *prisoners* [*desmōtas*]. That this entire verse is reminiscent of Jer 24:1 is further indicated by the fact that LXX[L] and the Syriac add, with Jer 24:1, "and the craftsmen" (see textual note *e*). The Hebrew hiphil participle *masgēr* can mean either "prison" (Ps 142[141]:8; Isa 24:22, 42:7) or "smith" (II Kings 24:14,16; Jer 24:1, 29[36]:2). In the LXX, in the four places where the Hebrew definitely means "smith" (but see J. Bright, *Jeremiah*, AB, vol. 21, 193), it is correctly translated by *sugkleion*, "smith," in II Kings 24:14,16, and incorrectly(?) by *desmōtas*, "prisoners," in Jer 24:1, 36[29 H]:2. Since the same mistranslation occurs here in vs. 9, i.e. *desmōtas* for *masgēr*, we may infer that the translator of at least this portion of Baruch was either the scribe who translated Jeremiah or had the Greek text of Jeremiah before him. As will be seen later, some other translation idiosyncrasies common to Baruch and Jeremiah also suggests these two possibilities.

the influential [*tous dunatous*]. Literally "the powerful," be it because of their physical and military prowess (cf. II Kings 24:14) or their political power (II Kings 24:15). Since Jer 24:1, the verse after which I Bar 1:9 is patterned, has "the prisoners and the wealthy [*tous plousious*]" going into captivity, "influential" is the best word to use here since influence can be the result of physical, political, or economic power.

the rank and file. Cf. Jer 1:18, Dan 9:6. Literally "the people of the land." These are the common, everyday people, in contrast to "the influential"; they are neither "the laity" as in Zech 24:14, nor "the dregs of society" as in II Kings 24:14 (*oi ptōchoi tēs gēs*).

10. *they wrote.* Literally "they said."

cereal offerings. This verse is strikingly reminiscent of Jer 17:26 ("burnt offerings and sacrifices, cereal offerings and frankincense,") not only because of their similar content but even more because of an identical error in their transliteration into Greek; for in all three of them the Heb. *minḥâ*, "cereal offering" or "gift," which is rightly transliterated as *manaa* in II Chron 7:7; II Kings 8:8, 20:12, was incorrectly rendered here in vs. 10 as *manna*, "manna" (cf. Num 11:7 of the LXX). This error in translation is one more indication that the translator of Baruch either was also the translator of Jeremiah or had the Greek translation of Jeremiah before him when he translated Baruch.

The LXX's reading "and for sin" (see textual note *g-g*) and the Vulgate's "for sin" (see textual note *i*) are direct and indirect attestations, respectively, to Hebraisms (cf. *peri amartias* in Isa 53:10; Ps 39:7[40:6]). For a discussion of sacrifices and offerings in general and of these in particular, see T. H. Gaster, *IDB*, IV, s.v. "Sacrifices and Offerings, OT."

on the altar. That sacrificial offerings were being made at the altar of the temple does not necessarily preclude the incident here from being essentially historical (so Stoderl, p. 20). As a matter of fact, some sort of offerings was made on the altar at Jerusalem after the destruction of the first temple (so Jer 41:5[48:5]) as well as the second, although the exact nature of these offerings after A.D. 70 is a matter of debate. *Taanith* iv 6, one of the oldest tractates of the Mishnah, states flatly, "On the seventeeth of Tammuz, the Tamid came to an end" (the *tāmid* was the burnt offering every morning and evening of a lamb, along with oil, flour, and wine, for all the people, in accordance with Exod 29:38-42 [for details, see the tractate *Tamid* in the Mishnah] while Josephus ca. A.D. 93 says, "Yet hath our legislator [i.e. Moses] nowhere forbidden us to pay honours to worthy men, provided they be of another kind, and inferior to those we pay to God; with which honours we willingly testify our respect to our emperors, and to the people of Rome; *we also offer perpetual sacrifices for them* [italics added]; nor do we only offer them every day at the common expenses of all the Jews, but although we offer no other such sacrifices out of our common expenses, no not for our own children, yet do we this as a peculiar honour to the emperors, and to them alone" *Against Apion* II 6, Whiston's translation). For a discussion of this possible conflict of evidence and other matters concerning sacrifices after A.D. 70, See Schürer, III, 653*ff*.

11. *pray for [proseuxasthe peri] . . . Nebuchadnezzar*. From an impartial and objective point of view, there is nothing unreasonable about such advice. Nebuchadnezzar (Bab. *Nabû-kudurri-uṣur*, meaning "Nabu protect my boundary") was a far more humane and admirable king than most Jews and Christians realize (for a brief but sympathetic sketch of Nebuchadnezzar [pp. 133-145], as well as other "villains" of the Old Testament, including Tiglath-Pileser III, Sargon II, and Sennacherib, see the delightful little book by W. von Soden, *Herrscher im Alten Orient* in the Verständliche Wissenschaft Series, ed. D. H. von Campenhausen [Berlin: Springer, 1954], 152 pages). Nebuchadnezzar and the city of Babylon did, however, get good press from Jeremiah (cf. Jer 27:6-8, 29[36]:4-7; vs. 7 of ch. 29 even has Jeremiah offer advice in the same words as I Bar 1:1, *proseuxasthe peri*, "pray for," the city) and Ezekiel (Ezek 29:17-20). Thus, in I Bar 1:11-12 the exiles urge the Jews in Jerusalem to practice what Jeremiah had originally urged the exiles to do (cf. Jer 29[36]:4-7).

In later exilic prophecy virtually all Jews had become embittered toward Babylon (cf. Isaiah 47; Jeremiah 50-51). That I Bar 1:11-12 expresses such a servile, if not sympathetic, attitude toward a foreign conqueror has considerable relevancy for dating I Bar 1:1-14, that is, there are some periods in Jewish history in which such a docile and cooperative attitude was almost inconceivable, for example, in the sixth through fourth decades of the second century B.C., and the fifth and sixth decades of the first century A.D.

his son Belshazzar [baltasar]. A serious anachronism here, Belshazzar (Bab. *Bêl-šar-uṣur*, meaning "Bel, protect the king") was not the son of Nebuchadnezzar but the son of Nabonidus, the last king of the Neo-Babylonian empire, its kings being Nabopolassar (626-605 B.C.), Nebuchadnezzar (605-562), Amel-Marduk (562-559), Neriglissar (559-556), Labashi-Marduk (556), Nabonidus (556-539 B.C.) and his crown prince and later co-regent, Belshazzar. On Belshazzar, see R. P. Dougherty, *Nabonidus and Belshazzar* (Yale University Press, 1929), 93-104.

Baruch's anachronism concerning Belshazzar is shared by Dan 5:2,11,18,22. To assert, as Stoderl does (p. 22), that Nebuchadnezzar probably had a son named Belshazzar but our extant cuneiform records are so scanty that no mention is made of him in any of them is, of course, "an invention from silence."

Such an argument proves nothing—except perhaps man's willingness to snatch at straws to support a deeply held idea, in Stoderl's case, the Baruchian authorship of I Bar 1:1-3:8. Just as unlikely but not as "disprovable" is the view of those following Kneucker who see Belshazzar as really representing Titus, and Nebuchadnezzar as representing the emperor Vespasian. According to this interpretation, Babylon would represent Rome.

their days . . . above the earth. The verbs are lacking in the LXX. The idiom, meaning "as long as the heavens and the earth exist," is an obvious hyperbole, first found in Deut 11:21 (but see also Ps 89:29[88:30], "and his throne as the days of the heavens").

12. *the Lord will give us strength.* Cf. Ps 29[28]:11.

sharpen our vision. Literally "enlighten our eyes"; cf. Pss 13:3[12:4], 19:8[18:9].

protection [skian]. Literally "shadow"; here more in the sense of Ezek 31:6 and Dan 4:12,21, where "shadow" is symbolic of protectiveness *and* power than in such expressions as "the shadow of God's hand" (Isa 49:2, 51:16) and "the shadow of his wings" (Pss 17:8, 36:7), where only protection is emphasized. Besides, "to live under the shadow of something" has in colloquial English today a decidedly pejorative tone.

for a long while. Literally "many days"; cf. Jer 29:5,28.

and find their favor. The argument is essentially that found in Jer 29:7: "Pray to the Lord on its [Babylon's] behalf, for in its welfare you will find your welfare."

13. *to date.* Literally "until this day"; cf. vs. 19.

the Lord's fury [thumos] nor his anger [orgē]. That these two terms are not exactly synonyms is clear from Eccles 48:10: "to calm the wrath [orgēn] of God before it breaks out in fury [thumou]."

14. *when making your confession [exagoreusai].* This verb can refer to congregational confession as here (so also Ezra 10:1; Neh 9:2) or to individual confession (Lev 5:5, 16:21; Num 5:7; Dan 9:20).

in the Lord's temple. See NOTE on "on the altar" in vs. 10.

festival day [ēmera eortēs]. Among Jews certain canonical books were prescribed reading at particular times or festivals, for example, The Megilloth: Song of Songs (Passover), Ruth (Feast of Weeks, or Pentecost), Lamentations (the Ninth of Ab), Ecclesiastes (Booths, or Tabernacles), and Esther (Purim). Presumably, since the LXX has no definite article here, the author of Baruch had no particular date or festival in mind (although the Hebrew text would have been the same in either case, namely, *bywm ḥg*). However, Thackeray (*The Septuagint and Jewish Worship*, 81-109) argued that our book was to be prescribed reading, as it was for the Syrian Jews, for the beginning of the Jewish New Year—as reckoned by the old Babylonian calendar which began in the spring (in the month of Nisan), not by the civil calendar which began in the fall.

and season [kai ēmerais kairou]. Cf. Eccles 33:8 (*kairous kai eortas*). The Syriac "on the days of the Lord" is obviously an inner-Greek error, *kuriou*, "Lord," being read for *kairou*, "season" (Heb. *môʿēd*). According to Thackeray's theory (p. 93), this "season" refers to a festival commemorating the three-week interval between the fall of Jerusalem on the seventeenth of Tammuz and the burning of the temple on the ninth of Ab.

COMMENT

Verses 1-14, functioning as an introduction and covering letter to the Book of I Baruch, raise for the reader more questions than they answer. Mistranslations of the Hebrew (see NOTES on "prisoners" in vs. 9, and "cereal offerings" in vs. 10) and errors originating during the transmission of the Greek text (see NOTE on "Ahava river" in vs. 4) account for some of our difficulties. Certain errors of fact (see NOTES on "the high priest Joakim" in vs. 7, and "his son Belshazzar" in vs. 11), as well as certain improbable assertions of "fact" (see NOTES on "in Babylon" in vs. 1, "to return them" in vs. 8, and "silver vessels . . . Zedekiah . . . had made" in vs. 8) further compound the difficulties.

But beyond all this is the general imprecision of content, for example, in vs. 2, *in the fifth year* after what? In what month? In vss. 7-8, exactly what happened *on the tenth of Sivan?* Is that the day the silver vessels of Zedekiah left Babylon or arrived in Jerusalem? In vs. 8, *who* took them to Jerusalem? In vs. 14, was the letter of Baruch originally designed to be read for any specific festival or season?

Then too, the sequence of events in the introduction is awkward and somewhat illogical, in that Baruch is said to have read aloud his message to those Jews in Babylon (1:3-4), to which the people reacted in several ways (1:5-9); then their covering letter is quoted (1:10-14), and finally, Baruch's message itself (1:15-5:9). The following sequence would be more logical: the Superscription (1:1-2), the setting (1:3-4), Baruch's message itself (1:15-5:8), the various reactions of the Babylonian Jews (1:5-9), including their covering letter to the Jews in Jerusalem (1:10-14). Eissfeldt (p. 594) believes that originally vs. 15 followed 1:2 and that vss. 3-14, which presuppose a different situation, were inserted later.

In sum, the effect of the introduction to Baruch's message is one of awkwardness and imprecision in both style and content which, in turn, heightens the reader's sense of the artificiality and secondary character of vss. 1-14. There is virtually nothing in them to support their claim to authenticity and much to discredit it. As for when they were written, all we can say at this point is at a time when a docile and cooperative attitude toward the Gentile masters was possible, if not palatable, for Jews (cf. vss. 11-12).

"It is obvious," wrote Oesterley (p. 259), "that the purported historical background of our book is merely a literary device adopted for the purposes of disguising the actual historical background."

II. A CONFESSION FOR THE PALESTINIAN REMNANT
(1:15 - 2:5)

1 15 And you shall say, "The Lord our God has been vindicated, but to us, to date, there's *a*open shame*a*—to the men*b* of Judah and the inhabitants of Jerusalem, 16 to our kings and nobles, and our priests and prophets, and our fathers— 17 *c*because we have sinned*c* in the Lord's*d* sight 18 and have disobeyed him and have not listened to the voice of the Lord our God *e*telling us*e* to follow the Lord's commandments which he had set before us.

19 "From the time when the Lord brought our ancestors out of the land of Egypt until now we have been disobedient to the Lord our God and *f*have been quick*f* not to listen to his voice. 20 So to this day *g*disasters have plagued us, namely, the curse which the Lord pronounced to his servant Moses at the time when he brought our ancestors *h*out of the land of Egypt*h* to give us a land flowing with milk and honey.

21 "Nevertheless, we did not listen to the voice of the Lord our God as found in the words of the prophets whom he*i* sent to us. 22 But we strayed, each following the dictates of his*j* own wicked heart, serving other gods and doing what is evil in the sight of the Lord our God.
2 1 So the Lord carried out his threat which he had made against us—against our judges who ruled Israel, and against our kings and nobles, and against the men of Israel and Judah.

a-a OL "redness of face"; see NOTE.
b LXX "man"; see NOTE.
c-c Emending *on*, "whose," to *oti*, "because"; LXX*L* omits; SyrH. has obelus here, and in its margin "This is not in the Hebrew"; see NOTE.
d Vulgate, Syriac have "Lord our God's"; see NOTE.
e-e See NOTE.
f-f So LXX*A*; Syriac "we rebelled"; see NOTE.
g LXX "the disasters"; many versions add a preceding "all."
h-h LXX*B* omits.
i LXX*A* "I"; cf. Jer 26[33]:5.
j "Our" in LXX*A*, OL, Vulgate.

2 *k*"*l*"What happened*l* in Jerusalem was unprecedented yet consistent with what is written in the law of Moses. 3 As for some among us, one ate the flesh of his son! Another the flesh of his daughter! 4 Moreover, he handed them over to all the neighboring kingdoms to be an object of reproach and horror*m* to all the neighboring peoples among whom the Lord had scattered them*n*. 5 Instead of prospering, they*o* became poor, because we had sinned against the Lord our God by not listening to his voice."

k With the exception of LXX^B, Greek MSS and versions add "By bringing upon us a great calamity such as"; see Note.
l-l LXX^B "what he did"; see Note.
m LXX "impassable"; see Note.
n LXX adds "there"; see Note.
o "We" in LXX^L and other versions.

NOTES

1:15. *The Lord our God has been vindicated.* Cf. 2:6. Literally "Righteousness [is] to the Lord our God." Cf. Dan 9:7: "You, Lord, have been vindicated" (*lk 'dny hṣdqh* MT). "Righteousness" (*dikaiosunē*) is used here in a legal sense; cf. 2:9. Verses 17-22 will spell out in greater detail the plight and punishment of the Jews as a vindication of God's honor, power, and justice.

to us. In the LXX this prepositional phrase is in the emphatic position and reflects accurately the Hebrew version of Baruch (cf. Dan 9:7: *wlnw bšt hpnym,* "but to us confusion of face").

to date. Cf. 1:20, 2:6,11,26. Literally "as this day," which represents the Heb. *kywm hzh,* as in Dan 9:7; I Kings 8:24.

there's open shame [*aischunē tōn prosōpōn*]. Cf. 2:6; II Chron 32:21; also Jer 7:19. Literally "confusion of faces." Although the reader may not be accustomed to seeing abbreviations used in biblical translations, it is nonetheless quite justified here and elsewhere (see Note on "What's the matter? . . . Relax" in Esth D 8, p. 218), for the Greek is both brief and emphatic. The phrase "to us, to date, there's open shame" is almost identical with Dan 9:7 ⊙, the only difference being that ⊙ has the singular, *tou prosōpou,* instead of the plural which both Bar and the LXX of Dan 9:7 have. The ultimate origin of this phrase in both Daniel and Baruch may be Ezra 9:7: "From the days of our fathers to this day we have been in great guilt; and for our iniquities we, our kings, and our priests have been given into the hand of the kings of the lands, to the sword, to captivity, to plundering, and *to utter shame, as at this day* [*en aischunē prosōpou ēmōn ōs ē ēmera autē*]" (italics added). The rendering of the OL, "redness of face," is somewhat misleading; for in I Bar 1:15 it is long-standing shame of the Jews, not just flushed embarrassment, which is the outward facial expression of their sin and failure.

to the men [anthrōpō] of Judah and the inhabitants of Jerusalem. Although the identical phrase occurs in Dan 9:7 (except that instead of *anthrōpō*, the LXX of Dan 9:7 has *anthrōpois*, and ⊖, *andri*), the entire phrase is essentially Jeremianic, occurring there (eight times, including Jer 4:4, 11:2,9, 17:25, 32:32, 35:13) and in II Kings 23:2; II Chron 34:30. In all these places, as well as Bar 2:1, the Greek renders the Heb. *'yš*, "man," used collectively, cf. GKC, § 123, *b*.

16. *kings . . . nobles . . . priests . . . prophets . . . fathers.* Although Dan 9:8 has a similar series (i.e kings, princes, fathers), Neh 9:32 [II Esd 19:32] is closer to Baruch by listing kings, princes, priests, prophets and fathers, while Jer 32[29]:32 is closest of all, having kings, princes, priests, prophets, men of Judah and the inhabitants of Jerusalem. (It should be noted that Jer 32:32 does not mention "our fathers" of I Bar 1:16, but in its place has "the men of Judah and the inhabitants of Jerusalem" [cf. Bar 1:15].) Other parallels to I Bar 1:16 are found in Jer 44[51]:17,21; and Neh 9:34[II Esd 19:34].

With some justice, Charles (p. 229) regards vss. 8-9 of Daniel 9 as expansions of Dan 9:7.

fathers. Possibly in the sense of "ancestors," including all generations (so Gifford); but more likely, especially since the entire verse enumerates people in authority, "fathers" here refers to the elders, the heads of families.

17. *because we have sinned.* The unemended Greek, with its *ōn* (see textual note *o-o*), makes little sense. The problem undoubtedly goes back to a mistranslation of the Hebrew Baruch which must have had *'šr*, as does the parallel passage in Dan 9:8 (*'šr ht'nw lk*, "because we have sinned against you") which is variously treated by the two Greek translations of Daniel (the LXX rendering *'šr* with *oti*, "because"; ⊖, *oitines*, "whoever").

In the Syro-Hexaplar, the presence of the obelus here and twice in 2:3, along with the marginal notes to the effect that the phrase is not found in the Hebrew, is very puzzling, especially since *the entire book* of I Baruch bore the obelus. (For details on the Hexapla and the obelus in general, and for the Syro-Hexaplar in particular, see *OTTV*, pp. 128-136, and 227-228, respectively.) The obelus in 1:17 must refer, therefore, to the biblical source for the author of Baruch, not to the Hebrew text of Baruch itself. (It cannot refer to Dan 9:8 because the latter *does have* the clause.) Harwell (pp. 8-9) argues that the obelus belongs to what he regards as the biblical source for Baruch here, namely, Dan 9:8, where the phrase "to our priests and our prophets" is lacking. However, the obelus is even more applicable to Neh 9:32 and Jer 32:32, where the phrase "because we have sinned" is not found, especially since both are closer to Bar 1:17 in content than is Dan 9:3.

in the Lord's sight [enanti kuriō]. In the Vulgate and Syriac the additional phrase, "our God," probably reflects their contamination by Dan 9:9, which begins with "Lord, our God."

18. While this verse is reminiscent of a number of passages in earlier biblical books (cf., for example, Deut 9:23; Jer 9:13[12], and especially 26[33]:4), its resemblance to them is more in thought content than Greek wording. Apart from I Bar 2:10, the closest parallel in Greek wording to Bar 1:18 is Dan 9:9c-10 ⊖.

telling us to follow. Literally "to follow"; "telling us" is supplied here in the interest of greater clarity.

the . . . commandments [*tois prostagmasin*]. Judging from Dan 9:10, one may assume that the Hebrew word lying behind this phrase in Baruch was *tôrōt*, the plural of *tôrāh*, in which case "commandments" refers, not to the Law of Moses, but to instruction, precepts, and statutes in general (see R. H. Charles, *A Critical and Exegetical Commentary on the Book of Daniel*, [Oxford at the Clarendon Press, 1929], pp. 229-230).

commandments which . . . before us. Cf. Deut 4:8, 11:32; Jer 9:13[12], 44[51]:10.

19. *From the time when . . . until now.* Literally "from the day which . . . and until this day." The author is speaking of an entire process, not emphasizing precise chronological points. Cf. II Kings 21:15; Jer 7:25.

we have been disobedient [*ēmetha apeithountes*]. This particular grammatical construction (cf. Deut 9:7,24 of the LXX) stresses the persistent, continuous character of the people's disobedience, i.e. it was not just a matter of occasional backsliding on their part.

been quick [*eschediasamen*]. The verb, which occurs in the LXX only here, has occasioned much discussion, and the adopted translation is far from certain. The verb, meaning "to be hasty," is understood to be used here in an ironical or sarcastic sense. But Whitehouse (p. 578) explains the LXX's "be hasty" as a misreading of Baruch's Hebrew text, namely, *mrdnw*, "we rebelled" (which the Syriac does have here) was misread as *mhrnw*, "we acted hastily"; but Harwell (p. 13) sees the Syriac as contaminated through the LXX of Dan 9:5,11, while Gifford (p. 259) regards the whole matter as one more indication of the independence of the translators of Daniel and Baruch.

20. Although a composite of biblical phrases, this verse is primarily Jeremiah (cf. Jer 11:4,5). The affinities between this verse and Dan 9:11 (especially "and the curse and the oath") and Dan 9:13 ("All this calamity has come upon us") are not nearly as great as Whitehouse (p. 578) would suggest.

have plagued [*ekollēthē*] *us.* Cf. 3:4. Literally "have stuck to us." The Greek verb is the same as in Deut 28:21,60 of the LXX; and contrary to many scholars (including Whitehouse, p. 578), it reflects in Baruch the Heb. *wattid-baq*, not *wattābō'*.

namely. Literally "and," the rest of the verse being appositional to "disasters have plagued us."

the curse which the Lord pronounced. For the sweeping comprehensiveness of the curse, see Deut 28:15-68; Lev 26:14-39.

21. *Nevertheless, we did not listen to . . . God.* Cf. 2:10, and Exod 15:26 of the LXX. Although identical with the Greek of Dan 9:10 (except that ☉ has *eisēkousamen* instead of *ēkousamen*), this clause in both its ideas and wording is common in the Bible, especially in Deuteronomy (cf. Deut 4:30, 9:23, 28:1,2,15) and Jeremiah (Jer 3:13, 9:13, 44[51]:23).

The concluding parts of I Bar 1:21 and Dan 9:10 are, however, quite different from one another, and each contains elements more reminiscent of Jer 26[33]:4-5 than of one another. Compare the following:

I Bar 1:21b   as found in [literally "according to all"] the words of the
                 prophets whom he sent to us. (Cf. Jer 26:5.)

Dan 9:10b ⊕   to walk in his laws [LXX "your law"] which he set before
                 us [LXX "you set before Moses and us"] by the hands of
                 his [LXX "by your"] servants the prophets. (Cf. Jer 26:4.)

Jer 26[32]:4-5   If you will not listen to me, to walk in my law [LXX
                 "laws"] which I have set before you, and to heed the words
                 of my servants the prophets whom I send to you urgently
                 [LXX adds "and I sent"], though you have not heeded.

22. *the dictates* [*dianoia*] *of his own wicked heart.* Cf. 2:8; I Chron 29:18 of
the LXX; Luke 1:51.

serving [*ergazesthai*] *other gods.* Only in Jeremiah (cf. Jer 27[34]:9,
30[37]:8,9) and Baruch (I Bar 2:21,23) is the Heb. *'bd,* "to serve a god," rendered by this Greek verb instead of the usual Greek equivalent *douleuein* (so
Thackeray, *JTS* 4 [1903], 263).

2:1. *carried out* [*estēsen*] *his threat.* Cf. 2:24. Literally "confirmed his
word." Here *estēsen* (Heb. *wayyāqem*) is understood in an unpleasant sense, in
contrast to its meaning in Deut 9:5; I Kings 8:20.

judges [*dikastas*]. Up to this point, I Bar 2:1 and Dan 9:12 are virtually
identical; but here Dan 9:12 uses a different word for "judges" (*kritas*), which
means rulers in general. Since I Bar 2:1 goes on to mention kings, nobles, and
people in general, none of whom are mentioned in Dan 9:12, "judges" in I Bar
2:1 refers to the historical judges. Given the audience listening to Baruch's
prayer (cf. 1:3-4), scholars find the specificity of Baruch's list of offenders here
highly appropriate.

2. Preceding the addition to this verse (see textual note *k*), the SyrH. has a
Hexaplaric asterisk, which, since all of Baruch was under the obelus, may mean
that the phrase was supplied from Dan 9:12. I Bar 2:1 makes sense without it,
but we cannot rule out the possibility of a copyist's error in LXX^B. The idea of
God's bringing great calamity is common enough in the Bible, especially in
Jeremiah (cf. Jer 35[42]:17, 36[43]:31).

What happened. Reading, with LXX^A and many versions, *epoiēthē* (Heb.
ne'eŝtâ, as in Dan 9:12) rather than with LXX^B ("what he did"). After all,
many of the terrible things that happened in Jerusalem were perpetrated by the
people themselves (cf. vs. 3), rather than caused by God.

was unprecedented. Cf. Dan 9:12. Literally "It was not done under the whole
heaven." For other ways of expressing in Hebrew a unique phenomenon, see
Ex 9:18, 10:6, 11:6. For the phrase "under the whole heaven," see I Bar
5:3; Deut 4:19; Dan 7:27.

yet consistent with (literally "according to") *what is written.* Cf. I Kings 2:3;
also II Chron 23:18, 35:12. The JB is too paraphrastic here with its "thus
fulfilling what was foretold." The point being made here is not that the terrible
unprecedented suffering in Jerusalem was predicted but that it was compatible
with God's justice (cf. vss. 6,9) and earlier threats.

in the law of Moses. Possibly this refers to the Decalogue; but more likely, it
is an allusion to passages such as Deut 28:15-68, and especially vss. 37,53-55.

3. *As for some among us, one . . . Another.* Literally "We ate, a man

[anthrōpon] . . . a man *[anthrōpon]*." The Gr. *anthrōpon* presupposes the Heb. *'yš*, "man," used in the distributive sense. Because none of the likely biblical sources for the verse have the distributive *'yš* (cf. Jer 19:9; Lev 26:29; Lam 2:20, 4:10), in the SyrH. an obelus was placed before each "a man" (so Harwell, pp. 8-9).

For a chilling example of cannibalism in all its gruesome detail, see Josephus' account of Mary the daughter of Eleazer eating her infant son during Titus' siege of Jerusalem (*Jewish Wars* VI 3.4).

4. *he handed them over to.* Literally "he put them in the hand of"; cf. the Hebrew and Greek of Gen 14:20.

to be an object of reproach and horror. Literally "for a reproach *[eis oneidismon]* and impassable *[kai eis abaton]*." The translation is far from certain. In the Hebrew Bible the word *šammâ* can mean either "a waste" or "a horror" (see BDB, p. 1031). Translated by various Greek words in the LXX, including *ainigma*, "taunt" (Deut 28:37) and *aphanismon*, "destruction" (II Kings 22:19; II Chron 29:8; Jer 25:9), *šammâ* is rendered by *abaton*, "impassable" only here and in those chapters of Jeremiah (e.g. Jer 25[32]:18, 44[51]:22, 48[31]:9) which Thackeray (*JTS* 4 [1903], 245, esp. 248, 263) has shown were done by the translator he designates as *beta*, who was responsible for translating Jeremiah 29:52 of the LXX. The biblical basis for vs. 4 is probably Jer 42[49]:18, where the Greek translator mistakenly chose the idea of "a waste" or "impassable land" instead of "a horror."

among whom the Lord had scattered them. Cf. 2:13; Deut 30:3; Jer 29:14, 40:12; and Dan 9:7. In all these places the Greek preserves a Hebraism, namely, *'ăšer . . . šām*, "where/whom . . . there" (see textual note *ⁿ*).

5. *Instead of prospering, they became poor.* Literally "they were below and not above." The JB's "Instead of being masters, they found themselves enslaved" is too paraphrastic and emphasizes too much the political aspects of their situation. The verse is ultimately based on Deut 28:13, where both the idea and our phrase occur and where the emphasis is far more on the financial and economic power of the Jews (see Deut 28:8-13) than on their political might. Cf. also Deut 28:43.

COMMENT

Unlike the confession in Dan 9:4-19, our passage is more a public acknowledgment of deserved punishment than a confessional prayer, that is, in I Bar 1:15-2:5 God is spoken *of*, not *to*. To give a modern analogy, one might liken I Bar 1:15-2:5 more to a public Pledge of Allegiance to the flag than to a communal confession to God in a worship service. (This analogy runs counter to I Bar 1:14; but presents no great difficulty since 1:1-14 and 1:15-2:5 may have had different authors [see introduction, p. 260].)

Strictly speaking, I Bar 1:14-2:5 is not so much a public confession as a didactic exhortation whose theme is "We have been very *justly* punished" or, as it is stated in vs. 15: "The Lord our God has been vindicated, but to us, to date, there's open shame—to the men of Judah and the inhabitants of Jerusalem."

In fact, 1:17 - 2:5 is essentially an elaboration of vs. 15. The present plight of the Jews is their *deserved* punishment; for as they themselves admit, ". . . we have sinned . . ." (1:17), "and have disobeyed him [the Lord] and have not listened . . ." (1:18), ". . . we have been disobedient . . . and have been quick not to listen to his voice" (1:19). Ignoring the warnings of Moses (see vs. 20) and the prophets (vs. 21), ". . . we strayed, each following the dictates of his own wicked heart, serving other gods and doing what is evil . . ." (1:22). Small wonder, then, that "the Lord carried out his threat . . ." (2:1), and that "What happened in Jerusalem was unprecedented yet consistent with what is written in the law of Moses" (2:1), i.e. instances of cannibalism (2:3), the exile and terrible humiliation of the Jews (2:4), and their continuing failure (2:5).

Taken at face value, 1:14 - 2:5 was designed by Baruch for the Jews who remained in Palestine during the exilic period, as I Bar 1:14 and 15b plainly indicate and as internal evidence seems to confirm. For example, the first person plural pronouns (*we, us, ours*) appear in every verse from 1:15 through 2:3, which surveys the period from the Exodus to the Exile. But beginning with 2:4, the point at which the period of the Exile begins, the third person plural pronouns appear for the first time: ". . . he handed *them* over to . . . all the neighboring [literally 'around us'] peoples among whom the Lord had scattered *them*. Instead of prospering, *they* became poor . . ." (italics added).

The problem of the relationship of I Bar 1:15 - 2:19 to Dan 9:4-19 will be discussed later on in detail in COMMENT II, pp. 291-293.

III. PRAYERS FOR THE EXILED
COMMUNITY
(2:6-3:8)

2 6 The Lord our God has been vindicated, but for us and our ancestors, to date, there is open shame. 7 All *those disasters*ᵃ ᵇwith
whichᵇ the Lord threatened us have happened to us. 8 But we have
not pacified the Lordᶜ by everyone turning away from the thoughts of
hisᵈ own wicked heart. 9 The Lord supervised these disasters; and the
Lord brought them upon us. So the Lord is just in all his actions
which he has ordered against us. 10 But we have not listened to his
voice telling us to follow the Lord's commandments which he had set
before us.

11 And now, Lord, the God of Israel, who brought your people out
of the land of Egypt with a strong hand, with portents and wonders,
with great power and outstretched arm ᵉso thatᵉ you made your reputation what it is today, 12 we have sinned; we have been irreligious; we
have broken, Lord our God, all your commandments.

13 Let your anger turn away from us since ᶠonly a few of usᶠ are left
among the nations where you have scattered usᵍ. 14 Listen, Lord, to
our earnest prayer. Deliver us for your ownʰ sake and grant us favor
before those who have taken us into exile 15 so that the whole world
may know that you are the Lord our God and that Israel and its descendants belong to you. 16 Lord, look down from your holy dwelling
place and give a thought to us. Strain your ears, Lord, and listen.
17 Open your eyes, Lordⁱ, and consider: those dead in the grave whose
breath has been taken from their bodies will not give glory or vindica-

---

ᵃ⁻ᵃ LXX *ta kaka tauta*, to which the LXX and versions add "which" (Gr. *a*). This is
probably a dittography with *tauta*.
ᵇ⁻ᵇ LXX *a;* LXXᴸ, OL, Vulgate, Syriac have "because."
ᶜ Vulgate adds "our God"; cf. Dan 9:13.
ᵈ So LXXᴬ ᴸ; LXX has "their"; see NOTE.
ᵉ⁻ᵉ LXX *kai,* corresponding to the Heb. *wa.*
ᶠ⁻ᶠ LXX "we few," to which LXXᴸ and most versions add "from many"; see NOTE.
ᵍ LXX adds "there"; see NOTE in 2:4.
ʰ LXXᴬ and many versions add "name's."
ⁱ Only LXXᴮ omits; cf. II Kings 19:16.

tion to the Lord; 18 but the person who remembers better days, who shuffles along with unseeing eyes, and the hungry person—these will give to you glory and vindication, Lord.

19 For it is not because of the merits of our fathers or our kings that we present our humble plea before you, Lord our God. 20 For you vented your furious anger against us just as you had promised through your servants the prophets *who said*, 21 Thus says the Lord:

> Bow your shoulders and serve the king of Babylon, and you will remain in the land which I gave your ancestors. 22 But if you do not listen to the voice of the Lord and serve the king of Babylon, 23 then I will silence the sounds of joy and merriment in the cities of Judah and *in the streets* of Jerusalem—the voice of the bridegroom and the voice of the bride—and the whole land shall be a waste, without inhabitants.

24 But we did not listen to your voice and serve the king of Babylon, and so you carried out the threat which you made through your servants the prophets, namely, that the bones of our kings* and the bones of our ancestors would be taken from their *resting places*. 25 And indeed they were exposed to the heat of the day and the frost of the night. *The people* died a dreadful death by famine, sword, and plague. 26 And so, because of the wickedness of the house of Israel and the house of Judah, you have made the* house that bears your name* as it is today.

27 And yet, Lord our God, you have treated us with complete fairness and with all your great tenderness 28 just as you had promised through your servant Moses on the day you commanded him to write your Law in the presence of the sons of Israel, and said,

> 29 If you do not listen to my voice, this large, swarming crowd will certainly be reduced to a small number among the nations where I will scatter them. 30 And I know that they will not listen to me, for they are a stubborn people. But in the land of their exile they will come to their senses, 31 and they will realize that I am the Lord their God. And I will give them *a receptive* heart

---

j-j LXX "saying"; LXX^B, SyrH. omit.
k-k LX "outside"; see Note.
l LXX^A adds, with Jer 8:1, "and the bones of our princes."
m-m LXX "place"; Jer 8:1.
n-n "They" in LXX and versions.
o Many LXX manuscripts and versions have "your."
p OL, Vulgate, Syriac, and SyrH. add "a waste" (Gr. *erēmon*).
q-q So LXX^L and versions: LXX has "a heart"; see Note.

and attentive ears. 32 They will praise me in the land of their exile and will remember my name. 33 They will repent of their stubbornness and wicked deeds, for they will remember the fate of their ancestors who sinned in the Lord's sight. 34 Then I will restore them to the land that I promised their forefathers, to Abraham, Isaac, and Jacob, and they will possess it; and I will increase their number, and they shall not dwindle. 35 And I will make with them an eternal covenant: I will be their God, and they shall be my people. Never again will I drive my people Israel out of the land that I have given them.

3 1 Almighty Lord, the God of Israel, a soul in anguish and a wearied spirit cries out to you. 2 Listen, Lord, and have pity*r*, for we have sinned in your sight. 3 You are enthroned for ever while we are continually passing away. 4 Almighty Lord, the God of Israel, hear the prayers of the men*s* of Israel and of the sons of those who sinned in your sight, who did not listen to the voice of *t*the Lord their*t* God, so that misfortunes have dogged us. 5 Remember not the misdeeds of our ancestors, but do remember right now your power and your reputation. 6 For you are the Lord our God, and we will praise you, Lord. 7 It is for this reason that you put the fear of you in our hearts: that we should call upon your name. And we will praise you in our exile, for we have purged our hearts of all the iniquity of our ancestors who had sinned in your sight.

8 *u*Consider us*u* today in our exile where you have scattered us— reproached, accursed, and devastated*v*—for all the misdeeds of our ancestors who rebelled against the Lord our God.

r Some Greek MSS, including LXX^A, and some versions add: "for you are a merciful God and have mercy."
s LXX and versions have "the dead"; see NOTE.
t-t "Your" in LXX^B, SyrH.; LX^A, Ethiopic omit.
u-u Literally "Behold, we are."
v LXX and versions "for penalty [*eis ophlēsin*]"; see NOTE.

NOTES

2:6. *and our ancestors.* Cf. Ezra 9:7. Literally "and our fathers." Cf. 1:16, where, the same Greek phrase occurs but probably with a different meaning (see NOTE on "fathers" in 1:16). I Bar 2:6 is identical with 1:15, except that this phrase replaces "to the men of Judah and the inhabitants of Jerusalem."

7. *All those disasters . . . have happened to us.* Cf. Dan 9:13.

with which the Lord threatened (lit. "spoke against") *us.* Cf. Jer 19:15, 35[42]:17, 36[43]:31, where *elalēsen epi,* "spoke against," is used in the sense of "threatened." The translation of the entire verse is uncertain, probably because of the imprecision of the Hebrew which used *'ašer,* which can be treated either as a relative pronoun as done here or as a conjunction (see textual note *b-b*).

8. *pacified [edeēthēmen] the Lord.* See Dan 9:13. Literally "entreated the face of the Lord." The Hebrew idiom represented (*hlh 't-pny*) is quite common and means "to make the face pleasant"; cf. Jer 26[33]:19; Exod 32:11; I Sam 13:12.

thoughts [noēmatōn] of his own wicked heart. Instead of "thoughts," in the corresponding phrase in I Bar 1:22 we have "dictates," and in Dan 9:13, "our wickedness."

his own. Since with respect to number Biblical Hebrew was not as insistent as English upon agreement of antecedents, the plural possessive adjective used by the LXX here, "their," may very well be original; but in the interest of our sense of English it has been emended; see textual note *d*.

9. In contrast to Dan 9:14 which this verse closely resembles, I Bar 2:9 is far from clear, as evidenced, for example, by such paraphrastic renderings as the JB's "And so the Lord has watched for the right moment to bring disaster on us, since the Lord gives a just return for what we do of all that he has ordered us to do." The verse in I Baruch may be an echo of the threat in Jer 44:27: "Behold, I am watching over them for evil and not for good."

supervised ("watched over") *these disasters.* Cf. Dan 9:14; Jer 1:12, 31[38]:28, 44:27. Since God had kept an eye on the impending calamities, their coming was not an expression of God's ignorance or helplessness but his justice (so vs. 9b).

brought them. "Them" is lacking in the LXX, but Vulgate and Syriac rightly supply it. See also Dan 9:14 ⊕.

the Lord is just. I.e. God was justified in doing what he did to his people (see first NOTE on 1:15). Cf. Jer 12:1; Lam 1:18.

in [epi] all his actions. For this unusual use of *epi* (Heb. *'l,* as in Dan 9:14), see Neh 9:33.

he has ordered against us. Translation is uncertain; for whatever it is worth, the corresponding passage in Dan 9:14 makes better sense, namely, "he has done."

10. With the substitution of "his voice" in place of "the voice of the Lord our God," this verse is identical with 1:18 (cf. also Dan 9:10 ⊕).

But we . . . voice. Identical with Dan 9:14 of the LXX.

11. *And now, Lord, the God of Israel.* The first prayer of the Exiled Community begins here (2:11-35). In the corresponding place in Dan 9:15, God is addressed in the LXX as "Master, Lord, our God," and as "Lord, our God" in ⊕.

with portents . . . outstretched arm. With the exception of this phrase which Daniel omits, I Bar 2:11 and Dan 9:15 ⊕ are strikingly similar, even to the point of reproducing Jer 32[39]:20-21 *in reverse order,* i.e. in both Baruch and Daniel the quote from Jer 32:20c ("and you made your reputation what it is today") comes *after* the quoted material of Jer 32:21. (For the significance of this agreement between Baruch and Daniel, which can hardly be coincidental, see COMMENT II, pp. 291-293.) Jer 32:21 is, in turn, reminiscent of Deut 6:21-23.

you made your reputation what. Literally "you made for yourself a name as." See Jer 32[39]:20c and Dan 9:15; also Neh 9:10; Gen 11:4; Isa 63:12.

12. *sinned [ēmartomen]* . . . *been irreligious [ēsebēsamen]* . . . *broken [edikēsamen].* This passage and its counterpart in Dan 9:15 ℮ (*ēmartomen ēnomēsamen* [LXX *ēgnoēkamen*]) are imperfect echoes of the concluding portion of I Kings 8:47: *ēmartomen ēnomēsamen ēdikēsamen* (cf. also Ps 106[105]:6).

been irreligious. Literally "acted impiously."

13. *Let your anger turn away from us.* Identical with the corresponding clause in 9:16, except that the latter has "anger *and wrath*" as in Num 25:4; Jer 30:24. With the exception of this clause, the rest of vs. 13, including the phrase "from many" (see textual note *f-f*), is virtually the same as Deut 4:27.

since only a few of us are left. If we accept the additional phrase "from many" (see above), then the Greek here is identical with Jer 42[49]:2.

Taken at face value, this statement in Baruch is relevant for the dating of this portion of I Baruch inasmuch as many scholars have dated it between the first century B.C. and the first century A.D. Yet as Pfeiffer has observed (p. 416), to claim that the Jews of the Diaspora are few in number is an absurd statement for a Jew of the first century A.D. to make; for by then the Jews were virtually everywhere. In fact, as early as 85 B.C. the Greek geographer Strabo wrote: "It is hard to find a place in the habitable earth that has not admitted this tribe of men [i.e. Jews], and is not possessed by them" quoted by Josephus *Ant.* XIV 7.2).

14. *Listen, Lord, to our earnest prayer.* "Earnest prayer" is literally "our prayer and our entreaty," which is hendiadys. Cf. Dan 9:17, especially ℮, which is closer than I Bar 2:14 to the original source for both Baruch and Daniel, namely, II Chron 6:19.

for your own sake. Cf. Jer 14:7; cf. also Isa 48:11; Dan 9:17.

15. *Israel . . . belong to you.* Cf. Deut 28:10; Jer 14:9. Literally "your name has been called upon Israel and upon his descendants." To have one's name "called upon" something meant to have proprietary rights to it, as in II Sam 12:28, where Joab said to David, ". . . encamp against the city, and take it; lest I take the city and it be called by my name [lit. "my name be called upon it"]."

In the corresponding verse in Daniel (Dan 9:18), it is the devastated city of Jerusalem, not the people, which bears God's name.

16. *look down from your holy dwelling place.* So Deut 26:15 and Isa 63:15 of the LXX. Literally "your holy house," our phrase refers not to the temple but to Heaven (cf. the Hymn of the Three Young Men, vs. 31[53]). To suggest that the clause repeats Dan 9:18 (so Whitehouse, p. 586) is not valid: Dan 9:18 ℮ represents almost exactly Hezekiah's words as recorded in II Kings 19:16.

Strain your ears ("Bend down your ear"), *Lord, and listen.* Identical with the Greek of II Kings 19:16.

17. *Open your eyes . . . and consider.* Identical with Dan 9:18 and II Kings 19:16.

those dead in the grave. Cf. Isa 38:18. The view of death and afterlife expressed here is the normative one of the Old Testament (cf. Pss 30:9, 88:10-12, 115:17; Eccles 3:19-22; see also Sira 17:27,28). For brief surveys on the subject, see E. Jacob, *IDB*, I, s.v. "Death," and II, s.v. "Immortality."

To view the verse as a Sadducee correction of a Pharisee interpolation (so Oesterley, *The Books of the Apocrypha*, 499-502) is to put the literary evidence of Baruch into a first-century Procrustean Bed, i.e. Oesterley regards as an interpolation all the evidence which does not fit into a first-century A.D. date.

breath. I.e. the "wind [Heb. *rûaḥ*] of life," as in Gen 6:17 of the LXX.

bodies [*splagchnōn*]. Literally "the viscera," i.e. the heart, lungs, intestines, etc.

will not give glory or vindication [*dikaiōma*] *to the Lord.* Identical with 2:18, except that there we have *dikaiosunēn* instead of *dikaiōma*, both of which presuppose the Heb. *ṣᵉdāqâ*, "justice." Our choice of the word "vindication" is debatable. Evidently the Jews are saying that the dead can neither praise God nor testify to the justness of his actions towards his people (see NOTE on "the Lord is just" in 2:9).

18. *who remembers better days.* Literally "who grieves over greatness." None of the ancient versions and no modern scholar has translated this particular clause to anyone's satisfaction other than his own. As Gifford so ominously put it, "There lurks behind it [i.e. the LXX] a corrupted Hebrew original" (p. 263).

The verse reflects the spirit and imagery, but not the wording, of Deut 28:65: "And among these nations you shall find no ease . . . but the LORD will give you there a trembling heart, and failing eyes, and a languishing soul."

who shuffles along. Literally "who goes stooping and weak."

with unseeing eyes. Literally "the eyes which omit." These are the eyes of those who are dazed and crushed in spirit, not by physical injury or aging.

and the hungry person. Cf. Jer 31[38]:25. Not the "hungering soul" as in the JB, but the individual who is physically hungry.

these ("they") *will give . . . vindication.* Cf. 2:17. Although the exiled Jews are broken in body and spirit, nonetheless they will by word and deed proclaim God's power and justice.

19. *not because of the merits* [*dikaiōmata*] *of our fathers.* Either this is a repudiation of the Jewish doctrine of the Merits of the Fathers (*zkwt 'bwt*) or, more likely, it antedates the formation of that doctrine (cf. Deut 9:4-6). Instead of *dikaiōmata*, "righteous deeds," Dan 9:18 has *dikaiosunais ēmōn*, "our upright deeds." For a brief discussion of the Talmudic doctrine of *zakut*, "merits," see Solomon Schechter, *Aspects of Rabbinic Theology* (New York: Shocken, 1961), 170-98.

present . . . you. Literally "throw down a plea before your face." Apart from this passage and Dan 9:18 (where the Hebrew is differently rendered by both the LXX and Ⓖ), the Hebrew idiom (*mpylym tḥnwnynw lpnyk*) occurs only in Jeremiah (Jer 36[43]:7, 37[44]:20, 38[45]:26, 42[49]:2).

20. *furious anger.* Hendiadys, literally "fury and anger." The verse is inspired by Jer 36[43]:7.

21. *Bow . . . and serve.* For imagery and concept, see Jer 27[34]:11-12.

23. *sounds of joy and merriment.* Literally "voice of joy and voice of merriment." The verse is based on Jeremiah (cf. Jer 7:34, 16:9, 33:10-11).

in the streets. LXX has *exōthen,* "outside," a mistranslation here and elsewhere in Jeremiah (cf. Jer 33[40]:10, 44[51]:6,9) of the Heb. *mēḥûṣôt,* "from the streets."

24. *threat which you made.* Literally "words which you spoke," referring to what follows in vss. 24-25a, namely, the contempt shown the bones of honored ancestors, as predicted in Jer 8:1-2a.

25. *exposed to . . . frost of the night.* Based on Jer 36[43]:30, which refers to King Jehoiakim who had treated Jeremiah's scroll in such a high-handed fashion as burning it, column by column, as it was being read to him (cf. Jer 36:20-27).

a dreadful death. Literally "in great miseries."

famine, sword, and plague. This terrible trinity occurs frequently in Jeremiah (cf. 14:12, 24:10, 32:36, 38:2), Ezekiel, and elsewhere (cf. Lev 26:25; II Sam 24:13; I Kings 8:37). "Plague" (LXX *apostolē,* "a sending forth") occurs also in Jer 32[39]:36; the Greek noun is probably derived from the Gr. *apostellein thanaton,* "to send forth death," as in Lev 26:25; II Chron 7:13; Jer 24:10, and elsewhere.

26. *because of the wickedness of . . . the house of Judah.* So Jer 11:17.

that bears your name. Cf. Dan 9:18. Literally "where your name has been called over it," an indisputable Hebraism (as in 2:4,13,17,29, 3:5).

as it is today. Contrary to some ancient translations of the LXX (see textual note *p*; also 1:2), the Greek does not say that the temple was "in ruins" (cf. 1:14); possibly one should understand here that the temple was merely run-down, standing in sharp contrast to its more glorious days. Scholars who follow Kneucker see here an allusion to the temple's state after A.D. 70.

27. *with complete* ("according to all your") *fairness* [*epieikeian*]. *Epieikeia* usually means "compassion" or "mercy" (cf. The Prayer of Azariah, vs. 19[42]; Wisd 2:19; II Macc 10:4); but it can also mean "equity," as in Wisd 12:18.

your great tenderness. Cf. Dan 9:18 Θ.

29. *large, swarming crowd.* Literally "large and numerous buzzing," the image being that the people are like a swarm of bees. As a noun, *bombēsis,* "buzzing," occurs only here in the LXX, where it renders the Heb. *hāmôn,* which in the LXX is variously rendered as *ochlos,* "crowd" (I Kings 20[21]:13), *ethnē,* "people" (Isa 13:4), and *plēthos,* "multitude" (Ezek 30:15). For the ultimate source of vs. 29, cf. Deut 28:62.

30. *come to their senses.* Literally "return to their heart"; cf. I Kings 8:47; II Chron 6:37; Dan 4:34,36; also Luke 15:17. In Hebrew thought the heart, not the brain, was the seat of the intellect. For a brief introduction to biblical psychology regarding "the heart," see R. C. Dentan, *IDB,* II, 549-550.

31. *heart.* The unemended Greek text (see textual note *q-q*) seems incomplete, for the people already had a heart. What they needed was either "another heart" (Jer 32[39]:39); "a new heart" (Ezek 18:31), "a heart to know" God (Jer 24:7); or, most likely, "a receptive (*sunetēn*) heart."

32. *in the land of their exile.* Cf. vs. 30. In the LXX, *apoikismou,* "exile" (Heb. *šᵉbî*) is used only in Jeremiah, e.g. Jer 43[50]:11.

33. *stubbornness.* Literally "their stiff back"; cf. "stubborn," literally "stiff-necked" (Heb. *qšh ʻrp*) in vs. 30.

the fate. Literally "the road" (i.e. their road of hardship and punishment); cf. *drkk,* "your way," in Ps 37:5.

34. *Then I will restore . . . possess it.* Cf. Jer 33[37]:3, which ultimately goes back to Lev 26:42-45 and Deut 30:1-5.

35. The first sentence in this verse is reminiscent of Jer 31[38]:33, while the second sentence roughly corresponds to the thought, but not the wording, of Jer 24:6 and 42[49]:10.

3:1. *Almighty [pantokratōr]. Pantokratōr* renders the Heb. *ṣb'wt,* "hosts," in II Sam 5:10, 7:8,26.

3. *enthroned.* Literally "seated," as in Pss 9:7, 29:10, and Lam 5:19, where the Heb. *škb* hints at that eternal majesty and transcendence of God described in more detail in passages like Isa 57:15. Cf. also Ps 9:4; Esth 5:1.

we. I.e. the remnant in exile, but cf. Jer 40:15, 27:10,15.

4. *men.* The Greek has "dead," which was undoubtedly a misreading of Heb. *mᵉtê,* "men," for *mētê,* "the dead," an error which also occurs in Isa 5:13, as well as in Aquila's rendering of Isa 41:14; Ps 17:14. Moreover, that "the dead" are not intended here is clear from I Bar 2:17. Prior to the general recognition of this error in translation (but see Isa 59:10; Lam 3:6, where "the dead" are those Israelites *close* to death), much ingenuity and imagination were used to identify these "dead" (for details on this as well as on other mistranslations of *mētîm,* see Gifford, pp. 266-268).

who sinned. That is, the parents and ancestors of the suppliants, not the exiles themselves. That this interpretation is correct is confirmed by the concluding clause of the verse where the sinners and *"their* God" are clearly distinguished from the "us" whom "misfortunes have dogged," i.e. the exiles, the attitude of the latter being in keeping with views expressed in Ezek 18:2; Lam 5:7; and Jer 31:29 (see COMMENT III, pp. 293-294).

7. *It is for this reason.* Literally "on account of this," referring to the people's praising God (cf. vss. 6b and 7b). Cf. also Jer 32:40b.

we have purged. The verse is a fulfillment of God's predictions mentioned in I Bar 2:30-32.

our ancestors who had sinned. This is another indication that the suppliants here are exiles, distinct from the suppliants of the prayer in 1:15 - 2:15.

8. *reproached, accursed, and devastated.* Literally "for a reproach and a curse and a penalty *(eis ophlēsin).*" Cf. 2:4, and Jer 42[44]:18. *Ophlēsin,* which in the LXX occurs only here, has occasioned much discussion (see Whitehouse, p. 588); the adopted reading follows Harwell (p. 16), who suggests that *mᵉšō'āh,* "devastation" (cf. Job 30:3, 38:27), was misread as *maššā'āh,* "loan," "debt" (cf. Prov 22:26.).

COMMENT I

I Bar 2:6-3:8 consists of three parts, each of which may originally have been independent: (1) the confession of the exiled community (2:6-10); (2) a prayer stressing their repentance (2:11-35); and (3) a prayer emphasizing their suffering innocence (3:1-8). All three of these components give unequivocal evidence of being Greek translations of a Semitic text (see NOTES on 2:6,11,13,26,29; 3:4,8).

If we say that faint echoes of older books such as Deuteronomy and Kings can be heard in these passages of I Baruch, then we must say that the Book of Jeremiah literally shouts out at us, the latter book being represented in almost every verse of this section of I Baruch (see NOTES *passim*). Not only that, but there are a number of readings in I Bar 2:6-3:8 which are peculiar to either the Hebrew text of Jeremiah (see NOTES on I Bar 2:13,19,25) or the Greek (see NOTES on I Bar 2:21,23,32). (On the very close parallels between I Bar 2:6-19 and Dan 9:4-19, see COMMENT II, below.)

In contrast to I Bar 1:15-2:5, which was designed for Jews who remained in Palestine during the exilic period (see COMMENT, pp. 281-282), I Bar 2:6-3:8 is clearly appropriate for a Jewish community living outside of Palestine, e.g. 2:13b ("only a few of us are left among the nations where you have scattered us"); 2:14b ("Deliver us . . . and grant us favor before those who have taken us into exile"); and 3:8a ("Consider us today in our exile where you scattered us"); cf. also 2:30c,32, 3:7c.

Apart from the claims made in I Bar 1:1-14 (whose veracity is certainly open to question) there is no indication of where these prayers originated, whether in the Babylonian remnant, the Egyptian, or one in each (cf. 2:13: "only a few of us are left among the nations where you have scattered us"; 2:29: "this large, swarming crowd will certainly be reduced to a small number among the nations where I will scatter them"). In any case, these prayers seem equally applicable to all Jewish communities of the Diaspora. As for when they may have been written, see below.

COMMENT II

As many scholars have observed and as the NOTES *passim* illustrate, there is a close relationship between the prayer in I Bar 1:15-2:19 and the one in Dan 9:4-19. (For a more detailed discussion of this matter, see the writer's article, *CBQ* 36 [1974], 312-320.)

The Greek translations of these two Hebrew prayers share a number of identical readings (e.g. I Bar 1:15b,21a, 2:1a,7b,10a, and 17a are identical with Dan 9:7b,10a,12a,13b,14 [last portion], and 18b, respectively) as well as a number of parallels which are closer to one another than either is to an older biblical source (e.g. I Bar 1:15a,18, 2:2,8,9,10,11,13a, and 19 are parallel to Dan 9:7a,9c-10,12c-13a,13c,14b,10,15,16b, and 18, respectively).

Are the two prayers so similar because one is based upon the other, or are they independently based upon a common source such as, for instance, a temple or synagogal liturgy? The great majority of scholars have argued that Baruch is based on Daniel, the most recent detailed presentation of this view being that by B. N. Wambacq, *Biblica* 40 (1959), 463-475, while Wenzel Stoderl (*Zur Echtheitsfrage von* Baruch 1-3,8 [Munster: Aschendorffschen, 1922]) is one of the few twentieth-century scholars to argue in detail for Daniel being based upon Baruch. A few scholars, including J. T. Marshall, R. H. Charles, and Louis Hartman, have subscribed to the view that both prayers are based upon a common source. The question is an important one, for one's view of the relationship of the two prayers is crucial for fixing the upper and lower limits for the prayer in I Baruch, if not the book itself.

Those scholars who defend the priority of Daniel's prayer are correct in pointing out that (1) Baruch's prayer is more diffused and repetitious than Daniel's, and is 47 per cent longer; and (2) in some of the parallel passages, the reading in Daniel is closer to the older biblical sources than is the one in Baruch (e.g. whereas I Bar 2:14 has, literally, "Hear, O Lord, our prayer and our supplication," Dan 9:17a ⊕ has "Now therefore, O Lord our God, hearken to the prayer of your servant and to his supplications," which is much closer to II Chron 6:19: "Yet have regard to the prayer of your servant and to his supplication, O Lord, my God." (For discussion of other possible examples, see B. N. Wambacq, *Biblica* 40 [1959], 463-475.) On the other hand, those scholars who think that Baruch is the basis for Daniel or that both prayers are based upon a common source, regard the first argument for Daniel's priority as unconvincing. As for the second reason, they point out that the same argument can be made for Baruch, i.e. in some of the parallel passages the reading in Baruch is closer to the older biblical source than is the one in Daniel (e.g. compare I Bar 1:16 and Dan 9:8 with Neh 9:32, also I Bar 2:12a and Dan 9:15c ⊕ with I Kings 8:47c, I Bar 2:15b and Dan 9:18c with Deut 28:10).

In any case, Daniel's prayer is *sui generis,* at least as far as the rest of the MT of Daniel is concerned, i.e. the prayer was not originally a part of the "final" form of Daniel but either an inclusion or an interpolation. Indications of its intrusive character include the following: (1) apart from Dan 1:2, the word "Yahweh" never occurs in Daniel outside the ninth chapter, where it occurs eighteen times; (2) the needless repetitions in the prayer's setting at the beginning (cf. vss. 3 and 4a) and the end (cf. vss. 20 and 21); (3) Dan 9:4-19 is written in "good" Biblical Hebrew (i.e. with no Aramaisms), in contrast to the rest of the Hebrew sections of Daniel, i.e. 1:1 - 2:4a, 8:1 - 12:13; (4) Daniel's prayer is inappropriate to the tone and emphasis of the Book of Daniel in general (see Pfeiffer, p. 774), and to the ninth chapter in particular (the context demands a prayer for personal illumination, not a communal confession, but see B. W. Jones, "The Prayer in Daniel ix," *VT* 18 [1968], 488-493); moreover, one can skip directly from vs. 2 to vs. 21 without losing anything in terms of either information or inspiration.

Regardless of the origin of Daniel's prayer, it is a mosaic of older biblical passages, liturgical in character and Deuteronomistic in style, being patterned after Deuteronomy, I Kings 8, and Jeremiah (esp. 26:2-6, 32:17-25, and ch. 44). (Maurice Gilbert, "La prière de Daniel, Dn 9, 4-19," *Revue théologique de Louvain* 3 [1972], 284-310, while regarding Baruch's prayer as based on Daniel's, nonetheless regards the latter as taken probably from a synagogal liturgy of the day [p. 292].)

As for fixing the upper and lower dates of the prayer's composition, we can say that since none of the prayer's concepts or phrases are peculiarly post-Ezra/Nehemiah, the prayer itself, or its *Vorlage* if it and Baruch are based upon a common source, may go back as far as the fourth century B.C. The *terminus ad quem* for the prayer is the first century B.C., the probable time of the book's translation into Greek (see p. 29).

The date-span for Daniel's prayer is of considerable importance for fixing the *terminus a quo* of I Baruch. (It is not in itself, however, the sole consideration for establishing the upper date of I Baruch since a comparable problem exists concerning the relationship of I Bar 4:36 - 5:9 to the eleventh chapter of the Psalms of Solomon, the latter being a pseudepigraphic work of the first century B.C. [see COMMENT II, pp. 314-316].) Even if Baruch's prayer be based upon Daniel's—a view which is far from certain—Baruch's prayer must be much older than is generally thought, especially since it also has no elements in either concept or wording which are peculiar to post-Ezra/Nehemiah books. Regardless of whether one prayer is dependent upon the other or both are dependent upon a common source, there is within Baruch's prayer itself no linguistic, literary, or theological reason why the Hebrew form of that prayer could not go back to the late fourth century B.C.

COMMENT III: I Bar 3:1-8

Whether these verses had the same author as 1:15 - 2:35 has been debated by scholars, with but little being settled. There is no external evidence to suggest that 3:1-8 is secondary, but the internal evidence may point in that direction. For instance, a word like the divine epithet *pantokratōr* (3:1) is nowhere else applied to Yahweh in 1:15 - 2:35; but on the other hand, an unusual phrase such as *eis oneidismon* in 3:8 also appears in 2:4. What little justification there is for thinking that 3:1-8 is secondary lies in a difference of tone and attitude, that is, while the prayer of the exiles in 2:6-35 is characterized by a deeply repentant mood (cf. 2:9c,12,24,27a), the prayer in 3:1-8 reflects an innocent, almost self-righteous attitude (cf. 3:4b-5a: "hear the prayers . . . of the sons of those who sinned . . . [and] did not listen to the voice of the Lord their God, so that misfortunes have dogged us. Remember not the misdeeds of our ancestors"; 3:7: "we have purged our hearts of all the iniquity of our ancestors who had sinned in your sight"; and 3:8b: "reproached, accursed, and devastated—for all the misdeeds of our ancestors who rebelled against the Lord our God").

The difference in tone and spirit between 2:6-35 and 3:1-8 is real, 3:2b notwithstanding. But if these two passages did have different authors, then, given the lack of external evidence, it must have been in the Semitic stage rather than the Greek.

IV. A POEM IN PRAISE OF WISDOM
AS EMBODIED IN THE LAW
(3:9 - 4:4)

3   9 Listen, O Israel, to the commandments that mean life;
    hear, and learn what wisdom means.
10 Why, Israel, why is it that you are in the land of your enemies,
    that you are growing old in a foreign country,
11 That you have been polluted with the dead,
    that you are numbered with those who *go down* to the
    grave?
12 It is because you have abandoned the spring of wisdom!

13 If you had walked in God's way,
    you would always have lived in peace.
14 Learn where wisdom is, where strength, where understanding
    is, and so learn where longevity and life are,
    where there is light for the eyes, and peace.

15 Who has found where she lives,
    or who has entered her treasure house?
16 Where are the rulers of the nations,
    and those who tamed the beasts of the earth;
17 Who dallied with the birds of the air,
    who hoarded up the silver and gold in which men trust,
    and whose possessions were unlimited,
18 Who *schemed for money* and were anxious,
    whose activities were beyond fully discovering?
19 They have vanished and gone down into the grave
    while others arose in their place.
20 A new generation was born and possessed the earth,
    but they did not know the way to knowledge,
21 Nor did they understand her paths or have any grasp of her.

a-a So most versions; Greek omits; see NOTE.
b-b Greek and Latin have "who worked the silver"; see NOTE.

Their sons have strayed far from her[o] way.

22 She was never heard of in Canaan,
    nor seen in Teman.

23 The sons of Hagar who search for worldly wisdom,
    the merchants of Medan[d] and Tema[e],
    the storytellers and those who seek understanding
    have neither discovered the way to wisdom
    nor understood her paths.

24 O Israel, how great is the house of God!
    And how vast his domain!

25 It is infinitely wide and immeasurably high!

26 In it were born the giants, famous from antiquity,
    very tall, expert in war.

27 But these God did not choose:
    he did not give them the way to knowledge.

28 So they perished for lack of wisdom;
    they perished through their own folly.

29 Who has ever gone up to heaven and taken her,
    and brought her down from the clouds?

30 Who has ever crossed the sea and found her,
    or has bought her with fine gold?

31 No one knows the way to her,
    or is concerned about the path to her.

32 But he who knows all things knows her;
    he has discovered her through his own intellect.
    He who created the earth for all time
    has filled it with four-footed creatures.

33 He sends forth the lightning, and it goes;
    he called it, and shimmering it obeys him.

34 The stars shone joyfully in 'their night watches';

35 He called them, and they answered, "Here we are!"
    They twinkled for the one who created them.

36 This is our God;
    no other can compare with him.

37 He grasped the whole way to knowledge,
    and gave her to his servant Jacob
    and to Israel whom he loved.

---

[o] So Syriac; Greek and other versions have "their"; see NOTE.
[d] "Merran" in the LXX and other versions; see NOTE.
[e] LXX and versions have *thaiman;* see NOTE on "in Teman" in vs. 22.
[f-f] Syriac "their places."

³⁸ After that she⁹ appeared on earth and lived among men.

4   ¹ She is the book of the commandments of God,
>   the Law that will last for ever.
>   All who keep her will live
>   while those who abandon her will die.

² Turn back, Jacob, and seize her;
>   approach the radiance of her light.

³ Do not surrender your glory to another,
>   or your privileges to a foreign people.

⁴ Israel, we are happy
>   because we know the things that please God!

⁹ "He" in Latin and Syriac; see NOTE.

NOTES

3:9. *Listen, O Israel, to the commandments.* While very reminiscent of Deut 5:1b, where Moses introduces the people to the Law, this command to listen and be attentive is even more a characteristic preface to advice-giving in the Wisdom genre (cf. Prov 1:8, 4:1,10, 5:7, 8:32-33).

commandments that mean life [*entolas zōēs*]. Literally "commandments of life." Here *zōē* is more than either the Gr. *bios*, "life," in a physiological sense, or even in a quantitative sense, "longevity" (Gr. *makrobiōsis*, as in 3:14); here and in vs. 14 *zōē* also includes, to use a much used phrase, "the quality of life" (cf. Prov 4:20-23; Rom 7:9-10.)

wisdom [*phronēsin*]. Cf. NOTE on "wisdom" in vs. 14.

10. *you are growing old* [*epalaiōthēs*]. The Greek, as in the rest of 3:9-4:4, suggests that the Jews have now been in exile for a long time and not for just a few years as the material in 1:1-3:8 would suggest (esp. 1:2,11).

11. *you have been polluted with* [*sunemianthēs*]. Possibly the Greek translator misread *nidmêtā*, "you are similar to," for *niṭmêtā* (so Kneucker, pp. 280*f*); but more likely, we should understand our author to be emphasizing either the exiles' sorry situation or, as in Jer 2:23 and Ezek 20:31, their pollution through idolatry.

numbered with . . . to the grave. Cf. 3:19 and Ps 88:4a[87:5], the latter probably being the basis for our verse, except that the LXX has *lakkon*, "pit," instead of *adou*, "grave." Cf. also Ps 55:15.

12. *It is because.* Although neither the Greek nor the other versions have this phrase, it is clearly presupposed, vs. 12 here being the speaker's answer to his rhetorical question posed in vss. 10-11.

the spring of wisdom [*tēn pēgēn tēs sophias*]! I.e. God himself, as in Jer 2:13: "they have deserted me, the spring of living waters," and Sira 1:1: "All wisdom [*sophia*] comes from the Lord, and is with him for ever" (but see also Sira 1:5: "The source of wisdom [*sophias*] is God's word in the highest heaven," and II Esd 14:47: "For in them [i.e. in certain books dictated by God through the mouth of Ezra] is the spring of understanding, the fountain of wisdom, and the river of knowledge").

13. *God's way.* Cf. Ps 27:11: "Teach me your way, Lord, and lead me on a level path"; cf. also Micah 4:2.

14. This verse, mentioning as it does, wisdom, understanding, longevity, life, and peace, is very reminiscent of Prov 3:13-18; cf. also Job 12:13.

wisdom [*phronēsis*]. By this point, three synonyms for wisdom have appeared which will occur repeatedly throughout the poem: *phronēsis* (Heb. *bînâ*), "prudence," "discretion" (vss. 9, 14); *sunesis* (Heb. *tᵉbûnâ*), "understanding," "intelligence" (vs. 14); and *sophia* (Heb. *ḥokmâ*), "wisdom" (vs. 12). While these differences in nuance and emphasis can be made concerning these synonyms, on occasion each word can represent all the others, e.g. *sophia* in vs. 23, *phronēsis* in vs. 28, and *sunesis* in vs. 23, although *sophia* seems to be the most comprehensive term.

strength [*ischus*]. Not physical, but moral and spiritual strength, as in Micah 3:8: "I am filled with power [LXX *ischun*], with the spirit of the Lord, and with justice and might [LXX *dunasteias*]."

life. More than just longevity, life (Gr. *zōē*) includes abundant joy and happiness, as in Ps 16:11.

15. *Who has found . . . or who has entered.* Cf. Job 28:12,20. Not until vs. 32ff is this question answered. Like Job 28:13-28, I Bar 3:16-31 answers in the negative, saying, "No mortal!" but then, in more positive fashion, I Bar 3:32 - 4:4 goes on to say that God, who alone possesses wisdom, granted it to Israel in the Law.

her treasure house. Cf. the Greek of Job 38:22 and Ps 135:7.

16. *rulers . . . tamed* ("ruled over") *the beasts.* Possibly this is a subtle allusion to Nebuchadnezzar (cf. Dan 2:37-38, 4:20-21; Jer 28:6, 28:14; Judith 11:7); but more likely, it refers to men of wealth and power in general.

17. *Who dallied with* [*empaizontes*] *the birds.* Although these men had the wealth and leisure to own sporting birds (but see Job 41:5, where the verb means "to tease"), the wealthy have not learned from the creatures the wisdom that they should have: "But ask the beasts, and they will teach you; the birds of the air, and they will tell you. . . . Who among all these does not know that the hand of the Lord has done this?" (Job 12:7,9); cf. also Job 35:11.

18. *schemed for money.* This verse has been very troublesome to translators (for details, see Whitehouse, p. 589), the primary reason being that this phrase, which is basic to a proper understanding of the entire verse, is far from clear. Instead of any mention of silversmiths, which both the Greek and Latin texts have and which seems inappropriate to the poet's argument, the Syriac has "who acquired silver," which suggests that the Hebrew verb here was *qōnê* (which can be translated either as "worked" or "acquired") and not *ḥārāšê*. Hence our "who schemed," refers to the rich and powerful of the preceding verses.

whose activities were beyond fully discovering. Literally "there is no searching out of their works"; cf. Prov 25:3; Job 5:9; Isa 41:28.

20. *A new generation was born.* Literally "the young saw the light"; cf. Job 3:16: "as infants that never see the light."

21. *Their sons.* I.e. the third generation, those mentioned in vs. 20 being their fathers, and those in vs. 19 their grandfathers.

from her (Greek "their") *way.* Most translators follow the Syriac and emend *autōn,* "their," to *autē,* "her," i.e. to Wisdom's way; but cf. Job 17:9, and Prov 5:8.

22. *in Canaan.* In later usage, as here, the Canaanites were the Phoenicians (cf. Zeph 2:5: "O Canaan, land of the Philistines"; and Matt 15:21-22), famous for their wealth and for their knowledge and skill in commerce (cf. Isa 23:8).

Elsewhere, the Old Testament recognizes the wisdom of the Phoenicians, as in Ezek 28:3-5: "You [i.e. the prince of Tyre] are indeed wiser than Daniel; no secret is hidden from you; by your wisdom and your understanding you have gotten wealth for yourself, and have gathered gold and silver into your treasuries; by your great wisdom in trade you have increased your wealth"; cf. also Zech 9:2-5; II Chron 2:7.

in Teman [*en thaiman*]. Although the same Greek word appears here and in vs. 23, two different cities were probably intended; for in the Septuagint *thaiman* is used to render two distinct Hebrew proper names (*tymn,* "Teman," and *tym',* "Tema"). Teman, the *thaiman* mentioned here, was an Edomite city famed for its wisdom, as in Jer 49:7: "Concerning Edom, thus says the Lord of hosts: 'Is wisdom no more in Teman? Has counsel perished from the prudent?' "; cf. also Obad vss. 8-9. In the Book of Job, a work from which our poet draws much inspiration, Eliphaz was a Temanite (cf. Job 2:11).

23. *sons of Hagar.* I.e. the Ishmaelites (cf. Gen 16:15; Ps 83:6), bedouin caravaneers who traded with Egypt (Gen 37:25).

worldly wisdom. Literally "understanding on earth," that is, they sought wisdom in the practical and material spheres of life.

Medan. The Gr. *merran,* which occurs here and nowhere else in the Bible, is probably a corruption of either Medan or Midian, these being the names of two of Abraham's sons by Keturah (cf. Gen 25:2). Such a corruption could easily have occurred first in the Hebrew, where the *r* and the *d* of the Hebrew script are very similar in appearance, and then in the Greek where the doubling of the *r,* while very rare in Hebrew, occurred frequently in the transliteration of Hebrew proper names, for example, Sarah (Heb. *śrh,* and Gr. *sarra* in Gen 17:19) and Gomorrah (Heb. *'mrh,* and Gr. *gomorras* in Gen 18:20).

Medan, being the name of a founder of a clan, was presumably also the name of a city in Arabia, probably located south of Tema, see S. Cohen, "Medan," *IDB,* III, 318.

Tema. Like Medan, Tema (Heb. *tym'*) was located in Arabia (see Gen 25:15; I Chron 1:30; Job 6:19; Isa 21:14; Jer 25:23); it is located approximately two hundred miles NNE of Medina and two hundred fifty miles SE of Aqaba (see S. Cohen, "Tema," *IDB,* IV, 533).

storytellers [*muthologoi*]. In the LXX, this word occurs only here and probably refers to foreigners who, like those mentioned in the Bible (cf. Ps 49:3-4), posed riddles and fables not unlike those in Judg 9:8-15; Ps 78:2; Ezek 17:2-10.

24. *house of God!* Here *oikos tou theou* is neither the temple nor an awesome place (as in Gen 28:17), nor even Heaven (cf. NOTE on "look down from your holy dwelling place" in 2:16), but, in keeping with its description in vss. 25-26, the entire universe (as in Philo *On the Incorruptibility of the World* XXI).

domain. Literally "place of possession."

25. *It is infinitely wide.* Literally "Great, and it does not have an end." By stressing here and in subsequent verses the immensity of God's universe the poet is, in effect, underscoring God's great grace in giving wisdom to Israel (cf. vss. 37-38.).

26. *the giants* [*oi gigantes*]. This is an allusion to the antediluvian semidivine beings of Gen 6:4 (the Nephilim) rather than to their "descendants," i.e. to such Palestinian tribes as the Anakim (cf. Num 13:28,33) or the Rephaim (cf. Deut 2:10-11,20-21). While instances of giantism were undoubtedly known to the Israelites (cf. I Sam 17:23-54; II Sam 21:16-22), a principal reason for inhabitants of Palestine believing that giants once ruled Canaan was the presence of megalithic structures in their midst (for a brief article on uninscribed, unfigured stones [or *maṣṣēbôt*], see Carl Graesser, "Standing Stones in Ancient Palestine," *BA* 35 [1972], 34-63). Anyone who has seen the Gezer "High Place" or, like the present writer, has excavated at the base of the Middle Bronze II Tower at Gezer, gazing up at its enormous stones each weighing several tons, can readily understand how a tradition concerning giants arose. For these features at Gezer, see William G. Dever, H. Darrell Lance, and G. Ernest Wright, *Gezer I: Preliminary Report of the 1964-66 Seasons* (Hebrew Union College: Jerusalem, 1970), I, 41-44.

In I Baruch, as elsewhere in the intertestamental literature, the antediluvian giants are viewed in an unfavorable light, as arrogant (so Wisd 14:6), rebellious creatures (Sira 16:7), who literally devoured people (I Enoch 7:4) as well as one another (Jub 7:22-23).

28. *they perished.* I.e. the Nephilim: cf. Wisd 14:6: "For even in the beginning, when arrogant giants were perishing, the hope of the world took refuge on a raft, and guided by your hand left to the world the seed of a new generation"; cf. also III Macc 2:4.

29. *Who has ever gone . . . and brought her down.* The interrogative pronoun (as in Deut 30:12-13; Prov 30:4; and Isa 40:12-18) anticipates a negative answer (so vs. 31). Although vss. 29-30a are reminiscent of the phraseology and imagery of Deut 30:12-13, almost the exact opposite idea is expressed there, where it is the close proximity and easy availability of the desired object which is stressed, not its unattainability by man unassisted by God.

from the clouds. Says Wisdom of herself in Sira 24:4-5a: "I dwelt in high places, and my throne was in a pillar of cloud. Alone I have made the circuit of the vault of heaven"; cf. also Wisd 9:4a.

30. *or has bought her with fine gold?* For the same idea, much expanded, see Job 28:12-19.

32. *for all time.* Here as elsewhere in the Old Testament, the earth is "eternal" in comparison with man rather than in any absolute time sense (cf. Eccles 1:4: "A generation goes, and a generation comes; but the earth remains for ever").

four-footed creatures. "Creatures" might be a better translation since *ktēnōn tetrapodōn* probably stands for all animals and not, as in Acts 10:12, for a particular subdivision of the animal kingdom.

33. *lightning [phōs].* Literally "light"; but see Job 36:30,32, 37:11,15, where the Heb. *'ôr,* "light," refers to lightning. Moreover, our verse, as well as vs. 35, seems to be based on Job 38:35: "Can you send forth lightnings, that they may go and say to you, 'Here we are'?" (cf. also Job 37:3).

shimmering. Literally "quivering" or "trembling," referring to the appearance of the lightning rather than, as interpreted by most scholars, fear personified.

34. *shone joyfully.* Literally "shone and were glad." While the metaphor of the stars doing guard duty is clearly present here (as in Sira 43:10), the phrase is even more concerned with stressing their beauty and light as witnessing to God's power (cf. Ps 148:3b, "Praise him all you shining stars").

35. *He called them.* Cf. Isa 40:26: "He who brings out their host [i.e. the stars] by number, calling them all by name; by the greatness of his might, and because he is strong in power not one is missing." The stars do not *come* out: they are *brought* out. Unlike the Greek view of the ordered universe (Gr. *kosmos*), where law or secondary causation prevails, the Hebrew view of Nature was personal, "natural" events being immediately dependent upon divine activity. On the Hebrew concept of Nature, see H. Wheeler Robinson, *Inspiration and Revelation in the Old Testament* (Oxford at the Clarendon Press, 1946), 1-15; also Walther Zimmerli, *Die Weltlichkeit des Alten Testamentes* (Göttingen: Vandenhoeck & Ruprecht, 1971), 20-31.

"Here we are!" The "we" refers to the stars, notwithstanding the fact that in Job 38:35, it is the lightning that says this. Cf. also Judith 9:6. The Syriac's "behold us" reproduces the Hebrew original, *hinnēnû.*

twinkled. Literally "shone with joy."

36. The verse's thought is Deutero-Isaianic (cf. Isa 43:10-11, 44:6, 45:18).

37. *He grasped . . . knowledge [epistēmēs].* Here the question first posed in vs. 15 is finally answered; cf. also Job 28:23: "God understands the way to it [i.e. to wisdom], and he knows its place."

gave her to his servant Jacob and to Israel. Cf. Sira 24:8, where God said, "Make your [i.e. Wisdom's] dwelling in Jacob, and in Israel receive your inheritance"; see also Isa 44:1: "But now hear, O Jacob my servant, and Israel whom I have chosen."

38. *After that [meta touto].* I.e. after Wisdom was given to the Jews via the Law; but many scholars regard the phrase as a clumsy introduction to a verse which, they argue, is a Christian interpolation.

she appeared [ōphthē]. No other verse in I Baruch has been more commented upon or has created more controversy than this one, primarily because in the Greek no subject is expressed apart from the verb. Greek and Latin Fathers, especially during and after the Arian Controversy of the fourth century A.D., saw the verse as a prediction of the incarnation of Jesus Christ (cf. John 1:14: "And the Word became flesh and dwelt among us, full of grace and truth; and we have beheld his glory, glory as of the only Son from the Father"). In the nineteenth century, many Protestant scholars followed Kneucker and Schürer in regarding the verse as a Christian interpolation, which it may have been.

For an exhaustive list of Church Fathers who discussed vss. 36-38, see Reusch, including his Appendix.

Nevertheless, the present context indicates that Wisdom (the "her" of vs. 37 and the "she" of 4:1), and not God (the "he" of vs. 37), is intended. Such an interpretation is consistent with Sira 24:10-12, where Wisdom says: "In the holy tabernacle I ministered before him [i.e. God], and so I was established in Zion. In the beloved city likewise he gave me a resting place, and in Jerusalem was my dominion. So I took root in an honored people, in the portion of the Lord, who is their inheritance"; cf. also Wisd 9:10, where Solomon prays for Wisdom: "Send her forth from the holy heavens, and from the throne of your glory send her, that she may be with me and toil, and that I may learn what is pleasing to you." Cf. also Prov 8:1-4,31.

Referring to Wisdom here as "she" is not without its dangers; for as K. V. H. Ringgren has observed, "Wisdom is depicted [in 2:9-4:4] as an independent entity, but it is not very clearly shaped as a personal being. It should be noted that the terms vary: . . . phroēsis . . . sophia . . . epistēmē" (Word and Wisdom [Lund: Hakan Ohlssons, 1947], p. 114).

4:1. *She is the book of the commandments . . . , the Law.* Wisdom, then, is given to Israel in the form of the Torah. Identification of Wisdom with the Pentateuch is found also in Sira 24:23: "All this is the book of the covenant of the Most High God, the law which Moses commanded us as an inheritance for the congregations of Jacob." Pfeiffer (p. 421) and others have suggested that *prostagmatōn*, "commandments," represents the Greek translator's misreading of the Heb. *tôrat*, "law of," for *tôrôt*, "laws of."

that will last for ever. Cf. Sira 1:15: "She [Wisdom] made among men an eternal foundation, and among their descendants she will be trusted."

keep her. I.e. hold Wisdom, although the "her" could as easily refer to the "Law" (Heb. *tôrāh*) which, like "Wisdom" (Heb. *ḥokmāh*), is in the feminine gender.

2. *the radiance of her light.* Cf. Prov 6:23a: "For the commandment is a lamp and the teaching a light."

3. *your glory.* I.e. Israel's possession of Wisdom in the form of the Law. Cf. Deut 4:8: "And what great nation is there, that has statutes and ordinances so righteous as all this law which I set before you this day?" Cf. also Deut 4:32-37, where Israel's glory, or privileges, is spelled out in greater detail.

a foreign people [*ethnei allotriō*]. Whether this is an allusion to the Hellenists and their pretensions to "wisdom" in Greek philosophy (so Tov, p. 557) or to the Christians who reject the Law of Moses (so Kneucker, Marshall, and others) depends upon the date one assigns to the poem, i.e. whether or not one regards the poem as pre-Christian in date.

4. *that please God!* Cf. Wisd 9:18b: "And men were taught what pleases you [God], and were saved by wisdom."

COMMENT

The poem, a very clear and coherent statement on the nature and importance of Wisdom, consists of three parts: (1) the introduction, in which the problem (3:9-11) and its solution (3:12-14) are stated briefly; (2) the main body of the argument (3:15-4:1), and (3) the conclusion (4:2-4), in which Israel is again enjoined to embrace Wisdom, i.e. to observe the Law, just as Israel knows she should.

In the main passage of the poem, the problem is concisely stated ("Who has found where [Wisdom] lives?" [3:15]) and is then answered, first in negative terms (3:16-31), and then in positive (3:32-36). As for the negative statement, neither the powerful nor the wealthy (vss. 16-19), nor later generations (vss. 20-21), nor the reputedly wise (vss. 22-23), nor even the antediluvian giants (vss. 24-28)—absolutely no mortal through his own unaided power (vss. 29-31) has truly possessed Wisdom. On the other hand, the all-knowing, omnipotent God *does* know Wisdom (vss. 32-36), and that wisdom he has given to Israel in the form of the Law (3:37-4:1).

In the poem's literary type as well as its theology and phraseology there are faint biblical and intertestamental echoes, if not always exact parallels. In terms of both literary form and content (see NOTES *passim*), Job 28:12-22,23-27 provides the model for I Bar 3:29-31,32-37. The view that Wisdom is to be identified with the Law (I Bar 3:37-4:1) is also found in Sira 24:8-23. In addition, ch. 9 of the Wisdom of Solomon figures prominently in our psalm (see NOTES *passim*). To a lesser extent, there occurs in our poem phraseology and theology reminiscent of Psalms, Proverbs, and Deutero-Isaiah (see NOTES *passim*), but virtually nothing of Jeremiah!

The material in 3:9-4:4 differs from what preceded it in a variety of ways: it is poetry, not prose; it breathes a different spirit and has a different point of view (i.e. didactic rather than prophetic); its name for the Deity is different ("Lord" is not used at all); and most important of all, it either had a different Greek translator or was originally composed in Greek.

Scholars have been very much divided over the question of the original language of the poem, although the majority, past and present, favor Hebrew. (J. T. Marshall [*HDB*, I, 253] argued for its having been composed originally in Aramaic; but Whitehouse [pp. 571-572] refuted Marshall's argument point for point.)

While there is evidence of a Hebrew origin (cf. NOTES on "schemed for money" in 3:18; "Medan" in 3:23; and "Here we are!" in 3:35), it is by no means conclusive. For instance, Harwell's evidence of a Hebrew basis for all of I Baruch (pp. 53-55) comes mostly from I Bar 1:1-3:8; on the other hand, Harwell has succeeded reasonably well in translating the Greek of I Baruch into good Biblical Hebrew. The unit 3:9-4:4 is rendered in regular 3/3 meter.

That the poem was translated by the same Greek editor who did I Bar 1:15-3:8 is improbable (see Kneucker, pp. 76-80; and H. St. J. Thackeray,

JTS 4 [1903], 261-266), inasmuch as basic words and phrases in the Greek of the two parts of I Baruch. 1:15-3:8 and 3:9-4:4, are very different. For example, the Heb. *wa,* "and," is translated by *kai* in the Greek prose part, but in the poetry part by *de* or is omitted; the Heb. *kî* is rendered by *oti* in the prose, and by *gar* in the poetry.

It is difficult to date the poem. The second century B.C. and the first century A.D. represent the extreme limits among the overwhelming number of scholars, past and present. Relevant to fixing the poem's *terminus a quo* is the fact that the Diaspora is depicted in the poem as being of long-standing (see NOTE on "you are growing old" in 3:10). More important, the poem was certainly written after Job, and possibly after both the Wisdom of Sira of the second century B.C. and the Wisdom of Solomon, dating from the first century B.C. Whether the poem, or better, all of I Baruch, was written in the first century B.C. or later depends upon the relationship one sees between I Bar 4:36-5:9 and Ps of Sol 11:3-8 (those who think the poem is based upon Psalm of Solomon 11 usually date I Bar 3:9-5:9 to the first century B.C. or later). But since I Bar 4:36-5:9 is not dependent upon Ps of Sol 11:3-8 (see COMMENT II, p. 315), there is no internal or external evidence to date the poem any later than the first century B.C. Where the poem was written is unknown, although, if it was originally in Hebrew, then a Palestinian provenance is probable.

In its present form, Poem is quite incongruous with what precedes (1:15-3:8) and follows it (4:5-5:9). Poem's sapiential character, for instance, is in sharp contrast to the prophetic stance of the psalms around it. Then too, whereas the God of Israel is regularly called "the Lord" (Gr. *o kurios*) in 1:15-3:8, and in 4:5-5:9 "the Eternal" (Gr. *o aiōnios*), in the Wisdom poem the regular title is "God" (Gr. *theos;* Heb. *'elōhîm*). The name preferred for the Deity is significant; for as Pfeiffer observed, "In this poem God is the universal sole Creator, whose outstanding attribute is wisdom. . . . Anthropomorphisms occur elsewhere (2:11,16f,29; 3:4), but not in the poem on wisdom; the same is true of human feelings and mental functions attributed to God (1:13; 2:13, 20; 3:5; 4:9,25,27; 5:5)" (pp. 423-424).

V. A PSALM OF ENCOURAGEMENT
AND HOPE
(4:5 - 5:9)

4   5 Take courage, my*a* people,
     who keep Israel's name alive.
6 It was not for destruction
     that you were sold to the nations:
Because you provoked God
     you were handed over to your enemies.
7 For you angered him who made you
     by sacrificing to demons and not to God.
8 You forgot the eternal God
     who had reared you;
You also grieved Jerusalem
     who had nursed you.
9 For when she saw the anger
     that came upon you from God,
     she said:

Listen, you neighbors of Zion,
     for*b* God has brought great sorrow upon me.
10 For I have witnessed the captivity of*c* my sons and
     daughters, which the Eternal has brought upon them.
11 Joyfully I had nurtured them,
     but in tears and sorrow I sent them away.
12 Let no one exult over me,
     a widow and deserted by so many.
I have been left desolate because of the sins of my
     children: because they turned away from God's law.
13 They did not know*d* his statutes

a "God's" in several versions.
b So LXX^A and most versions; LXX omits.
c LXX^A and Latin add "my people."
d "Observe" in LXX^A.

or walk in the ways of God's precepts
or tread the paths of discipline
as he justly required.

14 Let the neighbors of Zion come here.
   Remember the captivity of my sons and daughters
   which the Eternal has inflicted upon them.
15 For he brought upon them a nation from far away,
   a ruthless nation of strange speech,
   who had neither respect for the aged
   nor pity for the young.
16 They carried off the widow's dear sons
   and deprived the *e*lonely woman*e* of her daughters.

17 But I, how can I help you?
18 For he who brought these disasters *f*upon you*f*
   will also deliver you from the power of your enemies.
19 Go your way, my children, go,
   for I am left desolate.
20 I have taken off the robe of peace
   and put on the sackcloth of suffering.
   I will cry out to the Eternal*g* as long as I live.

21 Take courage, my people, cry to God;
   and he will rescue you *h*from tyranny*h*,
   from the power of your enemies.
22 For I have put my hope for your rescue in the Eternal
   and joy has come to me from the Holy One because
   of the mercy which will soon come to you from
   your deliverer, the Eternal.
23 For in sorrow and tears I sent you away,
   but God will give you back to me in joy and
   gladness for ever.
24 For just as the neighbors of Zion have already witnessed your captivity, so they will soon see your
   deliverance,
   which will come upon you with great glory and with
   the splendor of the Eternal.

---

e-e LXX*A* *monogenē*, "desolate."
f-f So LXX*A* *L*.
g "The Most High" in LXX*A* and Latin.
h-h LXX*A* omits; probably a gloss.

²⁵ My children, patiently endure the wrath that has come
   upon you from God;
   yourⁱ enemy has hounded you,
   but soon you will witness his destruction
   and will put your foot upon ^jhis neck^j.
²⁶ My pampered ones have traveled difficult roads;
   they were carried off like a flock snatched by
      enemies.

²⁷ Take courage, my people, and cry to God,
   for you will be remembered by him who brought
      ^kthese disasters upon you^k.
²⁸ For just as you had the idea of straying from God,
   so now turn around and seek him ten times as hard.
²⁹ For he who brought these disasters upon you
   will bring with your deliverance unending joy.

³⁰ Take courage, Jerusalem:
   he who named you ^lwill console^l you.
³¹ Those who abused you and gloated over your fall will
   be wretched.
³² The cities which enslaved your children will be wretched.
   She who received your sons will be wretched.
³³ For just as she gloated over your fall
   ^mand was happy about your ruin^m,
   so shall she grieve over her own desolation.
³⁴ And I will take away her prideⁿ in her great population,
   and her insolence will be turned into sorrow.
³⁵ For fire from the Eternal will burn in her for many a day,
   and she will be inhabited by demons for a long time.

³⁶ Jerusalem, look around to the east, and see the joy that
   is coming to you from God.
³⁷ See, your sons whom you sent away are coming!
   They're coming, gathered from east and west at the Holy
   One's command, rejoicing in God's glory.

ⁱ LXX^B omits.
^{j-j} So, many versions; LXX has "their necks."
^{k-k} LXX and versions omit; cf. vs. 18.
^{l-l} "Consoles" in LXX^A and many Greek MSS.
^{m-m} Syriac omits; possibly a gloss.
ⁿ LXX^A has "idol"; see NOTE.

5   1 Jerusalem, take off your dress of sorrow and distress,
           and put on for ever the glorious beauty that is from God.
         2 Wrap about you the cloak of righteousness that comes from
               God;
           place the tiara of the glory of *the Eternal* on your head.
         3 For God will display your splendor to every nation[p]
           under heaven.
         4 For you shall ever have as your name from God
           "Peace through Righteousness
           and Glory through Devotedness."

         5 Jerusalem, arise and stand upon the height and look to the
               east,
           and see your children gathered from west to east at the
           Holy One's command,
           rejoicing that God has remembered them.
         6 Although they left you, led away on foot by their enemies,
           God is bringing them back to you
           borne aloft in glory, like *a royal throne*.
         7 For God has commanded that every high mountain and the
           everlasting hills be flattened and the valleys filled up
           to make the ground level so that Israel may walk
           safely in God's glory.
         8 The woods and every fragrant tree provided shade
           for Israel at God's command.
         9 For God guided Israel with joy by the light of his glory,
           with the mercy and justice that come from him[r].

o-o LXXᴬ, Ethiopic, "the Holy One."
p LXX and versions omit.
q-q LXXᴬ, OL, Vulgate, "sons of the kingdom"; see Note.
r LXXᴬ, OL, Syriac have "God."

Notes

4:5. *Take courage, my people.* So also vss. 21 and 27. Here through vs. 9,
the psalmist is speaking in the name of the Lord, gently chiding the people even
as he consoles them. The universal God of the Wisdom poem is now once more
Yahweh, the personal God of Israel, who is concerned for his chosen people of
the covenant.

who keep Israel's name alive. Literally "the memorial [*mnēmosunon*] of Israel." Cf. Exod 3:15 and Job 18:17, where the Heb. *zēker* (LXX *mnēmo-sunon*) is parallel to the Heb. *šēm* (LXX *onoma*, "name"); cf. also Pss 9:7, 33:17, 108:15 of the LXX, where *mnēmosunon* is used in the sense of "memory of a name." According to the author, the Jewish remnant he is addressing preserves not only the name/memory of the patriarch Jacob/Israel (cf. Gen 32:28), but by implication, the promises God made to the people through him.

An alternate explanation is that of Harwell and Torrey who regard "the memorial of Israel" (Heb. *zkrwn yśr'l*) as a misreading of *zkrw yśr'l*, "remember, Israel" (cf. Isa 44:21; 46:8,9).

6. *not for destruction . . . sold.* Cf. Esth 7:4 of the LXX. In keeping with Isa 50:1 and 52:3, where God affirms that Israel was not sold for money, "sold" here is used by the psalmist in a metaphorical sense of "go into servitude or exile" (cf. Lev 25:39; Deut 28:68; Rom 7:14).

7. *to demons* [*daimoniois*]. I.e. to false gods and idols, as in Deut 32:17-18, the passage on which the verse is based; cf. also Pss 106:37-38, and 96:5: "For all the gods of the peoples are idols [Heb. *'elîlîm*; LXX *daimonia*]." Given the possibility, however, that the poem dates to the intertestamental period, one could interpret these "demons" as a distinctive order of malevolent spirits, subject to the Devil or Belial, as in the Twelve Patriarchs (Test Asher 1:9; Test Benjamin 5:2; Test Levi 19:1, Test Zebulun 9:8) and the Dead Sea scrolls, e.g. *The Manual of Discipline* iii 22-24. For an excellent but brief introduction to the subject of demons in the Bible and intertestamental literature, see T. H. Gaster, "Demon, Demonology," *IDB*, I, 817-824.

8. *the eternal God.* Cf. Isa 40:28 and Sus vs. 42.

had reared [*tropheusanta*]. Literally "had nursed," as in Exod 2:7, where a wet nurse was sought for the infant Moses. Given the strongly patriarchal character of Yahwism, one might argue that "nursing" was an inappropriate activity for a male deity like Yahweh; but see Hosea 11:4, where Yahweh seems to refer, quite literally, to nursing when he says, "And I bent down to them and fed them"; see also Ezek 16:4-7.

Jerusalem. From here to the end of the book, this personification of the city as the long-suffering mother of her people is sustained with great consistency and effectiveness. Cf. Isa 54:1-6; Tobit 13:9.

9. *neighbors.* That is, neighboring cities and peoples (cf. vss. 14 and 24, and Jer 49:18), be they Jewish or Gentile; ordinarily *paroikoi* in the LXX means "stranger."

10. *the Eternal.* Cf. Isa 26:4, 40:28. *O aiōnios*, which does not occur in I Bar 1:1 - 4:4, is a favorite appellation for God in the poem (cf. 4:14,20,22,24, 35, 5:2), the other names being "God" (4:7,12), "the God" (*passim*), and "the Holy One" (4:22,37, 5:5). "Lord" (YHWH) does not appear.

12. *a widow and deserted.* The imagery is reminiscent of Deutero-Isaiah (cf. Isa 49:21, 54:1,4).

they turned away from God's law. The Greek is identical with Job 34:27 of the LXX.

13. *discipline* [*paideias*]. The Greek word probably represents the Heb. *mûsār*, which means both "corrective punishment" (cf. Jer 2:30) and "instruction" (cf. Prov 1:2,7).

as he justly required. Literally "in his righteousness."

14. *Remember.* It is impossible to say whether this change in the verse from the third person ("let . . . come") to the second person ("remember")— which seems so awkward in English—is original or whether the person in either the first or second verb was changed; all three views have their defenders (see Whitehouse, p. 592).

15. While either the Roman or, more likely, the Seleucids were probably intended here, this verse is based upon Deut 28:49-50, where the oppressors are obviously the Babylonians: "The Lord will bring a nation against you from afar . . . a nation whose language you do not understand, a nation of stern countenance, who shall not regard the person of the old or show favor to the young." Cf. also Jer 5:15, 6:22-23 and Ezek 3:5.

17. Having spoken to the neighboring cities up to this point (vss. 9b-16), Jerusalem now comforts her exiled children, insisting that while she herself cannot help them, God will (vss. 17-29).

20. *taken off the robe . . . put on the sackcloth.* For the reverse process, see Isa 52:1.

sackcloth of suffering [*tēs deēseōs*]. *Deēsis* literally means "prayer," "request"; but in Ps 22:24[25] it is used to translate the Heb. *'ānût,* "suffering."

as long as I live. Literally "in my days," as in Isa 39:8 and Ps 116:2.

22. *the Holy One.* Cf. 4:37, 5:5; see also Isa 41:20; Hab 3:3; Pss 71:22, 78:41; Sira 48:20.

mercy . . . from your deliverer. Cf. the LXX of Ps 24:5: "He shall receive blessing from the Lord, and mercy from God, his deliverer."

24. *glory and . . . splendor* [*lamprotētos*]. Cf. Isa 60:1-3 of the LXX.

25. *put your foot upon his neck.* Literally "walk upon their necks"; cf. Greek of Deut 33:29.

26. *pampered ones* [*trupheroi*]. The word occurs in Deut 28:56; Esth D 1; Isa 47:1,8; Micah 1:16.

like a flock snatched by enemies. In the interest of maintaining the metaphor, Harwell (p. 54) suggests that "enemies" (Heb. *'ybym*) is a misreading of *z'bym,* "wolves," an ingenious suggestion but one without any manuscript support.

28. *turn around . . . ten times as hard.* Those who would reconstruct the Hebrew text of I Baruch have considerable difficulty in expressing this idea in Biblical Hebrew (for details, see Whitehouse, p. 573; Harwell, p. 55), all of which suggests either that this verse, if not the poem itself, was originally Greek or that the Greek translator sometimes translated rather freely (so Pfeiffer, p. 423).

30. Speaking now as a prophet for God (cf. vs. 34), the poet begins the second part of his poem (4:30 - 5:9), speaking to Jerusalem and offering her hope and salvation.

who named you. This is not an allusion to the name of the city (so KJ: "for he that gave thee that name") but to the fact that God had adopted the once-pagan city and had even built his temple there (cf. Ps 46). In the Old Testament, the city of Jerusalem is given many titles, including "the City of the Lord" (Isa 60:14); "the City of the Lord of Hosts" (Ps 48:8); "the city of God" (Pss 48:1, 87:3); "the Holy City" (Isa 48:2, 52:1); "the city of Righteousness" (Isa 1:26); "Hephzibah" (Isa 62:4); see also Isa 62:2: "You shall be called by a new name." In discussing the word "Jerusalem," Millar Burrows has observed, "The meaning of the name is undoubtedly 'foundation of Shalem [Shalem, or Shulmanu, being a Canaanite god].' The traditional interpretation, 'city of peace' is as inaccurate etymologically as it is inappropriate historically" (*IDB*, II, 843).

32. *The cities*. That is, the Babylonian cities where the Jewish exiles were scattered.

She. That is, Babylon, although some scholars, following Kneucker, would understand this as an allusion to Rome.

34. *pride* [*agalliama*]. LXX^A reads *agalma*, "idol," a corruption of *agalliama*, while the Syriac has "idols and pride," which is clearly a conflation and indicates that the Syriac was a translation of a Greek, not a Hebrew original.

into sorrow [*eis penthos*]. The Greek seems to be a Hebraism, *le'ēbel*.

35. *fire from the Eternal*. Although this statement refers to the fate of Babylon, it is also applicable to other situations and circumstances; but Kneucker certainly exceeded the bounds of evidence and credibility in seeing here an allusion to the eruption of Mount Vesuvius in A.D. 79, in which Pompeii was destroyed.

inhabited by demons [*daimoniōn*]. The verse is inspired by Isa 13:19-21: "And Babylon . . . will be like Sodom and Gomorrah. . . . It will never be inhabited. . . . But wild beasts will lie down there, and its houses will be full of howling creatures; . . . and there satyrs [Heb. *śā'îr;* Gr. *daimonia*] will dance"; see also Isa 34:14; and NOTE on "to demons" in 4:7.

36. In the manner of the prophets (cf. Isa 49:18, 60:4), the psalmist, who means us to understand that he is Baruch, foresees for the moment with such great vividness the return of the exiles that he even speaks of the event in the past tense (but see textual notes ^r-r and ^8-8, as well as COMMENT II, p. 315.

37. *gathered from east and west*. Cf. Ps of Sol 11:3. I.e. from everywhere, as in Isa 43:5, 59:19; Zech 8:7. Cf. I Bar 5:5 for a restatement of the entire verse.

God's glory. "Because," says Theodoret, "it is not in their own power . . . but God who . . . restored their liberty." Apart from the dominant idea of the return of the people to Jerusalem, the concept most stressed in 4:36-5:9 is God's Glory (Gr. *doxē*), which is mentioned seven times in just eleven verses (4:37, 5:1,2,4,6,7,9). Glory, a difficult word to define with precision in both Hebrew (*kbwd*) and English (see G. Henton Davies, *IDB*, II, s.v. "Glory"), here refers to God's rather than man's.

5:1. *dress of sorrow and distress*. Cf. 4:20. To delete "and distress" here as well as other phrases in the psalm on the grounds of "metrical considerations" (so Rothstein) is to assume too much here about our knowledge of Hebrew meter and poetic structure.

and put on. This is a familiar metaphor in Isaiah (cf. Isa 52:1: "put on strength . . . put on your glory, Jerusalem," and 61:10: "put on . . . garment of salvation").

glorious beauty that is from God. Literally "the beauty of the glory from God." Cf. Ps of Sol 11:8a: "Put on, Jerusalem, the garments of your glory." The striking parallels between I Bar 4:36-5:9 and ch. 11 of the Psalms of

Solomon, a pseudepigraphic work, are discussed in some detail in COMMENT II, pp. 314-316.

2. *Wrap . . . cloak [diploida] of righteousness.* A clear echo of Isa 60:10; but see also Job 29:14: "I put on righteousness, and it clothed me," to which the LXX adds "like a cloak."

the tiara [tēn mitran]. Here, neither a helmet (so Syriac) nor a turban (such as the *mitra* worn by Aaron in Exod 28:37 of the LXX), the *mitra* is a head decoration worn by both married (cf. Judith 10:3, 16:8) and unmarried women (cf. Isa 61:10).

The image in these verses of I Baruch is that of Jerusalem as a lovely woman, not the mighty warrior.

4. *you shall ever have as your name.* For other honorific names given to Jerusalem, see Isa 1:26; "the city of righteousness, the faithful city"; Isa 60:14: "city of the Lord, the Zion of the Holy One of Israel"; Jer 33:16: "The Lord is our righteousness" and Ezek 48:35: "The Lord is there."

Peace through Righteousness. This phrase, like many religious names and slogans in all religions, is a type of "religious shorthand" for expressing ideas which are quite clear to the initiates but not necessarily to the outsider or to later generations. Presumably the idea here is that Jerusalem's peace is the fruit of her righteous living, as in Isa 32:17; see also James 3:18.

Glory through Devotedness [theosebeias]. Literally "glory of the fear of God." Cf. Gen 20:11 and Job 28:28 of the LXX. Again, the idea seems to be that Jerusalem's glory results from her fear of the Lord. "Fear" here, however, probably involves love as well, hence, the appropriateness of the Vulg.'s *pietas,* "devotion."

5. Although this verse is an elaboration of 4:36, it is even more a mosaic of Deutero-Isaiah phrases (compare "Jerusalem, arise," with 51:17; "stand upon the height" with 40:9; "and see your children gathered" with 60:4; and "from west to east" with 43:5), but most of all, the verse is a striking parallel to Ps of Sol 11:3: "Stand upon the height, Jerusalem, and see your children assembled together from the east and west by the Lord." One could construct our verse out of phrases from Deutero-Isaiah, but only by skipping around from chs. 51 to 40 to 60 and 43 (see COMMENT II, p. 314).

from west. Literally "from the setting of the sun."

that God has remembered them. Literally "in God's remembrance"; cf. 4:27-29.

6. *like a royal throne [ōs thronon basileias].* A troublesome phrase (see textual note *q-q*; also the debate on it between Whitehouse [p. 595] and his editor, R. H. Charles [pp. 573-574], the latter seeing *ōs thronon basileias* as a mistranslation of the Heb. *ks' mlkwt,* "as on a royal throne," where the Hebrew particle *k* was used in a pregnant sense [see BDB, p. 455, note b; also GKC, § 118*s*] and should have been rendered as *ōs epi,* "as on").

The striking contrast here is between the ignominious departure of the exiles and their glorious return, i.e. not the fact that they walked away but that they would be carried back (but see Isa 66:20, 49:22).

7. Ultimately, if not immediately, based on Isa 40:4-5a ("Every valley shall be lifted up, and every mountain and hill be made low; . . . And the glory of the LORD shall be revealed"), the verse is even more reminiscent of Ps of Sol

11:5 ("High mountains be flattened so as to be level ground for them"). This is especially to be noted in view of the other parallel between I Bar 5:5 and Ps of Sol 11:3.

in God's glory. An attribute of which is light, as in vs. 9.

8-9. *provided. . . . guided.* Predicting the return of God's children to Jerusalem in 4:36-5:9, our prophet perceives the glorious event with such force and vividness that he describes it, at first, as happening (cf. 4:36-5:7), and then in 5:8-9 as having already happened (for an alternate explanation of this phenomenon of change in tense, see COMMENT II, pp. 315-16).

Compare our verse with Pss of Sol 11:6b-7a: "The woods shaded them. . . . Every fragrant tree [*pan zulon euōdias*] God made spring up. . . ." (*Xulon euōdias* occurs nowhere else in the canonical Old Testament; but in Enoch 100:24 fragrant trees are a symbol of God's blessing.)

COMMENT I

The psalm differs from the preceding Poem in Praise of Wisdom (3:9-4:4) in several ways. Whereas the Wisdom poem drew its inspiration, content, and phraseology primarily from Job, Ecclesiastes, and the Wisdom of Solomon (see COMMENT, p. 303), the psalm drew its inspiration primarily, if not almost exclusively, from Deutero-Isaiah, i.e. Isaiah 40-55 (see NOTES on I Bar 4:8,12,15,20,24,30,35,37, 5:1,2,5,7).

Whereas the Wisdom poem had almost the character of a logical argument, complete with statement of the problem, presentation of evidence, and conclusion (see COMMENT, p. 303), this psalm is more of a dramatic rehearsal of the past and a prediction of the future. The psalm has two speakers: first the psalmist, speaking to the exiles in the name of the Lord (4:5-9a); then Jerusalem, speaking first to her hostile neighbors (4:9b-16), then comfortingly to her exiled children (4:17-29); and again, the psalmist comforting Jerusalem, assuring her that her enemies will be punished (4:30-35) and that her children will soon be restored to her (4:36-5:9).

The psalm consists of seven "stanzas" of unequal length, the first three beginning with "Take courage, my people [in 4:5; "my children" in 4:21,27]" while the fourth stanza, beginning with "Take courage, Jerusalem" (4:30), serves as a transition to the next three stanzas, each of which begins by having Jerusalem commanded to do something: "Look around to the east" (4:36); "Take off your dress of sorrow and distress" (5:1); and "Arise and stand upon the height" (5:5). It is these last two stanzas, especially 4:36-37, 5:5,7,8a, which parallel Ps of Sol 11:3-8 (see COMMENT II, p. 315).

There are other differences between the Wisdom poem and the psalm. In Psalm, God is regularly called "the Eternal," but never "Lord" (see NOTE on 4:10). While the Wisdom poem has about it an air of quiet calm, if not almost complete detachment, the psalm pulsates with a spirit of hope and expectancy—God is on the verge of doing something wonderful!

Scholars are much divided over the question of whether Psalm was originally composed in Greek (so Marshall, Whitehouse, Oesterley) or Hebrew (so Kneucker, Thackeray, Harwell, Pfeiffer, Eissfeldt). Although no Hebrew text is extant, Harwell has done a reasonably good job of translating the Greek back into Hebrew with 3/3 meter. Nonetheless, the indisputable examples of Hebraisms offered by Whitehouse (pp. 571-572), Harwell (pp. 53-55), and especially Kneucker (pp. 32-46), occur overwhelmingly in 1:1 - 3:8, rather than equally throughout 1:1 - 5:9.

COMMENT II

Reminiscent of phrases and concepts in Deutero-Isaiah (see esp. NOTES on 5:5,7), stanzas VI-VII (4:36 - 5:9) bear an even more striking resemblance to the eleventh chapter of the Psalms of Solomon, a pseudepigraphic work not to be confused with the canonical Book of Psalms. Composed originally in Hebrew but extant only in Greek and Syriac, the Psalms of Solomon consists of eighteen psalms. It dates from Pharisaic circles of first-century B.C. Palestine (see H. E. Ryle and M. R. James, *Psalms of the Pharisees, Commonly Called the Psalms of Solomon* [Cambridge University Press, 1891], pp. xxxvii-lxi; see also G. Buchanan Gray, *The Psalms of Solomon, APOT*, II, 625-652; but for the view that it may not be Pharisaic in origin, see Robert B. Wright, "The Psalms of Solomon, the Pharisees, and the Essenes," *Septuagint and Cognate Studies* 2 [1972], 136-147), and was evidently used in synagogal services (cf. technical musical terms in 8:1, 17:31, 18:10). Because of the apparent references to the Roman general Pompey (cf. 2:2,6,30-33, 8:16-23), many scholars would date the work ca. 70-40 B.C., although some, such as Eissfeldt (p. 612), regarding 17:9,13-16 as allusions to Herod the Great (39-4 B.C.), would lower the time span by a decade or so. If these psalms do not all come from the same hand, they come from the same generation, one which held strong beliefs in apocalypticism (chs. 15 and 17) and resurrection (3:12, ch. 18). Ryle and James (p. xc), on the basis of Greek style as well as their own conclusion that I Bar 4:36 - 5:9 is based on Ps of Sol 11:3-8, date the Greek translation to the middle of the first century A.D. For a brief introduction to this psalter, see P. Winter, *IDB*, III, s.v. "Psalms of Solomon"; see also Eissfeldt, pp. 610-615.

The striking similarity between I Bar 4:36 - 5:9 and Ps of Sol 11:3-8 cannot be coincidental (see NOTE on Bar 5:8), inasmuch as their parallels do not ever violate the relative verse sequence of either Baruch or the psalm, that is, vss. 5, 7, and 8 of ch. 5 of I Bar roughly correspond to vss. 3, 5, and 6-7, respectively, of ch. 11 of the Psalms of Solomon. (For a more detailed treatment of this whole problem, see the writer's article in *CBQ* 36 [1974], 312-320).

The problem, then, is identical with the one concerning the relationship between the prayers in I Bar 1:15 - 2:19 and Dan 9:4-19, that is, is I Bar 4:36 - 5:9 based upon Ps of Sol 11:3-8, is the reverse true, or are they independently based upon a common source such as a now-lost synagogal liturgy? The answer to this question is crucial for establishing not only the upper and lower dates for the composition of this particular portion of I Baruch but also the entire book, since many scholars regard 4:5 - 5:9 as the most recent portion of the entire book.

The great majority of scholars have followed Ryle and James (pp. lxxii-lxxvii, 100-103) in regarding I Bar 4:36 - 5:9 as dependent upon the psalm, Wilhelm Pesch being almost alone among "recent" scholars in arguing in detail for the opposite view (*ZAW* 67 [1955], 251-263). A few scholars, including R. H. Charles (see his Editor's Note in *APOT*, I, 573-574), Harwell (p. 65), Pfeiffer (p. 422), and Gelin (p. 286), have followed Kneucker (pp. 43*f*) in regarding these two psalms as probably dependent upon a common source.

As Pesch (p. 257) has rightly pointed out, I Bar 5:1-4 seems to be a composite of phrases in the earlier stanzas of I Bar 4:5-37 (that is, 5:1 // 4:20, 5:4 // 4:30), all of which suggests that, contrary to scholarly consensus, at least the components of stanza VI (5:1-4) are not based on Ps of Sol 11:3-8. (I Bar 5:2, for instance, is nothing more than a natural extension of the imagery and thought in 5:1)

With regard to stanza VII (5:5-9), however, the situation is quite different. Here the parallels with Ps of Sol 11:3-8 are incontestable:

I Bar 5:5	Jerusalem, . . . stand upon the height . . . and see your children gathered from west to east . . .
Ps of Sol 11:3	Jerusalem, stand upon the height and see your children gathered from east to west . . .
I Bar 5:7	God has commanded that every high mountain . . . be flattened . . . to make the ground level
Ps of Sol 11:5	high mountains he flattened to make the ground level . . .
I Bar 5:8	The woods and every fragrant tree provided shade for Israel at God's command.
Ps of Sol 11:6b-7a	. . . the woods shaded them . . . every fragrant tree God made to spring up . . .

As to which passage is prior, we can at least say that, contrary to Pesch, the psalm is definitely not based on Baruch. The fact that stanza VII is somewhat longer and more diffused than the psalm (cf. 5:5 with 11:3, and 5:7 with 11:5) plus the fact that the psalm is, as most scholars agree, "concise, well ordered and logically developed" (so Ryle and James, p. lxxiv) are two reasons for saying that the psalm is not based upon Baruch. (The psalm itself consists of three well-integrated parts: (1) the directions to trumpeters in Jerusalem [11:1]; (2) the first announcement to Jerusalem that the exiles have returned [11:2-7]; and (3) the instruction to Jerusalem to celebrate the wonderful thing God has done (11:8-9).)

But there is a third and most decisive reason: whereas in the psalm the description of God's treatment of his people is given in the past tense (cf. 11:3-7), the description in I Baruch is at first narrated as happening (cf. 4:36 - 5:7), and then in the middle of stanza VII (5:8-9), without any logic or justification, *as having already happened*. This illogical shift in tense from present to past in Stanza VII is best explained by concluding either that Stanza VII is based on the psalm or that both are independently based upon a now-lost liturgical piece which was cast in the past tense. But in either case, it is clear that the psalm is not based on Baruch.

Being the last paragraph in I Baruch, stanza VII (5:5-9) is at the precise place where a later addition could most easily have been appended, namely, at the very end of the book. Keeping in mind the importance attached to the number "seven" in the Bible, it is quite probable that a later editor chose to make the psalm seven stanzas long, and that he drew his inspiration from Psalm of Solomon 11, his attention perhaps being first drawn there by the similarity of 11:3 to the first line of stanza V (9:36). If this was indeed the case, then stanza VII may have been composed originally in Greek. The alternative explanation is that both the psalm and stanza VII are independently based upon a synagogal liturgy which would, in all likelihood, have been in Hebrew.

If the above is essentially correct, then the psalm, beginning with I Bar 4:5 and ending with 5:4 (not 5:9), must be dated on the basis of internal evidence *and without reference* to the date of Psalm of Solomon 11. Unfortunately, the internal evidence in 4:5-4 is not very helpful; there are no allusions to specific, identifiable contemporary persons or events. (To be sure, various statements in our psalm clearly describe a period sometime between the fall of Jerusalem in 597 B.C. [4:14,24,26,31-33] and the fall of Babylon in 539 B.C. [4:25,32b-35], but scholars regard these passages as symbols appropriate to later historical circumstances.) One can say, however, that time and time again it is Deutero-Isaiah and not later books that provide the imagery and wording for the psalm. In short, while I Bar 5:5-9 must be dated not earlier than the late first century B.C., when a later editor added it, the Psalm of Encouragement and Hope (4:4-5:4) may have been written any time between the fourth and the second centuries B.C., the first half of the second century being the most probable.

EPISTLE OF JEREMIAH

INTRODUCTION

The Epistle of Jeremiah is not an epistle, nor was it written by Jeremiah.
These two facts, which are accepted as such by virtually all scholars today,
best explain why the book is part of the Apocrypha. There is no compelling reason to regard the Epistle of Jeremiah as a letter. Indeed, with
the exception of its Superscription (vs. 1) and opening paragraph (vss.
2-7), all the evidence is to the contrary. The Epistle is really a homily, a
tirade, or harangue against idols and idolatry; it has none of the characteristic features of a letter, not even a closing. That all this is the case is
clear from a study of its contents and structure.

Contents of Epistle

The Epistle consists of ten strophes, or stanzas, of unequal length, each
one (with the exception of the first and last) ending with a slight variation
of essentially the same refrain, namely, "So how can anyone consider them
gods? So have no fear of them!" Because each stanza is but a restatement
of this theme, and because there is no perceivable progression of thought
in the "poem," capsule summaries of each stanza sound very much like
one another.

Vss. 1-7	As punishment for their sins, God says through his prophet Jeremiah that the Jews must live in Babylon for up to seven generations, surrounded by impressive scenes of idolatry; but they must worship only the Lord, whose angel will protect them.
Vss. 8-16	The Babylonian gods cannot help themselves, let alone others. They can neither speak nor dress themselves; even worse, they cannot protect themselves from insults, rust or moths, thieves or war.
Vss. 17-23	Helpless and unable to protect themselves or their property, the idols are also senseless, unable to see and unaware of being either mortally "injured" or defiled by soot and unclean animals.

Vss. 24-29	Although outwardly impressive, the idols are helpless, without feelings, breath, or the ability to move. Small wonder, then, that their priests are ashamed of them, and that the priests and their wives exploit them and that unclean women defile their offerings.
Vss. 30-40a	If these idols were really gods, they would not tolerate their defilement by female attendants, tabooed mourning practices, or dishonest priests. Unable to protect themselves, they cannot protect kings or widows, wealth or life.
Vss. 40b-44	Bel and other gods are dishonored by the Chaldeans themselves, especially by their women's acts of sacred prostitution.
Vss. 45-52	Idols are only the creation of men, the works of mortals who some day must themselves die. (The rest of the stanza is but a repetition of ideas expressed in earlier stanzas; cf. vs. 45a with vs. 8, vs. 47 with vss. 35-38, and vs. 48 with vs. 15.)
Vss. 53-56	In this brief strophe nothing new has been added to the argument. Old points have merely been restated (cf. vs. 53 with vs. 34b, vs. 55 with vss. 20, 48, and vs. 56a with vss. 15,34b, and 49).
Vss. 57-65	The most helpless and useless of all man's creations, idols are even less impressive when compared to God's creations in the sky. The forces of nature can bestow on men both blessings and judgment; idols can do neither.
Vss. 66-73	More helpless than inanimate heavenly bodies or dumb animals, idols are as helpless and ineffective as a scarecrow, a thornbush, or a corpse. "Better, then, is the virtuous man who has no idols, for he will be far above reproach."

Author

The Epistle was not written by the prophet Jeremiah, even though it does bear a strong resemblance to certain passages in the Book of Jeremiah, notably to Jer 10:2-15. Its unknown author, who evidently knew a great deal about Babylonian religion (see *Place of Composition*, pp. 328-329), chose to give his message additional authority by attributing it to the great prophet Jeremiah, an idea which doubtless was suggested to him by the fact that Jeremiah had written a letter to the Jewish exiles once they were in Babylon (cf. Jeremiah 29). Neither in the Book of Jeremiah nor in II

Kings, however, is there any mention of such a letter as our Epistle; yet these are certainly the two places in the Hebrew Bible where one would normally expect such information to be recorded.

As the next few pages will show in some detail, there are three reasons for the almost universally held view that the author of the Epistle was not Jeremiah. (1) The Epistle depends primarily upon OT passages which originated long after the prophet Jeremiah, namely, Isa 44:9-20, 46:5-7; Pss 115:3-8, 130:6-7,15-17; *and* Jer 10:2-15 itself. (2) In terms of literary quality, as well as religious depth and sensitivity, the Epistle is, by common consent, decidedly inferior to genuine Jeremiah materials. (3) Ultimately, the Epistle was not included in the canon of the Hebrew Bible.

Literary Dependence

As the NOTES *passim* will show, most of the material in the Epistle depends for its ideas, imagery, and phraseology upon a few classic descriptions of idolatry, the most important for our purposes being

Jer 10:2-5,8-11,13b-15

2 Thus says the LORD:
"Learn not the way of the nations,
　nor be dismayed at the signs of
　　the heavens
　because the nations are dismayed
　　at them,
3 for the customs of the peoples are
　　false.
　A tree from the forest is cut down,
　　and worked with an axe by the
　　hands of a craftsman.
4 Men deck it with silver and gold;
　they fasten it with hammer and
　　nails
　so that it cannot move.
5 Their idols are like scarecrows in
　　a cucumber field,
　and they cannot speak;
　they have to be carried,
　　for they cannot walk.
　Be not afraid of them,
　　for they cannot do evil,
　neither is it in them to do good."

8 They are both stupid and foolish;
the instruction of idols is but
wood!
9 Beaten silver is brought from
Tarshish,
and gold from Uphaz.
They are the work of the craftsman
and of the hands of the
goldsmith;
their clothing is violet and purple;
they are all the work of skilled
men.
10 But the LORD is the true God;
he is the living God and the
everlasting King.
At his wrath the earth quakes,
and the nations cannot endure his
indignation.
11 Thus shall you say to them:
"The gods who did not make the heavens and the earth
shall perish from the earth and from under the heavens."

13b He makes lightnings for the rain,
and he brings forth the wind from
his storehouses.
14 Every man is stupid and without
knowledge;
every goldsmith is put to shame
by his idols;
for his images are false,
and there is no breath in them.
15 They are worthless, a work of
delusion;
at the time of their punishment
they shall perish.[1]

Several other passages are also echoed more than once in the Epistle:

[1] John Bright writes of this poem: "Though of great power and depth, [it] is all but universally conceded to come from another hand than Jeremiah's. Striking similarities to various passages in the latter part of Isaiah . . . suggest an Exilic date," *Jeremiah*, AB, vol. 21 (1965), 79.

Isa 44:9-20

9 All who make idols are nothing, and the things they delight in do not profit; their witnesses neither see nor know, that they be put to shame. 10 Who fashions a god or casts an image, that is profitable for nothing? 11 Behold, all his fellows shall be put to shame, and the craftsmen are but men; let them all assemble, let them stand forth, they shall be terrified, they shall be put to shame together.

12 The ironsmith fashions it and works it over the coals; he shapes it with hammers, and forges it with his strong arm; he becomes hungry and his strength fails, he drinks no water and is faint. 13 The carpenter stretches a line, he marks it out with a pencil; he fashions it with planes, and marks it with a compass; he shapes it into the figure of a man, with the beauty of a man, to dwell in a house. 14 He cuts down cedars; or he chooses a holm tree or an oak and lets it grow strong among the trees of the forest; he plants a cedar and the rain nourishes it. 15 Then it becomes fuel for a man; he takes a part of it and warms himself, he kindles a fire and bakes bread; also he makes a god and worships it, he makes it a graven image and falls down before it. 16 Half of it he burns in a fire; over the half he eats flesh, he roasts meat and is satisfied; also he warms himself and says, "Aha, I am warm, I have seen the fire!" 17 And the rest of it he makes into a god, his idol; and falls down to it and worships it; he prays to it and says, "Deliver me, for thou art my god!"

18 They know not, nor do they discern; for he has shut their eyes, so that they cannot see, and their minds, so that they cannot understand. 19 No one considers, nor is there knowledge or discernment to say, "Half of it I burned in the fire, I also baked bread on its coals, I roasted flesh and have eaten; and shall I make the residue of it an abomination? Shall I fall down before a block of wood?" 20 He feeds on ashes; a deluded mind has led him astray, and he cannot deliver himself or say, "Is there not a lie in my right hand?"

Isa 46:5-7

5 "To whom will you liken me and
    make me equal,
  and compare me, that we may be alike?
6 Those who lavish gold from the
    purse,
  and weigh out silver in the scales,
  hire a goldsmith, and he makes it
    into a god;
  then they fall down and worship!

7 They lift it upon their shoulders,
    they carry it,
    they set it in its place, and it
    stands there;
    it cannot move from its place.
If one cries to it, it does not answer
    or save him from his trouble.

Ps 115:3-8[113:11-16H]

3 Our God is in the heavens;
    he does whatever he pleases.
4 Their idols are silver and gold,
    the work of men's hands.
5 They have mouths, but do not
      speak;
    eyes, but do not see.
6 They have ears, but do not hear;
    noses, but do not smell.
7 They have hands, but do not feel;
    feet, but do not walk;
    and they do not make a sound in
      their throat.
8 Those who make them are like
      them;
    so are all who trust in them.

PS 135[134H]:6-7,15-17

6 Whatever the LORD pleases he does,
    in heaven and on earth,
    in the seas and all deeps.
7 He it is who makes the clouds rise at
    the end of the earth,
    who makes lightnings for the rain
    and brings forth the wind from his
      storehouses.

15 The idols of the nations are silver
      and gold,
    the work of men's hands.
16 They have mouths, but they speak
      not,

> they have eyes, but they see not,
> they have ears, but they hear not,
> nor is there any breath in their
> mouths.

Deut 4:27-28

27 And the LORD will scatter you among the peoples, and you will be left few in number among the nations where the LORD will drive you. 28 And there you will serve gods of wood and stone, the work of men's hands, that neither see, nor hear, nor eat, nor smell.

When one compares the Greek text of the passages above with the comparable passages in the Septuagint version of the Epistle of Jeremiah, it is evident that the author of the Epistle was primarily dependent upon the Hebrew text of the Old Testament rather than upon its Greek translation. Otherwise, how can one explain the fact that in his Epistle he often reproduced the meanings and phrases of these Hebrew passages in Greek words and phrases quite different from their Septuagint translation? Additional evidence of the author's dependence upon the Hebrew rather than the Greek Bible is found also, for instance, in vs. 70 of the Epistle where he says that the idols "are like a scarecrow in a cucumber patch," which is clearly based on Jer 10:5: "Their idols are like scarecrows in a cucumber field," the latter being a clause which is absent from the Greek version of the Book of Jeremiah.

Literary Merit

Judging the literary merit of a work known only in translation is always risky, but doubly so when that translation is seriously flawed. Yet this is precisely the case with regard to the Epistle, as evidenced, for example, by two egregious Greek mistranslations of the Hebrew (cf. NOTES on "moths" in vs. 12, and "fine linen" in vs. 72), not to mention certain other infelicities and imprecisions of phrase, such as found in vss. 27 and 41 (see NOTES).

Apart from a not infrequent uncertainty as to the antecedents of pronouns (see textual notes *passim*), the Epistle is usually intelligible. The text, whether one is thinking here of the presupposed Hebrew original or its Greek translation, seems, however, quite pedestrian, with few, if any, images, analogies, or comparisons unparalleled by earlier biblical materials, i.e. the Epistle has little in the way of imagery or phraseology that is new or memorable—certainly the Church Fathers rarely even alluded to the Epistle.[2]

Perhaps most serious of all, the Epistle is lacking in clear organization and development of thought. To be sure, the "poem" has a superficial organization, with its ten strophes, each one (excepting the first and last) ending with some variation of essentially the same refrain, namely: "So how can anyone consider them gods? So have no fear of them!"

vss. 16   It is obvious, therefore, that *they are not gods so have no fear of them.*

23   From all this you may know that *they are not gods, so have no fear of them.*

29b   From all this you may know that *they are not gods, so have no fear of them.*

40   *So how can anyone consider* them gods or call them so?

44   Everything that relates to these idols is false. *So how can anyone consider* them gods or call them so?

52   *Can anyone fail to realize that* they are not gods?

56   *So how can anyone allow or believe* that they are gods?

65   Recognizing, therefore, that *they are not gods, have no fear of them.*

Wolfgang M. W. Roth may be correct in insisting that the ordering principle of the stanzas is that of catchword and "catchthought" associations,[3] but that ordering principle would not have been especially evident to the average ancient reader.

In general structure, then, the "letter" is not unlike Psalms 42-43 and 107, with their recurring refrains (cf. 42:5,11, 43:5, 107:1,8,15,21,31) and strophes of varying lengths.

After the first three or four stanzas of the Epistle there is no further development or progression of thought; rather, the same old observations and arguments are restated—or worse, rehashed—again and again in successive strophes. "It is," wrote Torrey, "a formless composition, rambling and repetitious" (p. 65). In arguing against an Egyptian provenance for the Epistle, Naumann rightly observed (p. 49) that neither its form nor logic would have appealed to members of the Alexandrine school of Egypt.

---

[2] Although not actually quoted, the Epistle seems to have much influenced the *Apologia* of Aristides of Athens, a defense of Christianity addressed to the emperor Hadrian (117-138). Brief portions of the Epistle were quoted by Tertullian of Carthage in his *de scorpiae* VIII, and by Cyprian of Carthage in his *de dominica oratione* V, while Firmicus Maternus, a fourth-century Sicilian rhetorician, quoted almost a third of it (vss. 5-10, 21-24, 28-31, 50-57) in his *de errore profanarum religionum* XXVIII.

[3] For example, "Catchwords: women 27/29; deceit 44/47; king 50/52; to be saved 54/57; cf. shame 71/72; catchthoughts: to blacken/to polish 20/23; cf. blind/mute 36/40; to do well/to bless 63/65," W. M. Roth, *CBQ* 37 (1975), 40.

With regard to determining the literary merit of a work, form and substance go hand in hand; certain weaknesses in one can sometimes be compensated by greater strengths in the other. Unfortunately, neither the form nor substance of the Epistle is strong enough to compensate for the failures of the other, a fact which helps to explain why the Epistle of Jeremiah did not become canonical among the Jews.

Canonical Status

Although the Epistle of Jeremiah was, evidently, excluded from the canon of the Hebrew Bible by the Council of Jamnia (ca. A.D. 90), it had already been accepted by Christians in Egypt as part of their Old Testament, continuing as such down to the Reformation, when it was rejected by Protestants and reaffirmed by Roman Catholics as deuterocanonical at the Council of Trent in 1546.

Alluded to only occasionally in antiquity (see fn. 2), the Epistle was nonetheless included, by name, in a number of the Canon Lists compiled by Church Fathers. In the Eastern Church, for instance, the Epistle was accepted as canonical by Origen, Athanasius, Cyril of Jerusalem, Epiphanius, bishop of Constantia in Cyprus, and the Laodicene Canons (343-381), while in the West it appeared in the list of Hilary who, it should be noted, did not mention I Baruch. Even when not mentioned by name in a Canon List, the Epistle was regarded as such, it being thought that the Epistle was merely an adjunct to the Book of Jeremiah rather than a separate book.[4] So far as we know, it was not until Jerome (340?-420), that the Epistle's canonicity was ever questioned by name.[5] Jerome, of course, regarded as non-canonical every Septuagint book which had no parallel in the then-current Hebrew canon.

In some of the later Greek manuscripts the Epistle follows immediately after I Baruch without a break, but it was not until Jerome that the Epistle was finally and consistently appended to I Baruch as the latter's ch. 6, thereby uniting two works which should have been kept quite separate.

Purpose

Why was the Epistle written? Ostensibly, it was designed to prevent Jews from worshiping false gods in Babylon (and, in effect, also in Palestine itself). But were there any other considerations? It is possible (but un-

---

[4] So, for instance, Irenaeus of Lyons (140-?202), Clement of Alexandria, Tertullian of Carthage, and Cyprian of Carthage.

[5] See Jerome's Preface to his *Commentary on Jeremiah* (Migne, *Patrologiae Latina*, XXIV, 706), where he called the Epistle a pseudepigraphon.

likely) that this little tract against idolatry was directed just as much, if not more so, toward the Gentiles, that is, the Epistle may have been a "defense" against the accusations of now-unknown anti-Semitic writers who, like Posidonius (130?-50 B.C.) and Appolonius Molon (fl. ca. 70 B.C.), later on charged the Jews with godlessness and despising the gods (so Pfeiffer, p. 432). Or, the Epistle may have been a veiled or indirect attack on Tammuz worship, the cult which flourished in the temple in Jeremiah's day (cf. Ezek 8:14) and, presumably, later as well.[6]

More likely, however, the Epistle is a homily, or brief sermon, inspired by the very puzzling phenomenon of Jer 10:11, which verse, alone in the Book of Jeremiah, is in Aramaic, namely: "Thus shall you say to them: 'The gods who did not make the heavens and the earth shall perish from the earth and from under the heavens.'"[7] This Aramaic verse, supported and illuminated by the Hebrew of Jer 10:2-15, inspired the author of the Epistle to expand upon it (so Torrey, pp. 64-65), even as the same Aramaic verse later on inspired the translator of the Targum on Jeremiah to add an Aramaic epistle to it (so Thackeray, *Some Aspects of the Greek Old Testament*, p. 59).

Original Language

Although most nineteenth-century scholars, including such giants as Otto Fritzsche and Emil Schürer, had no doubts that the Epistle was originally composed in Greek, twentieth-century scholars have thought otherwise, thanks primarily to the ground-breaking work of C. J. Ball in *APOT,* I. Most scholars today follow Ball in regarding the Epistle as being composed originally in Hebrew.[8]

That the Epistle was originally composed in Hebrew is based primarily upon three lines of linguistic evidence: (1) the presence of corrupt Greek readings which presuppose a particular Hebrew word of two very different meanings and where the Greek translator obviously chose the wrong one (see, for example, the NOTES on "moths" in vs. 12, "It is obvious" in vs. 16, and "fine linen" in vs. 72); (2) instances where variant readings are probably best explained by positing a Hebrew original (see, for example,

---

[6] So Thackeray. Whether Thackeray was correct in this matter, there is merit to his suggestion that this Epistle was a *Haftorah* (a prescribed synagogal reading from the Prophets) for the Jewish fast on the seventeenth of Tammuz (see *Some Aspects of the Greek Old Testament,* 57-60). Moreover, he maintains that this Epistle was part of a synagogal pericope in which the Book of Lamentations was used for the fast on the ninth of Ab, and portions of I Baruch were used for the three Sabbaths of Penitence before the ninth of Ab as well as for the ninth of Ab itself and the next seven Sabbaths (see *The Septuagint and Jewish Worship,* 107-111).

[7] "An obvious gloss," says John Bright in *Jeremiah,* AB, vol. 21, 79.

[8] C. C. Torrey and R. H. Pfeiffer, however, believed that the original text was in Aramaic; see NOTE on "on the roof" in vs. 11.

the Notes on "soot of the temple" in vs. 21, "helpless as the clouds" in vs. 54, and "hide" in vs. 68); and (3) the presence of other types of Hebraisms, including the repeated use of the Greek future tense for the present (see Notes *passim*), and the literalistic rendering of such distinctive Hebrew constructions as the infinitive absolute (see Note on "don't dare imitate" in vs. 5).

There is also a literary argument for a Hebrew original: as the Epistle now stands in the Greek, it has so little to commend it in terms of either content or literary style that one is hard pressed to understand how the Epistle would have ever been accepted by Greek readers had it not first been in Hebrew or Aramaic. One must distinguish, then, between the now-lost Hebrew original and its extant Greek translation, the latter accurately characterized as "a piece so formless, so confused, so utterly destitute of the graces of style" (Ball, p. 597). Whether the Greek translation was a paraphrastic rendering of the now-lost Hebrew or a slavishly literal one, it was not one that stirred the hearts of the ancient Church Fathers to the point that they loved to quote from it.

Date

The original version of the Epistle was written sometime between 540 B.C. (i.e. the earliest date for Deutero-Isaiah passages [Isa 44:9-20 and 46:5-7]) and the first century B.C., that century being the date both of II Maccabees, which alludes to the Epistle,[9] and of the earliest extant Greek translation of the Epistle, the one found in Dead Sea Cave VII (see Note on vs. 44). The Epistle evidently antedates the Wisdom of Solomon, a first-century apocryphon, else how can one account for the Epistle's failure to utilize any of the very effective satire and invective against idolatry in Wis 13:10 - 15:17?

But just how much before the first century B.C. was the Hebrew text

---

[9] II Macc 2:1-2,4: "One finds in the records [Gr. *en tais apographais*] that Jeremiah the prophet ordered those *who were being deported* [italics added] to take some of the fire, as has been told, and that the prophet after giving them the law instructed those who were being deported not to forget the commandments of the Lord, nor to be led astray in their thoughts upon seeing the gold and silver statues and their adornment. . . . It was also in the writing [*en tē graphē*] that the prophet, having received an oracle, ordered that the tent and the ark should follow with him, and that he went out to the mountain where Moses had gone up and had seen the inheritance of God" (*RSV*).

Since the Epistle of Jeremiah contains nothing about the tent or ark mentioned in II Macc 2:4, many scholars have concluded that II Maccabees was not alluding to our Epistle; but as Marshall pointed out ("Jeremy, Epistle of," *HDB*, II, 579), II Macc 2:4 does not say that the business about the ark and the altar were mentioned in the *same* writing as the one attacking idols, i.e. it is all a matter of what the author of II Maccabees defined as "Scripture."

written? There is no compelling reason not to accept the clue given us in vs. 3, where the author of the Epistle predicts Israel may have to stay in exile in Babylon "up to seven generations," i.e. until ca. 317 B.C. (see NOTE on "up to seven generations" in vs. 3). After all, why should the author of the Epistle have given this "future" date if he was already writing at a time long after the predicted event should have occurred and had not, i.e. why should he have cited a particular point in time which subsequent history *had already* proven not to be correct? Moreover, there is nothing in the Epistle itself which precludes a date as early as the end of the fourth century B.C. While it is admittedly an "argument from silence," it is nonetheless significant that the Epistle contains no literary parallels peculiar to biblical materials of the third through first centuries B.C.

The late fourth century B.C. was certainly a time when the message of the Epistle was relevant to the needs and dangers of the Eastern Diaspora[10] as well as of Palestine itself, where the Hellenization process was making serious inroads into Judaism. For us to accept a late fourth-century date for the Epistle is not, however, to deny either the special appropriateness of the Epistle's message or the Koine character of its Greek translation for the Maccabean-Hasmonean period (167-163 B.C.)—the period to which most scholars assign the book; but to assign the composition of the Hebrew text to that time is not justified.[11]

Place of Composition

There is no justification for asserting today, as was frequently done by scholars in the nineteenth century, an Egyptian provenance for the Epistle. (This error was primarily rooted in a failure to distinguish between the place where the Epistle was composed and the place where it was probably translated.[12]) Apart from a very cryptic mention of cats (see NOTE on vs. 22), there is no distinctive Egyptian religious element or practice mentioned in the Epistle. Conspicuous by its absence from the Epistle is any mention of Egyptian animal worship, which by the Ptolemaic period (323-30 B.C.) had become quite widespread as part of the state religion.

---

[10] Witness, for example, the situation in the Book of Esther where the Jewish hero and heroine not only had pagan theophorus names (see NOTES on "Mordecai" in 2:5, and on "Esther" in 2:7, in AB 7B), but Queen Esther did not observe the laws of *kašrût* (see NOTE in 2:9 on "and her delicacies" in 2:9 COMMENT, p. 28, in AB 7B).

[11] For a very detailed analysis of the Koine character of our Epistle's Greek, see Naumann, BZAW 25 (1913), 31-44.

[12] J. T. Marshall, for instance, was quite correct when he wrote of the Greek text, "The slightly inflated style of the Epistle is thoroughly Alexandrinian. The fondness for assonance and for long compound words . . ." (*HDB*, II, 579), but this says nothing about the Hebrew original.

Had the Epistle been composed in Egypt, it is inconceivable that an Alexandrian apologist would have made no allusion whatever to this practice.[13]

On the other hand, virtually everything said in the Epistle about the idols, their priesthood and cult is, as Naumann (pp. 3-31) has so convincingly documented, completely compatible with Mesopotamian religion in general and with the worship of the Babylonian Marduk in particular.[14] The few identifiable cultic practices mentioned are distinctly Babylonian, or at least Mesopotamian, namely, a Tammuz-type cult (see NOTE on vs. 32) and a rite of sacred prostitution (see NOTE on vs. 43). Moreover, the only god mentioned, apart from the Lord (vss. 1,2,6, and 62), is the Babylonian Marduk, or Bel (see NOTE on vs. 41). The proper "care and feeding" of the gods (cf. vss. 11-12,26-29,33,58,72) was a matter of great concern to the Babylonians; but in this matter the Babylonians were no different from other ancient peoples.[15]

It is important to observe, however, that some very distinctive pagan elements of the Babylonian religion go unmentioned in the Epistle. For instance, there is no mention of such a central and distinctive feature as divination, complete with all the mystery and trappings of astrology and extispicy. Nor does the author of the Epistle evidence a firsthand awareness of either the details of Babylonian sacred prostitution or the power and appeal of the Babylonian gods. (Perhaps worth quoting here is the observation of A. L. Oppenheim on the power of idols *for their believers:* "Not even a perfectly preserved image could indicate to us what it meant for the priest and the pious, how it functioned as the center of the cult, what its *Sitz im Leben* was for the community" [p. 174].) It is as though the author of the Epistle were criticizing a Mesopotamian religion and its gods *from afar.*

In sum then, the internal evidence agrees with the claims of the Epistle's Superscription (vs. 1) that the "letter" was designed for those who would encounter Babylonian idols and idolatry. There is no reason to reject a presumably Palestinian location (cf. vs. 1) as the Epistle's provenance. To affirm this is in no way to deny that the idolatry attacked by the Epistle was also a reality of the author's own time and place, namely, the late fourth- or early third-century Palestine.

[13] In the Epistle not one idol is described in either theriomorphic ("animal-form") or therioanthropomorphic terms.

[14] The only weakness in Naumann's argument is that he drew his supporting examples from *all* periods of Mesopotamian literature, not just from the Neo-Babylonian period (626-539 B.C.).

[15] On the complicated subject of Mesopotamian religion, see A. Leo Oppenheim, *Ancient Mesopotamia* (University of Chicago Press, 1964), pp. 171-227; and H. W. F. Saggs, *The Greatness That Was Babylon* (New York: Hawthorn, 1963), pp. 299-358.

The Versions

In Joseph Ziegler's excellent critical edition of the Epistle in the Göttingen series, he used 134 printed lines for the Greek text and then an additional 352 lines (almost three times as many!) for his very compact and abbreviated notes in the *apparatus criticus*. A careful study of Ziegler's *apparatus* shows, however, that the versions are not of much help in explicating the Greek text. (We should note in passing that significant differences between the various families of Greek manuscripts of the Epistle, such as Vaticanus [LXX^B], Alexandrinus [LXX^A], the Lucianic [LXX^L], and the Origenic recensions [LXX^O], are quite few in number, and that LXX^B seems to be the best text.)

The differences between the LXX and the versions based on it are not of great significance. The OL, Vulgate, and SyrH. are all very literal translations of the LXX, each having few variant readings which commend themselves. An additional phrase or clause, for instance, is exceedingly rare (but see the OL and Syriac reading of vs. 49, the Vulgate of vs. 52, and the Syriac of vs. 53); the same may even be said of one-word additions (see the OL and Vulgate reading of vs. 4, or the LXX^L, OL, Syriac, and SyrH. reading of vs. 62). Omissions are also infrequent; and, with the exception of an entire clause omitted by the LXX^A and Arabic in vs. 6, omissions are rarely more than a word or so. Nor are variants of very much help (but see textual notes *passim*). The Arabic version is also very faithful to the LXX, especially to LXX^A, nearly always agreeing with LXX^A when the latter disagrees with LXX^B. Only the Syriac is somewhat free, being a bit more expansive and sometimes unintelligible.

Verse Numbering

Among the English translations of the Epistle there is some disagreement as to the correct numbering of its verses, in part, because modern editors of the Greek text such as Swete, Rahlfs, and Ziegler do not include the Superscription (our vs. 1) in their verse numbering. Then too, modern translators do not always find the end of a particular thought at the same point, being variously influenced by the verse divisions and translations of the ancient versions, especially the Vulgate, where the Epistle is treated as ch. 6 of I Baruch. For purposes of convenience, the numbering adopted in this translation follows the most common one in English, although the present writer has not felt bound by that numbering in determining the sense and flow of the Greek itself.

BIBLIOGRAPHY IIIв

Commentaries

Ball, Charles James. *Epistle of Jeremy, APOT*, I, 596-611. *Cited as* Ball.

Fritzsche, Otto F. *Der Brief des Jeremia,* Kurzgefasstes exegetisches Handbuch zu den Apokryphen des Alten Testaments, eds. O. Fritzsche und C. Grimm, I. Leipzig: Hirzel, 1851. *Cited as* Fritzsche.

Gifford, E. H. *The Epistle of Jeremy,* Apocrypha of the Speaker's Commentary, ed. Henry Wace, II. London: John Murray, 1888. *Cited as* Gifford.

Gunneweg, A. H. J. "Das Buch Baruch," in *Historische und legendarische Erzählungen,* Judische Schriften aus hellenistisch-römischer Zeit, ed. Werner Georg Kümmel et al., III, 2. Gütersloh: Mohn, 1975.

Hamp, Vincenz. *Der Brief des Jeremia,* Die Heilige Schrift des Alten und Neuen Testaments. Würzburg: Pattloch, 1948.

Rothstein, Johann W. *Der Jeremiasbrief,* Die Apokryphen und Pseudepigraphen des Alten Testaments, ed. E. F. Kautzsch, I. Tübingen: Mohr, 1900. *Cited as* Rothstein.

Wambacq, Bernard N. *Jeremias, Klaagliederen, Baruch, Brief van Jeremias,* De Boeken van het Oude Testament. Roermond: Romen & Zonen, 1957.

Zöckler, Otto. *Der Brief des Jeremia,* Die Apokryphen des Alten Testamentes, Kurzgefasstes Kommentar zu den heiligen Schriften des Alten und Neuen Testamentes sowie zu den Apokryphen, eds. O. Zöckler und H. Strack, IX. München: Oskar Beck, 1891.

Other Books

Baillet, Maurice, Jozef T. Milik, and Roland de Vaux. *Les 'Petites Grottes' de Qumrân,* Discoveries in the Judaean Desert of Jordan, III. Oxford: Clarendon Press, 1962.

Bentzen, Aage. *Introduction to the Old Testament,* I, 6th ed. Copenhagen: G. E. C. Gad, 1961.

Eissfeldt, Otto. *The Old Testament: An Introduction, including the Apocrypha and Pseudepigrapha, and also the works of similar type from Qumran,* tr. from the 3d ed., by Peter R. Ackroyd. New York: Harper & Row, 1965. *Cited as* Eissfeldt.

Fraenkel, Isaac S. *K*e*tûbîm 'aḥarônîm* (a Hebrew translation of the Apocrypha). Warsaw, 1863.

Metzger, Bruce. *An Introduction to the Apocrypha.* Oxford University Press, 1957.

Oesterley, W. O. E. *The Books of the Apocrypha*. New York: Revell, 1914.
———— *An Introduction to the Books of the Apocrypha*. New York: Macmillan, 1935. *Cited as* Oesterley.
Pfeiffer, Robert H. *History of New Testament Times, with an Introduction to the Apocrypha*. New York: Harper, 1949. *Cited as* Pfeiffer.
Schürer, Emil. *Geschichte des jüdischen Volkes im Zeitalter Jesu Christi*, 4th ed., III. Leipzig: Hinrichs, 1909. *Cited as* Schürer.
Thackeray, Henry St. John. *The Septuagint and Jewish Worship*, 2d ed. Oxford University Press, 1923.
———— *Some Aspects of the Greek Old Testament*. London: Allen & Unwin, 1927.
Torrey, Charles C. *The Apocryphal Literature*. Yale University Press, 1945. *Cited as* Torrey.
Tov, Emanuel. *The Book of Baruch Also Called 1 Baruch (Greek and Hebrew): Edited, Reconstructed and Translated* in Texts and Translations, VIII, and Pseudepigrapha, VI, of the Society of Biblical Literature, ed. Robert A. Kraft. Missoula, Mont.: Scholars Press, 1975.
———— *The Septuagint Translation of Jeremiah and Baruch: A Discussion of an Early Revision of the LXX of Jeremiah 29-52 and Baruch 1:1 – 3:8*, in Harvard Semitic Museum and Harvard Semitic Monographs, VIII, ed. Frank Moore Cross. Missoula, Mont.: Scholars Press, 1976.

Articles

Artom, Elihu S., "L'origine, la data, et gli scopi dell' epistola di Geremia," *Annuario di Studi Ebraici* 1 (1935), 49-74.
Lee, G. M. "Apocryphal Cats: Baruch 6:21" *VT* 18 (1968), 488-493.
Marshall, J. T., "The Epistle of Jeremy," *HDB*, II, 578-590.
Naumann, Weigand, "Untersuchungen über den apokryphen Jeremiasbrief," *BZAW* 25 (1913), 1-53.
Roth, Wolfgang M. W., "For Life, He Appeals to Death (Wisd 13:18): A Study of Old Testament Idol Parodies," *CBQ* 37 (1975), 21-47.
Thackeray, Henry St. John, "Notes and Studies: The Greek Translators of Jeremiah," *JTS* 4 (1903), 245-26.
Vaux, Roland de, "Fouilles de Kirbet Qumrân," *RB* 63 (1956), 533-577.

Versions

Swete, Henry Barclay, ed. *Epistle of Jeremiah*. The Old Testament in Greek according to the Septuagint, III. Cambridge University Press, 1894.
Ziegler, Joseph. *Ieremias, Baruch, Threni, Epistula Ieremiae*. Septuaginta. Vetus Testamentum Graecum auctoritate Societatis Gottingensis editum, ed. J. Ziegler, XV. Göttingen, 1957.

VI. SUPERSCRIPTION AND INTRODUCTORY MATERIAL

(Vss. 1-7 [ch. 6 in Vulgate and KJ])

1 A copy of a letter which Jeremiah sent to those about to be led captive to Babylon by the king of the Babylonians, informing them of what God had commanded him*a*:

2 Because of the sins you have committed before God, you are to be led away captive to Babylon by Nebuchadnezzar, king of the Babylonians. 3 Once you have reached Babylon you will stay there for many years, for a long while, up to *b*seven generations*b*; but afterwards I will bring you away from there in peace. 4 Now in Babylon you will see carried on men's shoulders gods made of silver*c*, of gold, and of wood, filling the pagans with awe. 5 So beware: don't dare imitate the foreigners or be overawed by *d*their gods*d* 6 when you see the throng before and behind them worshiping them. *e*Rather, say in your hearts, "You only must we worship, Lord."*e* 7 For my angel is with you; he *f*is responsible for*f* your lives.

a "Them" in LXX*A* and Arabic.
b-b Syriac "seventy years"; see NOTE.
c OL and Vulgate add "and of stone."
d-d Greek "them."
e-e LXX*A* and Arabic omit.
f-f Syriac "will avenge"; see NOTE.

NOTES

1. *Jeremiah.* Although ten different Jeremiahs are mentioned in the Old Testament (cf. I Chron 52:24, 12:4,10,13; II Kings 23:31; Jer 1:1, 35:3; Neh 10:2, 12:1,34), *the* Jeremiah is intended here, even though the Epistle makes no further mention of him.

to those about to be led captive. If vs. 1 were taken at face value, then the letter would antedate the one quoted in Jeremiah 29, where Jeremiah offered to those exiles of 597 B.C. *already in Babylon* the revolutionary advice to settle down and make peace with their situation. Even though no mention of a letter such as the Epistle is made in the Old Testament, it was probably thought by the author of II Maccabees to have been part of "the records" alluded to in II Macc 2:1 (see COMMENT). Given all the heartbreaking experiences the Israelites of 597 B.C. had already been through (cf. II Kings 24:1-17), not to mention the uncertainties that still lay ahead of the exiles, most scholars have rightly observed that the message of the Epistle is not only inappropriate but lacking in that compassion and tenderness associated with the prophet Jeremiah.

There is no reason to regard the Superscription and its mention of Jeremiah as intrusive or secondary. After all, before this Epistle was appended to I Baruch, it would have needed some kind of introduction or background; and the Epistle's message was appropriate for a Jeremiah, albeit, not for this occasion!

In any case, those Jews who actually were taken to Babylon by King Nebuchadnezzar could not have helped being impressed by the greatness of the city, especially if they had been led into it through the justly famous Ishtar Gate (for a painting of it, based upon considerable archaeological evidence, see Plate 8).

2. *Because.* Speaking for God, Jeremiah was not predicting here but explaining. It is as if he were answering the question posed by the people in Jer 16:10b: "Why has the LORD pronounced all this great evil against us? What is our iniquity? What is the sin that we have committed against the LORD our God?" For the real Jeremiah's answer to these questions, see Jer 16:11-13.

by Nebuchadnezzar. This is perhaps another indication that the Jews to whom the Epistle was addressed were the exiles of 597 B.C. rather than 586 B.C., because, technically speaking, the latter group was led away to Babylon by Nebuzaradan, the captain of Nebuchadnezzar's bodyguard (cf. II Kings 24:10-16 and 25:8-11).

3. *for a long while.* Cf. Jer 32:14 and Bar 4:35. According to the false prophet Hananiah, the Babylonian exile would last for only a few years (cf. Jer 28:11).

up to seven generations. This prediction as to the length of the Babylonian exile conflicts sharply with the estimates in canonical Jeremiah, where the period is represented as being either seventy years (so Jer 25:12, 29:10) or three generations of Babylonian rulers (Jer 27:7) (These estimates are roughly equivalent.) Some scholars have explained the sharp disagreement between the Epistle and the canonical Jeremiah as resulting from an early confusion in the Epistle over the alphabetic equivalents for certain numbers, that is, a "seven" was read instead of a "three" in either the Hebrew stage (a *zayin* for a *gimel*) or the Greek (an *eta* for a *gamma*). But more likely, the estimate of "up to seven generations" represents an attempt to reflect more accurately the realities of the situation, that is, the Epistle was written late enough for Jeremiah's figures to be seen as patently incorrect. If a "generation" here represents approximately forty years (although it can represent as many as a hundred years, as in Gen 15:16), then the author of the Epistle was thinking of a period something like 280 years after the first deportation, in which case one might infer that the Epistle was written no later than ca. 317 B.C. Predicting future events in even the vaguest terms is, however, always fraught with perils, as evidenced by the fact that the writer of Daniel felt compelled to change Jeremiah's "seventy years" (Jer 25:12, 29:10) to "seventy *weeks of* years" (cf. Dan 9:24), i.e. four hundred ninety years!

I will bring. Here and in vs. 7, but nowhere else in the Epistle, God speaks directly to the people.

in peace. Cf. Gen 26:29 and Exod 18:23 of the LXX.

4. *carried on men's shoulders* [*ep ōmois airomenous*]. The allusion here and in vs. 6 is to the well-known Babylonian phenomenon of religious processions in which the image of a god was carried on men's shoulders (see Plate 9). In the *Akitu,* or Babylonian New Year Festival, for instance, on the sixth day of celebration the god Nebo of Borsippa, as well as various gods (i.e. idols) from other Babylonian cities, came to visit Marduk in Babylon, after which, on the eighth day, a statue of Marduk was carried from Babylon across the Euphrates River to Borsippa, and then back again to Babylon on the eleventh day (for details, see Elmer A. Leslie, *The Psalms* [New York: Abingdon-Cokesburg, 1949], pp. 56-60). Cf. also Isa 46:7: "They lift it [the idol] upon their shoulders, they carry it, they set it in its place, and it stands there; it cannot move from its place. If one cries to it, it does not answer or save him from his trouble." Cf. also Jer 10:5.

gods made of silver, of gold, and of wood. Cf. Pss 115:4, 135:15. The addition of "and of stone" in the OL and the Vulgate is probably under the influence of Deut 4:28: "And there [i.e. in Babylon] you will serve gods of wood and stone, the work of men's hands, that neither see nor hear, nor eat, nor smell." For some examples of gods from Canaan, Syria, and Mesopotamia, see Plates 10, 11, and 12.

Although idols were sometimes made of solid metal (cf. Isa 40:19a), more often they were of wood and trimmed with gold or silver, as in Jer 10:3b-4: "A tree from the forest is cut down and worked with an axe by the hands of a craftsman. Men deck it with silver and gold: they fasten it with hammer and nails so that it cannot move." Cf. also Isa 40:19b, 41:6-7, 44:10-17, 46:6. For a brief discussion of the various words for "idol," see J. Gray, *IDB,* II, 673-675.

5. *don't dare imitate* [*mē umeis aphomoiōthentes aphomoiōthēte*]. The Greek construction is emphatic and is also a Hebraism, i.e. the Greek reflects a Hebrew infinitive absolute construction.

or be overawed by their gods (literally "by them"). Cf. Ps 48:6; Exod 15:15.

For the logic, or argument, behind vs. 5b, see Deut 12:30: "Take heed that you be not ensnared to follow them, after they have been destroyed before you, and that you do not inquire about their gods, saying, 'How did these nations serve their gods?—that I also may do likewise.' " Cf. also Deut 18:19 and, especially, Jer 10:2-5.

6. *in your hearts* [*tē dianoia*]. Literally "in your understanding"; cf. *dianoia* in Gen 17:17 and 27:41 of the LXX.

"You only must we worship, Lord" [*soi dei proskunein despota*]. In the Greek the emphasis is upon the pronoun "you." Ball (p. 600) suggests that vs. 6b, which LXX^A and Arabic omit, may be an interpolation; but it could just as easily be haplography.

7. *my angel is with you*. I.e. to protect them, as an angel guarded Jacob (Gen 48:16); to lead them, as an angel led the Israelites in the Wilderness (Exod 23:23, 32:34); and to be in general charge of them, like Michael in Dan 12:1. Naumann (p. 1), however, regarded this mention of a guardian angel as further proof of the post-exilic origin of this passage, angels being, he claimed, of minor significance in pre-exilic literature.

responsible for [*ekzētōn*] *your lives*. Literally "seeks out your lives." The translation is uncertain. In the Old Testament, *ekzētō* is used to translate the Heb. *bqš npš* (II Sam 4:8; Pss 35:4, 38:12[13]; Prov 29:10) as well as *drš npš* (Gen 9:5), both Hebrew phrases expressing malevolent, not benevolent, intent. But see Ps 142:4[5], where *drš npš* evidently has a benevolent connotation.

COMMENT

Although the Epistle of Jeremiah is called a letter, it actually is not, the claims of the Superscription (vs. 1) notwithstanding. To be sure, vss. 3 and 7, where God speaks in the first person, seem somewhat personal and epistolary in character; but the total effect of the Epistle is that of a rambling, impassioned harangue against idolatry. Then too, the Epistle lacks anything resembling a conclusion appropriate for a letter.

Besides providing the context for "Jeremiah's" advice (vss. 2-4), the introduction also states the Epistle's theme: "Don't dare imitate the foreigners or be overawed by their gods. . . . You only must we worship, Lord" (vss. 5, 6b).

VII. ON THE HELPLESSNESS
OF THE IDOLS
(Vss. 8-16)

8 Their tongues are polished by a carpenter, and they are gilded and silvered; but they are a fraud and cannot speak. 9 As one might for a girl fond of jewelry, *these craftsmen*ᵃ take gold and make crowns for the heads of their gods. 10 Sometimes, even the priests filch gold and silver from their gods and lavish it upon themselves 11 and give some of it to prostitutes on the roof. They dress up *their idols*ᵇ in clothes like human beings—gods of silver and gold and wood! 12 Although draped in purple clothes, *these gods*ᶜ cannot save themselves from rust and moths*ᵈ*. 13 *Their faces have to be dusted*ᵉ because of the house dust which settles thick upon them. 14 Although *a god*ᶠ holds a scepter like a human judge of a province, he cannot put to death anyone who offends him. 15 Although he holds in his right hand a dagger and an axᵍ, he cannot defend himself against warʰ or thieves. 16 It is obvious, therefore, that they are not gods, so have no fear of them.

ᵃ⁻ᵃ Greek "they."
ᵇ⁻ᵇ Greek "them."
ᶜ⁻ᶜ Greek "they."
ᵈ So OL and Vulg. (*tinea*); LXXᴬ ᴮ "food" (*brōmatōn*); LXXᴸ "meat" (*brōseōs*); see NOTE.
ᵉ⁻ᵉ Greek "They wipe away their own face"; see NOTE.
ᶠ⁻ᶠ Greek "he."
ᵍ Syriac adds "in his left."
ʰ So LXXᴮ (*polemou*); "enemies" in LXXᴬ (*polemōn*) and Arabic.

NOTES

8. Some idols, because they were expected to announce oracles, had their mouths open and their tongues conspicuous. The verse echoes the thought of such passages as Pss 135:15-16a and 115:4-5a: "Their idols are silver and gold, the work of men's hands. They have mouths, but do not speak."

9. *fond of jewelry* [*philokosmō*]. Literally "ornament loving." A *hapax lego-menon* in the LXX, this word is found only in late Greek writers such as Plutarch (see LSJ, p. 1936).

10. *lavish* [*katanalōsousin*]. Cf. "Bel and the Snake" vs. 13; literally "they spend upon something"; but in the LXX the verb is used to translate the Heb. *'kl*, "to eat, consume" (cf. Jer 3:24; Deut 4:24, 9:3).

11. *on the roof.* Evidently, this was either the place where the sacred prosti-tutes slept during the summer nights, or it was the place where they performed their ritual acts. Torrey (p. 66) saw in the phrase indisputable proof that the Epistle was composed originally in Aramaic, his argument being that the Greek translator misread *'al agrā*, "for (their) hire," as *'al iggārā*, "on the roof." Torrey may very well be correct; but "on the roof" does make good sense here, especially since the Greek word used here, *stegos*, also means "brothel" in late Greek (see LSJ, p. 1636); cf. also Herodotus I 181.

12. *Although draped in purple clothes.* Since in the Greek text this phrase ac-tually comes at the end of vs. 12, it is taken by the Vulgate and Arabic with vs. 13. Even though it is a genitive absolute construction, it makes better sense for us to take it with vs. 12, the point being then that moths are no respecters of cloth, not even royal cloth.

moths. The Greek has "food" (LXX[L] "meat"), which makes no sense. As Ball (p. 601) long ago pointed out, the unpointed Hebrew word *m'kl*, which can be read either as "food" (so Gen 6:21) or as "moth" (so Mal 3:11; Job 13:28), was misread here as *ma'ᵃkāl*, "food," instead of *mē'okēl*, "from a devourer." A similar error in translation was made in Isa 55:10, where *l'kl*, "to the eater," was rendered as *eis brōsin*, "for food." Cf. also Matt 6:19.

13. *Their faces have to be dusted.* The use of the Greek middle voice (*ekmassontai*) makes little sense here. Granting a Hebrew *Vorlage*, one would assume an original something like "They are wiped as to their face," i.e. a He-brew passive verb was erroneously translated into a Greek middle.

Naumann regarded this "dusting" as a ritual ceremony, comparable to such well-known idol magic as "Opening the Mouth" or "Washing the Mouth" (pp. 15-17), but such an interpretation seems to fly in the face of the obvious, i.e. the helplessness of the idol was being alluded to, not some magic ceremony.

the house dust [*tēs oikias koniorton*]. In the LXX *oikia* usually denotes an or-dinary house, whereas *o oikos* refers to the temple.

14. *a god holds a scepter.* Here and in vs. 15 the ancient author may have had a particular idol in mind, one that was especially well known to him. Naumann (pp. 4-5) has described a number of statues and reliefs depicting a Babylonian god with a scepter in his hand.

15. *an ax* [*pelekun*]. While the scepter (*skēptron*) in the ancient Near East was an almost universal symbol for kings and gods, the ax was not. Since the author of the Epistle seems to have had a specific god in mind in his description in vss. 14-16, the Babylonian-Hittite god, Ramman-Adad, who was later identified with, or perhaps just subsumed under, the god Marduk, may have been the god described here (so Naumann, pp. 5-6).

16. This verse, which concludes the stanza, is repeated with slight variations in vss. 23,29,65, and 69. Cf. also vss. 4-5.

It is obvious [*gnōrimoi eisin*]. The Greek literally means "they are friends" (cf. II Sam 3:8). Evidently, the Greek translator erroneously read the Heb. *mwd'ym* as a noun instead of a participle (so Ball, p. 602).

COMMENT

Down through the ages people have worshiped gods for many reasons. But at the very least, men have worshiped this or that god because of either their hope of what that god could do for them or their fear of what he could do to them. Our stanza asserts that the Babylonian gods cannot help themselves, let alone others. The conclusion is obvious: "Since they are completely helpless, don't fear them!"

VIII. ON THE SENSELESSNESS
OF THE IDOLS
(Vss. 17-23)

17 For just as a man's*a* cracked pot is useless so are their gods: when they sit in their temples*b* their eyes are filled with dust raised by the feet of those who enter. 18 And just as the gates*c* are locked on all sides to one who has offended the king or*d* to one who is sentenced to death, so the priests secure their temples with doors and bolts and bars so that *e*these gods*e* won't be robbed by thieves. 19 They light *f*more lamps than they themselves need,*f* yet *g*the idols*g* cannot see one of them. 20 *h*Their idols are like one of the beams*h* of the temple: their "hearts," so to speak, are eaten out; creatures crawling out of the ground devour them and their fancy clothes. They are unaware of it 21 when their faces are blackened by the soot *i*of the temple.*i* 22 *j*Bats, swallows and other*k* birds flit around *l*the bodies and heads of the idols*l*—and so do the cats! 23 From all this you know that they are not gods, so have no fear of them.

a Syriac "potter's."
b So LXX (*oikois*); "gardens" in the LXXᴬ (*kēpois*) and Arabic; "house" in OL, Vulg. (*domo*), and Ethiopic.
c Reading with one Greek MS, the OL and Vulgate, instead of LXX's "courts"; see NOTE.
d "Or" is included only in LXXᴬ, OL, Vulgate, and Arabic.
e-e Greek "they."
f-f LXXᴬ "many lamps for them [i.e. for the idols]."
g-g Greek "they."
h-h Greek "And it is like a beam."
i-i "Lighting from the ground" in LXXᴬ and Arabic; see NOTE.
j For vs. 22, Syriac has "And on their heads bats and swallows and ravens sit together, and also weasels"; see NOTE.
k So SyrH.; LXX and other versions omit.
l-l Greek "over their body and over the head."

NOTES

17. *a man's cracked pot is useless.* Cf. Jer 22:28a: "Is this man Coniah a despised broken pot, a vessel no one cares for?" and Hosea 8:8: "Israel is swallowed up; already they are among the nations as a useless vessel." Cf. also vs. 59. The Gr. *skeuos anthrōpou,* "a man's pot," is somewhat awkward and may represent a mistranslation of the Hebrew, i.e. the Heb. *kly 'dmh,* "an earthen pot," was read as *kly 'dm,* "a man's pot" (so Ball).

when they sit in their temples. As a genitive absolute, the clause is better taken with what follows (so Vulgate) than with the clause which precedes it. The idea is that idols are useless and helpless with respect to their own condition.

18. *gates.* The LXX's "courts" makes no sense. As in Esth 2:19 (see AB 7B, NOTE on "at the King's Gate"), we have an inner-Greek corruption, i.e. *pulai,* "gates," was misread as *aulai,* "courts," a very easy error for a copyist to have made in the uncial stage of Greek manuscripts.

A gate, it should be noted, serves not only to keep undesirable people, like robbers, out: it also serves to keep people in, i.e. the gods are themselves prisoners!

19. *more lamps than they themselves need.* Literally "and lamps more than for themselves." A suggestion frequently made by scholars (but with very little to commend it) is that this verse is an allusion to the Festival of Lamps at Sais, Egypt (cf. Herodotus II 62).

20. *so to speak.* Literally "they say." This is a very puzzling phrase. Some scholars see it as referring to a now-forgotten proverb. Ball (p. 603) argued that it was a corruption of the biblical idiom "to say in one's heart," i.e. to think ("and he is like a beam of the temple, yet they think that he eats"). But since neither Biblical Hebrew nor ancient Greek had punctuation marks, the ancients often must have had to rely on explanatory phrases, such as "they say," to accomplish what we today accomplish through punctuation, e.g. the quotation marks about "hearts" remind us that wooden beams and idols do not really have hearts.

21. *soot of the temple.* Taking a clue from the absurd reading in the LXX^A ("lighting from the ground"), perhaps we should emend this phrase to "the rising soot," that is, the Heb. *hykl,* "of the temple," was somewhere along the way misread by a Jewish copyist as *h'lh,* "that goes up (from the ground)," which was, in turn, misread as *heʿelāh,* "lighting (from the ground)."

22. *flit around* [*ephiptantai*]. Literally "they fly over"; the Greek verb is a late form of *epipetomai* (cf. LSJ, 257). That the birds do these things around the idols is proof of the latter's helplessness and senselessness, whereas, when the sparrow or swallow finds shelter in Yahweh's temple, it is a symbol of God's beneficence and protection (cf. Ps 84:3-4)!

and so do the cats! Bats and birds fly; cats do not. In spite of numerous efforts to explain away the incongruous Greek word *ailouroi,* "cats" ("an Egyptian gloss," says Naumann [p. 29]), all such efforts have been farfetched and improbable. For the latest but ultimately unconvincing attempt, see G. M. Lee, "Apocryphal Cats: Baruch 6:21," *VT* 21 (1971), 111-112.

23. *them.* I.e. the idols rather than the gods, since the third person plural neuter pronoun (*auta*) is used here, although a few Greek manuscripts do use the masculine form (*autous*), which refers to the gods. Greek, with its masculine, feminine, and neuter pronominal forms in the third person often has, as here, greater precision and clarity than a literal English translation would suggest. Whether the Greek itself has correctly interpreted its Hebrew text here is impossible to say, especially since in vs. 16 the "them" (Gr. *autous*) refers to the gods, not the idols.

IX. IDOLS ARE DISHONORED EVEN BY THEIR OWN FOLLOWERS

(Vss. 24-29)

24 Although beautifully trimmed with gold, *ᵃthe idolsᵃ* will not shine unless someone rubs off the tarnish. While they were being cast, they did not feel it. 25 Although purchased at a high price, there is no breath in them. 26 Without feet, they have to be carried on men's shoulders, which shows people how worthless they are. 27 Even those who attend them are embarrassed because if ever *ᵇan idolᵇ* falls to the ground, *ᶜthey themselves have to pick it up;ᶜ* if anyone sets it upright, it cannot move of itself; if it is tilted, it cannot right itself. Yet offerings are set before them as before the dead. 28 Their priests sell *ᵈthe sacrifices offered to the idolsᵈ* and pocket the proceeds for themselves. Just as bad, their*ᵉ* wives cure some of the meat but share none of it with the poor and the helpless. 29 *ᶠOfferings to idolsᶠ* are handled by women who are having their menstrual periods or have just given birth. From all this you may know that they are not gods, so have no fear of them.

ᵃ⁻ᵃ Greek "they"; in OL and Syriac "it," referring to the gold.
ᵇ⁻ᵇ Greek "it."
ᶜ⁻ᶜ "It/they cannot pick itself/themselves up" in LXXᴬ ᴼ ᴸ, SyrH., Syriac; see NOTE.
ᵈ⁻ᵈ Greek "their sacrifices."
ᵉ So LXXᴬ ᴸ and SyrH.; LXX has "the."
ᶠ⁻ᶠ Greek "Their offerings."

NOTES

24. *Although beautifully trimmed with gold.* Literally "for the gold which goes around for beauty." In the Greek the first sentence of the verse is somewhat puzzling. Since it is in the very nature of gold not to tarnish, it is obviously not the gold (but see James 5:3) but other parts of the idols that tarnish or rust.

25. *Although purchased at a high price.* Literally "from all cost it is bought."
no breath in them. Cf. Jer. 10:14; Ps 135:17; also I Bar 2:17.

26. *have to be carried on men's shoulders.* Cf. Isa 46:7a; also Jer 10:5b: "They [the idols] have to be carried, for they cannot walk."

27. This verse, like vs. 26b, echoes the thought of Isa 46:7: "They lift it upon their shoulders, they carry it, they set it in its place, and it stands there; it cannot move from its place"; see also Wisd 13:16. In the LXX and its versions, the inconsistent use of either the singular or plural when referring to the idol/s in this verse probably reflects a Hebrew *Vorlage.*

offerings . . . as before the dead. Cf. Tobit 4:17: "Place your bread on the grave of the righteous, but give none to sinners"; but cf. Sira 30:18-19.

28. *pocket the proceeds for themselves.* Literally "they abuse" or "they consume."

Just as bad [ōsautōs]. Literally "In the same way," also vs. 35.

29. *women who are having their menstrual periods.* Literally "she who sits apart" (=Heb. *dwh*). For Jewish views on menstruation, see remarks on Esth C 27, p. 212.

or have just given birth [kai lechō]. I.e. a woman who is still ritually unclean after childbirth. Cf. Lev 12:2b-4a: "If a woman conceives, and bears a male child, then she shall be unclean seven days; as at the time of her menstruation, she shall be unclean. . . . Then she shall continue for thirty-three days in the blood of her purifying; she shall not touch any hallowed thing. . . ." Cf. also Lev 15:33.

X. "HONORED" BY THEIR FOLLOWERS, THESE IDOLS CAN HELP NO ONE

(Vss. 30-40a)

30 For how can they be called gods *when it is women*ᵃ who set offerings before gods of silver, gold, and wood? 31 And in their temples the priests sit apart, with their clothes torn, their heads and beards shaved, and their heads uncovered; 32 and they howl and cry before their gods as people do at a funeral feast. 33 The priests take the robes from ᵇthe idolsᵇ to dress their own wives and children. 34 Whether ᶜthese godsᶜ are treated badly or well by someone, they are unable to repay it. They can neither establish nor depose a king. 35 Just as bad, they cannot bestow wealth or moneyᵈ; if anyone makes a vow to them and does not honor it, they won't exact it. 36 They will never save a man from death, nor rescue the weak from the strong. 37 They can never restore a blind man's sight, nor rescue a man who is in trouble. 38 They do not pity a widow, nor treat well an orphan. 39 They are like rocks from aᵉ mountain—these wooden idolsᶠ plated with gold and silver—and those who attend them will be mortified. 40 So how can anyone consider them gods or call them so?

ᵃ⁻ᵃ Greek "For women."
ᵇ⁻ᵇ Greek "them."
ᶜ⁻ᶜ Greek "they."
ᵈ Greek has "copper"; LXXᴸ and Syriac "silver"; OL and Vulgate "evil"; Bohairic "favor."
ᵉ Greek "the."
ᶠ Missing in the Greek, but the adjectives here are neuter forms, not masculine.

NOTES

30. *when it is women [oti gunaikes] who set.* Inasmuch as Judaism had no priestesses, to the Jewish reader the practice described here would have been scandalous and one more indication that these gods were not real.

31. *priests . . . with their clothes torn, their heads and beards shaved . . . heads uncovered.* All these outward signs of mourning for the dead were, with few exceptions (cf. Ezek 44:25), prohibited for Jewish priests in general (Lev 21:1-6) and for the chief priest in particular (cf. Lev 21:10-12).

32. *howl and cry . . . as . . . at a funeral feast.* The allusion here is, primarily, to rites associated with the dying god motif, so widespread throughout the ancient Near East (cf. Dumuzi in Sumer, Osiris in Egypt, Baal in Canaan, Persephone and Dionysus in Greece, and Adonis in Syria) and testified to, for instance, in Ezekiel's vision of the idolatries at the northern gate of the temple: "And behold, there sat women weeping for Tammuz" (Ezek 8:14b).

The author of the Epistle may also have had in mind funeral feasts for everyday people, such as friends and relatives; cf. Jer 16:5,7a: "Do not enter the house of mourning, or go to lament, or bemoan them. . . . No one shall break bread for the mourner, to comfort him for the dead." For a brief treatment of funeral customs in the Old Testament, see W. L. Reed, *IDB,* I, s.v. "Burial" and E. Jacob, *IDB,* III, s.v. "Mourning."

34. *are treated badly or well.* Literally "they experience either an evil or a good."

they are unable to repay it. This inability of the gods to respond is in sharp contrast to the God of Israel who "makes poor and makes rich; he brings low, he also exalts" (I Sam 2:7). Cf. also Jer 16:18, and Job 2:10b: "Shall we receive good at the hand of God, and shall we not receive evil?"

35. *they won't exact it.* Their "conduct" is in sharp contrast to that of Israel's God: "When you make a vow to the LORD your God, you shall not be slack to repay it, for the LORD your God will surely require it of you, and it would be sin in you" (Deut 23:21).

36. *never save . . . from death.* Cf. Deut 32:39b, where Yahweh says, "And there is no god beside me; I kill and I make alive; I wound and I heal; and there is none that can deliver out of my hand"; cf. also I Sam 2:6.

37. *can never restore . . . sight.* This verse and the next seem to be inspired by Ps 146:8b,9b: "The LORD opens the eyes of the blind; the LORD lifts up those who are bowed down. . . . he upholds the widow and the fatherless."

39. *like rocks from a mountain.* I.e. solid, lifeless—and silent!

who attend them will be mortified. Cf. Hab 2:19: "Woe to him who says to a wooden thing, Awake; to a dumb stone, Arise! Can this give revelation? Behold, it is overlaid with gold and silver, and there is no breath at all in it."

40. Since in the Greek the construction of the verse is so awkward (so scholars from Fritzsche on), the problem may be a mistranslation of the Hebrew rather than a corruption of the Greek. The verse serves to conclude the strophe and to introduce the next!

XI. THE CHALDEANS THEMSELVES
DISHONOR THEIR IDOLS

(Vss. 40b-44)

40 Besides, even the Chaldeans themselves dishonor them: 41 when they see a dumb man who cannot speak, they bring Bel and pray *the mute* may speak—as if Bel[b] were able to understand! 42 But they cannot perceive this[c] and abandon *their idols* because they lack common sense. 43 Women sit in the streets, with cords around them, burning bran like incense; and when one of them is led off by a passer-by to have intercourse[e], she taunts her neighbor for not being thought as attractive as herself and for not having her cord broken. 44 Everything that *relates to* these idols is false. So how can anyone consider them gods or call them so?

a-a Greek omits; see NOTE.
b Greek "he."
c So LXX[A] and Arabic; Greek omits.
d-d Greek *auta*, "them."
e "To lie with him" in LXX[L], SyrH., Vulgate, and Syriac; "with her" in LXX[A], Bohairic, and Arabic.
f-f Greek "is done to" LXX[A], and Arabic "among" them.

NOTES

40. *Chaldeans*. The word is used here in its restricted sense of a priestly magician, astrologer, or diviner (cf. Herodotus I 181; Diodorus Siculus *Bibliotheca historica* II 29) rather than as a synonym for "the Babylonians." For a brief discussion of the term in its various meanings, see A. L. Oppenheim, *IDB*, I, s.v. "Chaldea."

41. The translation is uncertain, primarily because in the Greek the subject of the verbs "may speak" and "were able" is uncertain. Most translators understand the mute to be brought to Bel, i.e. to the temple precinct, rather than an idol to the mute, an assumption which strikes many as gratuitous.

Bel [*ton bēlon*]. The Mesopotamian counterpart of Canaan's Baal, Bel (Akk. *belu*, "He who subdues") was from the time of the Neo-Babylonian empire on the name, or title, of Marduk, the patron god of Babylon (cf. Jer 50:2, 51:44; Isa 46:1; and "Bel and the Snake"). In *Enuma Elish,* the Babylonian Creation Story, it is Marduk who created the universe out of Tiamat, the primordial water goddess, and then went on to fashion Man out of her slain consort, Kingu (for the full story, *ANET²,* 60-72). Marduk was also the god of health and healing, as proved by the many prayers for healing directed to him.

43. The practice described here is reminiscent of but not identical with the one described in Herodotus I 199:

> The Babylonians have one most shameful custom. Every woman born in the country must once in her life go and sit down in the precinct of Aphrodite, and there have intercourse with a stranger. Many of the wealthier sort, who are too proud to mix with the others, drive in covered carriages to the precinct, followed by a goodly train of attendants, and there take their station. But the larger number seat themselves within the holy enclosure with a wreath of string [*stephanon thōmiggos*] about their heads, and here there is always a crowd, some coming and others going; lines of cord [*schoinotenees diexodoi*] mark out paths in all directions among the women, and the strangers pass along them to make their choice. A woman who has once taken her seat is not allowed to return home till one of the strangers throws a silver coin into her lap, and takes her with him beyond the holy ground. When he throws the coin he says these words: "I summon you in the name of the goddess Mylitta." (Aphrodite is called Mylitta by the Assyrians.) [A rendering of Assyrian *mu'allidtu,* "She who causes to bring forth," which was a frequent epithet for Ishtar, the Mesopotamian fertility goddess. She was frequently associated with the god Tammuz (cf. Note on vs. 32).] The silver coin may be of any size; it cannot be refused, for that is forbidden by the law, since once thrown it is sacred. The woman goes with the first man who throws her money, and rejects no one. When she has had intercourse with him, and so satisfied the goddess, she returns home; and from that time on no gift however great will prevail with her. Such of the women who are tall and beautiful are soon released, but others who are ugly have to stay a long time before they can fulfill the law. Some have waited three or four years in the precinct. A custom very much like this is found also in certain parts of the island of Cyprus.

Strabo (born ca. 63 B.C.) described a similar practice (*Geography* XVI ch.1); his account, however, seems to be dependent upon Herodotus (see Naumann, pp. 19-20). The Epistle, however, is not. In the custom described in the Epistle there is no mention of *all* women being required to prostitute themselves or of their having to be in the temple precinct. On the other hand, in Herodotus there is no mention of the women burning bran (not as a burnt offering, according to Fritzsche and Zöckler, but as a magic aphrodisiac). The head cords mentioned in Herodotus do not resemble in either form or function the cords (*schoinia*) in the Epistle. Nor does the Epistle indicate whether it was a once for all act (so Herodotus) or a repeatable rite. In any case, all forms of prostitution, but especially sacred prostitution, were rejected by the biblical writers (cf. Deut 23:17-18), if not always by local attitudes and customs (cf.

Hosea 4:13-14; Gen 38:14*ff*). For a brief statement on the matter, see O. J. Baab, *IDB*, III, s.v. "Prostitution."

44. Two letters in the last Greek word of the preceding verse (*dierragē*, "broken") and twenty very scattered Greek letters in this verse on a very small fragment found in Cave VII at Qumran constitute the only attestation to the Epistle's existence in the first century B.C. (see Plate 13). The reading in the Dead Sea fragment seems to agree with LXX^L and Syriac, namely, "consider them to be gods or call them gods" (for details, see Maurice Baillet, Jozef T. Milik, and Roland de Vaux, *Les 'Petites Grottes' de Qumrân*, Discoveries in the Judaean Desert of Jordan, III [Oxford at the Clarendon Press, 1962], 27-30, 143).

XII. IDOLS ARE ONLY THE
CREATION OF MORTALS

(Vss. 45-52)

⁴⁵ They are made by carpenters and goldsmiths; they can be nothing but what ^athose craftsmen wish them to be^a. ⁴⁶ Their makers cannot prolong their own lives so how can the things made by them ^bbe gods^b? ⁴⁷ ^cThese idols^c have bequeathed fraud and disappointment to posterity; ⁴⁸ for when war or disasters strike ^dthese idols^d, the priests decide for themselves where to hide out with them. ⁴⁹ How then can anyone fail to realize that these are not gods^e since they cannot save themselves^f from war^g or disasters? ⁵⁰ Since they are of wood, plated with gold and silver, it will eventually be recognized that they are frauds. ⁵¹ It ^hwill be evident^h to all nations and kings that they are not gods at all but the creations of men and that there is no divine power in them. ⁵² Can anyone fail to realize that they are not gods?ⁱ

^{a-a} LXX^A and Arabic "they intend."
^{b-b} LXX^B omits.
^{c-c} Greek "For they."
^{d-d} Greek "them" (neuter plural in LXX^B; masculine plural in LXX^A).
^e LXX^L, OL, and Syr. add "but the works of men's hands."
^f "Them" in LXX^A.
^g "Enemies" in LXX^A and Arabic; cf. vs. 15.
^{h-h} LXX^A and Arabic "is evident."
ⁱ Vulgate adds "but the works of men's hands, and there is no work of God in them."

NOTES

45. *made by carpenters and goldsmiths.* Cf. Jer 10:9b: "They [the idols] are the work of the craftsman and of the hands of the goldsmith." Cf. also Isa 40:19.

46. *prolong their own lives.* Literally "be existing for a long time."

48. *these idols.* Literally "them"; in the presumed Hebrew *Vorlage* the word

'*Thm*, "upon them," could be taken to refer to either the idols (so LXX[B]) or the idolaters (so LXX[A]).

51. *divine power*. Literally "work of God."

52. *Can anyone fail to realize*. Literally "To whom then shall it not be known" ("be known" in LXX[B]).

XIII. IDOLS ARE COMPLETELY
HELPLESS
(Vss. 53-56)

53 They cannot set up a king over a country*a*; and they cannot give mankind rain. 54 They cannot decide a*b* case or right *c*a wrong*c*; for they are as helpless as the clouds*d* between heaven and earth. 55 And if fire breaks out in a temple of these wooden gods (or gilded or silvered ones), their priests run and save themselves while *e*these idols*e* burn up like timbers. 56 They can offer no resistance to a king or to enemies. So how can anyone allow or believe that they are gods?

a LXX*L* adds "or deliver"; Syriac adds "nor are they able to punish or reward."
b LXX*A* "their"; LXX*B* "their own."
c-c LXX*A* "one who is wronged."
d Greek and all versions have "crows"; see NOTE.
e-e Greek "they."

NOTES

53. *cannot set up a king.* But Israel's God *can* (cf. I Kings 14:14; Dan 2:44).

they cannot give mankind rain. Again, Israel's God can: "He will give the rain for your land in its season, the early rain and the later rain, that you may gather in your grain and your wine and your oil" (Deut 11:14); cf. also Ps 147:8. Although this clause in the Epistle offers no problem whatsoever in terms of either concept or grammar, ingenious scholars have sometimes invented them: Ball (p. 607) suggested that "mankind" (Gr. *anthrōpois*) here represents a misreading of the Heb. *h'dmh*, "of the ground" as *h'dm*, "to man"; and Reusch argued that the Heb. *mōreh*, which can mean either "teacher" (cf. Job 36:22) or "early rain," here was erroneously read as the latter. While both suggestions are ingenious, neither has manuscript support; nor does the Greek translation require any emendation.

54. *helpless as the clouds.* The Greek has "helpless as the crows," a most inappropriate adjective to apply to the wily crow—as every farmer and hunter well knows. The reading adopted here follows the brilliant suggestion of Ball (p. 607), who, noting that the Syriac had "and not like the ravens between heaven and earth," argued that the Greek translator read *k'bym*, "like the

clouds," in his Hebrew text as k'rbym, "like the ravens." The gods, then, are as helpless as clouds before the winds.

56. *can offer no resistance.* If the writer of the Epistle had in mind primarily the Babylonian Marduk (so Naumann), then the city of Babylon and her temples to Marduk were certainly a case in point. The city and her temples were captured and plundered a number of times (e.g. by the Hittites ca. 1600 B.C., by Tukulti-Ninurta I [1235-1198 B.C.], by Sennacherib in 689 B.C., by the Assyrians again in 648 B.C.), the last time being by the Persian king Xerxes (cf. Herodotus I 183). For a brief history of the city, see T. Jacobsen and P. S. Minear, *IDB*, I, 334-338.

XIV. UNLIKE GOD'S WORKS,
IDOLS ARE USELESS
(Vss. 57-65)

⁵⁷ Gods of wood, silvered or gilded, ^acannot save themselves^a from thieves and robbers. ⁵⁸ ^bMen who can^b will strip them and make off with the gold and the silver and the clothing they had on, and ^cthese idols^c will be powerless. ⁵⁹ So it is better to be a king who proves his prowess or a household pot that serves its owner's purpose, than to be these false gods; or even a house door that keeps its contents safe, than these false gods; or a wooden pillar in a palace, than these false gods.

⁶⁰ For sun and moon and stars shine: sent out for a purpose, they obey. ⁶¹ So too, lightning, when it flashes, is widely visible; and in the same way, the wind blows across every country. ⁶² When God commands the clouds to travel over the whole world, they execute that order; ⁶³ and the fire sent down from above to consume mountains^d and forests does what it is commanded. But idols^e are not to be compared to ^fany one of^f these in either form or power. ⁶⁴ Therefore, one must not consider them gods or call them so when they have no power either to administer justice or to confer benefits on people. ⁶⁵ Recognizing, therefore, that they are not gods, have no fear of them.

---

^{a-a} Reading, with many Greek MSS, *diasōthōsin,* instead of *diathōsin* LXX^B or *diasōsousin* LXX^A.
^{b-b} Greek "The strong."
^{c-c} Greek "they."
^d LXX^L, OL, SyrH., and Syriac add "and hills."
^e Greek "these."
^{f-f} LXX^B omits.

NOTES

57. *from thieves and robbers.* Evidently a danger for idols (cf. vss. 15,18,33).

59. *better to be a king.* Since this comparison seems somewhat inappropriate or overdrawn (instead of being an idol, who wouldn't prefer to be a human being, let alone a king?), Torrey (p. 65) argued that the Greek translator read the Heb. *pelek,* "crutch," as *melek,* "king," i.e. that the Hebrew *Vorlage* had "Better to be a crutch that has proved its strength," a simile which is, admittedly, more compatible with the other commonplace objects in the verse.

[than] *a king . . . pot . . . door . . . pillar.* For a similar catenation of comparisons, see Wisd 5:9-13.

its contents. Literally "the things which are in it."

61. The point of the verse is not too clear. Evidently we are to understand that lightning and wind, like the heavenly bodies mentioned in vs. 60, are obeying God's will, not being independent of it. Cf. Ps 135:7: "He it is who makes the clouds rise at the end of the earth, who makes lightnings for the rain and brings forth the wind from his storehouses."

widely visible [*euoptos*]. This is the earliest recorded occurrence of this word in Greek, its next appearance being in the writings of the stoic Musonius (ca. A.D. 80).

63. *fire . . . from above.* Evidently a special type of lightning, one which has a very specific purpose (cf. Num 16:35; II Kings 1:10; II Macc 2:10).

64. *administer justice.* Literally "decide a case."

XV. FINAL ARGUMENTS AND
THE CONCLUSION
(Vss. 66-73)

66 For they can neither curse kings nor bless them*. 67 They cannot provide portents in the heavens for the nations; nor shine like the sun nor shed light like the moon. 68 The animals are better off than they, for they can take cover and hide*. 69 We have no evidence at all that they are gods, so have no fear of them.

70 Their wooden, gilded, and silvered gods are like a scarecrow in a cucumber patch—protecting nothing! 71 Again, their wooden gods, gilded and silvered, are like a thornbush in a garden, on which every bird perches, or like a corpse tossed out into the dark. 72 From the purple and fine linen* rotting on *these idols* you can tell that they are not gods. Ultimately, they themslves will be eaten away, and they will be a disgrace throughout the land. 73 Better, then, is the virtuous man who has no idols, for he will be far above reproach.

a Greek omits.
b Greek "help themselves"; LXX*A B* "help them"; see NOTE.
c "Marble" in LXX and all versions except Syriac's "silk stuffs"; see NOTE.
d-d Greek "them."

NOTES

66. *can neither curse . . . nor bless.* Cf. Jer 10:5c: "Be not afraid of them [i.e. false gods], for they cannot do evil, neither is it in them to do good." Cf. also Num 22:6.

67. *portents in the heavens.* Cf. Jer 10:2: "Learn not the way of the nations, nor be dismayed at the portents of the heavens because the nations are dismayed at them."

68. *hide.* The Gr. *eauta ōphelēsai*, "to help themselves" probably represents (noted Ball, p. 609) a misreading of the Heb. *lᵉhēʿālēm* (niphal of *ʿlm*), meaning "to be hidden," for *lᵉhōʿīlēm* (hiphil of *yʿl*), meaning "to help them." This error would have been an easy one to make since, without the vowels, both Hebrew words were written exactly the same way: *lhʿlm*.

70. *like a scarecrow in a cucumber patch.* Cf. Jer 10:5: "Their idols are like scarecrows in a cucumber field." That the Septuagint version of Jeremiah omits this clause strongly suggests that the author of the Epistle was dependent upon the Hebrew text of Jeremiah and not the Greek.

71. *Again.* Literally "In like manner."

thornbush [*ramnō*]. The Bible mentions at least twenty different words for wild flora characterized by sharp projections on their branches, stems, or leaves; unfortunately, precise identification is virtually impossible for most of them. For a brief introduction to the problem, see J. C. Trever, *IDB*, I, s.v. "Bramble," III, s.v. "Nettle," and IV, s.v. "Thistle, Thorn."

a corpse tossed out. An expression which emphasizes the contempt of the living as well as the helplessness of the dead; cf. Jer 14:16: "And the people to whom they prophesy shall be cast out in the streets of Jerusalem, victims of famine and sword, with none to bury them"; cf. also Jer 22:19; Isa 34:3; and I Bar 2:25; I Macc 11:4.

72. *fine linen.* Here the LXX and ancient versions read "marble," an obvious error inasmuch as stone does not rot. The error does, however, point to the existence of an Hebrew original for the Epistle since the Hebrew word šēš can be translated as either "marble" (cf. Esth 1:6; Song of Songs 5:15) or "fine linen" (Exod 25:4). The Greek translator simply chose the wrong meaning.

73. *Better.* "Better" than what? Has something fallen out of the text, something like "than the idolaters/Chaldeans"? Possibly so; but as the verse stands, it is justly characterized as "an apparently lame conclusion . . . a *non-sequitur*" (Ball, p. 611). The translation of the verse by Torrey ("The Jew, then, is better off without any images, for he will be far from reproach" [p. 65]) is certainly a more appropriate conclusion for the Epistle, but it is far too paraphrastic. Perhaps it is just such weaknesses as those in vs. 73 that help to explain why the Epistle was not ultimately accorded canonical status by the Jews of Jamnia.

COMMENT

The final strophe contains three elements which are characteristic features of the Epistle of Jeremiah. First, as much as any strophe, this one illustrates a pronounced dependence on the Book of Jeremiah.

Jer 10:2-5	*Strophe (excerpts)*
2 "Learn not the way of the nations, nor be dismayed at the signs of the heavens because the nations are dismayed at them,	67 They cannot provide portents in the heavens for the nations; nor shine like the sun nor shed light like the moon.
3 for the customs of the peoples are false.	

A tree from the forest is cut
  down, and worked with an
  axe by the hands of a
  craftsman.
4 Men deck it with silver and
  gold; they fasten it with
  hammer and nails
  so that it cannot move.
5 Their idols are like scarecrows
  in a cucumber field,
  and they cannot speak;
  they have to be carried,
  for they cannot walk.

Be not afraid of them,
  for they cannot do evil,
  neither is it in them to do
  good."

70 Their wooden,

    gilded, and silvered gods

    are like a scarecrow in a
    cucumber patch—
    protecting nothing!
68 The animals are better off
    than they, for they can
    take cover and hide.
69b . . . so have no fear of them.
66 For they can neither curse
    kings nor bless them.

Second, the strophe offers incontestable evidence of a Semitic *Vorlage,* i.e. Heb. *šēš* in vs. 72 was translated by the Greek editor as "marble" instead of "fine linen."

Finally, the abruptness, illogic, and imprecision inherent in vs. 73 are often characteristic of other verses in the Epistle, a fact which helps to explain why the Epistle was ultimately rejected by the Jewish Council of Jamnia.

APPENDIX I: DATES OF CLASSICAL AND PATRISTIC WRITERS

Amphilochius of Iconium (d. after 394)
Appolonius Molon (fl. ca. 70 B.C.)
Aristides of Athens (fl. ca. 130)
Athanasius of Alexandria (295-373)
Athenagoras of Athens (fl. ca. 177)
Augustine (354-430)
Cassiodorus (478-573)
Clement of Alexandria (d. before 215)
Clement I, of Rome (30?-?99)
Cyprian of Carthage (d. 258)
Cyril of Jerusalem (d. 386)
Epiphanius (315-403), bishop of Constantia in Cyprus
Firmicus Maternus, fourth-century Sicilian rhetorician
Gregory of Nazianzus (329-390) in Cappadocia
Hermas (fl. 140-155)
Hilary (315-367)
Hippolytus of Rome (170-235)
Irenaeus of Lyons (140-?202)
Isidorus (560-636)
Jerome (340?-420)
John of Damascus (675-745)
Josephus (38 - after 100), his *Jewish Antiquities* ca. 93-94
Julius Africanus (d. after 240)
Junilius (fl. 542)
Justin Martyr (d. 165)
Leontius (485?-?543)
Melito of Sardis (fl. ca. 167)
Nicephorous (758?-829) of Constantinople
Origen (185?-?254)
Porphyry (233-?304)
Posidonius (130?-50 B.C.)
Ruffinus (345-410)
Tertullian of Carthage (160?-220)
Theodore of Mopsuestia (350?-428) in Cilicia

For brief introductions to the above, the reader may consult *The Oxford Classical Dictionary,* edited by N. G. L. Hammond and H. H. Scullard, 2d ed., Oxford at the Clarendon Press, 1970. For more detailed introductions to the Church Fathers, see Berthold Altaner, *Patrology,* translated by H. C. Graef, Edinburgh-London: Nelson, 1960.

APPENDIX II: LIST OF KINGS

The Achaemenian

B.C.
550-530 Cyrus the Great
530-522 Cambyses
522-486 Darius I, Hystaspes
486-465 Xerxes I
465-424 Artaxerxes I, Longimanus
423   Xerxes II
423-404 Darius II, Nothus
404-358 Artaxerxes II, Mnemon
358-338 Artaxerxes III, Ochus
338-336 Arses
335-331 Darius III, Codomannus
336-323 Conquests by Alexander the Great

The Seleucids

B.C.
312-280 Seleucus I, Nicator
280-261 Antiochus I, Soter
261-246 Antiochus II, Theos
246-226 Seleucus II, Callinicus
226-223 Seleucus III
223-187 Antiochus III, the Great

187-175 Seleucus IV, Philopator
175-163 Antiochus IV, Epiphanes
163-162 Antiochus V, Eupator
162-150 Demetrius I
150-146 Alexander Balas
146-142 Antiochus VI
142-138 Trypho
138-129 Antiochus VII, Sidetes
125-96   Antiochus VIII, Grypus
116-95   Antiochus IX, Philopator

The Ptolemies

B.C.
323-285 Ptolemy I, Lagi
285-246 Ptolemy II, Philadelphus

246-221 Ptolemy III, Euergetes

221-203 Ptolemy IV, Philopator
203-181 Ptolemy V, Epiphanes
181-145 Ptolemy VI, Philometer

145-117 Ptolemy VII, Euergetes II

117-108 Ptolemy VIII, Soter II
116-107 Ptolemy IX, Lathyrus

The Maccabeans

B.C.
167-161   Judas
161-143   Jonathan
143-135   Simon

The Hasmoneans

B.C.
135-105   John Hyrcanus
104   Judas Aristobulus I
104-78   Alexander Janneus
78-69   Alexandra
69-63   Aristobulus II
63   Rome enters Jerusalem

INDEX

I. AUTHORS

II. TOPICS

III. SCRIPTURAL AND OTHER REFERENCES

KEY TO THE TEXT

Book	Chapter	Verse	Section
THE ADDITIONS TO DANIEL			
"The Prayer of Azariah and the Hymn of the Three Young Men"	3	1-22[24-25 in LXX, ⊙, Vulg.]	I
		23-28[46-51]	II
		29-68[52-90]	III
"Susanna"	(13 in LXX and Vulg.)	1-27	IV
		28-41	V
		42-64	VI
"Bel and the Snake"	(13 in ⊙, 14 in LXX, Vulg.)	1-22	VII
		23-42	VIII
THE ADDITIONS TO ESTHER			
Mordecai's dream	A	1-17	I
Haman's letter	B	1-7	IV
Mordecai's prayer	C	1-11	VI
Esther's prayer	C	12-30	VII
Esther's audience	D	1-16	VIII
Mordecai's letter	E	1-24	XIV
Interpretation of dream	F	1-10	XI
Colophon	F	11	XV
THE ADDITIONS TO JEREMIAH			
I Baruch	1	1-14	I
	1	15-22	II
	2	1-5	II
	2	6-35	III
	3	1-8	III
	3	9-38	IV
	4	1-4	IV
	4	5-37	V
	5	1-9	V

Epistle of Jeremiah	(6 in Vulg. and KJ)	1-7	VI
		8-16	VII
		17-23	VIII
		24-29	IX
		30-40a	X
		40b-44	XI
		45-52	XII
		53-56	XIII
		57-65	XIV
		66-73	XV